# The Syracuse Community-Referenced Curriculum Guide
## for Students with Moderate and Severe Disabilities

edited by

**Alison Ford, Ph.D.**
**Roberta Schnorr, M.S.**
**Luanna Meyer, Ph.D.**
**Linda Davern, M.S.**
Division of Special Education and Rehabilitation
Syracuse University
**Jim Black, M.S.**
and
**Patrick Dempsey, M.S.**
Syracuse City School District
Syracuse, New York

·P·A·U·L·H·
**BROOKES**
PUBLISHING CO ®

**Baltimore • London • Sydney**

**Paul H. Brookes Publishing Co.**
Post Office Box 10624
Baltimore, Maryland 21285-0624
www.brookespublishing.com

Typeset by Brushwood Graphics, Inc., Baltimore, Maryland.
Manufactured in the United States of America by
Sheridan Books, Chelsea, Michigan.

Sixteenth printing, August 2014

*The Syracuse Community-Referenced Curriculum Guide* was developed under
Grant #G00-853-0151 awarded to Syracuse University by the Office of Special
Education Programs, U.S. Department of Education. The content, however,
does not necessarily reflect the position or policy of the U.S. Department of
Education and no official endorsement should be inferred.

**Library of Congress Cataloging-in-Publication Data**

The Syracuse community-referenced curriculum guide for students with
  moderate and severe disabilities / edited by Alison Ford ... [et al.].
      p.    cm.
    Bibliography: p.
    Includes index.
    ISBN-13: 978-1-55766-027-5
    ISBN-10: 1-55766-027-1
    1. Handicapped—Education—United States—Case studies.  2. Handi-
capped—Life skills guides—United States—Case studies.  3. Community
and school—United States—Case studies.  I. Ford, Alison.
LC4031.S96     1989
371.9—dc20
                                                            89-9876
                                                               CIP

# Contents

Editors ......................................................... v
A Note of Recognition from the Publisher ............................. vii
Preface ........................................................ ix
Acknowledgments ................................................. xi
Task Force Participants ............................................ xii

**SECTION I    Overview**

CHAPTER  1    Overview
*Alison Ford, Linda Davern, Luanna Meyer, Roberta Schnorr,*
*Jim Black, and Patrick Dempsey* ............................. 3

**SECTION II    Home-School Collaboration**

CHAPTER  2    Home-School Collaboration
*Luanna Meyer* .............................................. 17

**SECTION III    Community Living Domains**

CHAPTER  3    Self-Management/Home Living
*Alison Ford, Roberta Schnorr, Luanna Meyer, Linda Davern,*
*Jim Black, and Patrick Dempsey* ............................. 29

CHAPTER  4    Vocational Domain
*Alison Ford, Jim Black, Pat Rogan, Roberta Schnorr, Luanna Meyer,*
*Linda Davern, and Patrick Dempsey* .......................... 45

CHAPTER  5    Recreation/Leisure
*Alison Ford, Linda Davern, Luanna Meyer, Roberta Schnorr,*
*Jim Black, and Patrick Dempsey* ............................. 63

CHAPTER  6    General Community Functioning
*Alison Ford, Roberta Schnorr, Luanna Meyer, Linda Davern,*
*Jim Black, and Patrick Dempsey* ............................. 77

**SECTION IV    Functional Academic Skills**

CHAPTER  7    Reading and Writing
*Alison Ford, Roberta Schnorr, Linda Davern, Jim Black, and*
*Kim Kaiser* ................................................. 93

CHAPTER  8    Money Handling
*Alison Ford, Linda Davern, Roberta Schnorr, Jim Black, and*
*Kim Kaiser* ................................................. 117

CHAPTER  9    Time Management
*Alison Ford, Jim Black, Linda Davern, and Roberta Schnorr* ....... 149

**SECTION V    Embedded Social, Communication, and Motor Skills**

CHAPTER 10    Social Skills
*Susan M. St. Peter, Barbara J. Ayres, Luanna Meyer, and*
*Seunghee Park-Lee* .......................................... 171

CHAPTER 11    Communication Skills
*Pat Mirenda and Marsha Smith-Lewis* ......................... 189

CHAPTER 12    Motor Skills
*Beverly Rainforth, Mike Giangreco, and Ruth Dennis* ............ 211

**SECTION VI** **Implementation Strategies**

CHAPTER 13 Developing Individualized Education Programs
*Roberta Schnorr and Alison Ford* ............................. 233

CHAPTER 14 Scheduling
*Linda Davern and Alison Ford* ................................ 247

CHAPTER 15 Managing Classroom Operations
*Linda Davern and Alison Ford* ................................ 281

CHAPTER 16 Planning and Implementing Activity-Based Lessons
*Jim Black and Alison Ford* .................................. 295

APPENDIX A Parent Input Forms ....................................... 313
APPENDIX B Scope and Sequence Charts: Extended Versions ................. 323
APPENDIX C Blank Repertoire Charts ................................... 341
APPENDIX D Example Vocational Training Site Agreement and Brochure ........ 385
APPENDIX E Example Individualized Education Program Goals and Objectives ... 389

Index ............................................................ 399

# Editors

**Alison Ford, Ph.D., Division of Special Education and Rehabilitation, Syracuse University, 805 S. Crouse Ave., Syracuse, NY 13244-2280.** Alison Ford is an Associate Professor of Special Education at Syracuse University. She works collaboratively with the Syracuse City School District to prepare teachers, develop curricula, and design program models. Her recent work has focused on the development of community-referenced curricula and strategies for including students with severe disabilities in the life of the school.

**Roberta Schnorr, M.S., Division of Special Education and Rehabilitation, Syracuse University, 805 S. Crouse Ave., Syracuse, NY 13244-2280.** Roberta Schnorr is a doctoral student in the Division of Special Education and Rehabilitation at Syracuse University. She has served as the coordinator of the Syracuse Curriculum Project at the University, working directly with a number of school districts involved in curriculum development efforts for students with severe disabilities. She has had extensive experience as a special education teacher.

**Luanna Meyer, Ph.D., Division of Special Education and Rehabilitation, Syracuse University, 805 S. Crouse Ave., Syracuse, NY 13244-2280.** Luanna Meyer is a Professor of Special Education at Syracuse University, where she also coordinates the undergraduate program and works with educational agencies to prepare teachers to serve students with special needs in integrated schools and classes. She has served as editor of the *Journal of The Association for Persons with Severe Handicaps,* an associate editor of *The American Journal on Mental Retardation,* and published numerous articles and books on strategies to support the social integration of persons with disabilities into school and community settings across the lifespan.

**Linda Davern, M.S., Division of Special Education and Rehabilitation, Syracuse University, 805 S. Crouse Ave., Syracuse, NY 13244-2280.** Linda Davern is a doctoral student in the Division of Special Education and Rehabilitation at Syracuse University. Her past positions include that of research assistant with the Syracuse Curriculum Project, public school teacher, and adult service worker. Her primary research interest is focused on integration efforts in public schools.

**Jim Black, M.S., SETRC—Teacher's Center, Holy Trinity School, 501 Park St., Syracuse, NY 13203.** Jim Black is a Training Specialist in the Syracuse City School District, where he is involved in developing curriculum and instructional practices that prepare students with disabilities for active participation within integrated school and community environments. He is currently the president of the *Finger Lakes Chapter of The Association for Persons with Severe Handicaps.* He is also a doctoral student at Syracuse University where his research has focused on issues such as the social validity of work performed by persons with severe multiple handicaps and paraprofessional training.

**Patrick Dempsey, M.S., Special Education Department, Syracuse City School District, 725 Harrison St., Syracuse, NY 13210.** Patrick Dempsey is a Supervisor of Special Education in the Syracuse City School District, where he assumes responsibility for the education of more than 2,000 students with disabilities. He has been actively involved in the Syracuse Curriculum Project since its inception.

Also contributing to this volume are:

**Barbara J. Ayres, M.A.,** Division of Special Education and Rehabilitation, Syracuse University, 805 S. Crouse Ave., Syracuse, NY 13210.

**Ruth Dennis, M.Ed., OTR,** Center for Developmental Disabilities, University of Vermont, 499 C Waterman Building, Burlington, VT 05405.

**Michael F. Giangreco, Ph.D.,** Center for Developmental Disabilities, University of Vermont, 499 C Waterman Building, Burlington, VT 05405.

**Kim Kaiser, M.S.,** RR 2, Box 356, Jordan, NY 13080.

**Pat Mirenda, Ph.D.,** University of Nebraska-Lincoln, 204 F Barkley Memorial Center, Lincoln, NE 68583-0732.

**Seunghee Park-Lee, M.A.,** 5549 S. Ingleside Ave., Apt. 2, Chicago, IL 60637.

**Beverly Rainforth, Ph.D., PT,** School of Education and Human Development, State University of New York at Binghamton, Binghamton, NY 13901.

**Pat Rogan, Ph.D.,** Division of Special Education and Rehabilitation, Syracuse University, 805 S. Crouse Ave., Syracuse, NY 13210.

**Marsha Smith-Lewis, Ed.D.,** Department of Special Education, Hunter College, 625 Park Avenue, New York, NY 10021.

**Susan M. St. Peter, Ph.D.,** Department of Special Education, Pennsylvania State University, 125 Moore Building, University Park, PA 16802.

The addresses that are listed for the volume editors and contributing authors are those that were current at the time the book was developed and originally published.

# A Note of Recognition from the Publisher

The Preface that follows on page ix begins with the sentence: "The educational goal for every student is to become an active participant and contributing member of society." That statement is just as true today—in 2002 as this book goes to press for its *tenth printing*—as it was in 1989 when the editors first wrote these words.

In the decade plus since *The Syracuse Community-Referenced Curriculum Guide* was originally published, this volume has supported countless schools in their efforts to provide a meaningful education to every student served. *The Syracuse Curriculum* is still used across the United States and beyond this nation's boundaries. The table of contents, with its sections on Home-School Collaboration, Community Living Domains, Functional Academic Skills, Embedded Social, Communication, and Motor Skills, and Implementation Strategies, could be from a much more contemporary title. Indeed, *The Syracuse Curriculum* continues to maintain its relevance as schools strive to meet the mandates of the Individuals with Disabilities Education Act (IDEA) Amendments of 1997 and anticipate the next re-authorization of the law that was known as PL 94-142 when this book first published.

In these pages are strategies to accommodate diverse learning needs in ways that enable students to enjoy the benefits of inclusion with all of their peers. Look, for one example, to the Scope and Sequence charts for material that reflects the broad range of skill inventories that can—and should—be incorporated into individualized program planning to help each and every student gain access to the curriculum. The content is rich and spans the interests and needs of learners from kindergarten through high school and beyond.

The authors say it well on page 11: "The design of active, meaningful, and dignified ways for a student who has disabilities (regardless of the degree of disability) to participate fully as a valued classmate offers a powerful lesson not only to the entire school community, but to the individual student as well." Today's educator or administrator will supplement the content of this book with material found in other resources that expand on the important principles articulated in *The Syracuse Curriculum*. Brookes Publishing is pleased to offer many of these complementary materials (for a full listing, visit www.brookespublishing.com). Take the strategies that this book illuminates and fashion individualized learning that suits the aspirations of each student and reflects what best practices in education can offer. The responsibility rests with each reader; the opportunities to make a difference begin here.

*Melissa A. Behm*
*Vice President, Brookes Publishing Co.*
*January, 2002*

*This printing of the book bears a new cover design to pay tribute to this tenth printing and mark the milestone of more than 20,000 copies in print.*

# Preface

The educational goal for every student is to become an active participant and contributing member of society. In order for some students—particularly students with moderate and severe disabilities—to achieve this goal, the curriculum must extend beyond the classroom and school into the surrounding community to ensure the development of critical daily living skills. These students will be learning many important skills in their classes at school, but may also need to be taught how to cross streets, purchase items in a store, and work in a business or industry setting. This guide is intended to help parents and professionals make curricular decisions about those learners for whom a *portion* of their program must be devoted to direct instruction in the community living areas.

Not long ago, instruction for students with moderate and severe disabilities was often characterized by repeated practice on isolated skills. The skills themselves might have been derived from curricular sequences based on the developmental patterns of typical children in areas such as motor, language, and academic readiness tasks. Classroom activities following this developmental model frequently involved sorting objects, following basic directions, imitating movements and sounds, learning self-care skills, and—for more sophisticated and older students—working on early math and reading concepts. As students approached secondary school age, "prevocational" activities were added to the curriculum, often requiring more sorting, matching and nonfunctional seatwork. But students with severe disabilities generally take a longer amount of time to learn the skills that other students learn more easily. Consequently, the end result of this curricular approach was, all too often, the graduation of young adults whose skill repertoires resembled those of very young children, rather than those of adults ready to participate in the real world.

Just as schools seem to assume that typical fourth graders can understand and apply separate lessons in math, reading, and social studies to the activities of their daily lives, a similar assumption existed that students with severe disabilities would integrate their separate lessons in motor, speech, and preacademics and apply them to their daily lives. And just as typical students sometimes have difficulties seeing the relevance of their educational activities, so do students with moderate and severe disabilities. But, for the students with disabilities, the cost may have been greater. A skill taught in isolation from *other* necessary skills and from other people would often remain just that—an isolated skill of little use in the real world.

Outcomes such as these resulted not only from curricular orientation, but also from the isolation in which much of this instruction occurred. Even for those students placed in public schools, a typical day was often characterized by segregation—students spending the majority of their school day separated from other students in the school. This segregation results in great costs to the students' social, communication, and cognitive development.

In recent years, parents and professional educators have become increasingly aware of the importance of integration as well as the need to teach skills that are referenced to the performance demands of the real world. How does a school program incorporate the need for direct instruction in *community* activities along with an emphasis upon the social integration needs for students with disabilities? Without careful planning, these goals could actually be in conflict with one another. Indeed, the development of this guide in the Syracuse area grew out of the often expressed concerns of parents and teachers: "My child has been involved in community-referenced instruction—but how much is enough?"; "As it is, I don't think my child spends enough time with nondisabled peers—won't community-referenced instruction make it even more difficult to integrate her?"; and "What about academics, and art, music, physical education—where do these fit in?"

Our efforts to respond to these concerns began in 1983 when a district-wide task force was convened in the Syracuse City School District for the purpose of developing a community-referenced curriculum guide. Several years later—after many meetings, workshops, local demonstration efforts, and federal funding—the work of this task force resulted in the 1986 printing of a local guide. The local curriculum, which carries the same title as this guide, has since been implemented in the Syracuse City School District. In addition, it has served a role in field-testing effort with 12 school districts throughout the country. Finally, the local guide has been carefully reviewed by a group of distinguished people who were selected because of their expertise as curriculum developers or curriculum guide users. Each of these efforts has contributed greatly to the development of this guide.

Of course, even as this guide is published, new research and innovative practices are emerging that have important implications for improving the education of students with moderate and severe disabilities. How, then, can the project of developing a curriculum guide be completed when there is so much more input to consider? Our answer to this question lies with the user of *The Syracuse Community-Referenced Curriculum Guide:* The *Guide* can only be considered "complete" if the user brings not only his or her current knowledge to the decision processes conveyed throughout its sections, but is an active consumer of new knowledge by continuously updating skills and information. In this way, the *Guide* can become a constantly evolving tool that should be useful for as long as professionals and parents find its basic concepts and approaches sound and sensible.

# Acknowledgments

First and foremost, we want to acknowledge and give special thanks to all of the individuals who participated in task force activities within the Syracuse City School District. (See the listing of participants that follows.) Second, many additional districts helped with field-testing and provided us with numerous ideas for improvement: North Syracuse Central School District, New York; Utica Public Schools, New York; New York City Schools; Racine Unified School District, Wisconsin; Keene Public Schools, New Hampshire; Council Bluffs Schools and Iowa City Public Schools, Iowa; Portland City Schools, Maine; Grand Island and Lincoln Public Schools, Nebraska; Paradise Valley, Arizona; and West Point-King William School District, Virginia. Third, we benefited greatly from constructive suggestions made from reviewers across the United States and Canada. The following friends and colleagues have our continuing gratitude for their extensive reviews of an earlier draft of this guide: June Downing, Lori Goetz, Stephanie Lagaccia, Steve Maurer, Pat Mirenda, Jane Newton, Beverly Rainforth, Pat Rogan, Jeri St. Clair, Ellin Siegel-Causey, Mary Ulrich, Terri Vandercook, Cindy Wagner, and Wes Williams.

Finally, we also wish to thank the following people who helped us with preparation and final editing: Carol Johns for her ongoing assistance in manuscript preparation, Helen Anderson and Rosemary Alibrandi for their clerical assistance in various stages of its preparation, Eric Bauer and Doug Hansen for participation in photocopying and disseminating a multitude of drafts, and Pam Walker for her editorial work on the final draft.

# Task Force Participants

Syracuse City School District Administration and Task Force Advisors:

Patrick Dempsey, Supervisor of Special Education Programs and Task Force Advisor
Virginia Maroney, Supervisor of Special Education Programs
Anthony Maggesto, Administrator of Special Education
Edward Erwin, Director of Special Education
Henry P. Williams, Superintendent of Schools

Task Force Members (The teachers, parents, therapists, paraprofessionals, and university staff and students who took part in some or all of the curriculum development activities from 1983 to 1988):

| | |
|---|---|
| Corky Acevedo | Sarah Jenkins |
| Esther Adelson | Martha Jenks |
| Barb Ayres | Debbie Labs |
| Ann Beck | Joe Marusa |
| Sue Beisler | Luanna Meyer |
| Jim Black | Margaret Morone-Wilson |
| Donna Checkosky | Brian Nolan |
| Marty Clark | Marge Norton |
| Karen Colotti | Herb Okun |
| Janice Conaughty | Kathy Orzell |
| Nancy Copani | Floris Palmer |
| Cathleen Corrigan | Seunghee Park-Lee |
| Lisa Costanza | Mimi Roberts |
| Linda Davern | Lydia Rosero |
| Cathy Deery | Adrienne Rutkowski |
| Anne Dobbelaere | Jill Sargent |
| Mary Beth Domachowske | Hillery Schneiderman |
| Lois Eddy | Roberta Schnorr |
| Betsy Edinger | Mickey Schechter |
| Valerie Fenwick | Annegret Schubert |
| Alison Ford | Lisa Schutte |
| Pat Floyd | Elinor Solomon |
| Teresa Gavagan | Katie Sturtz |
| Maggie Gioya | Andrea Vasquez-German |
| Kim Kaiser | Susan Watson |
| Jerry Hartnet | Virginia White |
| Judy Hentges | Chris Willis |
| Melka Hermann | Cathy Ziels |

# SECTION I
# Overview

# CHAPTER 1

# Overview

Alison Ford, Linda Davern, Luanna Meyer,
Roberta Schnorr, Jim Black, and Patrick Dempsey

Growing numbers of students described as having moderate and severe disabilities have gained entrance to regular public schools since the late 1970s. Their entry into these schools poses some new curricular challenges. We know that many of the curricular offerings in today's schools (e.g., language arts, math, science, social studies, physical education, fine arts) can accommodate these new students when adaptations are planned and instructional supports are made available. But further examination reveals that the existing scope of most schools' curricula is not broad enough to encompass all the activities or areas of competence that may be appropriate for a given student. This is particularly evident in the community living areas. While it is true that most students in our public schools will not need explicit instruction in skills that fall within the community living areas, such as learning how to use a pay phone, getting dressed for swimming, or shopping in a grocery store, it is important to acknowledge that there are some students who will. If schools are committed to the mission of educating *all* students, then attention must be given to expanding the scope of public school curricula to include these community living areas.

## PHILOSOPHY

This community-referenced curriculum guide is based on the premise that every student, no matter how severe his or her disabilities, is capable of living, working, and recreating in the community. Therefore, this guide has been designed with the following principles in mind:

- When necessary, schooling should include direct preparation for the activities of daily life. Some members of a student body may need direct instruction in areas pertaining to community living in order to become active participants in everyday life.
- Social integration is an essential element of an appropriate education. Becoming a part of school life is viewed as an essential step toward becoming a part of community life.
- Home-school collaboration is vital to the success of an educational program. Sincere efforts to establish strong partnerships with parents must take place.
- Instructional decision making must be individualized. Decisions should reflect unique learner characteristics, chronological age, student and parent input, and so forth.
- Interdependence and partial participation are valid educational goals. Students should not be excluded from an activity because they will not be able to do it independently.

- Structured learning can occur in a variety of settings. Meaningful instruction is not limited to school settings; it can also take place in the surrounding community where students can learn and practice skills in real-life settings.

## INTENDED POPULATION

*The Syracuse Community-Referenced Curriculum Guide* is intended for teachers and parents of students with moderate and severe disabilities (ages 5–21). It is not intended, however, to be used as a prescription for the exact curriculum that would be offered a particular group or population of students. Rather, this guide provides a framework for decision making that should be applied to individuals on a student-by-student basis. We would expect individualized decisions to vary considerably depending on a range of factors, including the student's age, present ability to participate in community living activities, personal and parental preferences, and so forth.

The term "teachers" is used broadly throughout this guide. It is meant to include classroom teachers, therapists, teaching assistants, vocational teachers, and others who assume instructional responsibilities within a given school district. The term "moderate and severe disabilities" is also inclusive of many individuals. It includes students who traditionally have been labeled moderately, severely, or profoundly retarded, as well as individuals who may be labeled multiply handicapped, autistic, sensory-impaired, and/or deaf-blind.

## CONTENT AND COVERAGE

The core of *The Syracuse Community-Referenced Curriculum Guide* is devoted to the content areas that directly prepare a student to function in the real world: self-management/home living; vocational; recreation/leisure; and general community functioning. We have also included a section on functional academic skills. Finally, there is a section devoted to skill areas that we believe are best thought of as "embedded" within daily activities: social, communication, and motor. In addition to these sections that outline the content areas, the *Guide* contains sections on home-school collaboration, and other implementation strategies, including: developing individualized education programs (IEPs), scheduling, managing classroom operations, and planning and implementing activity-based lesson plans.

Each section offers practical strategies for decision making. The community living, functional academics, and embedded skills sections begin with a framework that organizes the content. There are scope and sequence charts for each community living area—self-management/home living, vocational, recreation/leisure, and general community functioning—and for functional academics. And, there are skill functions charts for embedded social, communication, and motor skills. Each of these charts is followed by a step-by-step decision process that will lead to the identification of individualized goals and objectives for a particular student. Examples and illustrations are used in various places; one case study example is carried throughout to afford the user a more complete picture of the *Guide*'s impact on one student to whom we refer as "Mary Z." A series of frequently posed questions appear in most chapters with answers based on the experiences of those who have implemented a community-referenced curriculum. Finally, at the end of each chapter we offer a list of suggested readings and resources that should assist the user to locate materials and to become more knowledgeable in a particular area of interest.

## SCOPE AND SEQUENCE CHARTS

The *scope* of a curriculum consists of the range of content areas for which knowledge and skills are delineated. As previously mentioned, the scope of the *Guide* consists of four major community living areas: self-management/home living, vocational, recreation/leisure, and general community functioning. It also includes functional academics and embedded social, communication, and motor skills. The *sequence* of a curriculum refers to the order in which learning activities occur, across ages or grade levels. The sequence of this guide covers an age span of 5 to 21, with the community living content organized into the following grade and age levels: kindergarten (age 5); primary elementary (ages 6–8); intermediate elementary (ages 9–11); middle school (ages 12–14); high school (ages 15–18); and transition (ages 19–21). Chart 1.1 depicts the areas covered by the scope and sequence charts in the community living section of the *Guide*.

Many community-referenced curriculum guides contain unwieldy lists of activities. (Some guides contain literally hundreds of activities that are listed with few guidelines as to their relative importance.) While these listings are helpful to teachers and parents, their usefulness is diminished unless they are accompanied by guidelines for decision making. Without such guidelines team members are left with many questions, such as:

- How can we possibly address *all* of the community living activities within the practical constraints of a typical school program?
- If we can't address all community living activities contained in the listings, which are the most essential to learn?
- At what age should a particular activity be introduced? (For example, should a student as young as 10 or 11 years old leave school for vocational training?)
- When are logical times of the day to provide instruction? Aren't some activities better suited to after school hours or on weekends?

The scope and sequence charts that are included in each community living chapter have addressed these questions in the following ways. First, we recognized that it is unrealistic to expect that all community living activities can be sufficiently addressed during a student's educational career. Therefore, the scope and sequence charts in the *Guide* are organized into an inventory of priority areas; they are intended to serve merely as a framework from which the team will select the *individual goals* that seem most important for a particular student at a given point in time.

Second, we acknowledged that learning does not stop at age 21. Too often, our curricular decisions are driven by a "now or never" attitude. That is, if a student does not master an important community living skill during his or her school years, he or she will never have the opportunity to learn it in adulthood. This belief has led to having young students learn activities such as how to prepare family meals, do laundry, work in several different jobs, and so on—sometimes long before most nondisabled peers would be expected to engage in these activities. To remedy this, we have designed the scope and sequence charts with typical age expectations in mind. Activities are sequenced according to the ages at which most children might be expected to participate in them.

Third, attention has been given as to when instructional opportunities more "naturally" occur. We recognize the overlap between many community living activities and the activities that already exist in the schedules of many regular education

Chart 1.1. Scope and sequence of community living areas

| Community living areas | | Age and grade levels | | | | | |
|---|---|---|---|---|---|---|---|
| | | Kindergarten (age 5) | Elementary school | | Middle school (ages 12–14) | High school (ages 15–18) | Transition (ages 19–21) |
| | | | Primary (ages 6–8) | Intermediate (ages 9–11) | | | |
| Self-management and home living | Eating and food preparation | | | | | | |
| | Grooming and dressing | | | | | | |
| | Hygiene and toileting | | | | | | |
| | Safety and health | | | | | | |
| | Assisting/taking care of others | | | | | | |
| | Budgeting/planning/scheduling | | | | | | |
| | Household maintenance | | | | | | |
| | Outdoor maintenance | | | | | | |
| Vocational | Classroom/school jobs and community work experiences | | | | | | |
| | Neighborhood jobs | | | | | | |
| | Community jobs | | | | | | |
| Recreation/leisure | School and extracurricular | | | | | | |
| | Alone—home and in the neighborhood | | | | | | |
| | Family/friends—home and in the neighborhood | | | | | | |
| | Family/friends—community | | | | | | |
| | Physical fitness | | | | | | |
| General community functioning | Travel | | | | | | |
| | Community safety | | | | | | |
| | Grocery shopping | | | | | | |
| | General shopping | | | | | | |
| | Eating out | | | | | | |
| | Using services | | | | | | |

students. Activities such as learning how to use the school cafeteria, manage belongings at one's locker, play games at recess, and perform school or community (work-study) jobs are just a few of the activities represented on the scope and sequence charts that are applicable to students with and without disabilities. Furthermore, many recreation/leisure activities can be addressed within the extracurricular program offered by the school district (e.g., ski club, gymnastics, band, art club).

Finally, we have seen how other community living activities—that do not necessarily overlap with typical school schedules—can be reasonably incorporated into students' programs (e.g., shopping for food items that will be used at snack time or in home economics; making a trip to the public library and later stopping at a restaurant). We have also addressed community living activities that more naturally occur at times and in settings that extend beyond the school program. Such activities might include preparing breakfast, keeping the bedroom neat, and raking the lawn. With this in mind, we have devised two separate kinds of charts. One kind appears within the body of the *Guide*, and contains activities for which instructional opportunities are already present or can be reasonably incorporated during the regular school day (including extracurricular activities). The other kind appears in Appendix B, and includes activities for which instructional opportunities typically occur apart from school—before school, in the evenings, or on the weekends—and that are considered better suited to instruction during these nonschool hours. (However, these activities may be incorporated into an individualized education program [IEP] under certain circumstances, particularly when a parent makes a specific request. These circumstances are further discussed within each of the community living chapters of the *Guide*.)

Each of these considerations has helped us sift through the extensive listings of community living activities and arrive at a more manageable framework for educational decision making.

## HOW AND WHERE COMMUNITY-REFERENCED INSTRUCTION FITS INTO THE OVERALL SCHOOL CURRICULUM

"Surely there is more to school than learning how to make a snack, cross a street, and work at a job!" This thought was expressed by a parent who became increasingly concerned with what she viewed as a lack of balance in her child's education program. In recent years, community living goals had become so dominant in the IEP that they threatened to monopolize the entire program. "It is getting more and more separate from the other kids' programs," the parent went on to say. She was not questioning her child's need for instruction in community living areas; in fact, she valued many of the skills her child was learning in these areas. Rather, she was concerned about the diminishing amount of time spent in other areas such as language arts, music, and physical education. "Aren't these areas important too? And if they are, where do they fit?" she asked.

Like this parent, we believe that a student's education program should not be limited to activities drawn solely from the community living areas. We view a community-referenced curriculum as only a *part* of the many curricular offerings that should be made available to the diverse group of learners attending today's schools. As parents and educators come together to plan an individualized program, we suggest that the broadest possible framework be used for decision making.

Although organized in various ways, the traditional scope of school curricula includes: language arts (reading, oral and written expression), mathematics, foreign language, health, science, social studies, fine arts (music, drama, and visual arts), physical education, industrial arts and home economics, and vocational/career education. Since many students with disabilities, particularly those considered moderately and severely disabled, were excluded from public schools in the past, it is not surprising that this traditional scope does not encompass all of the learning activities or content areas that may be relevant for a particular student (Ford & Black, 1989).

It is very important that the person(s) planning an instructional program not confuse content areas with classes or specific time blocks. This is a particularly important distinction because, in actuality, many schools do address the content areas as separate classes (e.g., math period, social studies class), and this faulty conceptualization of an "expanded" scope could lead to further isolation of students (e.g., separate community living programs or classes for students with disabilities). Many of the instructional activities subsumed under the community living domains can be incorporated during the informal parts of the school day. For example, activities such as dressing, toileting, maintaining one's appearance, and eating (all of which fall under the self-management/home living domain) can be addressed at natural times throughout the school day. Furthermore, recess or free time (or perhaps a free period in the student lounge for secondary students) is the natural time for students to learn play skills, games, leisure skills, and so forth (from the recreation/leisure domain).

## Adapting the Regular Curriculum

Some community living activities may fit within the existing classroom structure when appropriate adaptations are made. For example, a student might learn how to play a musical instrument in band class (recreation/leisure) or prepare food items in home economics class (self-management/home living). These examples further support the notion that the selection of *content* from the community living areas need not lead to the separation and isolation of students.

Students who have traditionally been excluded from participating with peers in the typical content areas can benefit from inclusion, given creative planning and commitment to the goal of active participation for all students. Two strategies for accomplishing this are: 1) multilevel adaptations, and 2) overlapping goals. Many levels of skills, including functional academics, can be incorporated into lessons in math and language arts when an experiential learning approach is used. Major projects and activities in classrooms often provide the vehicle through which students with very diverse needs can come together and learn. For example, consider the following. A fourth-grade class ran a hot chocolate business as a math project. This project allowed two students who needed direct preparation in money-handling skills to work on their individualized skill needs, while their nondisabled peers were expected to apply more sophisticated math functions from the regular curriculum (Ford & Davern, 1989). In this example, the same general curricular content (math) was a goal for all the students involved, but at different levels. Such *multilevel* adaptations can be designed— and often are—to reflect widely varying skill levels within a class or learning group.

In areas such as science and social studies, which are not addressed directly in this guide, a particular student may participate in order to learn skills that might be considerably different from the instructional goals for other students in the class. For example, a student with autism may be enrolled in high school biology because it provides an opportunity to learn social and communicative skills (instructional goals of primary importance) and basic science principles (instructional goals of secondary importance). These instructional goals are different from the biology goals for another student, but they might *overlap* nicely because of the nature of the activities that occur in a biology class. Laboratory experiments might involve learning to share and take turns, for example—skills that could be a priority for the student with severe intellectual handicaps. Embedded skills in particular (motor, social, and language/communication) can be practiced in traditional curricular areas as well as in community living domain content areas (Giangreco & Meyer, 1988).

Goals associated with many of the fine arts include individual expression, creativity, pride in craftsmanship, and so forth, making these curricular areas relevant to any student. Since many aspects of this content area are explored through the use of individual or group projects using varied materials, they are particularly conducive to the inclusion of students with a wide range of abilities. Physical education, as well, provides an invaluable opportunity to participate both individually and interdependently in activities that are geared toward physical development and health as well as lifelong leisure skills. Many enrichment or elective courses offered in secondary schools lend themselves to both multilevel and overlapping curricular adaptations, which make them well suited to addressing the unique needs of students with moderate and severe disabilities.

## Using An Expanded Curriculum: Summary Recommendations

In practical terms, what does using an expanded curriculum mean for teachers?

- In addition to drawing information from curriculum guides in math, language arts, science, and social studies, the teacher might also make use of a community-referenced curriculum guide when planning for a particular student.
- Teachers and parents should find *The Syracuse Community-Referenced Curriculum Guide* of considerable use when planning programs for students with moderate and severe disabilities, but of limited value for students with mild or no disabilities who do not typically require the kinds of direct and ongoing instruction in activities of daily living detailed here.
- The IEP of a student with moderate and severe disabilities should be written to reflect the broad scope of curriculum, covering the major content of the scope and sequence inventories—traditional as well as community-referenced areas. (In Chapter 13, "Developing IEPs," we present a planning process that takes into account an expanded array of content areas.)
- Although a common, broad framework for curricular planning is being proposed, *individualization* is fundamental to an appropriate education program. Such a framework could be used to construct an IEP for one student with only a small number of objectives drawn from the community living areas due to his or her young age, relatively strong repertoire in community functioning, parental preferences, and so forth. Conversely, the same broad framework used with an older student might result in a much higher percentage of objectives drawn from these areas.
- The needs of a student for direct instruction in community living do not require that the student be separated from his or her nondisabled peers in order to receive instruction. (In Chapters 14 and 15, "Scheduling" and "Managing Classroom Operations," respectively, we discuss ways to accommodate students with diverse learning needs.)

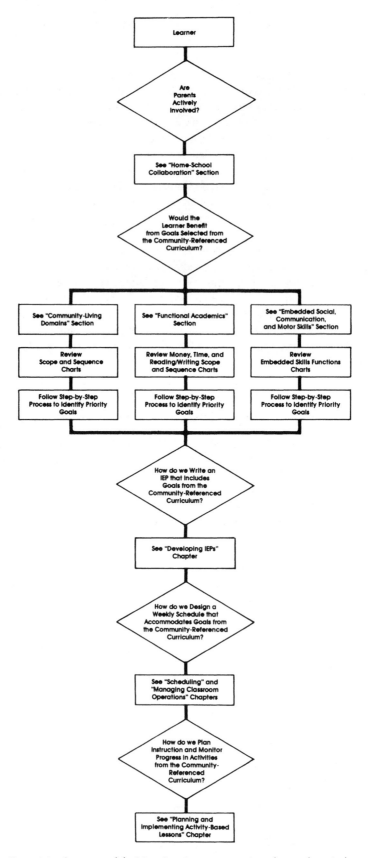

Figure 1.1. Sequence of decisions in using a community-referenced curriculum.

## The Implicit Curriculum

It is important to remember that learning, for any student, is never limited to only those items designated on an IEP or in a curriculum guide. What a teacher explicitly plans is only part of what a student experiences each and every school day. The school itself is a social system, and students learn many of the "rules" of their society by the many interactions they have with others across their school years. It is vital that all students, regardless of their learning characteristics, have opportunities to learn from both adults and one another on an ongoing basis in the school environment.

The significance of the implicit curriculum is evidenced by the fact that schools teach values (Apple, 1979; Goodlad, 1984). These values are shaped by the way learning is organized and facilitated. The design of active, meaningful, and dignified ways for a student who has disabilities (regardless of the degree of disability) to participate fully as a valued classmate offers a powerful lesson not only to the entire school community, but to the individual student as well.

## Curriculum Decision Making Begins with the Learner

The process of using a community-referenced curriculum follows a planned but flexible sequence of decisions. The flow chart in Figure 1.1 depicts the series of decisions that this guide covers. As can be seen on the chart, all decisions flow from knowledge of the learner.

## FINAL REMARKS

*The Syracuse Community-Referenced Curriculum Guide* has been written with the assumption that the user is familiar with basic principles of learning, assessment techniques, and task analysis procedures. It also assumes that the user has some knowledge of the regular education curriculum as well as a general understanding of how schools work. Finally, it assumes that the reader has developed an appreciation of the social and educational benefits of integrating students with moderate and severe disabilities in regular schools and classrooms. (For those users who are in need of background information in these important areas, an "Additional Readings and Resources" listing has been included at the end of this chapter.)

## REFERENCES

Apple, M.W. (1979). *Ideology and curriculum*. Boston: Routledge and Kegan Paul.

Ford, A., & Black, J. (1989). Community-referenced curriculum for students with moderate and severe disabilities. In D. Biklen, D. Ferguson, & A. Ford (Eds.), *Schooling and disability* (Eighty-eighth Yearbook of the National Society for the Study of Education) (pp. 141–167). Chicago: University of Chicago Press.

Ford, A., & Davern, L. (1989). Moving forward with school integration: Strategies for involving students with severe handicaps in the life of the school. In R. Gaylord-Ross (Ed.), *Integration strategies for persons with handicaps* (pp. 11–31). Baltimore: Paul H. Brookes Publishing Co.

Giangreco, M., & Meyer, L. (1988). Expanding service delivery options in regular schools and classrooms for students with severe disabilities. In J.L. Graden, J.E. Zins, & M. J. Curtis (Eds.), *Alternative educational delivery systems: Enhancing instructional options for all students* (pp. 241–267). Kent, OH: National Association of School Psychologists.

Goodlad, J. (1984). *A place called school: Prospects for the future*. New York: McGraw-Hill.

## ADDITIONAL READINGS AND RESOURCES

### Principles of Learning, Assessment Techniques, and Task Analysis Procedures

Albright, K.Z., Brown, L., VanDeventer, P. & Jorgensen, J. (1989). Characteristics of educational programs for students with severe intellectual disabilities. In D. Biklen, D. Ferguson, & A. Ford (Eds.), *Schooling and disability* (Eighty-eighth Yearbook of the National Society for the Study of Education) (pp. 59–76). Chicago: University of Chicago Press.

Baumgart, D., Brown, L., Pumpian, I., Nisbet, J., Ford, A., Sweet, M., Messina, R., & Schroeder, J. (1982). Principle of partial participation and individualized adaptations in educational programs for severely handicapped students. *Journal of The Association for the Severely Handicapped, 7,* 17–27.

Browder, D. (1987). *Assessment of individuals with severe handicaps: An applied behavior approach to life skills assessment.* Baltimore: Paul H. Brookes Publishing Co.

Brown, F. (1987). Meaningful assessment of people with severe and profound handicaps. In M. Snell (Ed.), *Systematic instruction of persons with severe handicaps* (pp. 39–62). Columbus, OH: Charles E. Merrill.

Gold, M. (1980). *"Did I say that?" Articles and commentary on the "try another way" system.* Champaign, IL: Research Press.

### Schooling in America

Biklen, D., Ferguson, D., & Ford, A. (Eds.). (1989). *Schooling and disability* (Eighty-eighth Yearbook of the National Society for the Study of Education). Chicago: University of Chicago Press.

Goodlad, J. (1984). *A place called school: Prospects for the future.* New York: McGraw-Hill.

Sarason, S.B. (1983). *Schooling in America. Scapegoat and salvation.* New York: The Free Press.

U.S. Department of Education. (1986). *What works: Research about teaching and learning.* Washington, DC: Author.

### School Integration

Berres, M., & Knoblock, P. (1987). *Program models of mainstreaming: Integrating students with moderate to severe disabilities.* Rockville, MD: Aspen Publishers.

Biklen, D. (1985). *Achieving the complete school: Strategies for effective mainstreaming.* New York: Teachers College Press.

Bogdan, R. (1980). "Does mainstreaming work?" is a silly question. *Phi Delta Kappan, 64,* 427–428.

Certo, N., Haring, N., & York, R. (Eds.). (1984). *Public school integration of severely handicapped students: Rational issues and progressive alternatives.* Baltimore: Paul H. Brookes Publishing Co.

Dobbins, J. (Producer/Director). (1987). Jenny's story [videotape]. Islington, Ontario: Integration Action Group (19 Rivercave Drive, MOB4Y8).

Elias, L. (1986). Jason goes to first grade. *The Exceptional Parent, 16*(5), 12–13.

Forest, M. (Ed.). (1987). *More education/integration: A further collection of readings on the integration of children with mental handicaps into regular school systems.* Downsview, Ontario: The G. Allan Roeher Institute (Kinsmen Building, York University Campus, 4700 Keele Street, M3J 1P3).

Gartner, A., & Lipsky, D. (1987). Beyond special education: Toward a quality system for all students. *Harvard Educational Review, 57*(4), 367–395.

Gaylord-Ross, R. (Ed.). (1989). *Integration strategies for persons with handicaps.* Baltimore: Paul H. Brookes Publishing Co.

Goodwin, T., & Wurzburg, G. (Producers). (1988). *Regular lives* [Videotape]. Washington, DC: State of the Art, Inc. (WETA, P.O. Box 2626, Washington, DC 20013).

Lipsky, D.K., & Gartner, A. (1989). *Beyond separate education: Quality education for all.* Baltimore: Paul H. Brookes Publishing Co.

Perske, R., & Perske, M. (1988). *Circle of friends: People with disabilities and their friends enrich the lives of one another.* Nashville: Abingdon Press.

Stainback, W., & Stainback, S. (1984). A rationale for the merger of special and regular education. *Exceptional Children, 51*(2), 102–111.

Strully, J., & Strully, C. (1985). Friendship and our children. *Journal of The Association for Persons with Severe Handicaps, 10,* 224–227.

Taylor, S. J. (1988). Caught in the continuum: A critical analysis of the principles of the least restrictive environment. *Journal of The Association for Persons with Severe Handicaps, 13,* 41–53.

Will, M. (1986). Educating children with learning problems: A shared responsibility. *Exceptional Children, 52,* 411–415.

# SECTION II

# Home-School Collaboration

# CHAPTER 2

# Home-School Collaboration

*Luanna Meyer*

The title of this section and chapter might be "Parent Involvement" or "Parent Participation"; instead, it is quite deliberately "Home-School Collaboration" to communicate the spirit and practice of a team effort between school and family in the educational process. As any parent knows, the relationship between home and school and the roles that parents have been expected to play are complicated and diverse. Schools generally have some sort of a philosophical statement written into programs that appears to encourage parent involvement and stresses the importance of parental support for educational goals and activities. In special education in particular, there has long been an emphasis upon the critical role of the parent as both decision maker and trainer. As decision maker, parents are encouraged to identify what they see as most important for their child to learn. As trainer, parents are often expected to "follow through" at home with opportunities for their child to practice the skills and behavior being taught at school. Parents might even be asked to provide basic instruction to their child, and the teacher might offer to train the parents how to do this. On the surface, such interactions between home and school sound highly appropriate and positive. But we believe that they can also be problematic if they reflect a primary consideration for *how many skills the child learns* rather than *how well the child functions at home and in the community.*

Strully and Strully (1985) pointed out in their article about their daughter Shawntell that she was learning many skills in school and would continue to learn even more in the years ahead. Yet, they emphasized that there were many other skills that Shawntell might not learn—some very critical ones—and ones that she might not completely master. They argued that how many skills Shawntell learned would only be an issue if Shawntell was expected to be completely independent. If, however, patterns of interdependence between Shawntell and her friends—including her best friend Tanya, a child who does not have a disability—are both recognized and supported, there would be few limits on what Shawntell could do. "No matter what a school program has to offer, if it prevents children like Tanya and Shawntell from sharing daily experiences and becoming friends, is 'special' good enough?" (Strully & Strully, 1985, p. 224).

We think that the collaboration between home and school should also reflect the recognition that while *skills* are important, so are *personal relationships*. Certainly, what any student can achieve in his or her lifetime will be affected by what he or she knows how to do. But it will also be affected by the extent to which that person has an interdependent support network—including both friends and family. All of us are interdependent with various other people in our lives, and our family in particular is a major source of support, encouragement, and even direct assistance when this is needed. Thus, this role of the family to provide support to the individual must be protected and valued—and not sacrificed in our endeavors to teach children more and more skills.

Another role that the family plays is to provide each member with a context of "rest and recuperation" as well as unconditional love and support. (For further information about families and their functions see the numerous Turnbull et al. references in the "Suggested Readings and Resources" section.) This might also be called *nurturance*. After a busy and perhaps even frustrating day at work or a day at school when things did not go well, coming home to your family can be a much needed respite from the pressures of an otherwise stressful day. Suppose, then, that a child with severe disabilities arrives home after a challenging day at school—to parents who themselves are arriving home after equally busy workdays and are especially looking forward to a quiet evening at home with one another. Add to this situation the presence of two other siblings—a brother and a baby sister perhaps—who themselves need care and support. Now imagine that a month ago that family agreed to conduct training sessions each night after dinner to enable their child with disabilities to work on a home living goal. Or, imagine that this is the evening that the teacher calls home to complain to the parents about a behavior problem that caused serious difficulty that day. How will this hypothetical family react to what, on the surface, seem to be small demands for "parent involvement"? Have you ever experienced an evening when you were so exhausted or there were so many conflicting demands upon your time that even a few minutes doing something only slightly stressful was more than you could handle?

Just as teaching is surely the most critical role the professional plays in the life of a child, being a family to that child is equally critical for parents. Thus, whatever image the school has for parent involvement or participation must recognize the many and extremely important roles of parent and family. And the extent to which a child will be able to adjust and participate in the activities of daily living will be influenced not only by *how much* he or she learns at school, but by the *support* he or she receives from others, especially the family.

This means that any model of home-school collaboration must balance its demands upon the family with the resources and supports that this collaboration provides to the family. Family adaptation is a function of reaching a balance among stressors, coping resources, and the ecological systems in which the family functions. You will want to examine closely whether the kinds of expectations your school has for parent participation really do consider the multiple roles of families and reflect a careful balance between the *demands* placed upon the family and the *resources* that such participation adds to support the family.

## PRINCIPLES OF HOME-SCHOOL COLLABORATION

While the mandate to include parents in the individualized education program (IEP) conference and overall planning of an IEP for their child is an important first step, it is not sufficient to ensure a productive partnership between parents and professionals, for several reasons:

1.  From a very practical perspective, if the only time during which parents are included in the educational planning process is the IEP conference, they will be at a distinct disadvantage as team members. Clearly, the various professionals will be far more likely to "have their act together" as a result of many occasions to work

and plan together in the absence of the parents. Thus, very often professionals already know what *they* want, and parents will be presented with a "draft" IEP for their review and approval. If a parent has a different idea about what that IEP should look like, he or she will be considerably out of step with the team. Thus, on the one hand, parents are generally expected to acquiesce to the plans of professionals, or on the other hand, be prepared for a possibly adversarial relationship with those same professionals. To avoid such situations, *parents must be active and visible participants in decision making throughout and across the school years.*

2.  Parents whose contact with the education program is limited to the IEP planning conference are not in a position to be effective advocates for their child and family needs. Parents may even themselves be alienated from schools as a result of their own personal histories or negative interactions with schools over the years regarding their child. As a consequence of this "distance," professionals will have a monopoly upon knowledge of the educational system and even what they choose to communicate to families about educational possibilities. This clearly unequal partnership makes it difficult for parents to argue their perspective and for professionals to listen to that perspective—particularly if the professionals believe as a result of lack of contact with them that the parents *are* uninterested or uncooperative. The professional team members could counter any request from parents with an authoritative response based upon having more information than they do, thus again giving parents the choice between agreeing or attempting to advocate without the information and experience to do so effectively. To be effective team members, *parents must have continuous and longitudinal experiences as team members.*

3.  This point is closely related to the one above, but parents need to have a *positive vision* about their child's future. Unfortunately, instead it is highly likely that from the moment of the birth of their child, they have been given negative images of what the future is likely to hold. Perhaps the obstetrician and the pediatrician, as well as close relatives, openly expressed their sympathy and even encouraged the family to institutionalize the child as the "only way to deal with the situation." As siblings and friends of children of similar age become increasingly independent and mature, the child with a severe intellectual impairment may continue to need basic care and support that seems extraordinary in comparison to other family situations. Thus, efforts must be made to ensure that parents are aware of and expect a positive future for their child, including the services and support that will enable him or her to live, work, and recreate in the community. We feel that the most persuasive as well as the most appropriate way for parents to develop such a vision of positive futures is by expanding their interactions with other parents of children with disabilities. Parents indeed appreciate contact with teachers and other professionals, but other parents—particularly those of children with similar disabilities who are older—are in the best position to share the "real thing." *Parents will be in a far better position to evaluate specific educational goals and opportunities if they can share personal experiences with other parents who have "been there."*

4.  Professionals also have a particular responsibility to ensure that parents are aware of and utilize the services and resources available to them. At a district, school, or classroom level, it is fairly easy for professionals to organize information on school and community resources and opportunities and make this infor-

mation available to families. This might represent a range of services from facilitating participation in extracurricular activities to "formal" transition planning
from school to adult support systems. Whenever transitions are to occur from
one level of education to another (e.g., from elementary to middle to high
school) or from one service to another (e.g., from school to work), professionals
are in a good position to organize information and facilitate this change process
for parents. Formal transition services to families as well as straightforward di-
rectories of resources should be provided without cost and with no expectations
placed on those families. Making such information and services available will
contribute a resource to family functioning, rather than entail yet another demand upon the family unit. As a minimal demonstration that schools do contribute resources to children's lives, *parents must be given ready access to knowledge about services and supports available to them.*

5. Finally, personal contact is essential to any meaningful relationship, and the relationship between teachers/professionals and parents is no exception. It will be
difficult for home and school to communicate with and understand one another if
there is little contact, or if the contact occurs only when there are problems. Instead, *ongoing and continuous positive contact between the child's teacher and
family must be developed and maintained in a manner that is perceived as being
rewarding to all participants.*

The home-school collaboration processes recommended in the remainder of this
chapter were designed by a task force of parents, teachers, university teacher-
educators, and support professionals in schools, with the above principles in mind.
(Members of the Syracuse City Task Force on Home-School Collaboration who contributed components of this section of this chapter are Marty Clark, Luanna Meyer,
Marge Norton, Seunghee Park-Lee, Mickey Schechter, Lisa Schutte, Sue Watson,
and Cathy Ziels. In addition, technical support was received from Jim Black in preparing materials on home-school collaboration and David Zawadski provided valued
input regarding the home-school interaction components.)

## PRACTICES OF HOME-SCHOOL COLLABORATION

A home-school collaboration model that actively seeks to support families and the
long-term development of their children is a critical element of any program. Table
2.1 provides an overview of the activities that could be included in such a model. Each
of the major activities and processes included in the model are discussed next.

### Parent-to-Parent Communication

In contrast to a traditional approach in which nearly all information that parents would
receive about services for their child would come from professionals, we recommend
a parent-to-parent process in which other parents are both a source of information as
well as a "resource" for families.

Parents often have access to information provided by professionals about services and supports for their child, and many parents take the initiative to attend and
participate in various training and information-sharing sessions that address educational, community living, and future employment options. While such sessions are no
doubt valuable and worthwhile for those parents who participate in these experiences,
we have been persuaded over the years that they are no substitute for sharing informa-

Table 2.1. Timelines for effective home-school collaboration

| Activity | When |
|---|---|
| 1. "Parent-to-Parent Night" at school. Parents and select staff at elementary, middle, high school, and postsecondary transition level come together for "parent-to-parent" presentations, followed by discussion and social interaction | End of school year |
| 2. Teacher sends a form home to parents: *Parent Preferences for Home-School Communication* (Appendix A) | Week 1 of school |
| 3. Each teacher sends home the *Parent Input: Determining Priorities in the Community Living Areas* forms (Appendix A) and follows-up with a call to each home a few days later | Week 3 of school |
| 4. Teacher completes his or her part of the *Conference Planning Form* (Chapter 13) for each student | Weeks 2–4 of school |
| 5. Whenever possible, teacher holds individual informal meetings with parents to review their priorities | Weeks 5–7 (depending upon district policy regarding time allotted before formal IEP meetings) |
| 6. Teacher arranges IEP conference and sends out written agenda that reflects parent input | At least 5 days in advance of formal IEP conference |
| 7. Formal IEP conferences held with educational team for each student (including parents and student) | Mid-to-late October (depending on district policy) |
| 8. Once IEP is fully developed, teacher ensures that parents, as well as each team member who will help to implement it, have a copy | |
| 9. Ongoing, regular communication between home and school, using strategies selected based upon *Parent Preferences for Home-School Communication* form (e.g., phone; daily log going back and forth between home and school) | Throughout school year |

Based on the work of the Syracuse City Task Force on Home-School Collaboration.

tion with another parent who has "been there." For example, a parent whose child also has a severe disability but who might be a few years older and is doing well in the community is in an excellent position to assist other parents in developing their vision for their own child's future.

Thus, the suggested timelines include a meeting at the end of the school year that has a purpose and focus different from the usual open house or more professionally led gatherings to which parents might be invited. Parents may be wondering about some of the changes that will occur in their child's program in the upcoming year. Some children may be transitioning from preschool to elementary; others may be enrolling in middle and high schools for the first time. The purpose of this meeting is to provide a forum in which one or two parents with an optimistic picture of their own child's experiences can share that vision with the "younger" parents in a teacher's program. Teachers might help the parent develop a slide show based upon the educational and community options available to students at the next level of schooling or as adults living in the community, but the *parent* should be the person sharing this information with other parents.

A second major purpose of the initial parent-to-parent meeting is to provide parents with an opportunity to meet one another and develop their own realistic and personally meaningful support networks and friendships. To allow this to happen, the meeting must maintain a "nonprofessional" feeling, with a social event flavor that does not take on the characteristics of a formal gathering or a lecture. The presentation by a parent should be short, with some discussion, but the group should move on to spending the larger portion of the evening talking informally with one another. It might be useful, for example, to organize the evening around a "potluck" dinner to which parents would contribute. Again, this should represent a typical social evening that families would enjoy as well as a pattern of social interaction that reinforces the principle that the purpose of the evening is for everyone to get to know one another and share their experiences as families. This is very different from a situation in which the teacher or other professional is the *source* of information, and parents are the "students" or consumers of whatever it is that professionals want them to know or hear. Thus, whatever occurs, the structure of the evening should reflect this non-professional nature and encourage such parent-to-parent sharing to take place.

## Initial Strategies for Home-School Communication

Good communication is as important on a week-to-week basis as it is to the design of an appropriate individualized education program. You may have already developed a standard system for sharing information with parents and involving them as team members in the IEP process. But, one standard way cannot possibly be suited to every family situation. Thus, an important initial step in our process involves asking the parents how *they* want to communicate with the school. Do they want to use a daily notebook system or would they prefer regularly scheduled phone calls? When it comes to the IEP conference, with whom would they like to meet? These and other questions are addressed on a one-page form entitled *Parent Preferences for Home-School Communication* (see Appendix A).

## IEP Planning

First of all, in the design of the IEP, parents are often asked to list their priorities in writing or complete a checklist of options. We have, in fact, designed and used the *Parent Input: Determining Priorities in the Community Living Areas* forms for use in obtaining parent input prior to the IEP meeting to actually write the IEP (see Appendix A). But, as mentioned in Chapter 13 of this guide, this form will need to be adapted to reflect your particular phase of the planning process and the family's interest in and ability to use this format. For example, the parent of a high school student may wish to hold a meeting for the purpose of reviewing the vocational section of the IEP. He or she might welcome some material that will help firm up his or her views about priorities. In this case, a teacher might send out the vocational section of the parent input form. Depending upon the parent, the teacher might also send along an article or two on promising practices in the area of employment or put the parent in contact with other resource people (including other parents). Of course, a "paperwork" approach is not suited to all families. You can probably think of at least a half-dozen other activities that would be much more appealing to do at the end of a busy day than complete a lengthy form. This is particularly true when parents have limited English proficiency or have difficulty reading printed materials. Thus, as you review the IEP planning chapter of the *Guide* (Chapter 13), it will be important for you to realize that, in order to be effective, the recommended communication strategies must be adapted to meet each family's needs.

## Strategies for Ongoing Home-School Communication

As previously mentioned, efforts to obtain active and meaningful parent involvement in the design of the IEP represent only one aspect of home-school collaboration. In addition, a useful system should be developed that allows the teacher and parents to communicate with one another on a *regular* basis. The teacher will need to share information with the parents about how well the student is doing on a new program—particularly whenever the skill involved is something that is likely to be used at home and in the community as well as at school—and parents will want to share information with the teacher about their child. There may need to be some strategy to let everyone know, for example, when the child has had a major seizure, has not eaten meals, seems to be ill, or is having difficulties for some reason. Particularly good days and news must also be shared, and will be valued by teacher and parents alike. Finally, if the parents and the teacher are generally comfortable in their communications with one another on a day-to-day basis, they are far more likely to be in a good position to work constructively together whenever important decisions must be made about program options, services, and supports.

## CONCLUSION

The home-school collaboration model presented in this chapter emphasizes the parents' role in educational decision making, rather than outlining an approach to involving the parents in direct instruction or even follow-up home training of students, counseling of families, and/or advocacy. Families may choose these other functions, and for those parents who wish to learn how to teach their child new skills at home, there should be options to obtain support from the school as to how to proceed. But all families play a critical role in guiding their child through activities and experiences that allow that child to be the best that he or she can be. To do this, parents must have a clear picture of what their child can be and must feel comfortable insisting that the educational services available for their child help him or her do what is necessary to "get there." Thus, parents must have a positive vision for their child as well as strategies to achieve that vision. The approach just described is designed to foster a home-school collaboration that emphasizes this primary role that only the family can play.

## REFERENCE

Strully, J., & Strully, C. (1985). Friendship and our children. *Journal of The Association for Persons with Severe Handicaps, 10,* 224–227.

## ADDITIONAL READINGS AND RESOURCES

Cutler, B. (1981). *Unraveling the special education maze: An action guide for parents.* Champaign, IL: Research Press.

Ferguson, P., & Asch, A. (1989). Lessons in life: Personal and parental perspectives on school, childhood, and disability. In D. Biklen, D. Ferguson, & A. Ford (Eds.), *Schooling and disability* (Eighty-eighth Yearbook of the National Society for the Study of Education) (pp. 108–140). Chicago: University of Chicago Press.

Skrtic, J.M., Summers, J.A., Brotherson, M.J., & Turnbull, A.P. (1984). Severely handicapped children and their brothers and sisters. In J. Blacher (Ed.), *Young severely handicapped children and their families: Research in review* (pp. 215–246). New York: Academic Press.

Turnbull, A.P., & Strickland, B. (1981). Parents and the educational system. In J.L. Paul (Ed.), *Understanding and working with parents of children with special needs* (pp. 231–263). New York: Holt, Rinehart & Winston.

Turnbull, A.P., Turnbull, H.R., Summers, J.A., Brotherson, M.J., & Benson, H.A. (1986). *Families, professionals and exceptionality: A special partnership.* Columbus, OH: Charles E. Merrill.

Turnbull, H.R., & Turnbull, A.P. (1982). Parent involvement in the education of handicapped children: A critique. *Mental Retardation, 20*(3), 115–122.

Turnbull, H.R., & Turnbull, A.P. (Eds.). (1985). *Parents speak out: Then and now.* Columbus, OH: Charles E. Merrill.

Turnbull, H.R., III, Turnbull, A.P., Bronicki, G.J., Summers, J.A., & Roeder-Gordon, C. (1989). *Disability and the family: A guide to decisions for adulthood.* Baltimore: Paul H. Brookes Publishing Co.

# SECTION III

# Community Living Domains

The community living domains are addressed in four chapters: self-management/ home living, vocational, recreation/leisure, and general community functioning. For each of these domains two different versions of scope and sequence charts that list activity routines have been included. The four basic scope and sequence charts that appear in the major text of the *Guide* address those activities and routines that teachers are likely to have opportunities to teach during the regular school day. In addition to these charts, Appendix B includes an extended version of the scope and sequence charts for each of the four community living domains. The extended scope and sequence charts include additional activities that may represent priorities for some learners—but instructional opportunities for these activities would more typically occur during nonschool hours. The activities on the extended charts would most likely be included on a student's individualized education program (IEP) only if they represent significant parent priorities for instruction.

The information contained on the scope and sequence chart in each chapter is arranged according to general *goal areas*. These goal areas represent fairly traditional categories that are often used in community-referenced curriculum materials. Within each goal area, you will find a listing of activities and routines across age levels from kindergarten to transition from school. The activity routines are sequenced according to the ages by which children without disabilities are usually expected *either* to partially participate in a routine or to perform it independently.

## ACTIVITY SELECTION

The scope and sequence charts are provided to give team members (parents, teachers, and therapists) an overall framework of the kinds of activities in which a student might participate throughout his or her school career. When planning the community-referenced portion of a student's IEP, a teacher can begin the process by utilizing information from parents, his or her own observations, and other sources to complete the following four steps:

- **Step 1:** Refer to the scope and sequence chart and examine the list of activities that appears in the column for the student's age group.
- **Step 2:** Look at the repertoire chart for the student's age group. (Blank repertoire charts are included at the end of the *Guide* in Appendix C.) Rate the student's

present level of performance for those activities considered to be part of his or her current repertoire. (For an activity to be considered part of a student's repertoire, he or she should experience a significant degree of participation in it.)

- **Step 3:** Based on these ratings, note priority activities that will strengthen the student's repertoire. (Of course, it is likely that some priorities may shift when more complete information about the student's repertoire is available from parents and other team members.)
- **Step 4:** Meet with parents and other team members to complete the *Conference Planning Form* (see Chapter 13). Make decisions about which goals will actually be included in the IEP. (As noted earlier, the goals from the community living areas will constitute only a part of any student's IEP, which would be likely also to include goals in traditional curriculum areas, participation in school routines, and embedded social, communication, and motor skills.)

This process reflects several general principles in planning the student's IEP. Professionals and parents must, of course, work together to decide on which particular goals and objectives will be given priority for this year's program. Both parent and professional team members are likely to have a great deal of information on what the student can already do. Contributions from all team members are necessary in order to establish individually appropriate goals based upon the student's present level of performance and overall educational needs. Just as teachers and therapists may have more information about school-based opportunities, parents are in the best position to identify current needs that are directly relevant to their child at home and in the community. Since some of the most important skills a student learns may be those that are immediately useful and interesting for his or her present situation, the family's priorities are obviously valuable.

The student must also be given opportunities to provide input into the selection of priority goals at whatever level is possible. For example, no matter how young the student, his or her interests must always be the basis for making decisions as to what leisure and recreation skills to teach. Likewise, for older students, valuable instructional time should not be invested in vocational experiences that involve a job that the individual clearly dislikes and in which he or she will probably never participate.

Another important consideration in the process is that priority activities are *not* determined by the student's potential for becoming independent in that activity. Priority activities must be reflected on the IEP, even if it is unlikely that the student will ever be able to master them. In these cases, the teacher and family should select a "least dependent alternative" that incorporates adaptations and assistance from others. Questions to ask when selecting a least dependent alternative strategy include:

1.  If I am going to design or use an adaptation, can I use familiar materials that are readily available rather than specialized, highly technical equipment?
2.  If help is going to be needed to complete the activity, can I identify someone in the natural environment (i.e., a nonhandicapped person) most likely to be available who can give that help (rather than the teacher or parent)?
3.  Are there some steps in the activity that could be mastered within a reasonable instructional time period? Can I teach the student to perform these steps independently so that he or she will not need to rely totally on the assistance of others?

These are general considerations. More specific criteria are discussed throughout other sections and chapters of the *Guide*.

## DECIDING WHERE, WITH WHOM, AND HOW OFTEN TO TEACH

Before the identified priority activities can be developed into instructional goals, the conditions for instruction need to be determined and clearly defined. Three major conditions that will have an impact on skill acquisition are "where," "with whom," and "how often" a particular activity will be taught.

When determining where to teach community living activities, teachers must weigh a number of factors. Consideration must be given to the actual environment in which an activity occurs, key features of particular activities and nonschool settings, characteristics that define an individual student's learning style, and the chronological age of the student. These and other considerations have been taken into account when developing guidelines and examples for the four community living chapters. Each chapter also includes a chart of instructional sites in which sample activities have been listed and evaluated regarding the potential for in-school or community-based instruction. No matter which settings become instructional sites, it cannot be assumed that a student has mastered an activity until he or she demonstrates success in the environment in which the activity would actually occur.

Equally important are decisions about with whom the activity will be taught. As stated earlier, the needs of a student for direct instruction in the community living areas do not require that the student be separated from her or his nondisabled peers. Teaching a student how to play games, prepare snacks, walk to destinations, and so forth *with a teacher and no peers* considerably diminishes the learning experience. Most of the community living activities listed on the scope and sequence charts are enriched greatly by the involvement of classmates who do not have disabilities. Thus, opportunities to receive instruction with nondisabled peers (and co-workers at the job site) must be a major consideration when developing IEP goals and objectives.

A final consideration has to do with how often a student participates in the learning experience. Using an example such as "riding a bus," an acceptable number of instructional sessions might range from daily to once or twice per week, depending on several factors related to the student. For many learners with moderate and severe disabilities, providing instruction in a particular activity less frequently than one time per week will contribute very little to the acquisition of skills for that activity. Systematic instruction requires regular, planned instruction and practice sessions as part of a predictable schedule over a period of months and years. Of course, logistical factors such as available staff, accessibility to community settings, and transportation will also influence the selection of instructional environments and frequency of sessions. Many of these factors are addressed in the "Questions and Answers" portion at the end of each chapter.

## FINAL REMARKS

In summary, a great deal of professional judgment and advocacy on behalf of each student's needs and interests must be reflected in the decision-making process for the community living domains. Perhaps more than any other area, the content decisions for community living must be made with every assurance that the activities selected are both meaningful and useful for the individual and his or her family.

## READINGS AND RESOURCES

Baumgart, D., Brown, L., Pumpian, I., Nisbet, J., Ford, A., Sweet, M., Messina, R., & Schroeder, J. (1982). Principle of partial participation and individualized adaptations in educational programs for severely handicapped students. *Journal of The Association for the Severely Handicapped, 7*(2), 17–27.

Brown, L., Branston, M.B., Hamre-Nietupski, S., Pumpian, I., Certo, N., & Gruenewald, L. (1978). A strategy for developing chronological age-appropriate and functional curricular content for severely handicapped adolescents and young adults. *Journal of Special Education, 13,* 81–90.

Brown, L., Nietupski, J., & Hamre-Nietupski, S. (1976). The criterion of ultimate functioning and public school services for severely handicapped students. In M.A. Thomas (Ed.), *Hey, don't forget about me: Education's investment in the severely, profoundly and multiply handicapped* (pp. 2–15). Reston, VA: Council for Exceptional Children.

Brown, L., Nisbet, J., Ford, A., Sweet, M., Shiraga, B., & Loomis, R. (1983). The critical need for nonschool instruction in educational programs for severely handicapped students. *Journal of The Association for the Severely Handicapped, 8,* 71–77.

Falvey, M.A. (1986). *Community-based curriculum: Instructional strategies for students with severe handicaps.* Baltimore: Paul H. Brookes Publishing Co.

Gaylord-Ross, R., & Holvoet, J. (1985). *Strategies for educating students with severe handicaps.* Boston: Little, Brown.

Goetz, L., Guess, D., & Stremel-Campbell, K. (1987). *Innovative program design for individuals with dual sensory impairments.* Baltimore: Paul H. Brookes Publishing Co.

Horner, R.H., Meyer, L.H., & Fredericks, H.D.B. (Eds.). (1986). *Education of learners with severe handicaps: Exemplary service strategies.* Baltimore: Paul H. Brookes Publishing Co.

Neel, R.S., Billingsley, F.F., McCarty, F., Symonds, D., Lambert, C., Lewis-Smith, N., & Hanashiro, R. (1983). *Teaching autistic children: A functional curriculum approach.* Seattle: University of Washington College of Education.

Orelove, F.P., & Sobsey, D. (1987). *Educating children with multiple disabilities: A transdisciplinary approach.* Baltimore: Paul H. Brookes Publishing Co.

Sailor, W., & Guess, D. (1983). *Severely handicapped students: An instructional design.* Boston: Houghton Mifflin.

Snell, M. (Ed.). (1987). *Systematic instruction of persons with severe handicaps* (3rd ed.). Columbus, OH: Charles E. Merrill.

Wehman, P., Renzaglia, A., & Bates, P. (1985). *Functional living skills for moderately and severely handicapped individuals.* Austin, TX: PRO-ED.

Wilcox, B., & Bellamy, G.T. (1982). *Design of high school programs for severely handicapped students.* Baltimore: Paul H. Brookes Publishing Co.

# CHAPTER 3

# Self-Management/ Home Living

*Alison Ford, Roberta Schnorr, Luanna Meyer,*
*Linda Davern, Jim Black, and Patrick Dempsey*

There are many self-management/home living activities that are essential to everyday functioning. Getting dressed and undressed (for physical education class, to remove or put on outer clothing) is just one example of such an activity. This activity poses a no-choice situation: If the student does not participate, it is likely that someone will act upon him or her, that is, dress him or her. Since this activity occurs frequently and by its nature requires the student's personal involvement, it makes sense to teach the student to become a more active participant and to exercise greater influence throughout the activity.

Other activities, such as preparing a snack or meal and managing a daily schedule, might also be considered essential. These types of activities are common in people's daily lives, and present frequent opportunities to make personal choices (e.g., what to eat, when to do something). By not teaching students to participate in such common and regular daily routines, we may seriously restrict their opportunities to influence decisions about their personal lives.

Finally, there are other activities in the self-management/home living domain that will carry less weight. They generally do not have survival value; nor are they necessarily prominent in the lives of all people. Thus, we might engage in some, but not all of them, based on our negotiations with others. For example, one person in your household might be responsible for doing the laundry, while another might take care of the pets, one might do the yard work, while another assumes responsibility for cleaning the kitchen. Whatever the arrangement, not all activities need to be performed (or mastered) by each individual. It is this reasoning that must be applied to the individualized selection of activities in the self-management/home living domain.

## SCOPE AND SEQUENCE

The self-management/home living domain includes six major goal areas: eating and food preparation, grooming and dressing, hygiene and toileting, safety and health, assisting and taking care of others, and budgeting and planning/scheduling. The sequence is the order in which a student might participate in such activities as he or she progresses through the school years. For instructional purposes, new activities are addressed while maintaining participation in previously established routines. This approach continuously builds upon and strengthens a student's existing repertoire.

Chart 3.1 illustrates the scope and sequence for self-management/home living

Chart 3.1. Scope and sequence for self-management/home living

Age and grade levels

| Goal areas | Kindergarten (age 5) | Elementary School | | Middle school (ages 12–14) | High school (ages 15–18) | Transition (ages 19–21) |
|---|---|---|---|---|---|---|
| | | Primary grades (ages 6–8) | Intermediate grades (ages 9–11) | | | |
| Eating and food preparation | Eat meals and snacks | Eat balanced meals | Eat balanced meals with appropriate manners | Eat balanced meals with appropriate manners | Eat balanced meals with appropriate manners | Eat balanced meals with appropriate manners |
| | Prepare simple snack for self; pour own drink | Prepare simple snacks for self; pour own drink | Plan and prepare simple snacks for self | Plan and prepare snacks for self | Plan and prepare snacks for self and others | Plan menu for self/family/roommates |
| | Serve snack to peers | Serve snack to peers | Serve food items to others | Serve food items to others | Serve food items to others | Serve food items to others |
| | Clean own place after snack/meal | Clean up table after snack | Clean up preparation area and table after snack | Clear table and do dishes after food preparation | Clear table and do dishes after food preparation | Clean up after meals |
| | | Choose nutritious foods: snack | Choose nutritious foods: snack | Choose nutritious foods: breakfast, lunch, snacks | Choose nutritious foods: breakfast, lunch, snacks | Choose nutritious foods (including when eating out) |
| | | | | Prepare simple meals: breakfast, lunch (some cooking) | Prepare various types of meals | Prepare meal for self/others |
| | | | | Store food and leftovers | Store food and leftovers | Store food and leftovers |
| | | | | | | Make weekly grocery list |
| Grooming and dressing | Brush/comb hair with reminders | Brush/comb hair reminders | Brush/comb hair when needed | Brush/comb and style hair (also choose hairstyle) | Brush/comb and style hair (also choose hairstyle) | Manage hair care |
| | Get dressed/undressed (school: shoes, outer clothes) | Get dressed/undressed (school: shoes, swimming, outer clothes) | Get dressed/undressed (school: shoes, swimming, outer clothes) | Get dressed/undressed (physical education, outer clothes) | Get dressed/undressed (physical education, outer clothes) | Get dressed/undressed |
| | | Maintain neat appearance throughout school day with reminders | Maintain neat appearance throughout school day | Maintain neat appearance throughout school day | Maintain appearance throughout school day | Maintain appearance |
| | | | | Use skin care products (cosmetics if desired) | Use skin care products (cosmetics if desired) | Manage skin care |
| | | | | Care for eyeglasses/contact lenses | Care for eyeglasses/contact lenses | Manage eye care needs |

| | | | | | | | |
|---|---|---|---|---|---|---|---|
| Hygiene and toileting | Use private and public toilets<br>Wash hands and face with reminders<br><br>Blow nose and dispose of tissue with reminders | Use private and public toilets<br>Wash hands and face: routine times (e.g., after toilet, before eating)<br>Blow nose and dispose of tissue as needed | Use private and public toilets<br>Wash hands and face: routine times and for specific activities (food preparation)<br>Follow acceptable hygiene practices | Use private and public toilets<br>Wash hands and face: routine times and for specific activities (food preparation)<br>Follow acceptable hygiene practices<br>Manage menstrual care | Use private and public toilets<br>Wash hands and face: routine times and for specific activities (food preparation)<br>Follow acceptable hygiene practices<br>Manage menstrual care | Use private and public toilets<br>Wash hands and face: routine times and for specific activities (food preparation)<br>Follow acceptable hygiene practices<br>Manage menstrual care | Use private and public toilets<br>Wash hands and face<br><br>Follow acceptable hygiene practices<br>Manage menstrual care |
| Safety and health | Follow safety rules on playground equipment and near traffic<br>Exit building for emergency/alarm<br>Show care with sharp or breakable objects<br>Inform adult when sick/injured<br>Take medicine with assistance<br>Avoid/report sexual abuse<br>Report emergency to adult<br>Use caution with strangers<br>Make emergency phone calls | Follow safety rules (playground, traffic, poison, etc.)<br>Exit building for emergency/alarm<br>Show care with sharp or breakable objects<br>Inform adult when sick/injured<br>Take medicine with assistance<br>Avoid/report sexual abuse<br>Report emergency to adult<br>Use caution with strangers<br>Make emergency phone calls | Follow safety rules<br>Exit building for emergency/alarm<br>Take care with utensils, appliances, and tools<br>Inform adult when sick/injured<br>Take medicine with adult supervision<br>Avoid/report sexual abuse<br>Report emergencies<br>Use caution with strangers<br>Make emergency phone calls<br>Avoid alcohol and other drugs | Follow safety rules<br>Exit building for emergency/alarm<br>Take care with utensils, appliances, and tools<br>Inform adult when sick/injured<br>Take medicine with supervision<br>Avoid/report sexual abuse<br>Report emergencies<br>Use caution with strangers<br>Use phone to obtain emergency help<br>Avoid alcohol and other drugs<br>Use appropriate first-aid procedures: minor injuries (cuts, burns)<br>Maintain good personal health habits (diet, exercise) with supervision<br>Manage birth control as needed | Follow safety rules<br>Exit building for emergency/alarm<br>Take care with utensils, appliances, and tools<br>Inform adult when sick/injured<br>Take medicine as needed<br>Avoid/report sexual abuse<br>Report emergencies<br>Use caution with strangers<br>Use phone to obtain emergency help<br>Avoid alcohol and other drugs<br>Use appropriate first-aid procedures: minor, major incidents (choking, bleeding, artificial respiration)<br>Maintain good personal health habits<br>Manage birth control as needed | Follow safety rules<br>Exit building for emergency/alarm<br>Take care with utensils, appliances, and tools<br>Inform adult when sick/injured<br>Take medicine as needed<br>Avoid/report sexual abuse<br>Report emergencies<br>Use caution with strangers<br>Use phone to obtain emergency help<br>Avoid alcohol and other drugs<br>Use appropriate first-aid procedures: minor, major incidents (choking, bleeding, artificial respiration)<br>Maintain good personal health habits<br>Manage birth control as needed | Follow safety rules<br>Exit building for emergency/alarm<br>Take care with utensils, appliances, and tools<br>Inform other(s) when sick/injured<br>Take medicine as needed<br>Avoid/report sexual abuse<br>Report emergencies<br>Use caution with strangers<br>Use phone to obtain emergency help<br>Avoid alcohol and other drugs<br>Know appropriate first-aid procedures: minor, major incidents (choking, bleeding, artificial respiration)<br>Maintain good personal health habits<br>Manage birth control as needed |

*(continued)*

Chart 3.1. (continued)

|  | Age and grade levels | | | | | |
|---|---|---|---|---|---|---|
|  | Elementary School | | | | | |
| Goal areas | Kindergarten (age 5) | Primary grades (ages 6–8) | Intermediate grades (ages 9–11) | Middle school (ages 12–14) | High school (ages 15–18) | Transition (ages 19–21) |
| Assisting and taking care of others (examples) | Help classmate clean up<br>Help teacher get materials<br>Help classmate learn game<br>Help new student learn routine<br>Share materials | Help classmate clean up<br>Help teacher with materials<br>Help classmate learn game<br>Help new student learn routine<br>Share personal belongings | Help classmate clean up<br>Help teacher with materials<br>Help peer learn game<br>Help new student learn routine<br>Share personal belongings | Help someone clean up<br>Help instructor with materials<br>Help peer learn game<br>Help new student learn routine and meet people<br>Share personal belongings<br>Do favor for classmate/peer | Help someone clean up<br>Help instructor with materials<br>Help peer learn game<br>Help new student learn routine and meet people<br>Share personal belongings<br>Do favor for classmate/peer | Help someone clean up<br>Help instructor with materials<br>Help peer learn game<br>Help new student learn routine and meet people<br>Share personal belongings<br>Do favor for someone |
| Budgeting and planning/scheduling | Gather belongings for outings/activities<br>Carry lunch/milk money<br>Follow daily/weekly schedule | Gather belongings for outings/activities<br>Carry lunch/milk money | Gather belongings for outings/activities<br>Carry money for small purchases: not only routine<br>Manage weekly/monthly schedule<br>Make plans with friends on daily basis<br>Participate in fundraising activities<br>Take care of personal belongings | Plan and gather items for outings/activities<br>Manage allowance and other money for personal purchases and gifts<br>Manage weekly/monthly schedule<br>Arrange activities with friends and family<br>Participate in fundraising activities<br>Take care of personal belongings | Plan and gather items for outings/activities<br>Manage own money for routine personal expenses and gifts<br>Manage weekly/monthly schedule<br>Arrange activities with friends and family<br>Participate in fundraising activities<br>Take care of personal belongings<br>Pay bills (credit card, magazine subscription) | Plan and gather items for outings/activities<br>Manage budget to cover personal expenses<br>Manage weekly/monthly schedule<br>Arrange activities with friends and family<br>Participate in fundraising activities<br>Take care of personal belongings<br>Pay bills (credit card, phone) |

activities. These activities are presented across six age and grade levels: kindergarten (age 5); primary elementary (ages 6–8); intermediate elementary (ages 9–11); middle school (ages 12–14); high school (ages 15–18); and transition (ages 19–21). The activities identified for a given age group should be given full consideration when developing the individualized education program (IEP) until a sufficient level of proficiency or participation has been attained. As for each of the other three domains, however, decisions for self-management/home living must be based on the input of team members, particularly students and parents.

The extended scope and sequence charts in Appendix B at the end of the *Guide* contain additional self-management/home living activities (and two additional goal areas: household maintenance and outdoor maintenance) that should be considered if parents indicate that they represent a family/household need, and/or are of particular interest to the student. For example, Tim's father suggested folding the laundry as a priority activity; he does most of the family's laundry on the weekends. This activity would help fill a household need, and also occurred at a time when Tim's work could be monitored by someone at home. Furthermore, because Tim's graduation was near, his father wanted him to share in the responsibilities as would any adult household member. It was decided that Tim's teacher would check with some of the coaches to see if he could participate in laundering team towels and uniforms once a week in the home economics room. If so, this instruction would be used to help target skills that Tim could perform in a laundry routine at home as well.

## ACTIVITY SELECTION

The scope and sequence chart provides a broad framework of self-management/home living activities for all students. The next task is to utilize this framework as a reference when making decisions regarding *individual* student programs.

In addition to examining potential activities on the scope and sequence chart, the teacher must also determine the existing repertoire of an individual student to identify the instructional priorities for that particular learner. A repertoire chart is presented in Form 3.1. Use of this chart should reveal gaps in a student's existing repertoire and lead to identification of new and revised priorities for domestic activities.

To illustrate this procedure, let us consider Mary Z., a 14-year-old student for whom a new IEP must be developed.

- **Step 1:** Refer to the scope and sequence chart (Chart 3.1) and examine the list of activities that appears in the column for the student's age group.

  *Mary Z.:* Mary is 14 years old. Therefore, we shall use the activities listed under the column heading "middle school" to compare her existing repertoire to what she might be expected to be able to participate in by the time she leaves middle school at the end of this year.

- **Step 2:** Look at the self-management/home living repertoire chart for the student's age group. (We will use the middle school repertoire chart [see Appendix C for blank copies] for Mary.) Rate the student's present level of performance for those activities considered to be part of his or her current repertoire. Fill in examples where needed, to note activities or clarify participation.

  *Mary Z.:* We have filled in information for activities that are considered to be a part of Mary's repertoire. She "eats meals" at home and in the school cafeteria with assistance on most steps. She also clears her place at the lunch table at school and disposes of garbage or

Repertoire chart for: __**Middle School (ages 12–14)**__  Student: __Mary Z.__

Domain: __Self-Management/Home Living__  Age: __i4__  Date: __9/18/90__

| Goal area | Present activities | Performance level — Check one | | | | Critical features — Check all that apply | | | | Note priority goal areas |
|---|---|---|---|---|---|---|---|---|---|---|
| | | Assistance on most steps | Assistance on some steps | Independent | Has related social skills? | Initiates as needed? | Makes choices? | Uses safety measures? | | |
| Eating and food preparation | Eat balanced meals with | | | | | | | | | • mealtime skills- |
| | appropriate manners | ✓ | | | | ✓ | | | | eating and social |
| | *Home and school* | | | | | | | | | |
| | *cafeteria* | | | | | | | | | |
| | | | | | | | | | | |
| | Choose nutritious foods: | | | | | | | | | |
| | breakfast, lunch, snacks | ✓ | | | | | | | | |
| | | | | | | | | | | |
| | *Occasionally points* | | | | | | ✓ | | | |
| | *to preference* | | | | | | | | | |
| | Plan and prepare snacks | | | | | | | | | • snack and meal |
| | for self | ✓ | | | | | | | | preparation — |
| | | | | | | | | | | increase par- |
| | | | | | | | | | | ticipation |
| | | | | | | | | | | |
| | Prepare simple meals: | | | | | | | | | |
| | breakfast, lunch (some | ✓ | | | | | | | | |
| | cooking) | | | | | | | | | |
| | | | | | | | | | | |
| | | | | | | | | | | |
| | | | | | | | | | | |
| | Serve food items to others | | | | | | | | | |
| | | | | | | | | | | |
| | | | | | | | | | | |
| | | | | | | | | | | |
| | Clear table and do dishes | | | | | | | | | |
| | after food preparation | | | | | | | | | |
| | *Clear place at* | | | | | | | | | |
| | *lunch (school)* | | ✓ | | | | | | | |
| | | | | | | | | | | |
| | Store food and leftovers | | | | | | | | | |
| | | | | | | | | | | |
| | | | | | | | | | | |
| | | | | | | | | | | |
| | | | | | | | | | | |

| | | Performance level | | | | Critical features | | | |
| | | Check one | | | | Check all that apply | | | |
| Goal area | Present activities | Assistance on most steps | Assistance on some steps | Independent | Has related social skills? | Initiates as needed? | Makes choices? | Uses safety measures? | Note priority goal areas |
|---|---|---|---|---|---|---|---|---|---|
| Grooming and dressing | Brush/comb and style hair | | | | | | | | |
| | (also choose hairstyle) | ✓ | | | | | | | |
| | | | | | | | | | |
| | | | | | | | | | |
| | Use skin care products | | | | | | | | |
| | (cosmetics if desired) | ✓ | | | | | | | • dressing and undressing |
| | | | | | | | | | |
| | | | | | | | | | |
| | Care for eyeglasses/contact | | | | | | | | |
| | lenses | NA | | | | | | | |
| | | | | | | | | | |
| | | | | | | | | | |
| | Get dressed/undressed | | | | | | | | |
| | (physical education, | | | | | | | | |
| | outer clothes) | ✓ | | | | | | | |
| | Pulls arms from coat sleeves | | | | | | | | |
| | Maintain neat appearance | | | | | | | | |
| | throughout school day | ✓ | | | | | | | |
| | | | | | | | | | |
| | | | | | | | | | |
| | | | | | | | | | |
| Hygiene and toileting | Use private and public | | | | | | | | |
| | toilets | ✓ | | | | | | | • use of public restrooms (school and community) |
| | Home and school | | | | | | | | |
| | Wash hands and face: | | | | | | | | |
| | routine times and for | | | | | | | | |
| | specific activities (food | | | | | | | | |
| | preparation) | ✓ | | | | | | | • shampooing |
| | Places hands under faucet | | | | | | | | |
| | Follow acceptable hygiene | | | | | | | | |
| | practices | ✓ | | | | | | | |
| | | | | | | | | | |
| | | | | | | | | | |
| | Manage menstrual care | ✓ | | | | | | | |
| | | | | | | | | | |
| | | | | | | | | | |

(continued)

| Goal area | Present activities | Performance level (Check one) | | | Has related social skills? | Critical features (Check all that apply) | | | Note priority goal areas |
|---|---|---|---|---|---|---|---|---|---|
| | | Assistance on most steps | Assistance on some steps | Independent | | Initiates as needed? | Makes choices? | Uses safety measures? | |
| Safety and health | Follow safety rules | ✓ | | | | | | | |
| | Exit building for emergency/alarm | ✓ | | | | | | | |
| | Take care with utensils | ✓ | | | | | | | |
| | Inform adult when sick/ injured | ✓ | | | | | | | |
| | Take medicine with supervision | ✓ | | | | | | | |
| | Avoid/report sexual abuse | | | | | | | | |
| | Report emergencies | ✓ | | | | | | | |
| | Use caution with strangers | ✓ | | | | | | | |
| | Use phone to obtain emergency help | | | | | | | | |
| | Avoid alcohol and other drugs | | | | | | | | |
| | Use appropriate first-aid procedures: minor injuries (cuts, burns) | | | | | | | | |
| | Maintain good personal health habits (diet, exercise) with supervision | ✓ | | | | | | | |

| Goal area | Present activities | Performance level (Check one) | | | Has related social skills? | Critical features (Check all that apply) | | | Note priority goal areas |
|---|---|---|---|---|---|---|---|---|---|
| | | Assistance on most steps | Assistance on some steps | Independent | Has related social skills? | Initiates as needed? | Makes choices? | Uses safety measures? | |
| Assisting and taking care of others (examples) | Shares tape player with friends | | ✓ | | | | ✓ | | |
| | | | | | | | | | |
| Budgeting and planning/scheduling | Plan and gather belongings for outings/activities | ✓ | | | | | | | • use hall locker at school for belongings |
| | Picks up pack-routines | | | | | ✓ | | | |
| | Take care of personal belongings | ✓ | | | | | | | |
| | Manage allowance and other personal purchases and money for personal gifts | | | | | | | | |
| | Manage weekly/monthly schedule | ✓ | | | | | | | • use a picture schedule to prepare for transitions |
| | Arrange activities with friends and family | ✓ | | | | | | | |
| | Participate in fundraising activities | | | | | | | | |

37

returns her tray (with assistance). (This is considered a significant degree of participation for Mary—for others greater participation may be expected.) Mary's participation in activities in other goal areas has also been noted.

- **Step 3:** Based on these ratings, note priority activities that will strengthen the student's repertoire. Also, note any features of the activity that will warrant special attention when finalizing goal selection.

   *Mary Z.:* Based on our ratings, we have noted priority activities in the righthand column of the repertoire chart. Priorities have been identified for four self-management/home living goal areas.

- **Step 4:** Use this information to fill in the teacher's portion of the *Conference Planning Form* (see Chapter 13 for a complete description of the conference planning process). This step is completed prior to, or during, the IEP conference.

   *Mary Z.:* The teacher's priorities from the self-management/home living repertoire charts have now been transferred to the *Conference Planning Form* for Mary. Parent and student priorities were filled in on the *Conference Planning Form* at the IEP conference. Parents and professionals were then in a position to look over the priorities and discuss any differences in how a student's needs are seen. In this case, Mary's parents and teacher agreed that there were needs in hygiene and scheduling. The teacher also felt that Mary should develop skills in meal preparation and the parents agreed with this goal. Her parents noted particular difficulty in getting Mary to participate and cooperate with washing her hair. They are requesting that this activity be addressed weekly after gym class. An IEP goal will be written for this activity.

After examining the scope and sequence chart, determining Mary's existing repertoire in this domain, and incorporating parent and other IEP team members' input, priorities in self-management/home living were identified for the revised IEP. These priority activities include: eating, preparing basic snacks and meals, using restrooms, shampooing, dressing, sharing and using a school locker, and following a picture schedule in school day routines.

## DETERMINING CONDITIONS OF INSTRUCTION

At this point, priority self-management/home living activities have been targeted by the team for inclusion in the revised IEP. Before these activities can be developed into instructional goals, however, conditions for instruction need to be determined and clearly defined. Three major considerations that will have an impact on skill acquisition are "where," "with whom," and "how often" a particular activity will be taught.

### Where Instruction Will Occur

Decisions about where an activity is taught can lead to very different interpretations of IEP goals. Consider the following example.
"Where should the activity be taught?"

- Mary will shampoo her hair *in the classroom sink.*
- Mary will shampoo her hair *in the locker room shower after swim class.*

   In this example, our attention is focused only on "where" an activity will be taught. Obviously, the gym locker room provides a more realistic setting for shampooing one's hair than would the classroom sink. Besides being a place where other people may shampoo their hair, it more closely approximates the criterion settings (e.g., home, the YWCA). Also, the instruction becomes a part of a hygiene routine that naturally occurs after physical education class. This would be more meaningful than scheduling isolated classroom instruction that is out of context.

Form 3.2 provides examples of possible instructional sites in both the community and school for a variety of self-management/home living activities. The sites that are considered to be undesirable are crossed off the chart, and are followed by brief explanations.

## With Whom Instruction Will Occur

Although the self-management/home living domain contains many activities that tend to be done alone or in privacy, there are others that are more enjoyable when friends are involved. Preparing a snack and eating lunch are examples of activities that often involve friends. Peers also serve as important models for learning the specific skills. Thus, when determining the conditions of instruction it is important to address with whom the instruction will occur.

FORM 3.2

### Self-Management/Home Living Activities: Possible Instructional Sites

| Example activities | Sites where activity typically occurs | Instructional options | |
|---|---|---|---|
| | | Possible instructional sites in the community | Possible instructional sites in school (undesirable options are crossed off) |
| Preparing and eating meals | Home Friends' homes | Actual home of students (during transition years) | Home economics room ~~Special Education classroom~~ (fails to teach students where activity is usually performed; unnecessary because more natural places exist) |
| Dressing self | Home Hall locker Gym locker room | YMCA | Gym locker room (e.g., after exercising, swimming) Hall locker area (outer clothing) ~~Classroom~~ (out of natural routine and context) |
| Brushing/ combing hair | Home School restrooms Public restrooms Locker rooms | Any setting where the need arises (e.g., upon arriving at the work site) | School restrooms Gym locker rooms ~~Classroom~~ (fails to teach students where activity is usually performed; unnecessary because more natural places exist) |
| Toileting | Home Homes of friends School restrooms Public restrooms | Any setting where the need arises (e.g., restaurant, mall) | School restrooms Private changing area |
| Clean up after meal | Home Fast-food restaurants Friends' homes | Fast-food restaurant (clear own place) Actual home of student (during transition years) | School cafeteria Home economics room |
| Reviewing daily/ weekly schedule and planning for upcoming events | Home | | Homeroom |

## How Often Instruction Will Occur

Equally important are decisions about how often the activity will be taught. Using the example "shampooing hair," an acceptable number of instructional sessions might range from daily to once or twice per week (depending on the student). "How often should the activity be taught?"

- Mary will learn to shampoo her hair *four times per year.*
- Mary will learn to shampoo her hair *once a week.*

While both of these goals address the activity "shampooing hair," they are likely to produce very different outcomes for the learner. In this example, shampooing hair will be taught either four times per year or one time per week. Needless to say, there is a significant difference between these two conditions. It is unlikely that a meaningful level of proficiency will be achieved in only four instructional sessions per school year. If, however, the activity "shampooing hair" is taught once a week, it is more likely that the student would make meaningful progress.

For many learners with moderate and severe disabilities, providing instruction on a particular skill less frequently than one time per week will contribute very little to the acquisition of that skill. Systematic instruction requires regular, planned instruction and practice sessions as part of a predictable schedule over a period of months and years.

## WRITING GOALS AND OBJECTIVES

Each goal should contain information about: 1) the activity, 2) where the activity will be taught, and 3) how often instruction will occur. Additional information indicating the level of student participation should also be included. Corresponding objectives that specify the skills the student will acquire related to each goal should be written. Consider the following example.

### Goals and Objectives for Mary Z.

#### Goal

When positioned at her school locker (approximately four to five times daily), Mary will remove or replace her outer clothing and other belongings to prepare for the next scheduled activity.

#### Objectives

- Mary will request help opening her locker by gesturing to a familiar classmate.
- When positioned at her locker before homeroom, Mary will grasp and remove her school bag for morning classes and replace it before lunch.
- When using her locker, Mary will greet familiar students nearby by smiling at them.

#### Goal

Mary will follow a picture schedule throughout each day to prepare belongings for transitions to activities in school and community settings.

### Objectives

- At the end of each period or activity, Mary will point (in response to a request) to the symbol on her picture schedule for the current activity and look at the symbol to the right for the next scheduled activity (successfully, throughout the day, for 5 consecutive days).
- After orienting to the next activity on her picture schedule, Mary will participate in gathering the appropriate belongings or items as needed.

### Goal

During daily situations that involve eating and drinking (home economics class, school cafeteria, and Burger King), Mary will increase her mealtime skills.

### Objectives

- Mary will pick up an appropriate amount of food (e.g., french fries), and complete chewing and swallowing before reaching for more (successfully, on four consecutive occasions).
- Mary will use an adapted spoon to eat soft food, independently (e.g., pudding, applesauce) ($1/2$-cup portion, on four consecutive occasions, with minimal spillage).
- When drinking from a glass (half full), Mary will take an appropriate amount of liquid into her mouth and pause between drinks (successfully, on four consecutive opportunities).
- When given her napkin by a peer or instructor, Mary will pick it up and bring it to her mouth and wipe (successfully, on four consecutive opportunities).
- Mary will seek eye contact with peers at her table.

### Goal

Mary will use public restrooms daily in familiar locations at school and in the community (hospital work site, Burger King).

### Objectives

- Mary will look at the commmunication board symbol for "restroom" as pointed to by her instructor before wheeling to the restroom.
- When positioned inside a familiar restroom (school or workplace), Mary will identify the accessible stall by wheeling to it (within 30 seconds, for five consecutive opportunities).
- When positioned next to the toilet, Mary will transfer from her wheelchair to the toilet by bearing weight while pivoting with assistance.
- When positioned in front of the air hand-dryer at the hospital or Burger King, Mary will push the button and hold her wet hands under the warm air (for at least 10 seconds, for three consecutive opportunities).

### Goal

Mary will increase her participation and speed in daily situations that require dressing and undressing (outerwear during arrivals and departures; swimwear for physical education class).

### Objectives

- While preparing for swim class, Mary will remove a pullover shirt by grasping and pulling it after her arms are removed from the sleeves (within 10 seconds of prompt, on five consecutive opportunities).
- Mary will participate in removing outerwear by pulling her hat off, pulling her mittens off, and pulling her coat off after it has been partially removed by a peer or instructor.
- Mary will participate in putting outerwear on by reaching for her coat in her locker, lifting her hat to her head, and pulling her mittens up after a peer or instructor has placed them part-way on her hands.

### Goal

Mary will increase her participation when shampooing (twice weekly) after swimming class.

### Objectives

- When shampoo is applied to her hair, Mary will use both hands to rub and lather her hair (for 20 seconds, for four consecutive occasions).
- Mary will hold a blow dryer to assist in drying her hair (for 60 seconds, on four consecutive opportunities).

### Goal

During home economics class (3 days/week), Mary will increase her participation in the preparation of snacks and meals with one to four classmates.

### Objectives

- When presented with premeasured amounts of liquid or dry ingredients in a 1- or 2-cup measuring cup (no more than half full), Mary will grasp the handle of the cup and pour ingredients into a mixing bowl or food processor positioned next to the cup (successfully, with minimal spillage, for five consecutive opportunities).
- When stirring ingredients, Mary will accept assistance from a peer/instructor to use a hand-over-hand method to assist her.
- Mary will request help to open a container by holding the container out to a classmate in the kitchen.
- In reponse to a question about what she wants, Mary will indicate whether she wants something to eat or drink using line drawings from her communication board (within 15 seconds, on four consecutive opportunities).
- Mary will assist in washing dishes with a partner after meal/snack preparation by placing rinsed items in the drainer. (Mary will be positioned in a parapodium stander with her knees straight during this activity.)

## QUESTIONS AND ANSWERS

Q: Aren't there some students who may never be able to engage in grooming and dressing independently?

A:   There are persons who will always require assistance with some activities. However, they can learn to participate in a more active manner by indicating preferences (e.g., what to wear, whom to receive help from, when to get dressed) and by gaining control over some aspect of the routine (e.g., using an adapted switch to control the power of a hair dryer or electric shaver). An individual may be expected to perform some steps within the routine such as opening his or her mouth without prompting during toothbrushing, or raising his head to have his neck shaved. Since a person will have to participate in such routines on a very frequent basis, every effort should be made to actively involve him or her in the activity.

Q:   What type of instruction would address the goal area "assisting and taking care of others"?

A:   Generally speaking, any activity that requires the student to recognize a need for help and respond to others by offering assistance might be appropriate. Often persons with moderate and severe disabilities are not taught to take notice of the needs of others or given opportunities to offer assistance. These skills are important and valued functions. It is unlikely that they will be developed by some learners without specific instruction. Examples of situations that might be addressed are: helping someone pick things up, taking note of someone whose arms are full and opening a door for them, getting the mail or newspaper in for parents without being requested to do so, and assisting with child care if there are young children in the household. More formal opportunities may include joining a helping organization and performing related duties as a volunteer (e.g., hospital volunteers, church volunteers, volunteer fire companies).

Q:   What types of assistive devices are available for feeding or self-care activities?

A:   Many adaptations are available for mealtime. These include varieties of special cups, glasses, plates, spoons, and plate guards (to build up a part of the plate to push food against). Other items to consider at mealtime are Dycem, a nonslip plastic material that acts as a "sticky" placemat; electric warming dishes to keep food warm throughout lengthy eating sessions; and foam rubber to "build up" spoon handles for self-feeding.

Dressing skills may be facilitated by modifying clothing in simple ways such as putting loops or tabs on zippers, and by choosing loosely cut sizes and styles; or by purchasing adaptive clothing such as Velcro-closure sneakers, or items from special catalogs.

Other suggestions include: washcloth mitts for bathing; liquid soap; electric toothbrushes; hand-held shower head; and adaptive switches to allow the students to control power on a hair dryer, a shaver, or a food appliance (e.g., blender).

## READINGS AND RESOURCES

Fraegon, S., Wheeler, J., Hill, L., Brankin, G., Costello, D., & Peters, W.M. (1983). A domestic training environment for students who are severely handicapped. *Journal of The Association for the Severely Handicapped, 4*(1), 49–61.

Orelove, F.P., & Sobsey, D. (1987a). Mealtime skills. In F.P. Orelove & D. Sobsey, *Educating children with multiple disabilities: A transdisciplinary approach.* (pp. 219–252). Baltimore: Paul H. Brookes Publishing Co.

Orelove, F.P., & Sobsey, D. (1987b). Toileting and dressing skills. In F. Orelove & D. Sobsey,

*Educating children with multiple disabilities: A transdisciplinary approach.* (pp. 253–284). Baltimore: Paul H. Brookes Publishing Co.

Perske, R., Clifton, A., McLean, B.M., & Stein, J.I. (Eds.). (1986). *Mealtimes for persons with severe handicaps.* Baltimore: Paul H. Brookes Publishing Co. (Original work published 1977)

# CHAPTER 4

# Vocational Domain

## Alison Ford, Jim Black, Pat Rogan, Roberta Schnorr, Luanna Meyer, Linda Davern, and Patrick Dempsey

In our society, it is considered appropriate for adults to work 8 hours a day, 5 days a week, for up to 51 weeks each year. While not all individuals are happy with their particular job at all times, involuntary lack of employment may result in a loss of self-esteem, and a loss of status in the eyes of others. For most citizens in our society, work is more than a means to earn money. It allows one to establish a positive self-image, gain the respect of others, and make a contribution to the community. The work environment is often a place where we broaden our social contacts and make friends.

Unfortunately, integrated employment has not been an option for most individuals with severe disabilities in our society. Follow-up studies of students who have exited special education programs have indicated the vast majority end up in sheltered settings or do not work at all (VanDeventer et al., 1981; Vogelsberg, Williams, & Friedl, 1980; Wehman, Kregal, & Seyforth, 1985). However, more recently we have begun to see a reversal of this trend due to changes in the vocational preparation of students and the development of supported employment programs, or integrated work options with appropriate supports, in adulthood. Consider, for example, the latest follow-up investigation of the Madison Metropolitan School District (Brown et al., 1987). Of the 32 students with severe disabilities who graduated during the 1984–1986 school years, 29 are working in community settings. This is a marked contrast from follow-up data reported on Madison graduates from 1971 to 1978, when 53 individuals graduated and only 1 worked in a community setting. Other districts around the country are working toward similar outcomes.

At least one important conclusion can be drawn from this follow-up information. If we continue to prepare students with severe disabilities for sheltered settings, it is likely they will be segregated as adults. However, if we attempt to change this pattern by providing longitudinal vocational training in community environments, we can increase the likelihood that integrated employment opportunities and supported work models will be developed in adulthood.

## SCOPE AND SEQUENCE

The scope of the vocational domain covers three major goal areas: classroom/school jobs and community-based work experiences, neighborhood jobs, and actual community jobs. Classroom/school jobs refer to helpful activities performed by students within the school building and during the course of the school day. Community-based work experiences also take place during the school day, but occur off-campus in typical businesses and work settings. These work training opportunities are considered a unique and critical aspect of a student's curriculum and, as such, are typically unpaid.

45

In contrast, neighborhood jobs occur during nonschool hours, may begin at a young age, and often provide opportunities to earn money. Families often encourage and support their young members to obtain and maintain neighborhood jobs. (Since these jobs typically occur after school and on weekends, they are listed in the extended version of the scope and sequence chart in Appendix B, at the end of the *Guide*.)

Finally, community jobs refer to actual employment situations where a student is hired as an employee during the transition phase of his or her high school career. Typically, students' community jobs parallel school hours and include wages.

The sequence reflects an accumulation of experiences in a variety of integrated environments, that build upon and strengthen an individual's vocational repertoire. The experiences can, and should, vary throughout a student's school career. The scope and sequence chart (Chart 4.1) provides examples of jobs that can be performed at various age levels.

## Elementary School

Community vocational training is longitudinal in nature. It requires a greater percentage of daily and weekly instructional time as a student approaches the completion of his or her schooling. Community-based vocational training would not be considered appropriate at the elementary level (students 5 to 11 years of age). However, there are many vocationally oriented experiences that can be performed within the students' classrooms and schools that would be considered appropriate. Some examples of classroom and school jobs available within the elementary school are included in Chart 4.1.

The purpose of classroom and school jobs at this age level is to develop positive work attitudes and behaviors. All students in elementary school should participate in a variety of activities that will help them learn to initiate assigned jobs, request help if needed, follow directions, work cooperatively with peers, accept criticism and correction, complete assigned responsibilities, and take pride in their own work.

The image value of specific jobs should be carefully considered before selecting them for instructional purposes. For instance, it would not be appropriate for students with severe handicaps to clean the bathrooms within their school. A useful general rule to follow is that the school jobs assigned to students with disabilities should be those that nonhandicapped students also do, or would feel comfortable doing, in the school environment (i.e., they would not be embarrassed in the presence of their peers). Students with disabilities should work together with their nondisabled peers to perform various work tasks in school.

## Middle School

Students enter middle school at age 12 and leave at approximately age 14. At around age 13, or at least 1 year before they move on to high school, they should receive community-based vocational training for a minimum of 1 half-day per week.

As with each of the community living areas, input from parents (and the student, when possible) should be secured. Parents should be encouraged to visit their child's vocational site to observe. Prior to transition to high school, school personnel should meet with parents to provide a cumulative written summary of each vocational experience provided during middle school years, and to discuss expectations for vocational instruction in high school.

Chart 4.1. Scope and sequence for vocational

| | Age and grade levels | | | | | |
| --- | --- | --- | --- | --- | --- | --- |
| | Elementary school | | | | | |
| Goal areas | Kindergarten (age 5) | Primary grades (ages 6–8) | Intermediate grades (ages 9–11) | Middle school (ages 12–14) | High school (ages 15–18) | Transition (ages 19–21) |
| Classroom/ school job and community-based work experiences (examples) | Carry out assigned classroom chores such as: Take attendance slip to office Get milk from cafeteria Serve snack | Carry out assigned classroom chores such as: Erase boards Collect papers Water plants Deliver messages to other locations | Carry out assigned classroom or school jobs such as: Erase and wash boards Clean erasers Pass back papers Take/record/deliver lunch count | Carry out assigned school jobs, such as: Work in school store Deliver/pick up A-V equipment Do clerical tasks in main office Sell lunch tickets Work at circulation desk in library   Have at least one community-based work experience: Prepare mailings in office building Bag groceries at supermarket Stamp forms at city hall Price records at music store | Carry out assigned school jobs, such as: Work in school store Work in guidance office (prepare passes) Work as teacher's assistant Work in athletic department (equipment manager)   Have at least four different community-based work experiences: Enter data into computer at insurance company Stock shelves in store Prepare food in restaurant Sterilize equipment in hospital Wash cars at public police/fire station Work as assistant in day care center | Enroll in specific job-training program Assume apprenticeship in particular trade Enroll in community college or university Work at community job (see examples under the goal area of "community jobs" below) |
| Neighborhood jobs (examples) | | | Fundraising in neighborhood for school activities | Fundraising in neighborhood for school activities | Fundraising in neighborhood for school activities | Fundraising: community group, club |
| Community jobs (examples) | | | | | | Work at: Supermarket or other store Restaurant Hospital Office Factory Day care center School |

47

## High School

Students enter high school at around age 15. Community-based vocational training should continue, for at least 2 half-days per week initially. Of course, the number of hours per day and days per week should be based on the individual, with the intent of gradually increasing hours throughout high school. By age 19, students should have experienced at least four work sites and types of work.

School personnel have the ongoing responsibility for providing specific information to parents regarding the upcoming transition process and the variables affecting the provision of integrated services and supports in adulthood. Parents should be encouraged to become actively involved with other parents in advocating for desired services, with teachers joining in this advocacy effort. Early contacts with adult vocational service providers in their community would enable parents to communicate the type of services they desire for their sons and daughters.

## Transition

During the last 3 years of a student's schooling, specific planning must occur to ensure a smooth transition from school to integrated adult services. Table 4.1 illustrates the major tasks that need to be undertaken and the times at which these tasks should

Table 4.1.    Transition planning guidelines

| Activities | Person(s) responsible | Timelines |
|---|---|---|
| Ongoing activities | | |
| 1. Teach transportation/mobility from home to school/work and return. | Classroom and vocational teachers | Ongoing |
| 2. Teach community and recreation activities to complement work schedules. | Classroom and vocational teachers | Ongoing |
| 3. Teach social/communication skills between student and nondisabled peers and co-workers. | All team members | Ongoing |
| 4. Maintain communication between student, parents, school, and agency staff. | All team members | Ongoing |
| Elementary school activities | | |
| 1. Discuss with parents the need to plan for vocational options after graduation. | Teacher | Yearly from age 9 as needed |
| 2. Discuss with parents the value of assigned chores at home to develop work skills and attitudes. | Teacher | Yearly from age 6 as needed |
| 3. Refer parents to local community advocacy groups and/or district special education advisory board. | Teacher | Yearly from age 6 as appropriate |
| 4. Include goals and objectives on the student's IEP to increase time-on-task, responsibility for classroom chores, and engaging in other functional daily living activities. | Teacher | Yearly from age 6 |
| Middle school activities | | |
| 1. Review, update, and complete actions on the elementary school list above. | Teacher | First year in middle school |

(continued)

**Table 4.1.** *(continued)*

| Activities | Person(s) responsible | Timelines |
|---|---|---|
| 2. Describe to parents the sequence of vocational programming from middle school through transition. Emphasize the importance of community-based training. | Teacher | First year in middle school and ongoing as needed |
| 3. Explain that school responsibility for services ends for students at age 21. Inform parents of the work options that exist in your community. Provide information on supported work. | Teacher | Yearly as needed |
| 4. Discuss with parents and students the types of work experiences desired in middle school. | Teacher, parents, and student | Yearly |
| 5. Write IEP goals for students that increase the types of work and amount of time spent at work sites each week. | IEP team | Yearly |
| 6. Maintain a cumulative record of all work experiences. | Classroom and vocational teachers | Yearly |
| 7. Increase involvement and responsibilities of student in chores at home and school. | Parents and teacher | Yearly |
| 8. Prior to transition to high school, discuss with parents and student the types of work experiences desired during high school. | Teacher, parents, and student | Last year in middle school |
| High school activities | | |
| 1. Continue to provide specific information to parents/guardians regarding the upcoming transition process and variables affecting their son/daughter's placement:<br>   a. Availability of services and funding<br>   b. Waiting list priorities and procedures for supported work<br>   c. The possibility of receiving less than full-time vocational services<br>   d. Effects on medical benefits and SSI | Vocational and classroom teachers | Yearly |
| 2. Encourage active involvement with other parents in advocacy efforts for support work services. | Vocational and classroom teachers | Yearly |
| 3. Assist parents to arrange visitations to services of interest. | Vocational and classroom teachers | By the time the student is 19 |
| 4. Provide names and numbers of key vocational and residential services providers. Assist parents to make contacts to express their need for services. | Vocational and classroom teachers | By age 19 and each year after |
| 5. Alert supported work agencies of the number of upcoming graduates each year for the next 5 years. | Vocational teacher | By fall of each year |
| 6. Meet with adult vocational agencies to discuss all upcoming graduates and begin transition planning. | Meeting set up by vocational staff. Includes vocational staff and teachers of graduates | By spring prior to last year of school |

These guidelines were adapted from those recommended by the Syracuse City School District Transition Planning Group (June, 1988). Members of this planning group included Jim Black, Marty Clark, John Emperor, Teresa Gavagan, Maggie Gioia, Melka Hermon, Martha Jenks, Sarah Jenkins, Virginia Maroney, Anthony Meggesto, Brian Nolan, Cheli Paetow, Dick Pratt, Pat Rogan, Tony Siracusa, Andrea Vasquez-German, Robert White, Virginia White, Chris Willis, and Prudence York.

occur. An individualized transition plan (ITP) should be developed by parents, school personnel, relevant adult services personnel, and significant others to ensure the coordinated involvement of all participants. This plan should include goals, strategies, and timelines for providing instruction in specific work and work-related skill areas through additional vocational experiences. By a student's last year in school, a job site should be secured that has the potential to continue after graduation. In order to achieve a good "job match," a site should be selected according to the individual's skills and preferences, proximity to home, availability of transportation options, and receptivity of employers. Even if a student is expected to require direct, ongoing supervision (rather than intensive initial training and subsequent "spot checks"), an *individual* community job (rather than an enclave or group site) should be secured. In other words, individual placements may be secured in different areas of the same building, but grouping two or more individuals with severe disabilities in the same work area should be avoided.

Timelines for fading school involvement and gradually "handing over" supervision responsibilities to receiving adult services and work-site personnel should be delineated in advance in the ITP. By the final months prior to graduation, individuals should be in their full work schedule, including daily community and recreational activities. If possible, wages should be negotiated while students are still in school. Examples of community-based vocational tasks and environments that might be selected during middle and high school years are presented in Table 4.2.

## ACTIVITY SELECTION

The scope and sequence chart (Chart 4.1) and the examples of "types of work" (Table 4.2) provide general guidelines for planning instructional programs for students in the vocational domain. These guidelines outline a preparatory vocational program that begins in kindergarten where all students are expected to help with some classroom jobs, and culminates in a transition from school to supported employment in the community. However, vocational preparation, like many other activities considered in this curriculum guide, must reflect each individual student's preferences, strengths and abilities, past experiences, and parental input. At this point, we turn our attention to the task of determining the priority vocational activities and environments of *individual* students. We follow a decision-making process similar to that offered in the other community living domains.

In the following example, we document, analyze, and build upon a student's vocational repertoire by using the repertoire chart in Form 4.1. The term "repertoire" is used here to refer to a student's current and past vocational performance in criterion and selected instructional environments. By comparing the student's vocational experiences to the scope and sequence chart, we can identify gaps in his or her repertoire. Then, we can determine priority vocational environments, activities, and skills for the student. To illustrate the activity selection process, we will continue with the example of Mary Z., a 14-year-old student for whom a new individualized education program (IEP) must be developed.

Table 4.2.  Community-based vocational training and transition sites for middle and high school students

| Types of work | Examples of tasks | Examples of vocational environments within which training might be provided |
|---|---|---|
| Stock | Price items<br>Stock shelves<br>Unload, load, and deliver supplies<br>Locate, stock, maintain, and put away supplies | Retail stores and shops<br>Hospitals (central supply departments) |
| Housekeeping | Clean rooms<br>Replace supplies (e.g., soap)<br>Make beds | Hotels/motels and hospitals |
| Building and maintenance | Maintain floors and carpets<br>Move furniture<br>Maintain grounds | Janitorial services, hotels/motels, and hospitals |
| Laundry | Sort laundry<br>Wash/dry laundry<br>Fold laundry<br>Deliver laundry | Hotels/motels, hospitals, and laundry services |
| Lawn and garden | Mow, rake, water, and trim lawn<br>Prune trees and shrubs<br>Plant trees and shrubs<br>Pot and water plants | Country clubs, parks, apartment buildings, residential areas, and greenhouses |
| Food service | Wash dishes and pans: by hand or by machine<br>Prepare food items<br>Serve food<br>Bus tables | Restaurants, cafeterias, and kitchens |
| Clerical and secretarial | File<br>Duplicate<br>Collate<br>Label<br>Sort<br>Stamp<br>Deliver<br>Enter data into computer<br>Microfilm<br>Answer phone | Offices |
| Industrial | Assemble<br>Disassemble<br>Salvage<br>Box<br>Package<br>Sort | Factories and plants |
| Customer service | Wait on customers<br>Bag purchased items<br>Answer questions | Stores and shops |

Repertoire chart for: **Middle School (ages 12–14)**    Student: Mary Z.

Domain: Vocational    Age: 14    Date: 9/18/90

| Goal areas and experiences | Performance level | | | | Critical features | | | | Note priority goal areas |
|---|---|---|---|---|---|---|---|---|---|
| | Check one | | | | Check all that apply | | | | |
| List the vocational experiences in the student's repertoire to the present date. Specify the environment, task, and sessions per week. | Assistance on most steps | Assistance on some steps | Independent | Has related social skills? | Broadens repertoire | Challenging | Student preference | Provides interactions with nonhandicapped co-workers | |
| Kindergarten and elementary school classroom/school jobs | | | | | | | | (Non H/C students) | |
| Wiped table (daily) | ✓ | | | | ✓ | | | | |
| Helped pick up | | | | | | | | | |
| attendance (daily) | ✓ | | | | ✓ | ✓ | ✓ | ✓ | |
| Collated school | | | | | | | | | |
| newspaper (2 x week) | ✓ | | | | | ✓ | | ✓ | |
| | | | | | | | | | |
| Middle school vocational training experiences | | | | | | | | | Develop community vocational site to: broaden repertoire |
| Stamped student | | | | | | | | | - offer opportunities for interactions |
| passes in | | | | | | | | | -2x/week |
| guidance office | | | | | | | | | (office or packaging work) |
| (2 x week) | ✓ | | | | | | | ✓ | |
| High school vocational training sites | | | | | | | | | - teach transportation and other work-related skills |
| | | | | | | | | | |
| | | | | | | | | | |
| | | | | | | | | | |
| | | | | | | | | | |
| Transition to community employment | | | | | | | | | |
| | | | | | | | | | |
| | | | | | | | | | |

- **Step 1:** Refer to the scope and sequence chart for the vocational domain (Chart 4.1) and review examples for the column representing the student's age group.

  *Mary Z.:* Since Mary is 14 years old, we refer to the "middle school" column. This provides a benchmark against which to measure her repertoire of experiences.

- **Step 2:** Look at the "vocational repertoire chart" (Form 4.1) for the student's age group. Write in all previous vocational experiences, settings, and tasks. Also, note the length and number of sessions per week of instruction that the student received. This longitudinal record provides an "at-a-glance" assessment of the student's vocational experience to date.

  *Mary Z.:* Mary is 14 years old. Therefore, we complete the kindergarten/elementary, and middle school sections of the "goal areas and experiences" column, listing her vocational experiences and specifying environments, tasks, and sessions per week. During elementary school, Mary was assigned the "chores" of picking up and delivering attendance envelopes, wiping tables in the classroom, and assisting with collating the school newspaper. Many of these tasks were performed with a nonhandicapped classmate. In her first year of middle school, Mary stamped passes in the guidance office. When we analyze Mary's repertoire compared to our guidelines, we can see that she is gaining an appropriate number of vocational experiences for her age.

- **Step 3:** Indicate the level of performance achieved by the student in each environment and task filled in on the repertoire chart. This provides a rough determination of the student's level of independence. Indicate whether the student demonstrated related social skills appropriate to that environment (e.g., greets co-workers). Also, check all "critical features" that applied to the environment or activity.

  *Mary Z.:* Mary's performance level data reveal that she needs "assistance on most steps" of the vocational activities within her repertoire. Additionally, she does not demonstrate many of the "related social skills" associated with work in community workplaces. The "critical features" column indicates that her recent training experiences were challenging and provided interactions with nonhandicapped co-workers. However, it also suggests that Mary does not enjoy this type of clerical work (stamping), and that her repertoire has *not* been broadened significantly.

- **Step 4:** Based on the listing and ratings, note priority vocational activities that will strengthen the student's vocational repertoire and fill any gaps identified in essential vocational experiences.

  *Mary Z.:* We determined that Mary needs a new vocational training site with a different type of work, one that will require more physical activity and has a better social climate. One possibility suggested was stuffing envelopes at an office. Another possibility is working in the packaging area of a hospital. These training experiences will allow a considerable amount of movement and the opportunity to interact with co-workers.

- **Step 5:** Fill in the teacher's column of the vocational section on the *Conference Planning Form*. This step is completed in conjunction with the IEP conference, which is described in Chapter 13.

  *Mary Z.:* The priorities identified in the repertoire chart are transferred to the *Conference Planning Form* with the priorities obtained from other team members. Mary's parents felt she should continue with office work. However, after discussion, it was decided by all the participants to go with packaging in a hospital setting for this semester, and to reevaluate this experience in January.

At this stage we have documented, analyzed, and identified priorities in an individual student's vocational repertoire. In our example of Mary Z., we have identified her priority need for a vocational experience that she would enjoy, and that would broaden her repertoire (e.g., dissimilar to her previous clerical experiences).

## DETERMINING THE CONDITIONS OF INSTRUCTION

Before we can write instructional goals and objectives for the student of concern, we first need to determine "where," and "how often," and "with whom" to teach the identified priority activity.

### Where Instruction Will Occur

There are a number of options to consider when determining where to teach priority vocational skills. Examples of possible instructional sites are listed in Form 4.2. Note that all simulated options are eliminated due to their inability to replicate key features of the criterion environments.

Community-based vocational sites are important during the middle school and high school years. It is typically not possible, or appropriate, to specify a criterion employment site prior to the student's last few years in school. To do so would result in restrictive "tracking" of students. In fact, the purpose of community-based vocational training experiences during the student's middle and early secondary schooling is to build a strong repertoire of *different* work experiences. This will provide opportunities for personal choice through a student's knowledge of alternatives, and perfor-

FORM 4.2

#### Vocational Activities: Possible Instructional Sites

| Example activities | Sites where activity would occur in adulthood | Instructional options | |
|---|---|---|---|
| | | Possible instructional sites in the community | Possible instructional sites in school (undesirable options are crossed off) |
| Packaging and unpackaging supplies | Hospital—central supply department Automotive parts company Games and toys factory | Hospital—central supply department Automotive parts company Games and toys factory | ~~Packaging small parts in classroom~~ (too many critical features cannot be replicated; e.g., social climate, co-worker support, transportation, quality, site-specific routines) |
| Stacking shelves | Grocery stores Drug stores Department stores Hardware stores Lawn and garden centers Hospital—central supply department Office supply store | Grocery store Drug stores Department stores Hardware stores Lawn and garden centers Hospital—central supply department Office supply store | ~~Practicing stocking shelves in a classroom or at a vocational training center~~ (too many critical features cannot be replicated; e.g., social climate, co-worker support, transportation, quality, site-specific routines) |
| Washing vehicles | Police/fire stations Parks and recreation department Highway department Taxicab companies Private businesses that use fleets of vans/ cars for delivery Auto dealers Rent-a-car companies | Police/fire stations Parks and recreation department Highway department Taxicab companies Private businesses that use fleets of vans/cars for delivery Auto dealers Rent-a-car companies | ~~Washing teacher's cars in school parking lot.~~ (too many critical features cannot be replicated; e.g., social climate, co-worker support, transportation, quality, site-specific routines) |

mance data with which to identify an optimum transition site for postschool employment. By virtue of being natural work environments, community-based training sites will share many similar features such as entering and exiting procedures, co-worker interactions, and break routines.

Potential postschool employment sites are particularly important to target during the transition years. Job-site modifications or individualized adaptations may need to be developed in order to enhance the functioning of an employee with disabilities. For example, special adaptive devices, co-worker or personal aide assistance, sub–minimum wage arrangements, and reduced work hours may be appropriate based on individual needs.

## How Often Instruction Will Occur

Because the goal of supported work typically involves full-time employment (unless contraindicated by individual employee needs), the vocational training experiences provided to a student should gradually build to full time, or the closest approximation of that level that is appropriate. The principle factor determining how often to provide instruction in the vocational domain involves *chronological age*. The older a student is and the closer he or she is to graduation, the greater the amount of time that should be spent in vocational instruction. The following section summarizes longitudinal guidelines for determining how often to provide vocational training during different stages of a student's education.

- *Kindergarten* (age 5): Students experience classroom chores on a daily basis. These are embedded within the daily schedule (e.g., handing out snacks and cleaning up afterward), and are the same or similar to those carried out by their nondisabled classmates.
- *Elementary school* (ages 6–11): The daily chores experienced in kindergarten gradually expand to more complex daily classroom and school "jobs." Students might spend 20–30 minutes a day engaged in meaningful, image-enhancing jobs within the school, with nonhandicapped classmates as partners whenever possible.
- *Middle school* (ages 12–14): The students experience community-based vocational sites for 1 half-day each week during middle school. This may increase to 2 half-day sessions prior to leaving middle school.
- *High school* (ages 15–18): Students receive training in community-based vocational sites for 2 half-day sessions at the beginning of their high school career and increase the amount of time spent in community work sites to a minimum of 3 half-days by age 18.
- *Transition to supported employment* (ages 19–21): During the final 2 years of a student's school career, a transitional employment site is developed. Students build to their postschool work schedule prior to graduation.

## With Whom Instruction Will Occur

Deciding with whom instruction will occur is as important as determining the nature of the vocational tasks. Community-based sites are used for teaching purposes because the conditions that exist in real work sites cannot be replicated adequately in the classroom, school setting, or other artificial environment. One of the primary conditions that students need to experience is adapting to and learning from the presence of co-workers who are not disabled. In many cases, individuals with disabilities lose jobs not because they cannot perform the work tasks, but because of their inappropriate behaviors and social skills. Consider the following two examples:

- A: John is learning to package supplies at Belmar Supply Company. He is stationed in an extra room that has been designed as his special work area.
- B: John is learning to package supplies at Belmar Supply Company. He is working side by side with other employees at Belmar who are completing similar tasks.

In example A, John has no opportunity to watch others perform the task. He cannot readily develop appropriate social skills and behaviors because he is isolated within the work setting. This situation also limits his opportunities to develop relationships with co-workers.

Example B allows John to experience the workplace in a manner similar to his co-workers. This increases the opportunities this training site can provide both in vocational and social skills development.

## Effect of Logistics

One additional factor may have an impact on your decisions regarding where and how often to teach vocational skills. This involves "logistics." As in other community living domains, transportation availability, staffing ratios, geographic location, necessary training-site development time, and many other issues may present apparent obstacles to the implementation of priority instructional activities. Many teachers and school districts are discovering a variety of strategies for overcoming logistical obstacles. In the "Questions and Answers" section at the end of this chapter some successful strategies and solutions are discussed.

## WRITING GOALS AND OBJECTIVES

At this point, IEP goals and objectives can be written. A goal statement should include the following information: 1) the activity, 2) the environment where the activity will be taught, and 3) how often the activity will be taught. Additional information may be added that targets the level of student participation. Instructional objectives should be written to correspond to each vocational goal. These instructional objectives provide a more specific and precise statement of the skills that a student is expected to acquire during the upcoming school year. Furthermore, these objectives will aid the instructional planning and monitoring phase of instruction.

In the vocational domain it is often logistically difficult to secure a community-based vocational training site, orient students to the site, and conduct assessments prior to writing the formal copy of the IEP. It may be necessary to write goals specifying *desired* activities and environments, and write objectives after more precise assessment of skills is possible at the training site.

Throughout this section, we have illustrated the proposed decision-making process with Mary Z., a middle school student. We continue that process and use the previous information gained from the scope and sequence chart (Chart 4.1), repertoire chart (Form 4.1), and the *Conference Planning Form* (see Chapter 13) to generate example goals and objectives for the vocational component of Mary's IEP.

## Goals and Objectives for Mary Z.

### Goal

When packaging and labeling items in the central supply department of Mercy Hospital (2 sessions/week), Mary will increase her rate and accuracy.

### Objectives

- When presented with plastic envelopes and corresponding supplies, Mary will place one item in each envelope (completing an average of 30 packets per hour, for five consecutive sessions).
- Mary will use a pincer grasp to place each package under the labeling machine, and remove it after labeling (completing an average of 25 packages per hour, for five consecutive sessions).
- When positioned standing with a belt supporting her hips, Mary will stand with her knees straight for 12 minutes out of each hour of her work session.
- After wearing a palmar splint for 20 minutes of packaging, Mary will maintain use of a pincer grasp (for the next three opportunities, for five consecutive sessions).

### Goal

Mary will look at symbols on a picture schedule to follow a prescribed routine at the hospital work site, including break.

### Objectives

When presented with a horizontal display of three work activities, Mary will look at the symbol for the next scheduled activity as pointed to by a co-worker or teacher.
- After being shown the symbol for "break," and being presented with her purse, Mary will remove her money envelope (within 10 seconds, on five consecutive opportunities).
- During her break, Mary will choose a snack or drink by pointing to a symbol on her communication board (from three choices, for five consecutive opportunities).
- Mary will order the desired items by pointing to a picture symbol (in plastic folder) for the cafeteria worker (within 5 seconds of clerk's attention, for five consecutive opportunities).
- Mary will pick up the money envelope (predetermined amount) from her tray and hand it to the cashier (within 5 seconds of clerk requesting payment, on five consecutive opportunities).

### Goal

While working at Mercy Hospital, Mary will increase her interactions with co-workers.

### Objectives

- Mary will greet familiar co-workers with a smile when she arrives for work and wave goodbye to them at the end of her shift.
- Mary will seek help from a nearby co-worker (Ann or Julie) by vocalizing and then pointing to a symbol on her board when she needs more work (as needed, for five consecutive work sessions).

## QUESTIONS AND ANSWERS

Q: Who should receive community-based vocational instruction?

A: Perhaps a more appropriate question is: Are there students with severe handicaps who should *not* be prepared to function in community vocational environments? In principle, *all* students, regardless of the severity of their handicap, should be prepared to work in the community. If we exclude someone from community-based vocational training, then in essence we are anticipating that during adulthood this student will lead a full life engaged in activities *other than work*. That is, we are envisioning that this person would be able to fill his or her day with meaningful domestic, recreational, and general community functioning activities—which is no easy task. Furthermore, if we deny certain individuals the opportunity to participate in an activity as highly valued as work, then we deny them the respect and dignity that is usually afforded workers in our society. Supported work options, which are now becoming available, enable adults who still require a great deal of supervision to work in community environments. These options will allow adults with severe disabilities to engage in productive, supported work within the mainstream, at a cost comparable to much more restrictive sheltered workshops and day activity centers.

Q: What is the best grouping of students and staff for community-based vocational instruction?

A: In general, the smaller the group size the better. Usually one or two students is appropriate. Heterogeneous grouping of students with a range of instructional and management needs facilitates the maximal placement of students per staff. The use of volunteers and student teachers to supplement staff at training sites is useful for program development. Teaching assistants, if trained on site and periodically supervised, may provide instruction at community sites. The use of related services personnel (e.g., language therapists, psychologists, physical therapists) to provide instruction and consultation within community vocational training sites holds great promise. Optimum group size must be weighed against the reality of limited staff resources. If we rely on a one-to-one model of vocational instruction, it is likely that not all students will receive community-based vocational instruction. In addition, one-to-one supervision is not readily available in adulthood due to limited resources.

Q: How do students get to and from community-based vocational training sites?

A: Students should use the public bus transportation system (if available). This provides meaningful opportunities to work on vocationally related skills such as pedestrian safety, appropriate social behavior in the community, time management, and so forth. In instances when it is absolutely impossible to utilize public transportation, school district buses can sometimes be arranged, particularly at times of the day when there is low demand. Teachers may transport students in their private vehicles, provided that they carefully follow district procedures, or students could walk. In any case, vocational sites located as close as possible to home/school should be secured.

Q: What vocational training sites have been developed by teachers?

A: A variety of vocational sites has been developed by teachers. Some examples include:

- Burnet Market, Inc.: The primary tasks performed included pricing and shelving items, and bagging groceries.

- Clean-All Products, Inc.: Products were labeled and boxed.
- Fairmount Athletic Club: Students were involved in maintenance and laundry.
- Fifield's Big M Grocery Store: Primary tasks performed were pricing items and stocking shelves, unloading trucks, and assisting the butcher.
- First Baptist Church Child Development Center, Inc.: The primary tasks performed were assisting the teachers during snack time, operating an industrial dishwashing machine, and putting away groceries.
- Great Games Video Arcade, Fairmount Fair Mall: The primary tasks performed included vacuuming, and cleaning video games.
- Kinney Shoes: Students stocked merchandise and performed light cleaning tasks.
- LeMoyne College Library: The primary tasks performed were labeling books, dusting shelves, and demagnetizing books.
- On the Rise Baked Goods: The primary tasks performed were chopping vegetables and making baked goods.
- Sheraton University Inn & Conference Center: The primary tasks performed were setting up and breaking down seating, setting tables, and running the dishwashing machine.
- City Police Garage: Two students received training in washing squad cars 2 days a week.
- J & T Automotive Inc.: The primary tasks performed were labeling and packaging automotive parts.
- Pizza Hut: The primary task performed was operating a commercial dishwasher.
- Phinney's Pet Supply: The primary tasks performed were sweeping out the store and cleaning cages.

Q: How are community-based vocational training sites secured?

A: Securing training sites requires a great deal of advanced planning. At the minimum, site development involves the following steps:

1. *Discuss with, and gain the support of your building level administrator, and parents of students.*
2. *Profile students.* Factors to consider when matching students to a vocational placement include: student age, work skills and behaviors, student interests, parental interest and support, and available staff resources and skills. Students with greater management and instructional needs may be grouped with more independent students in order to facilitate placement for all.
3. *Generate a list of possible training sites.* Factors to consider include accessibility, transportation requirements and options, opportunities for expansion in the site, opportunities for interactions with nonhandicapped people, the overall social climate of the site, and the availability of a range of vocational tasks appropriate to your student's needs and preferences. Consider listing businesses that employ friends and relatives, or those you patronize regularly.
4. *Prioritize site contacts.* Student profiles are then considered in light of the potential training sites. Instructional, administrative, and pragmatic issues are given appropriate consideration.
5. *Make an initial contact with a potential community training site.*
   a. Identify an initial contact person using a "walk-in" strategy, a tele-

phone call to a manager, or a telephone call to an acquaintance who is associated with the business.

b.  Briefly explain the purpose of the initial contact and request a meeting time to provide further information about your program.

c.  Send a letter of confirmation of the next meeting. Include any appropriate written information (e.g., a vocational program brochure).

6.  *Conduct the "planning" meeting.*

a.  Explain the purpose of your request to train at their site and discuss: the goals of education for your students, the limited effectiveness of simulated work experience, the need for real work experiences to teach appropriate work habits and attitudes, the fact that instruction will be provided by school personnel, the number of students that you are considering, and the amount of time per week that you would like to use the work environment as a training site.

b.  Provide suggestions of possible tasks that your students might do. For example, "I noticed some of your employees were labeling packages. What does this job entail? This might be a good task for some of my students to learn how to do."

c.  Mention the positive experiences of other community businesses that have participated in the program. Offer references of other places in which you or other teachers have developed successful training sites.

d.  Stress the fact that instruction and supervision will ensure quality control of completed work.

e.  Be prepared to respond to questions of liability for student injury. The training experience is part of the student's IEP. It is agreed to by parents and considered a part of the school day. Therefore, the school district is responsible. There is no pay involved because it is a training experience; therefore, there is no liability for Workers' Compensation.

f.  Ask for a tour and talk further about available tasks. Secure an agreement now, or attempt to arrange for a follow-up meeting.

g.  If agreement is reached, arrange a time to conduct a detailed ecological inventory of the tasks that students will perform.

7.  *Inventory the specific tasks that students will be trained to do.* Observe a nonhandicapped employee perform these tasks and note all significant details.

8.  *Write a training site agreement.* An approved *Community-Based Vocational Training Site Agreement* form (along with an example brochure of a vocational program) is included in Appendix D at the end of the *Guide.* This will clarify the responsibilities of both school personnel and the cooperating business. It should indicate the nature of the work to be performed by students, the days and times of training, the names of the supervising school personnel, and a statement regarding liability issues.

a.  File the agreement with the appropriate administrative office in the school district.

9.  *Verify that all district transportation and off-campus policies are complied with.*

a.  For training sites accessed by walking, personal vehicle, or public bus—specify site, transportation mode, days/times of the week, level of supervision, and target objectives in a permission slip to parents.

b. For training sites accessed by transportation in personal vehicles you may need to complete additional forms from the district central office.

## REFERENCES

Brown, L., Rogan, P., Shiraga, B., Zanella-Albright, K., Kessler, K., Bryson, F., VanDeventer, P., & Loomis, L. (1987). A vocational follow-up evaluation of the 1984 to 1986 Madison Metropolitan School District graduates with severe intellectual disabilities. *Monograph of The Association for Persons with Severe Handicaps, 2*(2).

VanDeventer, P., Yelinek, N., Brown, L., Schroeder, J., Loomis, R., & Gruenwald, L. (1981). A follow-up examination of severely handicapped graduates of the Madison Metropolitan School District from 1971–1978. In L. Brown, D. Baumgart, I. Pumpian, J. Nisbet, A. Ford, A. Donnellan, M. Sweet, R. Loomis, & J. Schroeder (Eds.), *Educational programs for severely handicapped students* (Vol. XI, pp. 1–177). Madison, WI: Madison Metropolitan School District.

Vogelsberg, R.T., Williams, W., & Friedl, M. (1980). Facilitating systems change for the severely handicapped: Secondary and adult services. *Journal of The Association for the Severely Handicapped, 5*(1), 73–85.

Wehman, P., Kregal, J., & Seyforth, J. (1985). Transition from school to work for individuals with severe handicaps: A follow-up study. *The Journal of The Association for Persons with Severe Handicaps, 10,* 132–136.

## ADDITIONAL READINGS AND RESOURCES

Bellamy, G. T., Rhodes, L. E., Wilcox, B., Albin, J. M., Mank, D. M., Boles, S. M., & Horner, R. H., (1984). Quality and equality in employment services for adults with severe disabilities. *Journal of The Association for Persons with Severe Handicaps, 9,* 270–277.

Brown, L., Shiraga, B., Ford, A., Nisbet, J., VanDeventer, P., Sweet, M., York, J., & Loomis, R. (1983). Teaching severely handicapped students to perform meaningful work in non-sheltered vocational environments. In L. Brown, A. Ford, J. Nisbet, M. Sweet, B. Shiraga, J. York, R. Loomis, & P. VanDeventer (Eds.), *Educational programs for severely handicapped students* (Vol.XIII). Madison, WI: Madison Metropolitan School District.

Brown, L., Shiraga, B., York, J., Kessler, K., Strohm, B., Rogan, P., Sweet, M., Zanella, K., VanDeventer, P., & Loomis, R. (1984). Integrated work opportunities for adults with severe handicaps: The extended training option. *Journal of The Association for Persons with Severe Handicaps, 9,* 262–269.

Mcloughlin, C.S., Garner, J.B., & Callahan, M.J. (Eds.). (1987). *Getting employed, staying employed: Job development and training for persons with severe handicaps.* Baltimore: Paul H. Brookes Publishing Co.

Nietupski, J., Hamre-Nietupski, S., Welch, J., & Anderson, R. (1983). Establishing and maintaining vocational training sites for moderately and severely handicapped students: Strategies for community/vocational trainers. *Education and Training of the Mentally Retarded, 18*(3), 169–175.

Pomerantz, D.J., & Marholin, D., II. (1977). Vocational habilitation: A time for change. In E. Sontag, J. Smith, & N. Certo (Eds.), *Educational programming for the severely and profoundly handicapped.* Reston, VA: Council for Exceptional Children.

Wehman, P., Moon, M.S., Everson, J.M., Wood, W., & Barcus, J.M. (1988). *Transition from school to work: New challenges for youth with severe disabilities.* Baltimore: Paul H. Brookes Publishing Co.

# CHAPTER 5

# Recreation/Leisure

*Alison Ford, Linda Davern, Luanna Meyer,*
*Roberta Schnorr, Jim Black, and Patrick Dempsey*

A substantial portion of a person's life requires the performance of constructive and personally significant recreation skills. Follow-up examinations of individuals with moderate and severe disabilities have revealed incredibly limited leisure skill repertoires. As adults, these individuals occupied most of their leisure time watching television, and if they did go out, they went in large, homogeneous groups. Consider the concern voiced by a parent of a high school student:

> I think he [my son] has got to be made aware that you don't just sit at home and watch television—that it isn't always your family that takes you places and does things with you. That you can go . . . you've got friends. Maybe they don't live right by . . . [but] you can meet them someplace and you can go.

This parent would like to see her son use his leisure time in a more active manner. She would like to see him go out more often and do things with his friends. To accomplish these goals, activities must be selected that will broaden and strengthen his recreation/leisure repertoire.

In addition to generally enhancing the quality of a person's life, the ability to occupy one's leisure time in a socially valued and acceptable manner may have a significant impact on where a person is able to live, whether he or she functions successfully on the job (e.g., utilizing "breaktime"), and the quality of relationships that develop with family, neighbors, and others in the community.

## SCOPE AND SEQUENCE

The recreational settings in which we expect a student to function should not differ significantly from those utilized by nonhandicapped peers. We would expect students to spend their free time in a variety of settings involved in a variety of activities. Therefore, the scope of the recreation/leisure domain includes five major goal areas:

1. School and extracurricular
2. Activities to do alone: at home and in the neighborhood
3. Activities to do with family and friends: at home and in the neighborhood
4. Activities to do with family and friends: in the community
5. Physical fitness

The first four goal areas specify the environment in which recreation occurs. Several goal areas indicate whether the individual participates alone or with others. The final goal area, physical fitness, is included to place particular emphasis on the importance of establishing and maintaining recreation routines that address physical well-being as well as personal enjoyment.

The scope and sequence chart (Chart 5.1) lists these goal areas as well as six age and grade levels: kindergarten (age 5), primary (ages 6–8), intermediate (ages 9–11), middle school (ages 12–14), high school (ages 15–18), and transition (ages 19–21).

Each goal area in Chart 5.1 is considered essential in that every student should either have an adequate repertoire of skills and activities in that area or be working on acquiring them. This does not necessarily mean that independence is expected, but that students participate in some activities within each goal area.

The array of activities that could be listed within each goal area is quite extensive and many activities do not fall exclusively under one goal area. For example, playing cards may be an activity engaged in alone (e.g., solitaire) or with family and friends (e.g., crazy eights). It may also occur at home, at school, or at a youth center.

The activities represented on the scope and sequence chart are just a *partial sampling* of activities that are appropriate for the given chronological ages. As the student grows older, certain activities that remain age appropriate are maintained in the student's repertoire, although the materials used may vary with age (e.g., looking at a teen-age magazine as opposed to a child's magazine, or playing Parcheesi as compared with Chutes and Ladders). Other activities are not maintained, but are replaced (e.g., playing with Legos, using playground equipment).

As the student progresses through school, there is a continual expansion of her or his activity repertoire. Thus, upon graduation from high school, the individual should be able to choose from a variety of activities when free time is available. Although the number of activities in which a student will be able to participate within each goal area is difficult to determine, most children and adults do have a large number of ways in which to spend leisure time. It would not be unusual for a young adult to routinely participate in 5–10 activities within most of the goal areas described. Although it may not be possible to provide instruction in this number of activities throughout a person's schooling, it is important to envision outcomes for students with moderate and severe handicaps that are similar to those expected for nonhandicapped students.

## ACTIVITY SELECTION

With the full range of recreation/leisure goal areas in mind, the task of determining specific activities for each individual begins. The following process noted earlier (with some modification) is recommended:

- **Step 1:** Refer to the scope and sequence chart (Chart 5.1), as well as other more extensive recreation/leisure activity listings, and identify activities that are appropriate for the chronological age of the student.

  *Mary Z.:* is 14 years old, and attending middle school.

- **Step 2:** Look at the repertoire chart (Form 5.1) and list the existing activities in the student's repertoire. This information will be gained from discussions with parents, reviews of existing school records, and teacher observations.

  *Mary Z.:* The activities listed on Mary's repertoire chart (Form 5.1) are those in which she engages on a fairly regular basis. Note that she does engage in activities in most goal areas, although the number of activities needs to be expanded.

- **Step 3:** Rate the student's present level of performance on each activity. Also check off which critical features are met by each activity.

  *Mary Z.:* All of the activities in Mary's repertoire are age appropriate. She obviously enjoys most of these. She needs assistance on most steps for many of the activities.

- **Step 4:** Based on these ratings, note any gaps that exist in each goal area. Other questions to consider when determining priority goal areas and activities include: Is the activity one that is enjoyed by the student, as well as widely accepted and highly valued by peers generally? Is there a balance between active and passive activities? Should specific activity/skills be strengthened or chosen for instruction because they will have long-term benefits (appropriate in adulthood also)?

    *Mary Z.:* Several gaps are revealed by Mary's repertoire chart (Form 5.1). For example, Mary engages in three activities while alone at home. All three are passive. She needs to expand her skills in this goal area. She also seems to spend little time with friends during nonschool hours.

- **Step 5:** Fill in the teacher's column of the recreation/leisure section on the *Conference Planning Form* (see Chapter 13 for an example of this form and more explicit suggestions on conducting individual education program [IEP] meetings). Since *student preference* plays a dominant role in this particular domain, note any information available at this time. Some activities may not be specified until the student has had the opportunity to express preferences, and choose from an array of activities.

    *Mary Z.:* Mary's parents completed the parent input form (see Appendix A for sample Parent Input Forms). During the conference, decisions were made as to certain priority areas for Mary's education. Several specific activities will be determined based on what Mary chooses.

Thus, after examining the scope and sequence chart (Chart 5.1) as well as other activity listings, completing the repertoire chart (Form 5.1), and incorporating the input from parents, the student, and other IEP team members, the priorities for Mary's upcoming IEP were identified. These included: joining an extracurricular club, using a tape player, introducing one or two new activities that can be engaged in alone or with friends, partially participating in playing Pictionary, using the public library (second semester), buying a snack at a fast-food restaurant, and continuing to attend swimming class. Mary will also be attending social events that occur throughout the school year.

## DETERMINING CONDITIONS OF INSTRUCTION

Once priority activities have been identified by the IEP team, several important decisions still remain before the IEP can be finalized. The conditions of instruction need to be determined. Three major conditions that will have an impact on skill acquisition are "where," "with whom," and "how often" instruction will occur.

### Where Instruction Will Occur

Determining the optimal site for instruction will be influenced by the nature of the activity. If learning how to play basketball is to be a priority activity for a student, that student will need to receive instruction in a gymnasium or outdoor basketball court, not in a special education classroom using a sponge ball and miniature net. Instruction in a special class using materials unlike those used in a gymnasium does not simulate the conditions of the activity closely enough to be an acceptable instructional situation. Examples of some of the demands that would be difficult to simulate include handling the ball, learning the rules of the court, and engaging in social interactions with teammates.

Chart 5.1. Scope and sequence for recreation/leisure

| | Age and grade levels | | | | | |
| | Elementary school | | | | | |
| Goal areas | Kindergarten (age 5) | Primary grades (ages 6–8) | Intermediate grades (ages 9–11) | Middle school (ages 12–14) | High school (ages 15–18) | Transition (ages 19–21) |
|---|---|---|---|---|---|---|
| School and extra-curricular (examples) | Look at books<br>Play computer games<br>Use crayons<br><br>Play catch<br>Engage in imaginary play | Read and look at books<br>Play computer games<br>Make simple crafts<br><br>Play catch<br>Play games at recess | Read books and magazines<br>Play computer games<br>Take art class<br><br>Shoot baskets/play catch<br>Play games at recess<br><br>Take instrumental lessons<br>Participate in school musical programs | Read books, magazines, newspapers<br>Play computer/electronic games<br>Take elective class in interest area (music, art)<br>Shoot baskets/play catch<br>"Hang out" with friends<br>Take instrumental lessons<br>Participate in school musical programs<br>Attend special events as spectator (games)<br>Attend school dances<br>Participate in clubs/activities (yearbook, newspaper) | Read books, magazines, newspapers<br>Play computer/electronic games<br>Take elective class in interest area (photography, electronics)<br>Shoot baskets/play catch<br>"Hang out" with friends<br>Take instrumental lessons<br>Participate in sports/chorus/band<br>Attend special events as spectator (sports, shows)<br>Attend school dances<br>Participate in clubs/activities (yearbook, pep rally, assemblies, science fair, student council) | Read books, magazines, newspapers<br>Play computer/electronic games<br>Take elective class in interest area (ceramics, drama)<br>Shoot baskets/play catch<br>"Hang out" with friends<br>Take instrumental lessons<br>Participate in sports/chorus/band<br>Attend special events as spectator (sports, concerts)<br>Attend school dances<br>Participate in clubs/activities (pep rally assemblies, mock U.N.) |
| Activities to do alone: at home and in the neighborhood (examples) | Look at books<br>Listen to music<br>Play computer games<br>Play musical instrument<br>Draw or color pictures | Read and look at books<br>Listen to music<br>Play computer games<br>Play musical instrument<br>Draw or color pictures | Read books and magazines<br>Listen to music<br>Play computer games<br>Play musical instrument<br>Write cards, letters | Read books, magazines, newspapers<br>Listen to music<br>Play computer/electronic games<br>Play musical instrument<br>Write cards, letters | Read books, magazines, newspapers<br>Listen to music<br>Play computer/electronic games<br>Play musical instrument<br>Write cards, letters<br>Cook/bake | Read books, magazines, newspapers<br>Listen to music<br>Play computer/electronic games<br>Play musical instrument<br>Write cards, letters<br>Cook/bake |

| | | | | | | |
|---|---|---|---|---|---|---|
| Activities to do with family and friends: at home and in the neighborhood (examples) | Play card games (fish, old maid)<br><br>Play simple board games (Chutes and Ladders)<br><br>Use swings/other playground equipment | Play card games (Uno, War)<br><br>Play board games (Sorry, Parcheesi)<br><br>Use swings/other playground equipment<br>Play kickball<br><br>Play computer games | Play card games (rummy, crazy eight's)<br>Play board games (Junior Trivial Pursuit, Monopoly, checkers)<br>Shoot baskets/play catch<br>Play dodgeball, kickball<br><br>Play computer games | Play card games (rummy, hearts)<br>Play board games (Pictionary, checkers/chess)<br>Shoot baskets/play catch<br>Play ball games (softball, basketball)<br>Play computer/video games | Play card games (pinochle, hearts)<br>Play board games (Trivial Pursuit, Pictionary)<br>Shoot baskets/play catch<br>Play ball games (softball, soccer)<br>Play computer/video games | Play card games (bridge, poker, gin, rummy)<br>Play board games (Trivial Pursuit, Pictionary, chess)<br>Shoot baskets/play catch<br>Play ball games and yard games (croquet, volleyball, bocce, basketball)<br>Play computer/video games |
| Activities to do with family and friends: in the community (examples) | | | Go to restaurant with friends | Go to restaurant with friends | Go to restaurant with friends<br>Go to shopping malls with friends | Go to restaurant with friends<br>Go to shopping malls with friends |
| Physical Fitness (examples) | Participate in exercise routine | Participate in exercise routine | Participate in exercise routine in physical education class<br>Participate in conditioning for team sport (soccer, track, football)<br>Play sport regularly for exercise (volleyball, basketball, cross-country skiing) | Participate in exercise routine in physical education class<br>Participate in conditioning for team sport (soccer, track, football)<br>Play sport regularly for exercise (tennis, basketball)<br><br>Lift weights<br>Participate in aerobic dance/exercise class | Participate in exercise routine in physical education class<br>Participate in conditioning for team sport (soccer, track, football)<br>Play sport regularly for exercise (tennis, basketball)<br><br>Lift weights<br>Participate in aerobic dance/exercise class | Participate in exercise routine in physical education class<br>Bike/swim/jog/walk for exercise<br><br>Play sport regularly for exercise (tennis, basketball)<br><br>Lift weights<br>Participate in aerobic dance/exercise class |

Repertoire chart for: **Middle School (ages 12–14)**  Student: _Mary Z._

Domain: _Recreation/Leisure_  Age: _14_  Date: _9/18/90_

| Goal area | Present activities | Assistance on most steps | Assistance on some steps | Independent | Has related social skills? | Obviously enjoys | Age appropriate | Interacts w/non-handicap peers | Note priority goal areas |
|---|---|---|---|---|---|---|---|---|---|
| School and extra-curricular (examples) | Attends Phys. Ed. (P.E. 7) | ✓ | | | | ✓ | ✓ | ✓ | • What extracurricular opportunities exist? |
| | | | | | | ✓ | ✓ | ✓ | • school-sponsored events (dances, concerts) |
| | Attends Art class | ✓ | | | | | | | • Continue Swim class – Pg 8 |
| | | | | | | | | | |
| | | | | | | | | | |
| Activities to do alone: at home and in the neighborhood (examples) | Watches TV | | ✓ | | | ✓ | ✓ | | • Strengthen use of tape player. |
| | Listens to radio | | ✓ | | | ✓ | ✓ | | • Home computer available – computer games? |
| | Uses cassette tape player | ✓ | | | | ✓ | ✓ | | |
| | | | | | | | | | |
| Activities to do with family and friends: at home and in the neighborhood (examples) | | ✓ | | | | ✓ | ✓ | | • need for expansion |
| | Goes out to eat w/ family | ✓ | | | | ✓ | ✓ | | • restaurant? • use public library |
| Physical fitness (examples) | Attends PE | ✓ | | | | ✓ | ✓ | ✓ | • Continue swimming |
| | | | | | | | | | |
| | | | | | | | | | |
| | | | | | | | | | |
| Activities to do alone: in the community (examples) | | | | | | | | | |
| | | | | | | | | | |
| | | | | | | | | | |
| | | | | | | | | | |
| Activities to do with family and friends: in the community (examples) | Sometimes watches sister play "Pictionary" | | | | | | | | • Teach target steps to participate in table games |
| | | | | | | | | | |

Some leisure or recreation activities may be successfully taught in school. Activities such as learning how to play a card game are not as dependent on unique environmental cues as others such as window shopping or using a restaurant.

Regardless of which environments become the instructional sites, it cannot be assumed that a student has mastered an activity until success is demonstrated in the target environment—that is, the environment in which the activity would naturally occur (e.g., home, a friend's house, recess at school, a gymnasium at school).

Form 5.2 lists possible instructional sites for activities in the recreation/leisure domain. Several instructional options are eliminated because they do not replicate the activity closely enough. Options such as teaching a student to play basketball in a classroom or teaching a student to ride a bike in the school hallways have been crossed off because they do not adequately replicate the complex features of the environments in which these activities would typically occur. Viable school sites (those not crossed out) can be selected and prioritized, considering additional factors such as the individual's learning style.

The learning style of some students is such that they are less able to apply what is learned in a simulated setting to other settings—that is, they do not generalize the acquired skills. This is an important factor to consider when determining the instructional site. In such a case, the instructional site will need to very closely replicate the features of the site in which the student will need to use the skills.

## With Whom Instruction Will Occur

Opportunities to receive instruction with students who are not handicapped is a fundamental component of the decision of where to provide instruction. Consider the following example:

- Mary will play computer games in a special classroom *with a teaching assistant*.
- Mary will play computer games in the media center *with two other eighth graders* and a teaching assistant who will monitor the activity.

Mary's teacher has determined that it is important for Mary to learn this leisure skill with others her own age. He has made this decision not only because he is interested in Mary learning from people her own age, but also because this is an opportunity for her to get to know others and possibly develop friendships. In addition, Mary shows much greater interest in the activity when she is in the media center. This is an attractive atmosphere with a lot of student movement and activity. Therefore the question of "with whom instruction will occur" weighs very heavily in determining the conditions of instruction.

## How Often Instruction Will Occur

Determining the frequency of instruction will have a significant impact on a student's progress. Consider the following:

- Mary will play computer games in the media center with two other eighth graders *four times during the school year*.
- Mary will play computer games in the media center with two other eighth graders *three times per week*.

If Mary enjoys computer games but only receives instruction in their use four times during the school year, it is unlikely that she will significantly improve her

FORM 5.2

Recreation/Leisure Activities: Possible Instructional Sites

| Example activities | Sites where activity would typically occur | Instructional options | |
|---|---|---|---|
| | | Possible instructional sites in the community | Possible instructional sites in school (undesirable options are crossed off) |
| Basketball | Gymnasium<br>Outdoor court | Recreation center<br>Park | Gymnasium after school<br>Gymnasium during physical education class<br>~~Mini-sponge basketball and not in special class~~ |
| Swimming | Family or neighbor's pool<br>Public pool<br>Beach<br>School pool | Public pool<br>YMCA | School pool during integrated physical education class<br>School pool during swim team practice (extracurricular) |
| Following a recorded aerobics routine | Home (VCR)<br>Friend's house (VCR)<br>Fitness club<br>School | Fitness club | Gymnasium during integrated physical education class |
| Biking | On sidewalks or streets in neighborhood<br>At a park—on a bike path | On sidewalks or streets in neighborhood<br>At a park—on a bike path | On sidewalks or streets surrounding the school<br>On the playground (if permitted by school policy)<br>~~School hallway~~<br>(Does not adequately replicate the real activity) |
| Playing a card game (rummy) | Home<br>Friend's house<br>Youth center<br>School | | Study hall (if permitted by school policy)<br>Cafeteria<br>Homeroom (if permitted) |
| Playing a computer game | Home<br>Friend's house<br>Public library<br>Youth center<br>School | Public library | Computer room<br>Media center<br>Classroom |
| Running or participating in field events | Neighborhood<br>Parks (sponsored events)<br>Health facility<br>School | Health facility | School track (team practice)<br>Playground/recess |

ability to participate. Frequency is determined by the nature of the activity, and the learning characteristics of the student. The frequency of instruction should allow the student to make significant gains over the school year.

The frequency of sessions may be affected by how often "free time" *naturally* occurs. For example, Sarah is an elementary school student who is learning to play Four Square during the daily recess period. In addition to taking advantage of the natural opportunities to engage in this activity, she will also gain the obvious benefit of interacting with her nonhandicapped peers.

## Effect of Logistics

As with all community living domains, "logistics" such as staff-to-student ratios, transportation, and cost will affect the frequency of instruction as well as the availability of specific environments chosen. Fortunately, there are many typical school settings and activities (including extracurricular opportunities) to choose from when learning recreation/leisure skills.

## WRITING GOALS AND OBJECTIVES

Once the questions of where, with whom, and how often to teach a priority activity have been addressed, IEP goals and objectives can be written. The goal statement should include at least the following information: 1) the activity, 2) where and with whom the activity will be taught, and 3) how often the instruction will occur. Objectives should be written to correspond to each goal. These objectives should provide a more specific indication of the skills that the student will acquire during the upcoming year. The recreation/leisure goals and objectives for Mary Z. follow.

### Goals and Objectives for Mary Z.

#### Goal

While preparing for swim class (four times/week), Mary will increase her level of participation, as well as her interactions with her classmates.

#### Objectives

- When positioned approximately 5 feet from her locker (which will be situated at the end of a bench) Mary will wheel to her locker (within 1 minute, on five consecutive opportunities).
- Mary will greet familiar classmates by smiling at them.
- Mary will request help opening her locker by gesturing to a familiar classmate (within 30 seconds, during four consecutive opportunities).

#### Goal

While participating in Swimming 8 (four times/week), Mary will increase her individual and group participation skills.

#### Objectives

- After being assisted to travel part of the width of the pool (while wearing a life jacket), Mary will use her arms to propel herself the last 6 feet to the side of the pool (within 2 minutes, on four consecutive opportunities).
- While supported by an adapted innertube, Mary will participate in water polo games by watching the ball and pushing it toward another student when it is nearby (for four of five opportunities, during four consecutive games).

#### Goal

Mary will increase her participation in using a cassette tape player in the school library when selected as a free-time activity (opportunities throughout week).

## Objectives

- Mary will greet the librarian, request headphones by pointing to symbols on her communication board, and thank the librarian by smiling (successfully, on four of five consecutive opportunities).
- Mary will demonstrate music preference by pointing to one of three tapes offered (from three choices, on four consecutive opportunities).
- Mary will gesture when a change in tape or activity is desired.
- After the tape is placed in the tape player, Mary will press the lid down as indicated by her partner (within 10 seconds, on four consecutive opportunities).

## Goal

Mary will participate in table games with eighth-grade friends during free time at school (several opportunities per week).

## Objectives

- When playing Pictionary with two pairs of familiar classmates, Mary will roll the dice for her team when requested.
- Mary will explore new leisure activities that are introduced to her by her peers. She will communicate her level of interest through facial responses, body language, and the amount of physical effort she puts forth to participate.

## Goal

In the computer room during after-school computer club (twice a week) and daily school-day opportunities, Mary will participate in computer games with another student.

## Objectives

- Upon entering the computer room with a peer, Mary will point to a symbol on her board to show interest in playing a computer game (from two familiar choices, within 10 seconds of questions, on four consecutive opportunities).
- While playing a computer game with a friend, Mary will respond to a friend's reminder of her turn by pressing the keyboard (single switch games will be used) within 10 seconds, on 5 consecutive opportunities.

## Goal

During the second semester, Mary will use the public library weekly.

## Objectives

- When presented with choices of books, Mary will indicate a preference by pointing to or taking the desired book.
- Mary will return the librarian's greeting by making eye contact and extending her library card.
- While an instructor or friend holds her pack open, Mary will place her library book in her pack (within 15 seconds, on four consecutive opportunities).

## Goal

While participating daily in Art 8, Mary will be encouraged to express herself creatively by contributing to the completion of individual and group art projects.

## Objectives

- When positioned approximately 5 feet from her table, Mary will wheel to the table and greet classmates who share her table by smiling at them (within 1 minute, for five consecutive classes).
- Mary will use a variety of art materials and tools to create artwork with her classmates (e.g., pottery, printmaking, papier mâché).
- When a supply or assistance is need, Mary will gesture to a nearby classmate to request help and, if necessary, point to the appropriate line drawing on her communication board.

## Goal

While participating in industrial arts class, Mary will contribute to the completion of woodworking projects with a classmate or group of classmates.

## Objectives

- Mary will use an adapted sander to smooth over the surfaces of pieces of a woodworking project.
- Mary will grasp an opened bottle of glue and respond to a request to squeeze the bottle as a classmate/instructor guides her hand over the surface to be joined.
- Mary will grasp the built-up handle of a foam paint brush to apply paint or stain to completed wood projects with her group.
- Mary will greet familiar classmates in her group by smiling at them as they join the table.
- After wearing a palmar splint for 10 minutes while handling individual fasteners, Mary will maintain a pincer grasp as she hands fasteners to a classmate during assembly of projects (for next five opportunities, for four consecutive classes).
- While sanding or finishing projects, Mary will be positioned in a parapodium stander for 10 minutes of each class. During this time she will stand with her knees straight.

## QUESTIONS AND ANSWERS

Q: In attempting to identify recreation/leisure activities, do parent, teacher, and student preferences all have equal weight?

A: No. This domain is unique in that *student preference* is the most heavily weighted consideration when identifying activities. Although certain factors such as age appropriateness and an activity's value in longitudinal planning may be overriding, student preference will ultimately determine whether the acquired skills are actually used during free time.

Q: How can we assure that the skills acquired during school hours "carry over" to nonschool hours?

A: Clear and frequent communication between school and home will facilitate carry over. If activity rules or materials are adapted to meet a particular student's needs, this information needs to be carefully conveyed to the family.

A nonhandicapped friend, an advocate, a university student, a sibling, or a city recreation employee could participate in a portion of the school program to gain an understanding of goals and instructional procedures. Carry-over sessions could be arranged to maximize the probability that the recreation skills acquired during school are used during after-school hours and weekends. For example: On Mondays, Wednesdays, and Fridays, Mary participates in Pictionary and other table games with several other eighth graders. One of the eighth graders is Nicole, who lives near Mary and frequently spends time with Mary and her sisters at their house. Nicole is familiar with how Mary participates and knows from the school sessions how to remind or encourage her. She helps Mary to participate in a similar fashion when they play with Mary's sisters at home.

Q: How much of a student's educational program should be devoted to teaching recreation/leisure skills?

A: As noted earlier, having recreation/leisure skills and knowing how to use them appropriately is an important part of a student's preparation. The amount of time devoted to this instruction will vary with the individual. As more services become available to address this domain outside of school hours, the need to provide instruction in these skills during the school day will be lessened.

Q: How about a student who has become attached to age-*in*appropriate toys and games?

A: "Attachment" is often offered as a reason for presenting age-inappropriate toys and games to students with severe handicaps (e.g., a 13-year-old using a toddler "busy box"). While it may be the case that the student enjoys the toy, it is usually possible (and definitely necessary) to find an activity that has similar features, but is appropriate for the student's age. For example, the student may enjoy the busy box because she is able to activate it by a simple movement and enjoys the sound. The same may be possible with a computer game that is not only appropriate for her age, but attractive to other students.

Q: Are there some recreation/leisure activities that have lifelong value, and should be encouraged for this reason?

A: There are many activities in which young teens engage that will remain appropriate well into adulthood. If a substantial amount of student and teacher time will need to be invested in gaining mastery of or maximal participation in an activity, it may be wise to encourage the use of activities with long-term value rather than those that are geared toward a more limited age group. Examples of such activities include: playing cards, board games such as Parcheesi, or electronic games such as Merlin, pinball, use of exercise equipment, use of a camera, skiing, and jogging.

## READINGS AND RESOURCES

Ford, A., Brown, L., Pumpian, I., Baumgart, D., Nisbet, J., Schroeder, J., & Loomis, R. (1984). Strategies for developing individualized recreation and leisure programs for severely handicapped students. In N. Certo, N. Haring, & R. York (Eds.), *Public school integration of severely handicapped students: Rational issues and progressive alternatives* (pp. 245–275). Baltimore: Paul H. Brookes Publishing Co.

Nietupski, J., Hamre-Nietupski, S., & Ayres, B. (1984). Review of task analytic leisure skill training efforts: Practitioner implications and future research needs. *Journal of The Association for Persons with Severe Handicaps*, *9*, 88–97.

Schleien, S.J., & Ray, M.T. (1988). *Community recreation and persons with disabilities: Strategies for integration.* Baltimore: Paul H. Brookes Publishing Co.

Walker, P., Edinger, B., Willis, C., & Kenney, M. (1989). *Involving students with severe disabilities in extracurricular activities.* Syracuse, NY: Center on Human Policy, Syracuse University.

Wehman, P., & Schleien, S. (1981). *Leisure programs for handicapped persons: Adaptations, techniques, and curriculum.* Austin, TX: PRO-ED.

Wuerch, B.B., & Voeltz, L.M. (1982). *Longitudinal leisure skills for severely handicapped learners: The Ho'onanea curriculum component.* Baltimore: Paul H. Brookes Publishing Co.

CHAPTER 6

# General Community Functioning

*Alison Ford, Roberta Schnorr, Luanna Meyer,*
*Linda Davern, Jim Black, and Pat Dempsey*

> I'd like him to be able to get around the community and be able to get involved in other activities and things that he could do. (Parent of a high school student)

Many individuals learn to cross streets, shop in stores, and use restaurants without the need for systematic instruction. This, however, is not the case for most students with moderate and severe disabilities. It cannot be assumed that they will acquire these critical skills on the basis of exposure alone. Thus, instructional sessions must be developed so that each student receives consistent and repeated opportunities to develop general community functioning skills, or—in the words of the parent quoted above—"to get around the community."

## SCOPE AND SEQUENCE

The scope of the general community functioning domain covers six major goal areas: travel, community safety, grocery shopping, general shopping, eating out, and using services. The sequence reflects the general order in which the experiences are presented across age groups. These experiences, which need to be defined for each individual, should continuously build upon and strengthen his or her existing repertoire.

The scope and sequence chart presented in Chart 6.1 contains general community functioning activities across six age and grade levels; kindergarten (age 5), primary elementary (ages 6–8), intermediate elementary (ages 9–11), middle school (ages 12–14), high school (ages 15–18) and transition (ages 19–21). It would be expected that these activities would be addressed during school years for most students with severe disabilities.

Notice from the chart that riding school and city buses, traveling to various destinations, and crossing streets are included as important activities. These kinds of community activities are likely to occur on a frequent basis and they present a no-choice situation; that is, if the student does not participate, someone else will move him or her through the steps necessary to complete the activity. Traveling requires some level of involvement on the part of the student and it occurs on a frequent basis, so why not teach him or her to become an active participant?

Grocery shopping, general shopping, and eating out represent another kind of community activity. These activities are represented because of their strong presence in most people's lives. By not addressing them in an individualized education program (IEP), we may be drastically limiting a student's opportunities for active par-

Chart 6.1. Scope and sequence for general community functioning

| | Age and grade levels | | | | | |
| | Elementary school | | | Middle school (ages 12–14) | High school (ages 15–18) | Transition (ages 19–21) |
| Goal areas | Kindergarten (age 5) | Primary grades (ages 6–8) | Intermediate grades (ages 9–11) | | | |
| --- | --- | --- | --- | --- | --- | --- |
| Travel | Walk or ride bus to and from school<br>Walk to and from school bus and to points in school (classroom, office)<br>Cross street: stop at curb | Walk or ride bus to and from school<br>Walk to and from school bus and to points in school (classroom, cafeteria, office, music room)<br>Cross street: familiar, low-traffic intersections | Walk, ride bus, or ride bike to and from school<br>Walk to various destinations in school and in the community (neighborhood grocery store, mailbox)<br>Cross streets safely | Walk, ride bus, or ride bike to and from school<br>Walk to various destinations in school and in the community (store, restaurant, job site)<br>Cross streets safely<br>Use public bus/subway for general transportation | Walk, ride bus, or ride bike to and from school<br>Walk to various destinations in school and in the community (store, restaurant, job site)<br>Cross streets safely<br>Use public bus/subway for general transportation | Walk, ride bus, or ride bike to and from home and community sites<br>Walk to various destinations<br>Cross streets safely<br>Use public bus/subway for general transportation |
| Community safety | | | Problem solve if lost in new places<br>Use caution with strangers | Problem solve if lost in new places<br>Use caution with strangers | Problem solve if lost in new places<br>Use caution with strangers | Problem solve if lost in new places<br>Use caution with strangers |
| Grocery shopping | | | Buy two to three items at neighborhood store for self (snack) or classroom snack activity | Buy items needed for specific planned menu | Buy items needed for specific meal or special event | Buy items needed for specific meal or special event |
| General shopping | | Buy item at school store | Buy item at school store | Buy few items in store with limited money amount<br>Purchase personal care items | Shop for desired items in shopping center<br>Purchase personal care items | Shop for desired items in shopping center<br>Purchase personal care items |
| Eating out | Carry milk/lunch money<br>Follow school cafeteria routine | Carry milk/lunch money<br>Follow school cafeteria routine | Carry milk/lunch money<br>Follow school cafeteria routine<br>Order and pay: familiar fast-food restaurants, snack stand<br>Buy snack/drinks from vending machine | Budget/carry money for lunch/snacks<br>Eat in school cafeteria<br>Order and eat in fast-food restaurant<br>Buy snack/drinks from vending machine | Budget/carry money for lunch/snacks<br>Eat in school/public cafeteria<br>Order and eat in fast-food restaurant<br>Buy snack/drinks from vending machines | Budget/carry money for meals and snacks<br>Eat in public cafeteria<br>Order and eat in fast-food restaurant<br>Buy snack/drinks from vending machines |
| Using services | Mail letter at corner mailbox<br>Use pay phone with help | Mail letter at corner mailbox<br>Use pay phone with help | Mail letters<br>Use pay phone | Use post office<br>Use pay phone<br>Ask for assistance in stores | Use post office<br>Use pay phone<br>Ask for assistance in stores, information booth | Use post office<br>Use pay phone<br>Ask for assistance appropriately in store, information booth |

ticipation in routines of everyday life. The regularity with which these routines occur often serves the purpose of connecting a person with severe disabilities with other members of his or her community.

## ACTIVITY SELECTION

The scope and sequence chart (Chart 6.1) provides a broad framework of general community functioning activities that can be applied to many students. Eventually the decision-making process must shift from this broad perspective to one that focuses on the individual. Thus, using the scope and sequence chart as a general reference point, we can now turn our attention to the needs of *each individual* student who requires instruction in this area.

Selecting individualized activities in the general community functioning domain follows a procedure similar to that used in the other commmunity living domains. A repertoire chart is presented in Form 6.1. This general community functioning repertoire chart should reveal the gaps in a student's existing repertoire and lead to the identification of new and revised priority activities. To illustrate the steps for completing the chart, we will continue with the example of Mary for whom a new IEP must be designed.

- **Step 1:** Refer to the scope and sequence chart (Chart 6.1) and examine the list of activities that appears in the column for the student's chronological age group.

  *Mary Z.:* Mary Z. is 14 years old. Therefore, we shall refer to the activities listed under the column heading "middle school" when comparing her existing repertoire.

- **Step 2:** Look at the general community functioning repertoire chart (Form 6.1) for the student's age group. Rate the student's present level of performance for those activities considered to be part of his or her current repertoire. Fill in examples, where needed, to note activities or clarify participation.

  *Mary Z.:* We have filled in the middle school repertoire chart with information for several activities that are part of Mary's repertoire. She rides the school bus to and from school and travels from the bus to her locker, although she needs assistance on most steps. As a part of her school program, Mary received ongoing instruction in using the school cafeteria, wheeling from school to the mailbox, and buying an item at the school store. Both the performance level and the critical features of each activity listed have been rated.

  As can be seen by the chart, Mary needs assistance on many steps for the activities in which she currently participates. It appears that little attention has been been given to the critical feature of choice making. Thus, this might be a feature that deserves special attention when designing the upcoming IEP.

- **Step 3:** Based on these ratings, note priority activities that will strengthen the student's repertoire. Also note any features of the activity that will warrant special attention when finalizing goal selection.

  *Mary Z.:* Based upon our ratings, we have noted priority activities in the right-hand column of the repertoire chart. Priorities have been identified for two of the six goal areas for Mary.

- **Step 4:** Use this information to fill in the teacher's portion of the *Conference Planning Form*. (More explicit suggestions for IEP conferences are discussed in Chapter 13.)

  *Mary Z.:* The teacher's priorities from the repertoire chart have now been listed on the *Conference Planning Form*. At the meeting, parent and student priorities were added. Parents and professionals discussed their priorities and differences in how they saw Mary's

FORM 6.1

Repertoire chart for: __Middle School (ages 12–14)__    Student: _Mary Z._

Domain: _____General Community Functioning_____    Age: _14_    Date: _9/18/90_

| Goal area | Present activities | Performance level — Check one | | | Critical features — Check all that apply | | | | Note priority goal areas |
|---|---|---|---|---|---|---|---|---|---|
| | | Assistance on most steps | Assistance on some steps | Independent | Has related social skills? | Initiates as needed? | Makes choices? | Uses safety measures? | |
| Travel | Walk, ride bus, ride bike | | | | | | | | |
| | to and from school | ✓ | | | | | | | |
| | | | | | | | | | |
| | | | | | | | | | |
| | *Wheel* ~~Walk~~ to various | | | | | | | | |
| | destinations | ✓ | | | | | | | |
| | *School to mailbox* | | | | | | | | |
| | | | | | | | | | |
| | Cross streets safely | | | | | | | | |
| | | | | | | | | | |
| | | | | | | | | | |
| | | | | | | | | | |
| | Use public bus/subway for | | | | | | | | |
| | general transportation | | | | | | | | |
| | | | | | | | | | |
| | | | | | | | | | |
| | | | | | | | | | |
| Community safety | Problem solve if lost in | | | | | | | | |
| | new places | ✓ | | | | | | | |
| | | | | | | | | | |
| | | | | | | | | | |
| | | | | | | | | | |
| | Use caution with strangers | | ✓ | | | | | | |
| | *Uncomfortable with* | | | | | | | | |
| | *strangers* | | | | | | | | |
| | | | | | | | | | |
| Grocery shopping | Buy items needed for | | | | | | | | |
| | specific planned menu, | | | | | | | | |
| | with help | ✓ | | | | | | | • *Purchase* |
| | *Purchases a* | | | | | | | | *familiar items from* |
| | *familiar item* | | | | | | | | *grocery store.* |
| | | | | | | | | | |

(continued)

FORM 6.1
(continued)

| Goal area | Present activities | Assistance on most steps | Assistance on some steps | Independent | Has related social skills? | Initiates as needed? | Makes choices? | Uses safety measures? | Note priority goal areas |
|---|---|---|---|---|---|---|---|---|---|
| General shopping | Buy few items in store with limited money amount | | | | | | | | |
| | *Used school store* | ✓ | | | | | | | |
| | Purchase personal care items | | | | | | | | |
| Eating out | Eat in school cafeteria | ✓ | | | | | | | • School cafeteria routine |
| | Order and eat in fast-food restaurant | ✓ | | | | | | | |
| | *Enjoys with family* | | | | | | ✓ | | • use fast food restaurant |
| | Buy food/drinks from vending machines | | | | | | | | |
| | Budget/carry money for lunch/snacks | | | | | | | | |
| Using services | Use post office | | | | | | | | |
| | Use pay phone  *N A* | | | | | | | | |
| | Ask for assistance in stores | | | | | | | | |

needs in this area. Members eventually agreed on two priority areas for general community functioning instruction.

Thus, after examining the scope and sequence chart, determining Mary's existing repertoire in this area, and incorporating the input from parents and other IEP team members, priorities for Mary's upcoming IEP were identified. These priority activities included: purchasing a familiar item from a grocery store, and eating out in a fast-food restaurant in addition to using the middle school cafeteria.

## DETERMINING THE CONDITIONS OF INSTRUCTION

Once the IEP team has identified priority general community functioning activities, the conditions of instruction must be determined before the IEP can be finalized. Three major conditions that will have an impact on skill acquisition are "where," "with whom," and "how often" instruction will occur.

### Where Instruction Will Occur

The nature of the activity must be considered when determining an appropriate site for instruction. For instance, if it is a priority for a student to learn to purchase an item from a grocery store, the student will need to receive regular instruction in a grocery store rather than role playing the shopping experience in a simulated "classroom store." It would not be possible to replicate the large array of items or many other store conditions in a classroom to create an acceptable instructional site. Some demands that would be difficult to simulate include maneuvering a cart through the aisles, awareness of employees and other customers, locating a target department and items, and determining a suitable checkout lane.

Some activities from the scope and sequence chart for general community functioning may be taught and practiced in school. These include traveling to and from school locations, eating in the school cafeteria, making purchases at the school store, using a vending machine, or using a pay phone. It is important to note that mastery of these school-based activities is *not* a prerequisite for related community-based activities. Indeed, if a school-based activity is being used, it seems best to use a community site concurrently (Brown et al., 1983; Horner, McDonnell, & Bellamy, 1986).

Form 6.2 lists possible instructional sites for activities in the general community functioning domain. Several options are crossed off because they do not replicate the activity in a meaningful way. Options such as street crossing in the school hallway, using a cardboard bus in the classroom, and locating items in a classroom store have been crossed off because they do not adequately replicate the complex features of the community settings where these activities would typically occur.

While some general community functioning activities may be virtually impossible to replicate effectively in school settings, others can be at least partially simulated in school with a degree of success—for some students. For example, George, age 13, receives instruction on restaurant use in the classroom. During the in-school sessions he practices reading real menus and calculating the cost of his order. He has demonstrated an ability to apply the skills learned in school to various restaurant settings. The situations that are difficult to replicate in school (e.g., problem solving how to position himself so that he can read the fast-food menu, responding to the requests of the waiter/waitress, maneuvering his way back to the table) become the focus of instruction during the weekly sessions at the actual restaurant. Again, viable

| | | | FORM 6.2 |
|---|---|---|---|

General Community Functioning Activities: Possible Instructional Sites

| Example activities | Site where activity would typically occur | Possible instructional sites in the community | Possible instructional sites in school (undesirable options are crossed off) |
|---|---|---|---|
| Pedestrian traveling | Routes from home to a familiar destination<br>Routes from one familiar destination (e.g., public library) to another (e.g., restaurant) | Routes from school to a familiar destination (if not enough natural opportunities exist in the current schedule, the teacher might incorporate short trips to the store or mailbox)<br>Routes from one familiar destination to another | ~~Practicing crossing the street adjacent to the schoolyard~~ (without a destination)<br>(lacks a meaningful purpose, students may begin to view it as an exercise rather than an important means for traveling to a destination)<br>~~Practicing with "walk" and "don't walk" signs in the~~ school hallway or classroom<br>(does not adequately replicate the real activity) |
| Riding the school bus or public bus | Bus routes between home and to a familiar destination (e.g., school, work)<br>Bus routes from one familiar destination (e.g., work) to another (e.g., friend's house) | Riding typical school bus or "late" bus for after-school activities<br>Bus routes from school to a familiar destination | Practicing with a cardboard bus in the classroom<br>(does not adequately replicate the real activity) |
| Grocery shopping | Grocery store(s) regularly used by student and family during non-school hours | Grocery store | Practicing portions of the skill sequence: calculating the cost of real items (that are kept on a shelf in the classroom or in a cabinet)<br>~~Setting up a classroom store so that students can practice locating items~~<br>(does not adequately replicate the complex array of items typically found in the grocery store) |
| Eating out in a fast-food restaurant | Fast-food restaurants used with family and friends during non-school hours | Fast-food restaurants | Practicing portions of the skill sequence: calculating the cost of menu items |
| Purchasing a snack from a vending machine | Vending machine in the workplace<br>Vending machines used regularly in other community settings (e.g., YMCA, bowling alley) | Vending machine in the workplace<br>Vending machines used regularly in other community settings (e.g., YMCA, bowling alley) | Vending machine in school (e.g., student lounge; possibly teacher's lounge if acceptable)<br>~~Vending machine board game~~<br>(does not adequately replicate the real world) |

school instructional sites (such as a classroom used to practice money handling) should be selected only if they match the individual's learning style (e.g., chronological age, learning pace, generalization) and only if they are used concurrently with instruction in community sites.

### With Whom Instruction Will Occur

The opportunity to receive daily instruction with students who are not handicapped is an essential element of determining where to teach. Consider the following example. "With whom should the activity be taught?"

- Mary will wheel from the school bus to her locker *with the teacher assistant*.
- Mary will wheel from the school bus to her locker *with two eighth-grade classmates* who have lockers nearby.

The presence or participation of others plays an important part in instruction. The priority activity of traveling from bus to locker is addressed in both alternatives. The condition of "with whom the instruction occurs" is obviously different. Other students in the setting may contribute to a presence (or absence) of natural cues for desired behaviors and skills. The motivation of individual students to participate may be strongly influenced by who the other participants are. In the case of students who are not yet proficient at an activity or who are partially participating, the availability of students who have complementary skills is particularly important. By limiting instructional situations to individual sessions (one-to-one) or groups of students with disabilities, we run the risk of fostering over-dependence on adults.

### How Often Instruction Will Occur?

The frequency at which an instructional session occurs is also strongly related to student progress. Consider the following example.
"How often should the activity be taught?"

- Mary will order and purchase a snack at Burger King during each of *four activity field trips during the school year*.
- Mary will order and purchase a snack at Burger King during *weekly instructional sessions throughout the school year*.

While the activity of ordering and eating at Burger King are targeted in both alternatives, the conditions (in this case frequency) under which it will be taught are noticeably different. If Mary's restaurant instruction is limited to four sessions during the school year, she is not likely to acquire new skills—skills that would increase her ability to participate actively in this setting. Frequency of instruction must consider the nature of the activity as well as the learning style of the student. The frequency of instruction must allow the student to make significant measurable gains over the school year.

Principles for determining the conditions of instruction can only be applied after considering the unique learning and performance characteristics of the student; that is, chronological age, learning pace, generalization, and motivation. For example, consider Jennifer, age 14. She is able to make purposeful responses only after large amounts of instructional time and trials. She retains few skills without ongoing practice and has difficulty generalizing performances across settings. Because of these learning characteristics, Jennifer receives all of her instruction within meaningful routines (within these routines, she might receive massed practice on certain component skills). In the general community functioning domain, virtually all of her instruction occurs in community instructional sites (e.g., wheeling to a familiar destination, eating/drinking a snack at Burger King and Pizza Hut, purchasing a familiar item from Lancaster Foods). In contrast, Jeffrey, age 14, has demonstrated an ability to acquire skills at a much faster rate and to apply skills taught in school to community settings. Thus, he receives some simulated instruction when he is in school (e.g., practicing reading a restaurant menu, practicing money handling). This simulated instruction is carried out concurrently with actual community instruction.

## Effect of Logistics

Again, we need to mention a significant factor that influences where, with whom, and how often an activity is taught. That factor is "logistics." Undoubtedly, the final decisions about instructional arrangements will be influenced by logistical factors such as staff-to-student ratios, transportation, and cost. For example, a teacher might need to select a large grocery store that will comfortably accommodate three to four students, rather than crowding into a little neighborhood market. A site might be selected because it is within walking distance to the school; thus reducing the need for transporting students in a wheelchair van. Potentially costly activities such as eating at restaurants might need to be scheduled less frequently or modified (e.g., purchase one item rather than an entire meal) to minimize the cost. Some of the common problems and solutions encountered in the general community functioning domain are discussed in the "Questions and Answers" section of this chapter and in Chapters 14 and 15.

## WRITING GOALS AND OBJECTIVES

Once the questions of where, with whom, and how often to teach a priority activity have been addressed, IEP goals and objectives can be written. The goal statement should include at least the following information: 1) the activity, 2) where and with whom the activity will be taught, and 3) how often the activity will be taught. Other information should be added when it helps to clarify the level of student participation. Objectives should be written to correspond to each goal. These objectives should provide a more specific indication of the skills that the student will acquire during the upcoming year.

In the beginning of this chapter, a repertoire chart was completed for Mary (Form 6.1) and several priority activities were identified. These activities have been translated into goals and objectives for her IEP. They are presented below.

---

### Goals and Objectives for Mary Z.

#### Goal

When preparing to buy a school lunch or a snack (at work or a fast-food restaurant), Mary will review available menu items to plan her purchase and use a picture-symbol strategy and gestures to communicate her request.

#### Objectives

- When presented with picture-symbol cards of food items, Mary will point to the items she would like to buy before entering the serving or ordering line (from three choices, on five consecutive opportunities).
- Mary will point for the food service worker to picture-symbol cards (displayed in a clear plastic folder) for items that she has selected (within 5 seconds of worker's attention, for five consecutive opportunities).

- After receiving the items she ordered, Mary will seek eye contact and smile to thank the clerk.
- At the appropriate time in a given routine, Mary will hand her money envelope to the cashier (within 5 seconds of clerk requesting payment, on five consecutive opportunities).

## Goal

When making routine purchases (school cafeteria, school store, snacks in community settings, store purchases), Mary will select the correct money envelope for the situation (predetermined amount strategy).

## Objectives

- When presented with two money envelopes with picture symbols for routine purchase situations, Mary will take the envelope she needs for the current situation (successfully, four of five times, for five consecutive opportunities).
- When making multiple purchases (when practical) Mary will choose the correct money envelopes and pool the money to cover the cost of all items (successfully, four of five times, for five consecutive opportunities).
- At the appropriate time in a given routine, Mary will hand her money envelope to the cashier (within 5 seconds of clerk requesting payment, on five consecutive opportunities).

## Goal

Mary will increase her level of active participation in grocery shopping for two to three familiar items using picture symbol shopping cards (an adapted shopping list) and money envelopes (an adaptation consisting of envelopes containing the amount of money necessary to purchase an item represented by a picture symbol on the outside).

## Objectives

- When positioned in front of grocery section containing the item for which she has a picture-symbol card, Mary will visually scan (horizontally) the shelf for an area of about 3 feet (successfully, on five consecutive shopping trips).
- Once the desired item is located, Mary will remove it from the shelf and place it in her shopping basket (successfully, with a given item, on four of five consecutive store trips).
- When positioned in front of the cashier, Mary will hand over her money envelope to the cashier (within 5 seconds of clerk requesting payment, for five consecutive opportunities).

## QUESTIONS AND ANSWERS

Q: Isn't elementary school too early to begin instruction in the community?

A: Elementary-age students are too young to spend a lot of school time in the community for instructional purposes. The guidelines reflect this concern by suggesting that just a *limited* amount of time be spent in the community so that most of the programmatic efforts can be devoted to integrating students into their elementary schools. However, there are some general community functioning skills that deserve our systematic attention at a very early age. Perhaps one of the most critical areas to address is the activity "crossing streets."

Successful street crossing requires very sophisticated judgment skills. In order to teach a student to be as independent as possible by the time he or she graduates from high school, instruction must begin early in elementary school. To ensure that students are provided with meaningful contexts to develop these skills, instruction could occur under the following conditions: 1) learning to walk to and from school with nonhandicapped students; 2) going to a nearby grocery store; 3) going to the mailbox to mail letters written as part of a regularly scheduled language experience exercise, or mailing the letters for office personnel.

At the middle and high school levels, greater emphasis should be placed on students learning to get to and from *a particular site* with a peer (teacher assistance should be faded as much as possible). Such instruction could occur when students are going to a job site, a grocery store, or other regularly scheduled community-site destinations. For example: Every Tuesday, John and Paula go to a grocery store where they are learning to stock shelves as part of their vocational program. The store is located 6 blocks away from the middle school. During the first 4 months, the teacher was within an arm's reach of the students as she provided the necessary street-crossing instruction. As the students became more proficient (this was carefully documented through weekly data collection procedures), the teacher faded the instructional cues to the point where, in month 6, the teacher was walking 5–8 feet behind them.

Q: How do we secure the necessary funds for these shopping and restaurant activities?

A: One temporary source of funding may be parents. If appropriate, they might be willing to give their sons and daughters a weekly allowance. As part of the school program, the student could learn how to budget his or her money for the week (e.g., $1.00 for breakfast on Tuesdays, $.50 for break at the work site on Wednesdays and Fridays). Of course, no student should be denied community-based learning experiences because of a lack of money. Thus, other sources of funding should be secured. Some strategies that have been used by teachers include having students purchase groceries for teachers or for home economics class. At some point, however, the funds necessary to carry out effective community-based instruction should be made available in the same way that funds are available for other instructional materials.

Q: How can I provide instruction in community sites with nonhandicapped peers?

A: Some elementary-level teachers have scheduled community activities such as grocery shopping as part of a class activity that addresses a wide range of goals for different students. The student group that goes to the grocery store may include one or two members who remain constant each week—students who need weekly instruction in the real setting. Other group members (nondisabled) may take turns, perhaps each student only going once every month or so. All participating students in this type of arrangement should be working on a targeted skill. Skills might range from practical steps in making a purchase to applying math concepts such as estimating or percentages.

Others who teach secondary-age students have sometimes recruited students from study hall, or utilized students who were scheduled as "peer partners" to participate in community activities.

## REFERENCES

Brown, L., Nisbet, J., Ford, A., Sweet, M., Shiraga, B., York, J., & Loomis, R. (1983). The critical need for nonschool instruction in educational programs for severely handicapped students. *Journal of The Association for Persons with Severe Handicaps, 8*(3), 71–77.

Horner, R., McDonnell, J., & Bellamy, T. (1986). Teaching generalized skills: General case instruction in simulated and community settings. In R.H. Horner, L.H. Meyer, & H.D.B. Fredericks (Eds.), *Education of learners with severe handicaps: Exemplary service strategies* (pp. 289–314). Baltimore: Paul H. Brookes Publishing Co.

## ADDITIONAL READINGS AND RESOURCES

Browder, D., & Snell, M. (1983). Daily living skills. In M.E. Snell (Ed.), *Systematic instruction of the moderately and severely handicapped* (pp. 358–409). Columbus, OH: Charles E. Merrill.

Browder, D., Snell, M., & Wildonger, B. (1988). Simulation and community-based instruction of vending machines with time delay. *Education and Training in Mental Retardation, 23,* 175–185.

Falvey, M. (1986). Community skills. In M.A. Falvey, *Community-based curriculum: Instructional strategies for students with severe handicaps* (pp. 61–76). Baltimore: Paul H. Brookes Publishing Co.

Gee, K., Harrell, R., & Rosenberg, R. (1987). Teaching orientation and mobility skills within and across natural opportunities for travel: A model designed for learners with multiple disabilities. In L. Goetz, D. Guess, & K. Stremel-Campbell (Eds.), *Innovative program design for individuals with dual sensory impairments* (pp. 127–157). Baltimore: Paul H. Brookes Publishing Co.

Vogelsberg, R.T., & Rusch, F.R. (1980). Community mobility training. In F.R. Rusch & D.E. Mithaug (Eds.), *Vocational training for mentally retarded adults.* Champaign, IL: Research Press.

Vogelsberg, R.T., Williams, W., & Bellamy, G.T. (1982). Preparation for independent living. In B. Wilcox & G.T. Bellamy, *Design of high school programs for severely handicapped students* (pp. 153–173). Baltimore: Paul H. Brookes Publishing Co.

Wheeler, J., Ford, A., Nietupski, J., & Brown, L. (1980). Teaching moderately and severely handicapped adolescents to shop in supermarkets using pocket calculators. *Education and Training of the Mentally Retarded, 15,* 108–112.

# Functional Academic Skills

Reading, writing and arithmetic (the three Rs) are often considered the "basics" of a curriculum. Elementary schools typically allocate a substantial amount of time to these areas (an average of 90 minutes daily for language arts—reading and writing—and 54 minutes each day for mathematics [Goodlad, 1984, p. 132]). In return for this investment, elementary school students are expected to learn to read, write, and perform basic operations in arithmetic. In the middle and high school years, students are expected to draw upon this foundation of basic skills as they pursue advanced applications that take the forms of English, geometry, algebra, and so forth. Throughout and beyond their school years, students are expected to apply these fundamental skills and concepts across a wide range of real-life situations.

By graduation, many students reach a level of academic mastery and specialization that should enhance their choices in adulthood—whether it be joining the work force or engaging in college studies. Few would dispute that these outcomes are of considerable value to the students who have mastered them. But what about those students who probably will not even closely approximate this level of academic proficiency? Should they follow the same curricular sequences but at a slower pace? Should we be willing to accept whatever outcome to which this "slower paced" approach leads—even if it results, upon graduation, in skills of little practical value such as reading at the early first-grade level or being able to rote count to seven? Or should we assume that, for some students, these academic skills are not worth pursuing at all? Certainly, academic skills *are* worth pursuing—but we now realize that in order to be meaningful to some students, careful consideration must be given to the curricular sequence that will be followed.

## ADAPTING THE REGULAR CURRICULUM

It is not unusual for students with moderate and severe disabilities to begin their educational careers by following the same curriculum as their peers without disabilities. The "regular" curricular sequences in preschools and kindergartens are generally designed to accommodate a wide range of learners and the academic lessons often occur within fun and meaningful activities (e.g., learning numbers while playing a game, interpreting words and pictures while preparing a snack). As students get older and academic sequences become more defined, discrepancies in performance are likely to become more pronounced. As this occurs, some decisions to adapt the curriculum will become necessary.

In the paragraphs that follow, we consider several students. JoAnn is a student who has received systematic instruction in reading and writing. The curriculum series was adapted—or streamlined—along the way to ensure that JoAnn was spending most of her time on the essential skills of reading (e.g., word identification, comprehension, reading interest, and fluency) as opposed to supplemental skills that were often included in the reading program (e.g., dictionary usage, map reading, using the card catalogue in the library, mastering more specialized vocabulary terms that pertain to a particular topic and are rarely encountered in everyday life). With this approach, she was able to acquire a reading level of approximately second grade by the time she was 14. With this degree of proficiency she was able to read selected books and magazines for pleasure. The fundamentals she acquired could be readily applied to real-life situations where she learned to read menus, grocery item labels, recipes, and other words frequently encountered in daily life. For JoAnn, the years of instruction in an adapted curriculum had a significant payoff.

Unlike JoAnn, many students have undergone years of academic instruction in regular academic sequences without any significant payoffs. These students "got stuck" in these sequences. Even with adaptations in the regular curriculum, their needs for useful skills were not met. Consider the following examples:

- Sarah is 21 years old. This year she will leave the school system and function as an adult member of her community. A major portion of her school career was devoted to a "prereading" program—almost an hour a day for 15 years. What did she gain from this considerable investment in prereading? She is now able to sight read (not decode) 13 words.
- Jeremy was in a regular math program that was adapted. In kindergarten and the first and second grade, this approach seemed to work well. He had been concentrating on learning basic number concepts and math operations. While he was nowhere near the proficiency level of most of his peers, it was felt this early investment was worth it in that it would serve as a strong foundation for more functional math applications. Unfortunately, Jeremy was not able to apply these skills as readily as his peers, and teacher decisions did not lead to direct instruction in a functional math approach. Instead he stayed in the math series and continued to work on the basic skills covered at the first-grade level. He graduated at age 21 knowing how to count to 30 and add and subtract double-digit numbers (without regrouping), but he didn't know how to handle money necessary for daily purchases and he couldn't tell time or manage his daily schedule.

These examples illustrate how a substantial educational investment can be made, yet result in a skill repertoire that is of little ultimate value to the student of concern. In each of these cases an alternative academic program should have been developed at some point in the student's educational career. For some students this alternative would be considered quite early, and for others, at a more advanced stage of their schooling.

## USING ALTERNATIVE FUNCTIONAL SEQUENCES

A minimal outcome of a student's academic program should be the achievement of useful skills—skills that will allow the student to enjoy a greater degree of participation in an enjoyable life-style. If a student, through systematic instruction, could learn to handle money, manage time, and read and write some of the words that are encountered in everyday life, would that not be a more desirable outcome than his or her having acquired a few rudimentary math and reading skills that were never developed to the point where they became useful? This is the question teachers need to answer as students move into the upper elementary grades (and perhaps before this point, where some students are concerned). Stated another way, teachers might ask, "Should I continue to adapt the regular curriculum, or should I use a more functional approach?" As we have learned from Jeremy's and Sarah's experiences, there are times when a departure to a functional academic program should be made so that usable skills are acquired by a student.

The functional academic sequences contained in this section may be considered when students: 1) are not benefiting significantly from adaptations in the regular curriculum; and/or 2) need more direct and systematic instruction in order to learn the money-handling, time management, and reading and writing skills used for basic functioning in everyday life. How instruction in functional academic skills is implemented may vary considerably. Depending on the learning style of the student, a functional academic program may be implemented during math and reading sessions in the classroom, combined with ongoing instruction and practice in real-life activities. For other students, instruction may be implemented strictly in an embedded manner—where the skills are taught only in the actual routines when they are needed (e.g., handling money is taught at the school cafeteria, school store, restaurant, and grocery store) and not at a separate time in the classroom.

## DETERMINING ACADEMIC PROGRAMS

Whether a teacher is adapting the regular curriculum, using a combined approach, or using a functional academic sequence, a thoughtful decision-making process must be followed. Like each of the decision processes described in this guide, the academic areas begin with a scope and sequence chart, which is followed by an individualized step-by-step process. Essentially, the steps involve:

- *First:* Gain an understanding of the student's existing repertoire in the particular academic skill area (i.e., mathematics, reading, and writing).
- *Second:* Analyze factors such as chronological age, learning style, progress in previous programs, and the integrity of previous programs, in order to determine the instructional approach best suited for the student.
- *Third:* Review the scope and sequence charts and specify which approach should be used with a particular student: regular, regular–adapted, functional, or functional–embedded.
- *Fourth:* Develop or adopt a program or skill sequence to match the outcome and approach selected.
- *Fifth:* Estimate where to place the student in the program or skill sequence and conduct a detailed assessment to establish baseline performance.

Whether you choose to use the functional academic sequences in this guide, or others that are available, we suggest that you evaluate the sequence in relation to the following criteria:

- Will the sequence lead to a *meaningful outcome* for the student? For example, the ability to "count coins" is not a worthwhile outcome by itself if it does not result in a usable skill, but "determining enough or not enough money in order to purchase a single item with pocket change" is.

- Have you developed or adopted a skill sequence that represents *a direct path* to the desired outcome? That is, have you identified the most essential skills in the sequence and pared away those that do not lead directly to the desired outcome?
- From the very beginning, and throughout the sequence, are skills taught by *referencing real-life experiences and applying the skills in actual situations?* The learner should never be expected to "wait until later in the sequence" before the skills can actually be used.
- Are there *decision points for departure* to an alternative approach in the event that the learner is not progressing at a reasonable pace? When a chosen path or sequence is not leading to the desired outcome, a departure may be necessary. Decisions to depart may be based on a student's lack of progress, his or her chronological age, the likelihood of achieving a meaningful outcome in the school years remaining, and so forth.

Each of the functional academic sequences presented in this section contains a set of guidelines that reflect these criteria—with the intention of assuring that students achieve the greatest degree of proficiency possible in reading, writing, money handling and time management.

## REFERENCE

Goodlad, J. (1984). *A place called school: Prospects for the future.* New York: McGraw-Hill.

# CHAPTER 7

# Reading and Writing

## Alison Ford, Roberta Schnorr, Linda Davern, Jim Black and Kim Kaiser

Learning to read and write serves a variety of purposes. In its most basic form, it enables one to interpret and use printed symbols that are encountered in everyday life (e.g., understanding labels on food items, signs, words/pictures on menus; making lists, signing your name) and is a source of enjoyment (e.g., looking at pictures in books and magazines, writing notes or cards). At a more sophisticated level, reading and writing can provide an important means of learning and communicating new information as well as a source of enjoyment (e.g., reading a book, keeping a diary, writing a letter). The reading process involves decoding printed symbols and comprehending their meanings. The writing process involves forming symbols, spelling words, and constructing comprehensible passages.

The ability to read and write, once considered unattainable by students with moderate and severe disabilities, has become achievable by many. In particular, there are students with moderate disabilities who, beginning at a very young age, received systematic reading and writing instruction. As a result of this instruction, they have been able to acquire some rather sophisticated reading and writing skills. Consider JoAnn, for example. By age 14, she was able to read (and comprehend) text written at least at a second grade level. The passage below, which was extracted from a second grade reader, is representative of the material that she could read with ease.

> When you race or jog, it's important to prepare with warm-ups. Warm-ups are exercises that help keep your body loose and healthy so that you can run better and not get hurt.
> Marathon runners must be careful. They must begin to prepare for a marathon race at least a year ahead of time. To do this they may run as much as ten miles a day.
> Joggers and runners prepare by doing stretching exercises. One kind of stretching exercise is to try to touch your toes without bending your knees. This exercise is always done slowly and carefully. Another stretching exercise is called "reaching for the sky." To do this you must stand on your toes. Then you put your hands above your head and reach up as high as you can. (Lampert, 1981, p. 292)

JoAnn has acquired a similar level of proficiency in writing. On the next page is a letter that she sent to one of us. As you can see, she is able to express herself by spelling words from memory or by sounding them out (using phonics).

Needless to say, JoAnn's sophisticated reading and writing skills have greatly enhanced her life-style. She is not limited to using specifically adapted menu cards in restaurants. She can read and write simple messages and shopping lists. She reads magazines (she enjoys reading "People" and other popular magazines) and books for enjoyment. The skills she has acquired will be of value throughout her lifetime. For JoAnn, it was important to choose an instructional approach that reflects the complex sequence of skills that leads to this type of outcome.

Dear ALison
Thank You FoR The
PhoTo ALbum
I Likeed iT ueRY
munch.
when aRe you
comeing back To
Madison,
be SuRe To See us
AGin.
and I hope you wiLL en Joy
This LiTTeR.
How is The waThe R in
SYRacuse.

This letter is reprinted with the permission of its author.

## SCOPE AND SEQUENCE

The reading and writing scope and sequence chart (Chart 7.1) outlines four general approaches to instruction that are geared toward achieving meaningful outcomes. Most of us are familiar with the *regular* curriculum—an approach used with most students. Although JoAnn and other students with similar characteristics have benefited from some components of the regular reading curriculum, adaptations needed to be made in order to achieve meaningful outcomes. The following best describes the *regular–adapted* approach used to teach JoAnn how to read and write:

- For reading: This is an approach that recognizes the complexity of the skills necessary to reach at least a second grade reading level, and therefore calls upon the teacher to use a reading series or program (preferably the one adopted by the school district). Once the reading program has been adopted, the teacher modifies it on an ongoing basis to ensure that the most essential skills/concepts are being stressed and to ensure application to everyday life.
- For writing: This is an approach that recognizes the complexity of the skills necessary to form and spell words such that meaningful passages can be expressed. It therefore calls upon the teacher to use a writing/spelling program (preferably the one adopted by the school district). Once the program has been adopted, the teacher is asked to analyze the program's scope and sequence chart to determine the most direct path to proficient writing.

Not all students will be able to acquire the degree of proficiency attained by JoAnn. Yet, these students can learn to interpret and use symbols encountered in everyday life. They might also learn to enjoy browsing through magazines and books during leisure time. As for writing, a student might learn to form basic symbols to write his or her name and other important information. To accomplish these functional outcomes, the following alternative approaches should be considered:

- *Functional–Language Experience:* This approach is aimed at developing an expansive sight-word vocabulary such that the words and phrases encountered in everyday life can be meaningfully interpreted. Decoding, spelling, and comprehension skills are taught in relation to naturally occurring events or language experience stories rather than through a formal reading series.
- *Functional–Embedded Symbol Usage:* This approach is aimed at building a set of symbols that a student can meaningfully interpret within naturally occurring events. A special time is not set aside to teach these skills. Instead, the symbols are systematically introduced and practiced when they serve an immediate purpose (e.g., the symbol for milk is introduced when the individual is following a recipe that requires milk).

Thus, when it is unlikely that a student will progress meaningfully through the regular reading sequence, several other viable approaches should be considered: regular–adapted, functional–language experience, and functional–embedded symbol usage. Chart 7.1 depicts each of these approaches and provides an outline of the skill development expected by various ages. Given this range of approaches, all students, including students with the most severe disabilities, should be equipped with at least one strategy for interpreting symbols.

## OPPORTUNITIES TO USE FUNCTIONAL READING AND WRITING SKILLS

What makes printed symbols functional? Increasingly, we see lists of words and kits that purport to contain "functional sight words" or "survival words." Among the words included in these kits are "exit," "stop," "yield," and "danger." When was the last time one of your students actually needed to read the word "stop" or "yield"? Unless he or she was driving, it is unlikely that these words required interpretation in daily life. Furthermore, since these are familiar traffic signs, the student might be just as likely to attend to the color and shapes of the signs as he or she would the printed word. The point is, that while some words or symbols may initially appear to have functional value, further examination of the actual *opportunities* to apply them in real life may lead to a different conclusion. Thus, an important step in your planning process is to determine what opportunities your students have to use reading and writing skills. Of course, these opportunities should not be limited to functional purposes. We are equally concerned about using reading and writing for enjoyment. If the options in your school program seem limited, your task becomes one of expanding and enriching opportunities throughout the school day. Table 7.1 offers some examples of the opportunities students have at different age levels to use reading and writing skills for both functional and enjoyment purposes.

## DETERMINING THE READING AND WRITING PROGRAM FOR A PARTICULAR STUDENT

In this section we outline the steps a team might follow to determine which approach to reading and writing is best suited to a particular student. We illustrate this decision process by carrying out the example of Mary Z., the student whose individualized education program (IEP) was being constructed in previous chapters of the *Guide*.

Chart 7.1. Scope and sequence for reading and writing

| Approach | | Elementary school — Primary (by age 8) | Elementary school — Intermediate (by age 12) | Age-level goals — Middle and high school (by age 18) | Outcome upon graduation (by age 21) |
|---|---|---|---|---|---|
| **Regular** <u></u><br>The teacher uses the scope and sequence that is outlined in the reading/writing program adopted by the school district. | Reading | • Word identification: Has strong sight-word vocabulary; uses phonics, contextual cues, and structural analysis to decode new words at approximately the 2nd-grade mastery level. | • Word identification: Has strong sight-word vocabulary; uses phonics, contextual cues, and structural analysis to decode new words at least at the 4th-grade mastery level. | • Word identification: Has strong sight-word vocabulary; uses phonics, contextual analysis to decode new words beyond a 5th-grade mastery level. | • Uses a 5th–12th+-grade reading ability to comprehend printed material for the purpose of gaining new information from literature, for pleasure and for functional use in everyday life. |
| | | • Materials: Reading series or program adopted by the school district, magazines and books; also, language experience stories, personal journal, and functional reading activities.<br>• Comprehension: Develops comprehension skills outlined in reading series or program.<br>• Reading interest and fluency: Develops reading interest and fluency in accordance with the guidelines in the reading series or program. | | | |
| | Writing | • Writes words, phrases, sentences, and passages in accordance with the guidelines in the writing program, spells from memory. | | | • Writes papers, reports, letters and other products for school/work, pleasure, and everyday use. |
| **Regular–adapted** <u></u><br>The teacher modifies the reading/writing series or program by placing greater emphasis on essential skills/concepts and ensures simultaneous application to everyday life. | Reading | • Word identification: Sight reads 50+ words; uses basic phonics, contextual cues, and structural analysis to decode new words. | • Word identification: Has growing sight-word vocabulary (150+); uses phonics, contextual cues, and structural analysis to decode new words at the 1st-grade mastery level. | • Word identification: Has strong sight-word vocabulary; uses phonics, contextual cues, and structural analysis to decode new words at least at the 2nd-grade mastery level. | • Uses at least a 2nd-grade reading ability to read books and magazines (e.g., "People" magazine) and interprets words, sentences, and passages encountered across settings in everyday life. |
| | | • Materials: Reading series that has been adapted or streamlined to ensure steady progress in essential skills or high-interest—low-vocabulary reading program; also, language experience stories, personal journal, and functional reading events. | | • Materials: High-interest—low-vocabulary reading program, magazines and books; also, language experience stories, personal journal, and functional reading events. | |
| | | • Comprehension: Forms mental pictures or acts out situations described, recalls facts or details, relates key points or main ideas, understands basic relationships between ideas (cause and effect, sequential happenings), summarizes content, thinks creatively beyond passage.[a]<br>• Reading interest and fluency: Enjoys being read to, expresses preferences for favorite reading materials, applies reading skills to novel situations, reads phrases and sentences with appropriate intonation patterns and pacing. | | | |

| | | | |
|---|---|---|---|
| **Regular–adapted** (continued) | Writing | • Writes words, phrases, and sentences that are connected with a language experience story, personal journal, and functional writing events. | • Writes words, phrases, sentences, and passages that are connected with the structured writing program, language experience story, personal journal, and functional writing events. | • Writes letters, journal/diary and other passages for pleasure, and writes key words and sentences as needed in everyday life. |

| | | Column A | Column B | Column C |
|---|---|---|---|---|
| **Functional–language experience**<br>The teacher uses the experiences of the student, his or her interests, and language repertoire to create printed materials and develop basic reading skills. | Reading | • Word identification: Reads set of key words and pictures.<br>• Materials: Experience stories written by teachers (5–6 sentences), information charts, messages, signs and labels, selected books, names, cards, lists.<br><br>• Comprehension: Forms mental pictures or acts out situations described, relates key points or main ideas, understands basic relationships between ideas (e.g., cause and effect, sequential happenings), summarizes content, thinks creatively beyond passage.<br>Reading interest and fluency: Enjoys being read to, expresses preferences for favorite books and other reading materials, applies reading skills to novel situations, reads phrases and sentences. | • Word identification: Reads 100+ words; uses basic phonics, contextual cues, and structural analysis to decode new words.<br>• Materials: Collection of experience stories written by student or teacher (of varying length), information notices, messages, signs and labels, lists, journal/diary, letters/cards, phrases in magazines and books. | • Reads phrases in magazines and selected books, looks at pictures, and enjoys being read to; uses an expansive sight-word vocabulary and basic decoding skills to interpret words, phrases, and passages in everyday life (e.g., reads key words/symbols on recipes, menus, lists). |
| | Writing | • Traces, copies, and writes words that are connected with a language experience story, personal journal, and/or functional writing event. | • Writes phrases and sentences that are connected with a language experience story, personal journal, and/or functional writing event. | • Writes key words and phrases in journal/diary and letters as they are needed in daily routines (e.g., name on belongings, messages, calendar reminders, making lists). |
| **Functional–embedded symbol usage**<br>The teacher identifies ways for a student to interpret and use graphic symbols as they occur within daily routines. | Reading | • Interprets increasing numbers of pictures, line drawings, and objects within naturally occurring events (may also interpret some words).<br>• Listens and enjoys story that is being read; looks at pictures in magazines and books. | • Interprets increasing numbers of pictures, line drawings, and objects within naturally occurring events; looks at pictures in magazines and books. | • Looks at pictures in magazines and books, and enjoys being read to; interprets key symbols (words, pictures, line drawings, objects) within naturally occurring events. |
| | Writing | • Uses an identifiable stroke (or rubber stamp) for writing name or actually writes out name and other key words needed in daily routines. | | • Uses a controlled stroke (or a rubber stamp) for writing name; or actually writes out name and other key words needed in daily routines. |

ªThe selection of these essential comprehension skills was based on Smith and Johnson (1980).

Table 7.1.    Reading and writing opportunities

| School level | For pleasure | For functional use |
|---|---|---|
| Elementary school: reading | Looking at books during free time<br>Checking out books from the library<br>Listening to stories read aloud (by peers, by teacher, by librarian)<br>Participating in structured reading time<br>Reading self-composed stories aloud to classmates<br>Reading books | Following sequence cards for classroom jobs<br>Reviewing daily lunch menu<br>Reviewing daily schedule<br>Managing weekly/monthly calendar<br>Using communication booklet<br>Reading portions of newsletters or "notes" to go home<br>Reading signs, posters, and bulletin boards<br>Following recipe for snack preparation |
| Elementary school: writing | Writing stories (or drawing pictures to illustrate message)<br>Writing cards and letters<br>Constructing photo albums and writing captions<br>Writing journals | Writing name on school projects<br>Writing name on card to check out library book<br>Filling out "emergency cards" and other forms that require name, address, and telephone number<br>Leaving notes or messages for a friend or teacher<br>Signing up for classroom job |
| Middle school and high school: reading | Looking at books during free time<br>Checking out books from the library<br>Participating in structured reading program in English class or reading lab | Following sequence cards at job site<br>Following written daily schedule<br>Reading the weekly cafeteria menu and menus in restaurants<br>Managing weekly/monthly calendar<br>Using communication booklet<br>Looking at school newspaper<br>Reading signs, posters, and bulletin boards<br>Following recipe in home economics class<br>Identifying labels on items in store |
| Middle school and high school: writing | Writing collection of stories<br>Writing cards and letters<br>Constructing photo album or essay with captions<br>Writing journals/diaries | Writing name on belongings (papers, books)<br>Writing name on library cards<br>Writing name on sign-up sheets<br>Filling out forms requiring identifying information<br>Leaving notes or messages for friends or teachers<br>Writing events/reminders on personal calendar<br>Writing grocery lists<br>Writing address and phone number down for friend |

## Step 1: Gain an understanding of the student's existing repertoire in reading and writing.

Here, the teacher wants to gather information that will help the team decide which approach is best suited for the student. This information could be gathered from cumulative records, direct observation, informal reading and writing inventories, and interviews with the student, family, and other teachers. If needed, a listing of skills for a functional reading/writing approach is presented in the appendix at the end of this chapter and can be adapted and used to record information about the existing repertoire of the student. Below are some guiding questions to help with this information-gathering step:

1. How would you describe the student's present reading performance in terms of *word identification*?
    a. Sight-word vocabulary or basic symbol interpretation?

    *Mary Z.:* Mary is not able to recognize any sight words, including her name. She is able to recognize black-and-white line drawings representing approximately 20 places, objects, people, activities, or events (when they are presented in context), including: "eat," "drink," "outside," "art," "music," "gym," "game," "book," "bathroom," "friend," and "work." She is also able to recognize a few photographs of family members, teachers, and friends.

    b. Phonics?

    *Mary Z.:* Not applicable.

    c. Written contextual cues?

    *Mary Z.:* Not applicable.

    d. Structural analysis?

    *Mary Z.:* Not applicable.

2. What types of materials does the student read and what is the highest level of difficulty in which the text can be written?

    *Mary Z.:* Not applicable.

    Other students, however, may show evidence of a marked reading ability. If the school records and direct observations do not give you a clear idea of what level of text the student can read (without frustration), you may want to perform an informal reading inventory or diagnostic test (see the discussion in Smith & Johnson, 1980; also, consult a reading specialist in your district).

3. What is the student's comprehension ability for written materials?

    *Mary Z.:* Mary is able to recognize select symbols when they are presented in context. For example, when her sheet of symbols for gym class is put into her communication board in the girl's locker room, she is able to recognize and use the symbols for "game," "shower," and "towel." If these symbols are mixed with others and presented at other times, she has difficulty using them.

4. What are the student's reading interests, and how fluent is his or her reading ability?

    *Mary Z.:* Mary enjoys being read to by friends. She appears to become relaxed by the rhythm in the voice of the reader. Also she enjoys looking at pictures in magazines with her peers and family members.

5. What are the student's writing abilities?
    a. Mechanics?

    *Mary Z.:* Mary is not able to write her name. She could learn to use a stamp for her full name and make a controlled stroke for her signature.

b.   Conveying messages and ideas?

> *Mary Z.:* Mary's symbol interpretation skills are used in conjunction with her communication board.

## Step 2: Analyze several important factors such as chronological age, learning style, extent of progress in previous reading programs and the integrity of previous programs. Use this information when determining the instructional approach best suited for the student.

Step 1 gives you a general profile of the student's reading/writing skills. Before you use this information for decision making, you will need to consider other pertinent factors. For example, Mary Z.'s profile suggests that she used reading and writing skills in their most basic form—using line drawings and pictures. Given her age of 14 and current functioning level, you might be inclined to continue with an approach that emphasizes the use of symbols as they occur in everyday routines, such as the embedded symbol usage approach. But what if her age were 5 or 6? And what if you learned that her exposure to books, words, pictures, and line drawings has been extremely limited? Most likely, this information would lead you to select a more sophisticated approach. There will always be factors that should be weighted against the information collected in Step 1. Below is a list of some of them.

1.   What is the student's chronological age?

> *Mary Z.:* Mary is 14 years old.

2.   How would you describe his or her learning style (particularly as it may influence the development of reading and writing skills)?

> *Mary Z.:* Mary appears to learn through all major instructional modes (e.g., auditory, visual, and tactile). Her ability to respond verbally is quite limited. She uses pointing to pictures/line drawings, facial and body gestures, and eye gaze as her primary means of responding.

3.   What was the rate of progress in previous reading programs?

> *Mary Z.:* It is unclear from Mary's records how much instructional emphasis was placed on her learning to interpret symbols in meaningful contexts. Apparently, the 20 line drawings she is able to use were acquired in the past year. This may suggest that she can learn many more this year as long as they are taught in the context in which they will be used.

4.   What is known about the integrity of previous reading programs?

> *Mary Z.:* The information gathered about previous programs was too limited to judge their effectiveness.

An analysis of the integrity of some students' previous programs may lead to a decision to pursue a more sophisticated approach. Some students' abilities have been grossly underestimated due to the existence of a particular educational label. For example, an 8-year-old student who may be capable of making meaningful progress in a regular–adapted approach may have been previously confined to strictly a functional approach.

## Step 3: Review the scope and sequence charts and specify which approach should be used with a particular student.

Like all students, students with moderate and severe disabilities represent a very diverse group of learners. A functional–embedded symbol usage approach may be very appropriate for one learner, but unnecessarily limiting for another. Similarly, while the use of a regular–adapted approach led to meaningful outcomes for JoAnn (the student mentioned in the introductory paragraphs of this chapter), it may have left others with very little usable skills (e.g., limited sight word vocabulary and a few basic phonic skills). Therefore, after gathering critical information about a student's reading and writing repertoire and considering other important factors, it is important for the team to specify which approach seems optimal for the student. When making this important decision about which instructional approach to adopt, consideration should be given to the following guideline.

It is better to *overestimate* than underestimate a student's capability. If, for example, you are vacillating between a regular–adapted approach and functional–language experience approach, you should choose the one that will lead to the more proficient outcome (the regular–adapted approach). If, later on, it becomes apparent that this approach is not appropriate, you can depart to the functional–language experience approach.

*Mary Z.:* Based on Mary's chronological age and performance repertoire, a functional–embedded symbol usage approach will be used.

## Step 4: Develop or adopt a program or skill sequence to match the specified approach.

If you plan to use a regular or regular–adapted reading approach, you will most likely be relying on the same kinds of materials used by the students without special needs. If you have older students who are using an adapted approach, you will want to consult with a reading specialist in your district to locate appropriate high-interest, low-vocabulary materials. (These materials will avoid the stigma and motivational problems associated with age-inappropriate materials.) Many middle and high school teachers have also found the local adult literacy center to be a valuable resource.

The functional–language experience approach will require some amount of sequencing of learning activities in order to reach the desired outcomes (see Chart 7.1). In the appendix at the end of this chapter we have included an inventory that consists of three skill clusters that are arranged in order of difficulty. This functional reading/writing inventory can help you develop a profile of the student's existing repertoire and determine which new skills to build into the reading/writing program.

The functional–embedded symbol usage approach does not require a detailed easy-to-hard sequence. Rather, it requires decisions about: 1) what type of symbol will be used (including tactile symbols for a student with significant visual impairment), 2) in what contexts the symbols will be taught, and 3) how many symbols will be introduced over a period of time.

*Mary Z.:* Mary will learn to interpret line drawings (except when people are being represented, in which case she will use photographs). She will expand the 20 symbols in her existing repertoire that she uses for communication purposes. After she masters the two to four symbols she uses in a particular context, an additional symbol will be added. Since Mary has communication sheets for 10 different contexts (e.g., physical education class, art class, work) this could mean the introduction of 10 new symbols. Vocabulary selection will be based on her communication needs for a particular context. She will also expand the number of photographs of people—perhaps by developing a photo album.

## Step 5: Estimate where to place the student in the program/skill sequence and conduct a detailed assessment to establish baseline performance.

Once a reading and writing sequence has been developed or adopted, the next step is to place the student in it. Placement is often imprecise because of the many variables that enter into the decision-making process. Nonetheless, it is far better than having students start at the beginning of a sequence when they have already mastered many of the skills!

This step involves conducting a detailed assessment based on the actual skill sequence that you plan to use. For this step, you convert the skill sequence (or a portion of it) into an assessment tool. When assessing the student, locate the point in the sequence where errors start to appear. This is the point where you should begin instruction. More specifically:

1.  Use past progress reports and informal observations and assessments to estimate where to place a student in the sequence.
2.  Based on your estimate, conduct several assessment sessions measuring performance on the skills listed in the sequence. (For further information on curriculum-based assessment, see "Curriculum-based assessment," 1985.) The initial skills tested should be performed successfully. If this does not occur, move back in the sequence to ensure success. Then gradually test more difficult skills until revealing errors are made. These data will serve as a baseline measure.
3.  Identify the place in the sequence where errors began to appear. Begin instruction at this point.

*Mary Z.:* The skill inventory contained in the appendix at the end of this chapter was modified and used to assess Mary's reading and writing repertoire. Information was gained about the symbols Mary currently uses. This assessment tool will also be used to record and monitor the additional symbols she will be learning during the upcoming year.

## WRITING GOALS AND OBJECTIVES

The reading and writing skills derived from the decision process above must be translated into IEP goals and objectives. As with all objectives, it is important to state the conditions under which priority reading/writing skills will be developed. Continuing with our example of Mary Z., an eighth grader, we would expect to see objectives that indicate which natural opportunities will be used to further develop her symbol interpretation skills. Since she is learning to use line drawings for communication purposes, symbol interpretation skills should be embedded throughout the day (e.g., when she wants to request something to eat or comment on the next activity). It is less clear, however, when she will have the opportunity to listen to stories and look at pictures in magazines. One possibility is English class. Mary's eighth-grade English teacher has a brief time scheduled almost every day for silent reading. Students use a variety of materials, including current magazines and newspapers available in the classroom. Mary might look at magazines and other books alone or with a classmate during this time. Another emphasis in this English class is oral presentations. Individuals and small groups of students are frequently assigned poetry and plays that are rehearsed for presentation to the class. Several students are also selected each week to deliver their creative writing assignments orally. Mary might enjoy listening to "rehearsals" as well as the group presentations. In terms of opportunities to use her writing skills, she could learn to use her signature (a controlled stroke with a stamp) whenever she has a notice to bring home, an art project to put her name on, and so forth. Given these considerations, the following goals and objectives were developed and incorporated into her IEP.

## Goals and Objectives for Mary Z.

### Goal

While participating daily in English 8, Mary will select and look at books and magazines.

### Objectives

- When presented with three books or magazines by a classmate (from the classroom bookshelf), Mary will indicate her preference by pointing/reaching.
- Mary will turn pages one at a time and look at pictures as a classmate points and comments (for 10 minutes, on three consecutive tries).

### Goal

While participating in English 8, Mary will construct a photo journal of a familiar school scene or event with a classmate during each journal-writing session.

### Objectives

- When a classmate presents pairs of photos from a familiar school scene or event (e.g., an assembly, a recent school dance), Mary will select photos to be included by touching or pointing to one of each pair.
- Mary will look at individual photos as her partner points to each and reads each caption.
- Mary will grasp and turn each page independently or when her partner indicates.

### Goal

While participating in English 8, Mary will listen to a small group of classmates as a story or passage is read orally (e.g., small group rehearsals of *Romeo and Juliet*).

### Objectives

- When positioned approximately 5 feet from the group's table, Mary will wheel to join the group (within 1 minute, for five consecutive classes).
- Mary will orient to the speaker.

### Goal

During English 8 class, Mary will use the school library two times per week.

### Objectives

- Mary will make a choice between listening to an audio tape, using the computer, or looking at a book by pointing to a line-drawn symbol on her communication board (within 15 seconds of prompt, for four consecutive opportunities).
- When presented with three choices of library books or magazines related to

her personal interests, Mary will indicate a preference by pointing to one item.
- As needed by members of her English 8 class, Mary will accompany a partner to check out research materials. After her partner has located the item, Mary will assist in checking it out by holding the item while being wheeled to the counter, placing it on the counter, and retrieving it from the librarian at the appropriate time.

### Goal

Mary will produce a written signature as needed by using a stamp carried in her pack (at library, marking projects, putting name on forms).

### Objectives

- As a teacher or peer helps to set the stamp up, Mary will look at the surface to be stamped.
- Mary will place the stamp on the spot indicated by a teacher or peer (successfully within 10 seconds of gesture, on five consecutive opportunities).

## MONITORING ACADEMIC PROGRESS AND MAKING DECISIONS FOR DEPARTURE TO ALTERNATIVE SEQUENCES

As noted earlier, the pace at which students progress through a reading and writing sequence will influence the outcomes achieved. We have developed the following chart of three students to illustrate their different learning paces and the outcomes that result.

| Three Students' Pace in Acquiring Reading and Writing Skills | | |
|---|---|---|
| age 5 | age 10 | age 21 |
| Matthew | Regular–Adapted | |
| Valery | Regular–Adapted | Functional–Language Experience |
| Lori | Functional–Embedded Symbol Usage | |

As can be seen by this illustration, Matthew began his school career in a regular–adapted approach. He continued to progress successfully with this approach throughout his school years. Matthew eventually graduated with a reading and writing ability at approximately the third-grade level.

Valery began in a regular–adapted approach, but did not make significant progress. When she was 10 years old, she still had not acquired more than 10 to 15 sight words. The decision was made at that time to depart from the regular–adapted approach and implement a functional–language experience program. With this approach she continued to expand on her sight word vocabulary to the point where she could use approximately 200 words *functionally* by the time she graduated. Furthermore, Valery enjoys keeping a diary (using words and symbols that she could draw), looking at books and magazines, listening to others read, and listening to tape-recorded books and stories.

Lori began her school program using a functional–embedded symbol usage approach and continued to benefit from this approach throughout her school years. She gradually expanded the number of symbols she could interpret in familiar contexts to 25–30 symbols.

Each of these outcomes is meaningful. None of them could be achieved without systematic instruction, careful review, and good decision making. The decision making process must be carried out on an *ongoing* basis to ensure that students are accomplishing the most meaningful outcome possible.

## QUESTIONS AND ANSWERS

Q: If a student is not following the regular reading curriculum, doesn't this mean that he or she needs separate instruction?

A: If by "separate" you mean isolating the student from his or her nonhandicapped peers, the answer is clearly "no." There will be students who will need an individualized, functional approach to reading and writing. But, individualization need not lead to separation. While reading is very often taught in homogeneous groups while other students do individual work at their desks, some are beginning to challenge this method of organizing instruction. Slavin, Stevens, and Madden (1988) describe a cooperative model for teaching reading that could be modified to accommodate students who are several grade levels below the majority of peers in their class. In their model, students rotate through teacher-led reading groups that are ability based, but then they engage in activities that occur in heterogeneous teams. This heterogeneous team, for example, might be asked to do partner reading (students take turns reading a story, following comprehension questions, practicing newly introduced words, and retelling the story for their partners).

Language experience opportunities can also be incorporated into various activities. Often students rotate through teacher-led stations in order to receive individualized assistance with writing projects. A student may use this time to review a language experience story developed by or with the teacher. Journal writing is a common activity in many classrooms. This writing time can be used to let partners develop language experience stories. One student can assist another in creating the story and reading it aloud.

Finally, cross-age tutoring is receiving attention from those who are aware of the benefits of having a skilled, responsive partner for reading sessions. A class of fifth graders may pair up with students from a first or second grade for 20 minute sessions several times a week for individualized attention. Regardless of the reading ability of the younger student, each can benefit from this instructional model.

Q: I have an 8-year-old student who seems to fall between two approaches: regular–adapted and functional–language experience. Would it be appropriate to use both approaches?

A: Absolutely. The approaches outlined in the scope and sequence chart (Chart 7.1) are designed to help you firm up *your* direction for instruction. Keep in mind that the chart offers a very broad framework for decision making and that you, and your team, do most of the work by carefully considering the repertoire of the student. If you are not sure which outcome is the most appropriate (this is often the case for younger children) then it is best that you continue to stress the more sophisticated outcome (i.e., regular–adapted) while also ensuring meaningful daily application through a functional–language experience approach.

## REFERENCES

Cohen, M., & Gross, P. (1979). *The developmental resource: Behavioral sequences for assessment and program planning* (Vols. I and II). New York: Grune & Stratton.

Curriculum-based assessment [Special issue]. (1985) *Exceptional Children, 52*(3).

Lampert, J. (1981). *Crystal kingdom* (Level Six Reader). Glenview, IL: Scott, Foresman.

Nietupski, J., Williams, W., & York, R. (1979). Teaching selected phonic word analysis reading skills to TMR labeled students. *Teaching Exceptional Children, 11,* 140–143.

Slavin, R.E., Stevens, R.J., & Madden, N.A. (1988). Accommodating student diversity in reading and writing instruction: A cooperative learning approach. *Remedial and Special Education, 9*(1), 60–66.

Smith, R., & Johnson, D. (1980). *Teaching children to read.* Menlo Park, CA: Addison-Wesley.

## ADDITIONAL READINGS AND RESOURCES

Bender, M., & Valletutti, P. (1982). *Teaching functional academics.* Baltimore: University Park Press.

Browder, D., & Snell, M. (1987). Functional academics. In M. Snell (Ed.), *Systematic instruction of persons with severe handicaps.* Columbus, OH: Charles E. Merrill.

Newman, J.M. (1985). *Whole language: Theory in use.* Portsmouth, NH: Heinemann.

Otto, W., McMenemy, R., & Smith, R. (1973). *Corrective reading and remedial teaching* (2nd ed.). Boston: Houghton Mifflin.

Palloway, E., Payne, J., & Patton, R. (1985). *Strategies for teaching retarded and special needs learners.* Columbus, OH: Charles E. Merrill.

Snell, M. (1983). Functional reading. In M.E. Snell (Ed.), *Systematic instruction of the moderate and severely handicapped.* Columbus, OH: Charles E. Merrill.

# APPENDIX: INVENTORY OF
# FUNCTIONAL READING/WRITING SKILLS

The following pages contain skill listings for the functional approaches included in the scope and sequence chart: language experience and embedded symbol usage. Many references were used when constructing these listings including samplings of basal reading series, the *Developmental Resource* books by Cohen and Gross (1979), and an article by Nietupski, Williams, and York (1979) for the phonics portion of the skill sequence. The reading and writing skills contained on the charts have been organized into three major clusters. Each of these skill clusters should lead to a meaningful outcome by itself. In addition, each skill cluster is designed to teach the underlying strategies and concepts necessary to move to the next skill cluster that represents a more proficient level of functioning. Finally, the skill listings are accompanied by a set of guidelines for implementation.

| An overview of the reading and writing inventory | | |
|---|---|---|
| Functional approach | | Skill cluster |
| Functional–embedded | I. | Using line drawings/pictures in everyday life |
| Functional–embedded and/or language experience | II. | Using a basic sight-word vocabulary to interpret words in everyday life |
| Functional–language experience | III. | Using an expansive sight-word vocabulary and basic decoding skills to interpret words, phrases, and passages in everyday life |

## SKILL CLUSTER I: USING LINE DRAWINGS/PICTURES IN EVERYDAY LIFE

This cluster is devoted to the development of basic symbol-interpretation skills—interpreting and using line drawings/pictures. To determine whether the skills in this cluster are appropriate for a particular student:

- *First:* Review the entire list of skills in this cluster.
- *Second:* Check off the skills listed in the cluster that are already present in the student's repertoire. (Most of the information you will have as a result of daily observations of the student. Additional information can be secured by setting up *meaningful* opportunities for the student to demonstrate particular skills.)
- *Third:* If the student already interprets many line drawings/pictures without formal instruction, then move on to the Skill Cluster II.
- *Fourth:* If the student's ability to use line drawings/pictures is limited, identify which items on this checklist need to be taught.

### Word Identification

Does the student:

_____ associate a line drawing/picture with a familiar object, action, or event? List the line drawings/pictures that the student can interpret:

_____

_____

_____

_____ choose the appropriate line drawing/picture to indicate a preference?
  _____ from an array of two symbols (e.g., selects "milk" or "Coke" at restaurant)
  _____ from an array of three symbols
  _____ from an array of four symbols
_____ use two or more symbols to follow a sequence of steps (e.g., daily schedule, recipe)?

### Materials

What is the student looking at and interpreting?

For pleasure:
_____ photo album
_____ pictures in books and magazines
_____ pictures on greeting cards

_____ _____

_____ _____

For functional use:
_____ pictures in communication booklet
_____ daily schedule cards
_____ picture recipe
_____ job sequence cards
_____ name on personal belongings
_____ pictures on grocery list
_____ pictures for restaurant items

_____ _____

_____ _____

## Comprehension

The student comprehends line drawings/pictures:

_____ only when presented in highly familiar contexts.

_____ across many settings without formal instruction.

## Reading Interest and Fluency

Does the student show an interest in reading materials by:

_____ listening to stories read aloud?

_____ choosing to look at books during a free period?

_____ looking through books and magazines in a purposeful manner?

## Writing

Does the student:

_____ make a consistent distinguishable stroke as a form of signature (a rubber stamp with the full name could be used under the "signature" to identify the person)?

## Suggestions for Implementation

The symbol-interpretation skills in this cluster should be taught within meaningful routines and activities (during snack preparation, when doing a classroom job, in the cafeteria line, and so forth). A separate "reading" period where students sit at a table and "touch" the correct picture would not be appropriate.

Activities such as constructing a photo journal and looking at books should be incorporated into the schedule at the same time that nondisabled peers are involved in similar activities.

## SKILL CLUSTER II: USING A BASIC SIGHT-WORD
## VOCABULARY TO INTERPRET KEY WORDS IN EVERYDAY LIFE

This skill cluster has been designed for those students who are just beginning to acquire sight words. To determine whether the skills in this cluster are appropriate for a particular student:

- *First:* Review the entire list of skills in this cluster.
- *Second:* Check off the skills listed in the cluster that are already present in the student's repertoire. (Most of the information you will have as a result of daily observations. Additional information can be secured by setting up *meaningful* opportunities for the student to perform particular skills.)
- *Third:* If the student already has a beginning sight-word vocabulary (approximately 20 words) used across settings, then move on to Skill Cluster III.
- *Fourth:* If the student's ability to read select words has not yet been developed, identify which items on this list need to be taught.

### Word Identification

Does the student:

_____ read a single word associated with a familiar person, place, thing, action, or event (e.g., recognizes name on classroom materials, on sign-in sheet at work)?

List the words that the student is able to read:

_____

_____

_____

_____

_____

_____ read materials that contain one or two word items (e.g., shopping list, schedule, informational signs, captions to pictures and cartoons)?

### Materials

What is the student reading?

As a structured reading program:

_____ a collection of language experience stories

_____ a personal journal/diary

_____ _____

_____ _____

For pleasure: The materials listed above, plus:

_____ pictures and key words in photo album/scrapbook

_____ pictures and key words in books and magazines

_____ pictures and key words on greeting cards

_____ _____

_____ _____

For functional use:

_____ key words in communication booklet

_____ key words on daily schedule cards

_____ key words in recipes

_____ key words on job sequence cards

_____ names of self and others on calendar, personal belongings, and so forth

_____  _____

_____  _____

## Comprehension

The student comprehends key words:

_____ only when presented in highly familiar contexts.

_____ when presented across many settings.

_____ when presented in a variety of printed materials.

## Reading Interest and Fluency

Does the student show an interest in reading materials by:

_____ listening to stories read aloud for extended periods?

_____ choosing reading materials over other free-time materials?

_____ looking through books and magazines in a purposeful manner?

_____ having favorite books and magazines?

_____  _____

_____  _____

## Writing

Does the student:

_____ write (and spell) familiar words from memory (or use a personal dictionary or word bank) in meaningful contexts?

    _____ captions for photo journal

    _____ messages

    _____ shopping lists

    _____ signs

    _____ forms

    _____  _____

    _____  _____

_____ form recognizable letters when writing key words in a meaningful context (e.g., write first and last name on sign-up sheet at work site, write name of grocery item on list, write greeting on card)? The student might begin with:

_____ tracing words, then

_____ copying from a model.

## Suggestions for Implementation

Similar to the previous skill cluster, word-identification skills should be taught in meaningful contexts rather than during an established reading time. A possible exception would be a student who can benefit from a language experience approach. Using this approach, the teacher would construct a story based on student input. The story would be written in picture symbols and words so that the student could read it back successfully. Select words would be targeted for mastery.

Activities such as listening to stories, developing a collection of language experience stories, and looking at books should be scheduled at a time when nondisabled classmates are also involved in them.

## SKILL CLUSTER III: USING AN EXPANSIVE SIGHT-WORD VOCABULARY
## AND BASIC DECODING SKILLS
## TO INTERPRET WORDS, PHRASES, AND PASSAGES IN EVERYDAY LIFE

This skill cluster has been designed for those students who will be expanding their sight-word vocabulary and developing basic phonic skills to decode new words. (The word-identification skills listed here generally fall within the first- and second-grade reading levels.)To determine whether the skills in this cluster are appropriate for a particular student:

- *First:* Review the *entire* list of skills in this cluster.
- *Second:* Check off the skills that are already present in the student's repertoire. You may want to use an informal reading inventory (see Smith & Johnson, 1980, or consult a reading specialist) to determine which word-identification skills have already been acquired.
- *Third:* If the student already has a strong repertoire of basic phonic skills, that is, most of the items listed here, then consider using a more sophisticated approach (see the regular–adapted approach on the scope and sequence chart).
- *Fourth:* If the student's ability to decode words has not yet been developed, identify which items on this list should be taught next.

### Word Identification

Does the student:

_____ use *sight-word vocabulary* to read words in language experience stories and in everyday life?

    _____      5 sight words
    _____    10 sight words
    _____    15 sight words
    _____    20 sight words
    _____    30 sight words
    _____    40 sight words
    _____    60 sight words
    _____    80 sight words
    _____  100 sight words
    _____  120 sight words

_____ use *phonics* to decode words when encountering words in language experience stories and during everyday events?

    _____ sound out letters in initial position:
m, t, b, h, p, n,
d, g, c, j, v,
f, s, w, l, k,
r, x, y, z, q,
a, e, i, o, u,
(short vowel sound)

    _____ sound out short vowel-consonant combinations:
an, at, am, ap, ag, od, og, ot, ob, op, it, in, im, id, ig, un, ug, ut, um,
en, ed, et

    _____ sound out short vowel-consonant families:
(e.g., pan, man, can, tan)
(e.g., wig, pig, fig, jig)

_____ sound out two-letter consonant blends in one-syllable words:
bl, cl, fl, pl, sl,
br, cr, dr, fr,
gr, pr, tr, wr,
dw, sw, tw,
sc, sk, sm, sn, sp, st

_____ sound out consonant blends—short vowel-consonant families:
(e.g., slap, flap, clap)
(e.g., grim, trim, prim)

_____ sound out consonant digraphs when appearing in the initial position:
ch, sh, th, wh

_____ sound out words with double consonants appearing at end or middle of word:
-ff, -bb, -dd, -gg, -ll, -mm, -ss

_____ sound out words with vowel digraphs and diphthongs:
ow, ew, aw,
ou, au,
ay, ue, ie,
oi, ey, eigh, augh

_____ sound out words that are influenced by "r"s:
er, ir, or,
ire, are, ore

_____ use *structural analysis* to interpret words?

　　_____ add endings to known root words:
　　　　-s, -es
　　　　-ed
　　　　-ing
　　　　-er
　　　　-est

　　_____ use contractions:
　　　　can't, don't, isn't, didn't, wasn't, let's, that's, here's, there's, he'll, I'll, she'll, we'll, I'm

　　_____ interpret compounds (e.g., anywhere, campground, something)

_____ sound out consonant digraphs and blends when appearing in the final position of a word:
digraphs: -ch, -sh, -th
blends: -nd, -ng, -nk, -nt, -rk, -it, -st

_____ sound out three-letter consonant blends:
sch-school, scr-screen, shr-shrink, spl-splash, spr-spring, squ-squash, str-string, thr-throw

_____ sound out long vowels:
silent e: ate, i(t) e, o(t)e, e(t)e, u(t)e
double vowel: ai, ee, oa, ea, oe

_____ sound out soft "c" and "g"

_____ sound out multisyllabic words that contain familiar sound units:
a-, in-, al-, to-, per-, en-, etc.
-on, -age, -ent, -it, etc.

_____ interpret possessives ('s)

_____ interpret common prefixes and suffixes:
un-, ex-, be-, dis-, sub-, re-, etc.
-ful, -less, -ness, -ment, -ly, etc.

## Materials

What is the student reading?

As a structured reading program:

_____ a collection of language experience stories

_____ a personal journal/diary

_____ selected books

_____ _____

_____ _____

For pleasure: The materials listed above, plus:

_____ words and phrases in photo album/scrapbook

_____ phrases and sentences in books and magazines

_____ phrases and sentences in letters

_____ _____

_____ _____

For functional use:

_____ words and phrases in communication booklet

_____ words on daily schedule and personal calendar

_____ phrases and sentences in recipes

_____ words in menus

_____ _____

_____ _____

## Comprehension

The student comprehends phrases and sentences:

_____ when presented in functional materials encountered in everyday life.

_____ when presented in language experience stories and books.

Understands literal meaning:

_____ identifies main character

_____ recalls key events

_____ sequences the events

_____ recalls critical details (who, what, when, where)

_____ _____

_____ _____

Understands beyond literal meaning:

_____ relates personal experience with the printed message

_____ recognizes motives of characters

_____ distinguishes between fact and fantasy

_____ indicates likes/dislikes of parts of story

_____ _____

_____ _____

## Reading Interest and Fluency

Does the student show an interest in reading materials by:

_____ listening to stories for an extended period of time?

_____ choosing reading materials over other free-time materials?
_____ having favorite books and magazines?
_____ readily applying reading skills to novel situations?
_____ demonstrating fluency in reading ability (reads passage at an appropriate speed; pauses in proper places; uses correct intonation with question marks, exclamation marks, and periods)?

_____ _____
_____ _____

## Writing

Does the student:

_____ write words by spelling them phonetically (e.g., spells the word bread, "bred") in a meaningful context (e.g., grocery list, notes to friends, listing events on personal calendar)?
_____ write phrases and sentences (spelling words from memory, word banks, and phonics) in meaningful contexts?
    _____ keeping a journal/diary
    _____ messages
    _____ letters and cards

    _____ _____
    _____ _____

_____ form letters with increasing control?
    _____ from larger to smaller letters
    _____ from irregular to regular sizes
    _____ from irregular to regular spacing

### Suggestions for Implementation

To ensure that a student at this reading level continues to progress and become more proficient in decoding skills, it will be important for the teacher to use materials that allow for the systematic monitoring of performance. One possible strategy is the development of a language experience booklet or journal (a collection of the students' stories that is typed and placed in a binder).

Similar to the other skill clusters, every effort should be made to embed reading skills into activities that occur throughout the day. Thus, the student acquires new reading and writing skills while preparing a shopping list, reading a menu or recipe, and managing a weekly calendar. Activities such as reading books and magazines, developing and reading a collection of stories, and writing a journal, should be incorporated into the schedule when nondisabled classmates are also involved in them.

# CHAPTER 8

# Money Handling

*Alison Ford, Linda Davern, Roberta Schnorr,
Jim Black, and Kim Kaiser*

Math programs encompass a broad spectrum of skills and concepts that allow students to explore and solve problems for purposes of: 1) functioning in everyday life, and 2) developing advanced reasoning abilities that may lead to a more varied participation in today's highly technical society. For some students, a math program will focus solely on the former purpose—that is, acquiring some of the basic skills and concepts necessary to manage math-related operations that are dominant in everyday life. In this chapter, we outline strategies to address one set of math-related skills that is frequently used in daily life—money handling. The chapter that follows addresses a second math application area—time management.

The underlying rationale for providing money-handling instruction is to enable individuals to make purchases. Some of the routine purchasing situations that students are likely to encounter include: purchasing a snack at a local grocery store or restaurant, buying food items at a corner grocery store for their parents, purchasing an item from the school store, buying a snack at the bake sale, buying a school lunch, and purchasing items from gumball machines or vending machines. In order to purchase an item successfully, an individual must determine whether he or she has sufficient funds to pay for it. The determination of "enough or not enough money" is undoubtedly the most difficult skill required in these purchasing transactions. Thus, sequences designed to address money-handling must account for the skills necessary to determine affordability.

Many of the purchasing situations that arise during the daily lives of students can be organized into two categories:

- *Purchasing a single item.* Buying one item requires: 1) counting money, 2) locating the price of the desired item, and 3) determining affordability. If the buyer does not have enough money, he or she might select another item and repeat the process.
- *Purchasing multiple items.* Buying more than one item requires: 1) counting money, 2) accounting for the *total* of the prices of the desired items, and 3) determining affordability of each item added to the total. If the buyer does not have enough money for all the items desired, he or she must determine which will be exchanged for less expensive items or not purchased.

Many students with moderate and severe disabilities receive money handling instruction throughout their school careers. Too often, however, this instruction is limited to step one: "counting money." Consequently we know of students who can count combinations of coins and bills when they are arranged neatly on the classroom table, but are not able to figure out whether $.78 is enough to purchase a candy bar at the corner store.

It will be important to teach students to *use* money skills from the onset of instruction. At the very minimum, the skill sequences designed by teachers must directly prepare students to make single- and multiple-item *purchases*. Of course, we would expect a student to be involved in purchases even if he or she were not able to count money and make determinations of affordability. As with the other academic sequences, a variety of approaches are suggested to accommodate a wide range of learners.

## SCOPE AND SEQUENCE

The money-handling scope and sequence chart (Chart 8.1) is designed in a manner consistent with the other academic areas. The content is organized under four approaches:

- *Regular*: The teacher uses the scope and sequence that is outlined in the math program adopted by the school.
- *Regular–Adapted*: The teacher modifies the regular math program by placing greater emphasis on essential skills and concepts and ensures application to everyday life.
- *Functional–Money-Handling Sequence*: The teacher develops or adopts a functional, easy-to-hard sequence that leads to the ability to determine whether an item or items are affordable.
- *Functional–Embedded Money-Handling Skills*: The teacher identifies ways for a student to exchange money as the need arises within daily routines.

For purposes of this guide, we focus on the latter two strategies: functional–money-handling sequence and functional–embedded money-handling skills.

Assuming that systematic money-handling instruction begins at age 5 (or earlier), we can expect significant accomplishments by age 21. For obvious reasons, the preferred outcome is one that is generalizable (the student can use it across a variety of settings) and unaided (the student does not need to rely on adaptations such as calculators or money cards). Indeed, some students have been able to use a generalizable and unaided strategy—a numberline strategy—to purchase single items with combinations of bills and coins. For multiple-item purchases, however, an unaided strategy requires rather complex addition, subtraction, and/or estimation skills. To handle this complexity, many students have learned to use a calculator. Both the numberline and calculator strategies are described below:

- *Numberline strategy*: Determinations of "enough" and "not enough" are based on an understanding of the relative positions of two numbers on the numberline: 1) the number representing the price of an item, and 2) the number representing the money to be spent. A student first learns to determine affordability by using a numberline marked from 1 to 10. After demonstrating mastery of the strategy with this simple numberline, he or she is asked to transfer the strategy to a more complex numberline that is marked in units of 10s to 100.

  The numberline strategy can be illustrated best through an example. Sarah, a 6-year-old student with moderate disabilities, wants to purchase an item from the school store. On this occasion she counts the eight pennies she has in her pocket

Chart 8.1. Scope and sequence for money handling

| Approach | | Age-level goals | | | |
|---|---|---|---|---|---|
| | | Elementary school | | Middle and high school (by age 18) | Outcome upon graduation (by age 21) |
| | | Primary (by age 8) | Intermediate (by age 12) | | |
| **Regular** The teacher uses the scope and sequence that is outlined in the math series adopted by the school district. | Math concepts and operations | • Has developed a solid understanding of numbers, place value, numeration, and basic operations of adding and subtracting and multiplying (at approximately the 2nd-grade level). | • Has developed the math concepts and operations necessary to approach problems requiring adding and subtracting (with regrouping), multiplying, dividing, estimation, graphing, measurement, and time (at least 5th-grade mastery level.) | • Has developed math concepts and operations beyond the 5th-grade mastery level. | • Uses a 5th–12th+-grade math level to question, estimate, explore, and solve problems as a means for developing advanced reasoning skills and furthering educational/career options; is able to apply basic math concepts and operations to everyday money-handling needs. |
| **Regular–adapted** The teacher modifies the regular math series by placing greater emphasis on essential skills and concepts and ensures application to everyday life. | Basic math concepts and operations | • Has developed an understanding of sets or classification, one-to-one correspondence, ordinality, rational counting (symbol association), place value (compare value of sets, numerals), combining sets (basic addition), and the inverse of addition (subtraction). | • Has developed an understanding of numbers, place value, numeration, and basic operation of adding and subtracting and multiplying. | • Has developed the math concepts and operations necessary to approach problems requiring adding and subtracting (with regrouping), multiplying, dividing, estimation, graphing, measurement, and time (at least 5th-grade mastery level). | • Uses at least a 5th-grade math ability to approach problems requiring adding, subtracting, multiplying, dividing, estimation, graphing, measurement, and time. |
| | Money applications | • Counts pennies, interprets and writes these money amounts, uses knowledge of place value to determine affordability of items. | • Counts all combinations of coins and bills, reads and interprets all prices; uses estimation, place value, and addition and subtraction skills to determine affordability of items. | • Applies math concepts and operations to purchasing items and other daily money-handling needs. | • Applies basic operations to handle money when purchasing items, banking, paying bills, and budgeting. |

(continued)

Chart 8.1. (continued)

| Approach | | Elementary school | | Middle and high school (by age 18) | Outcome upon graduation (by age 21) |
| --- | --- | --- | --- | --- | --- |
| | | Primary (by age 8) | Intermediate (by age 12) | | |
| Functional—money-handling sequence — The teacher develops or adopts a functional, easy-to-hard sequence that leads to the ability to determine whether an item or items are affordable. | Numberline and calculator strategies | • Numberline strategy: Uses a numberline strategy to determine the affordability of an item (e.g., with pennies to 10¢, then dimes to $1.00).<br>• Calculator strategy: Uses a price subtraction system on the calculator to determine the affordability of several inexpensive items with bills. | | • Numberline strategy: Increases ability to use a numberline strategy to determine the affordability of an item (e.g., with combinations of quarters, dimes, and nickels to $1.00 and dollar items to $20.00). | • Uses a numberline strategy to determine the affordability of a single item and a calculator to determine the affordability of more than one item when shopping, using restaurants, and in other purchasing contexts. |
| Functional—embedded money skills — The teacher identifies ways for a student to exchange money as the need arises within daily routines. | Predetermined amounts and money cards | • Money cards: Uses increasing numbers of money cards (cards that display the coins and/or bills needed to cover the cost of a particular item) to make routine purchases.<br>• Predetermined amounts: Uses increasing numbers of money envelopes (containing predetermined amounts of money) to make purchasing choices. | | | • Uses money cards to determine how much money is needed for items in routine purchasing situations.<br>• Uses a predetermined amount of money to pay for an item in routine purchasing situations. |

*Age-level goals*

and marks the number "8" on the numberline. She locates a pencil that costs "10¢." She compares the price of the pencil with her money. The relative positions of these numbers leads her to conclude that there is "not enough" money for the purchase. In time, the numberline will be faded and Sarah will demonstrate her understanding of the relative positions of the numbers without the use of a visual aid.

If Sarah has a solid understanding of the numberline strategy with 1–10, then she should be able to transfer her knowledge to the use of a numberline marked in 10s to 100. This premise, depicted below, serves as the basis for numberline skill sequences contained in this guide.

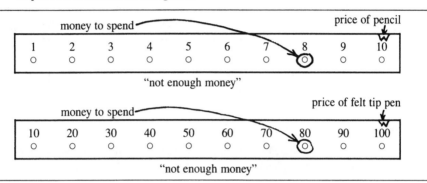

Students progressing through the numberline sequence will learn to make single-item purchases with increasingly complex combinations of coins/bills and prices.

- *Calculator strategy*: A cumulative subtraction system is used to determine the affordability of more than one item. This system was first described by Wheeler, Ford, Nietupski, Loomis, and Brown (1980). Students who learn this system perform the following steps: 1) count the money to be spent; 2) enter amount into calculator disregarding decimals; 3) press minus sign and the price of the item; 4) repeat step 3, unless the display shows a minus sign which means "not enough" money to purchase that particular item. More sophisticated uses of the calculator are taught once the basic system is mastered.

Not all students will be able to accomplish outcomes with this degree of proficiency. These students should still be expected to handle money in purchasing situations using alternative strategies. Possible alternatives include:

- *Money-card strategy*: A student might use pocket-size money cards to assist him or her in determining the correct amount of money to purchase an item(s). Money cards would be designed for a set of frequently purchased items. Each card would contain a symbol of the object and the price (the price would be rounded off and would include sales tax). Next to the symbol of the item, a configuration of coins/bills would be presented. This configuration could be depicted with pictures and/or indentations (such as those in coin collection books). A student would then match coins/bills to the card to determine the affordability of an item.
- *Predetermined-amount strategy*: A wallet might be adapted that contains envelopes with symbols of the items to purchase. Dollar/coin amounts to cover the cost of each item would be predetermined and placed into corresponding envelopes before leaving for the store or restaurant.

Given this range of possibilities, all students, including those with the most severe disabilities, should be equipped with at least one of these strategies for handling money. Skill sequences that incorporate each of these functional strategies are included in the appendix at the end of this chapter.

## OPPORTUNITIES TO USE MONEY-HANDLING SKILLS

As we have already discussed, it is important to teach the value or use of money from the onset of instruction. Thus, the task becomes one of identifying opportunities throughout the day or week when the student can apply his or her money-handling skills. Each of these opportunities becomes a "teachable moment." Table 8.1 contains a listing of the opportunities available to use money (*real money*) during elementary and middle/high school years. Young elementary school students should learn to hold onto their lunch money, carry field trip money, and purchase small items in the school store and corner grocery store. As students get older, the opportunities to use money expand significantly, requiring more complex calculations and budgeting.

## DETERMINING THE MONEY-HANDLING PROGRAM FOR A PARTICULAR STUDENT

What skills will the student learn this year that will enable him or her to make purchases in a more proficient manner? To answer this question effectively, the teacher must have information about the student's current repertoire as well as knowledge of the opportunities available to *use* money-handling skills. These information-gathering steps are incorporated into a series of steps that should help you determine money-handling goals for a particular student. We have continued to carry out our example of Mary Z. to provide an illustration of each step in the process.

### Step 1: Gain an understanding of the student's existing repertoire in math—and, specifically, money handling.

Sound decision making should begin with an understanding of the student's existing repertoire in math. This information can be gathered through cumulative records, direct observation, basic math skill inventories, and discussions with family and other teachers. Below are some guiding questions to help you with this information-gathering step.

How would you describe the student's *present math performance* in terms of:

Table 8.1.    Money-handling opportunities

| Elementary school | Middle and high school |
| --- | --- |
| Buys items from school store | Buys items from school store |
| Brings in money for field trips | Manages own money during field trips or community-based instruction (e.g., grocery store, department store, restaurant, snack bar) |
| Carries lunch money to cafeteria | |
| Buys familiar item at grocery store | |
| Collects money for fundraising activity | Purchases items from menu in school cafeteria |
| | Uses vending machines in lounge at job site |
| | Collects and manages money for club fundraising activities |
| | Uses coins or tokens for riding city bus |
| | Handles coins necessary to use pay telephone |
| | Purchases items from school snack bar, popcorn sales, and bake sales |

1. **Basic concept development?** Does the student show an ability to: 1) group similar objects together (classification); 2) place objects in order, such as arranging items from smallest to largest (ordering concepts or seriation); 3) estimate the number of items (two to three) without counting, rote count to 5 or 10, and rational count by applying number names to each item (cardination concepts); 4) create another set of items using one-to-one correspondence and later compare sets to determine sameness in size, more or less (set concepts); and 5) acknowledge that the set of objects is the same even though it has been transformed in some way (conservation)? (See Cohen & Gross, 1979, or other resources based on developmental theory for a description of these basic concepts.)

   *Mary Z.:* Mary is just beginning to recognize when familiar configurations are incomplete. For example, her typical place setting includes an adapted plate, a spoon, and a cup. She seems to notice when the spoon is missing. She is also beginning to group similar objects together (e.g., putting the paint brushes in one container and the colored chalk in another in art class).

2. **Rational counting?** What number of objects can the student count accurately? Can he or she "count out" a select number of objects from a larger amount?

   *Mary Z.:* Not applicable.

3. **Numeral identification?** What numerals can the student recognize? Which numerals can the student write?

   *Mary Z.:* Not applicable.

4. **Place value?** Can the student arrange numerals in order (1–5, 1–10, 1–20)? Can the student use a numberline to determine if a set is the same, has more, or is less ("not enough")?

   *Mary Z.:* Not applicable.

5. **Addition and subtraction?** Does the student demonstrate an understanding of addition (combining sets results in an increase in the total number of objects) and subtraction (removal of a set results in a decrease in the total number of objects)? When presented with an addition (4 + 3 = ____) or subtraction problem (8 − 3 = ____), is the student able to solve it using manipulatives? Which addition and subtraction facts have been mastered by the student?

   *Mary Z.:* Not applicable.

6. **Estimation?** How accurately does the student estimate quantities (e.g., the number of pencils left in the box, which container will hold more water)?

   *Mary Z.:* Not applicable.

7. **Money handling?** Does the student understand that money can be used to purchase a desired object? Is the student careful when handling money? Which coins and bills does the student recognize? Does he or she know the value of each coin and bill? Can the student determine whether he or she has enough money to purchase an item? Is the student able to count coins and bills in order to purchase an item? Can the student interpret actual price tags?

   *Mary Z.:* Mary has had limited experience with money. It is unclear whether she appreciates the purchasing power of money.

**Step 2: Consider the chronological age of the student and other important factors such as learning style, extent of progress in previous math or money programs and the integrity of previous programs. Use this information when determining the instructional approach best suited for the student.**

After completing Step 1 you should have an understanding of the student's repertoire in money handling and other basic math skills. Before determining which approach to use with a particular student, however, it is important to consider some additional factors. What if you learned that a student never received instruction in math or money skills? Or what if you learned that a student received money instruction for an hour each day during the past year on the numberline strategy—and still is on the very first step in the sequence? Information about past programs as well as these other factors needs to be considered before your team determines the best approach for the student:

1.  What is the student's chronological age?

    *Mary Z.:* Mary is 14 years old.

2.  How would you describe his or her learning style (particularly as it may influence the development of money-handling skills)?

    *Mary Z.:* Mary will have some difficulty manipulating money. Consideration should be given to designing a money envelope that she can grasp with ease. Also, it is important that the envelope is transparent so that she can actually see the money (object permanence is the concern here).

3.  What was the rate of progress in previous money or math programs?

    *Mary Z.:* Mary has not been expected to handle her own money in the past.

4.  What is the integrity of the previous money or math programs?

    *Mary Z.:* No systematic efforts have been made to teach Mary how to handle her own money.

### Step 3: Review the scope and sequence chart and specify which approach should be used with a particular student.

The information collected in Steps 1 and 2 should help you decide which approach is best suited for a student. If your team is debating between two approaches, it is generally better to select the more sophisticated approach rather than take the risk of under-challenging the student.

*Mary Z.:* Based on Mary's chronological age and performance repertoire, a functional–embedded money skills approach will be used. Mary will learn to use predetermined amounts of money that will be placed in envelopes.

### Step 4: Develop or adopt a program or skill sequence to match the specified approach.

If you plan to use a Regular or Regular–adapted math approach, you will probably be using many of the same materials used by the students without special needs. For older students using an adapted approach, you might want to consult with your colleagues about appropriate consumer math materials.

The functional–money-handling sequence and functional–embedded approaches will also take some careful planning. If these approaches are to lead to using coins and bills to make everyday purchases, then attention must be given to the sequence of skills necessary to achieve this outcome. In the appendix at the end of this chapter, we have included a sequence that was designed to correspond with these functional approaches. Whether you use this sequence or others it is important to resist teaching skills in isolation of the purchasing context (e.g., practicing sorting money, repeated trials of simply counting coins, reading price tags). From the very beginning of the sequence, the student should learn to appreciate the purchasing power of money.

*Mary Z.:* Based on Mary's chronological age and performance repertoire, a *predetermined-amount strategy* will be used.

## Step 5: Estimate where to place the student in the program or skill sequence and conduct a detailed assessment to establish baseline performance.

The procedures outlined in the reading and writing chapter also apply here (see Step 5 in Chapter 7). By this point in the decision process you have probably secured enough information to estimate where to place a student in a sequence or program. Your assessment information should lead to a precise determination of which skills will be targeted for instruction.

*Mary Z.:* The skill sequence contained in the appendix at the end of this chapter was modified and used to assess Mary's money-handling repertoire. Anecdotal data were also gathered to record how she handled money in actual purchasing situations.

## WRITING GOALS AND OBJECTIVES

The five-step decision-making process should lead to the determination of which skills/concepts will be addressed during the upcoming year. As we have stressed throughout this section, the functional use of academic skills must be an integral part of the instructional process. Thus, when writing individualized education program (IEP) goals and objectives, every effort should be made to communicate the *purchasing context* in which the student will develop or apply specific money or math skills. Consider the following examples from Mary Z.'s IEP.

### Goals and Objectives for Mary Z.

#### Goal

When preparing to buy a school lunch or a snack (at work or a fast-food restaurant), Mary will review available menu items to plan her purchase and use a picture-symbol strategy and gestures to communicate her request.

#### Objective

- At the appropriate time in a given routine, Mary will hand her money envelope to the cashier (within 5 seconds of clerk requesting payment, on five consecutive opportunities).

#### Goal

When making routine purchases (school cafeteria, school store, snacks in community settings, store purchases), Mary will select the correct money envelope for the situation (predetermined-amount strategy).

#### Objectives

- When presented with two money envelopes with picture symbols for routine purchase situations, Mary will take the envelope she needs for the current situation (successfully four of five times, for five consecutive opportunities).
- When making multiple purchases (when practical), Mary will choose the correct money envelopes and pool the money to cover the cost of all items (successfully, four of five times, for five consecutive opportunities).

- At the appropriate time in a given routine, Mary will hand her money envelope to the cashier (within 5 seconds of clerk requesting payment, on five consecutive opportunities).

### Goal

Mary will increase her level of active participation in grocery shopping for two to three familiar items using picture-symbol shopping cards (an adapted shopping list) and money envelopes (an adaptation consisting of envelopes containing the amount of money necessary to purchase an item represented by a picture symbol on the outside).

### Objective

- When positioned in front of the cashier, Mary will hand over her money envelope to the cashier (within 5 seconds of clerk requesting payment, on five consecutive opportunities).

## MONITORING ACADEMIC PROGRESS
## AND MAKING DECISIONS FOR DEPARTURE TO ALTERNATIVE SEQUENCES

The pace at which students progress through the sequence will influence the outcomes achieved. Some students may not progress within the sequences at a pace that will allow for the acquisition of the most proficient outcome—the abilities that accompany the use of the regular or regular–adapted curricular approach. In such cases, a teacher will need to pay greater attention to the alternative outcomes derived through the money handling sequence (numberline and/or calculator strategy ) or embedded money-handling skills (money cards or predetermined-amount strategy). Departures from one approach to another can be made in various directions. Consider the examples illustrated below:

| Three Students' Pace in Acquiring Money-Handling Skills | | |
|---|---|---|
| age 5 | age 10 | age 21 |
| Jennifer | Regular–Adapted _____ | |
| | | Money-Handling Sequences— Numberline Strategy and Calculator |
| Sally | Money Cards | Calculator |
| John | Predetermined Amount | |

Since kindergarten, Jennifer has followed an adapted version of the regular math program. In her early elementary school years she learned many basic math skills and concepts. When she was about 10 years old, her teachers became increasingly concerned about the fact that she was not effectively applying these math skills in purchasing contexts. Thus, in addition to continuing with an adapted math program, they incorporated instruction on the money-handling sequence. By graduation, she had a solid understanding of the basic math operations of addition and subtraction and some estimation skills, which she applied to banking, paying bills, and budgeting. She was also able to purchase single items without the use of an adaptation (she had internalized the numberline strategy). Furthermore, she could purchase multiple items with the calculator that she carried in her purse.

Sally progressed through the skill sequences at a slower pace. She developed her ability to use a money-card strategy during her first few years of elementary school. By age 8, she began to receive concurrent instruction in the use of the calculator (for both single and multiple items). During high school, the calculator strategy became her primary method for making everyday purchases.

John received intensive and systematic instruction in money handling. He began by learning to hold onto a predetermined amount of money and exchange it for a desired item in restaurants and stores. Later in elementary school, he learned to select the appropriate money envelope to cover his anticipated purchases. Now, at age 21, as he moves through his daily routine, he is able to select from an assortment of money envelopes to locate the one that will enable him to buy a desired item. For example, his work binder contains money envelopes for several snacks that can be purchased in the hospital cafeteria: 1) he selects the envelope carrying the symbol of ice cream, 2) he shows the ice cream symbol to the cafeteria worker to express his order, and 3) he hands the money envelope to the cashier to pay for the ice cream.

Of course the pace at which a learner progresses through the skill sequence is influenced by the degree to which instruction is intensive and systematic. Reasonable progressions can be expected when well-developed instructional plans are carried out on a daily basis. If a student is not moving through the sequence, the teacher might ask him or herself the following questions:

- Have I broken the skill sequence down enough?
- Have I presented the skills within a meaningful context such that learner motivation will be enhanced?
- Have I used teaching techniques that have been proven effective with this student?
- Have I devised an accurate data collection system, so that progress is noticeable and measurable?
- Have I provided enough opportunities for the student to learn the targeted skill?

In other words, the skill sequence only provides a framework for targeting specific skills. Once the skills are targeted, instructional plans must be developed and carried out effectively.

Chronological age is a particularly important factor when considering instruction in the use of a numberline strategy. If an older student has had little systematic instruction in money handling in the past, a time-limited program of instruction may be warranted. For example, a 3-month period might be devoted to instruction on the numberline strategy. If mastery of the basic strategy (using 1–10 cents) is not achieved, a departure to an alternative strategy should be taken (e.g., money cards, basic calculator system). Having a high school student count pennies for a year would be an inappropriate use of instructional time, as well as an activity that does not reflect the student's chronological age. In conclusion, careful planning must accompany the use of the money-handling skill sequence. If progress is not occurring at a reasonable rate, we must re-evaluate our instructional approach.

## QUESTIONS AND ANSWERS

Q:  I have a student who is 8 years old. Her math skills are at the "readiness" level (recognizes a few numerals, rote counts to six, identifies a penny and a nickel). Shouldn't I make sure she has mastered the prerequisite skills before she starts the money-handling sequence?

A:  We would encourage you not to think in terms of "prerequisites." Yes, skills and concepts such as numeral recognition, one-to-one correspondence, and counting are integral elements of the money-handling sequence (particularly the numberline strategy). However, rather than thinking that these skills need to be taught *first* (which often leads to lessons that are rather artificial), we recommend that you teach them *while* you teach the money handling skill sequence. Numeral recognition can be taught as you teach the numberline, one-to-one correspondence occurs when student places the coins on each number, and so forth. Other additional natural opportunities may arise throughout the day to address concepts such as one-to-one correspondence and counting.

Q:  The calculator procedure described in the appendix to this chapter is based on a subtraction system. Wouldn't it make more sense to use addition?

A:  An addition system is considerably more difficult than a substraction system. With the subtraction system the student enters the total amount of money to spend and cumulatively subtracts each item. He or she only needs to check the display (the subtotal) for the cue that indicates that there is "not enough" money for an item (the cue is a "minus" sign). To use addition, the student must: 1) keep track of the total amount that she or he has to spend (by memorizing it, writing it down, or some other strategy), and 2) check the display after adding in an item and compare the total with the amount she or he has to spend. The need to *compare* the amount in the calculator with the available money to spend makes this a much more difficult procedure.

Regardless of the system selected, it is important that efforts are made to communicate and demonstrate the calculator procedures to persons who are likely to accompany the student in purchasing situations (e.g., family members, other teachers, nonhandicapped peers). This will enhance the likelihood that consistent strategies are used across settings.

Q:  There are so many different types of calculators available. Is there a certain type that I should buy?

A:  While there is no specific type or brand that we would recommend, there are some features that you might want to consider carefully:

1.  Power source: Some teachers have found that the use of solar calculators creates some unnecessary problems. For example, if the lighting is not intense enough or if the calculator is moved out of the light, the entries may be cleared. Battery-operated calculators are often a better choice.

2.  Size: Calculators should be small enough to be carried easily. However, they should not be so small that students have difficulty locating and pushing the buttons.

3.  Sensitivity of the buttons: Some calculators have very sensitive buttons that students could easily press unintentionally. Calculators should be examined before purchasing to determine how much pressure must be applied to the buttons. In addition, it is possible to adapt the calculator by placing a keyguard over the buttons, which could enhance motoric accuracy.

4. Number of keys/buttons: Some students may be confused or distracted by the functions on the calculator that he or she will not need (e.g., multiplication, division, square root). This problem may be eliminated by simply covering the unnecessary buttons with black adhesive tape.

5. On/off button: Some calculators automatically shut off after a certain amount of time. This may be an advantage for the student who frequently forgets to turn the calculator off. However, it could be a disadvantage for the individual who requires a significant amount of time to locate items in the store. Conceivably, the calculator could turn itself off in the middle of shopping.

6. Batteries: Consideration should be given to the maintenance of the calculator. Some calculators come with rechargeable batteries, which may be a better buy for some students.

Q: How can students who are working on a functional approach in math receive instruction with students who are in a more advanced academic sequence?

A: It is possible to develop activity-based lessons that allow students with greatly different educational objectives to learn together. For example, David is learning how to make multiple purchases at the store with a calculator. His learning style is such that he is able to benefit from practice sessions aside from the actual purchasing opportunity. Today, he is part of a small math group that is assigned the task of comparison shopping. While the other students in his group are expected to apply their newly acquired division skills to this task, David is expected to practice deducting the price of the items on his calculator.

## REFERENCES

Cohen, M., & Gross, P. (1979). *The developmental resource: Behavioral sequences for assessment and program planning* (Vol. I and II). New York: Grune & Stratton.

Wheeler, J., Ford, A., Nietupski, J., Loomis, R., & Brown, L. (1980). Teaching moderately and severely handicapped adolescents to shop in supermarkets using pocket calculators. *Education and Training of the Mentally Retarded, 15* (27), 105–112.

## ADDITIONAL READINGS AND RESOURCES

Borakove, L. S., & Cuvo, A. J. (1976). Facilitative effects of coin displacement on teaching coin summation to mentally retarded adolescents. *American Journal of Mental Deficiency, 81*, 350–356.

Browder, D., & Snell, M. (1987). Functional academics. In M. Snell (Ed.), *Systematic instruction of persons with severe handicaps*. Columbus, OH: Charles E. Merrill.

Connis, R. (1979). The effects of sequential picture cues, self-recording, and praise on the job task sequencing of retarded adults. *Journal of Applied Behavioral Analysis, 12*, 355–361.

Cuvo, A. J., Veitch, V. D., Trace, M. W., & Konke, J. L. (1978). Teaching change computation to the mentally retarded. *Behavior Modification, 2*, 531–548.

Peterson, D. (1973). *Functional mathematics for the mentally retarded*. Columbus, OH: Charles E. Merrill.

Resnick, L. B., Wang, M. C., & Kaplan, J. (1973). Task analysis in curriculum design: A hierarchically sequenced introductory mathematics curriculum. *Journal of Applied Behavioral Analysis, 6*, 697–710.

Trace, M.W., Cuvo, A. J., & Criswell, J. L. (1977). Teaching coin equivalence to the mentally retarded. *Journal of Applied Behavioral Analysis, 10*, 85–92.

# APPENDIX: MONEY-HANDLING SKILL SEQUENCES

The following pages contain skill sequences for each of the approaches included in the *functional* section of the scope and sequence chart (Chart 8.1): predetermined amounts, money cards, numberline strategy for single-item purchase, and calculator for multiple-item purchase. The skill sequences are organized into three major "skill clusters" that reflect an easy-to-hard format. Teaching suggestions and decision points have been included to assist the teacher in implementing this approach.

An overview of the money-handling sequences

| Approach | Skill cluster: single-item purchase | Skill cluster: multiple-item purchase |
|---|---|---|
| | I. | I. |
| Prede-termined amount | Using a predetermined-amount strategy, makes a single-item purchase:<br>a. by using a given money envelope<br>b. by choosing the correct money envelope | Using a predetermined-amount strategy, makes a multiple-item purchase:<br>a. by using a given money envelope<br>b. by choosing the correct money envelopes and pooling the money to cover the cost of all items |
| | II. | II. |
| Money cards | Using a money-card strategy, determines the affordability of a single item:<br>a. by matching a single coin/bill to a money card | Using a money-card strategy, determines the affordability of more than one item:<br>a. by matching a single coin/bill to a money card corresponding with each item desired and pooling the money to cover the cost of all items |
| | b. by matching quarters, dimes, nickels, and bills in different combinations to a money card | b. by matching quarters, dimes, nickels, and bills in different combinations to a number of money cards and pooling the money to cover the cost of all items |
| | III. | III. |
| Numberline strategy and calcu-lator use | Using a numberline strategy, determines the affordability of a single item:<br>a. with pennies to 10¢<br>b. with a dime<br>c. with dimes to $1.00<br>d. with quarters to $1.00<br>e. with two quarters plus dimes to $1.00<br>f. with nickels to $1.00 | Using a calculator strategy, determines the affordability of more than one item:<br>a. with bills and price subtraction system<br>b. with bills, price subtraction system, and tax table<br>c. with bill and coins (added into calculator), price subtraction system, and tax table |

| An overview of the money-handling sequences | | |
|---|---|---|
| Approach | Skill cluster: single-item purchase | Skill cluster: multiple-item purchase |
| | g. with quarters plus nickels to $1.00 | |
| | h. with dimes plus nickels to $1.00 | |
| | i. with quarters plus dimes to $1.00 | |
| | j. with quarters, dimes, and nickels to $1.00 | |
| | k. with singles to $10.00 | |
| | l. with $5 bills plus singles to $20.00 | |
| | m. with a $10 bill plus singles to $20.00 | |
| | n. with a $10 bill, a $5 bill, and singles to $20.00 | |

## SKILL CLUSTER I: USING A PREDETERMINED-AMOUNT STRATEGY

This skill cluster involves using a money envelope containing a dollar/coin amount to cover the cost of an item. A wallet, communication booklet, or purse is adapted so that one or more money envelopes can be inserted. Each envelope is labeled with a picture or line drawing of the item to be purchased (e.g., a picture of a bus for the envelope that contains bus fare, a picture of a soda can for the envelope that contains vending machine money, a picture of a favorite food item for the grocery shopping envelope). The student learns to select the appropriate envelope and remove the money before engaging in the purchasing routine. To make multiple-item purchases (purchasing a shake and hamburger), the student selects separate money envelopes for each item and pools the money from the envelopes.

| Single-item purchase | Multiple-item purchase | Decision points and suggestions for implementation |
| --- | --- | --- |
| ___ A. Matches a single coin/bill to a money card to complete a transaction<br><br>___ B. Matches different combinations of coins/bills to a money card to complete a transaction | ___ A. Chooses the appropriate money envelopes and pools the money to cover the cost of all items<br>1. With two or more envelopes chosen from an array of four, then five, and so forth<br>2. In at least three purchasing situations (e.g., restaurant, grocery store, school store) | Line drawings, photos or actual product labels may be used to identify envelopes (e.g., juice label or gum wrapper is attached to envelope containing money). Small transparent plastic holders (with zippers or Velcro) make good money envelopes.<br><br>  If necessary, written instructions might be attached to the envelopes indicating, "Please remove my money and place the change inside."<br><br>  A money envelope can also be used as an aid in locating an item (the symbol serves as a reminder and can be matched to the product) or in communicating an order in a restaurant. Care should be taken so that materials do not elicit unnecessary attention due to size and age inappropriateness.<br><br>  *Decision point:* If the student has progressed to this point at a significant pace, a decision to move on to Skill Cluster II may be in order. For other students, expansion of this strategy may be appropriate. |

| Single-item purchase | Multiple-item purchase | Decision points and suggestions for implementation |
|---|---|---|
| | | (The use of a predetermined-amount strategy might be maintained for some purchasing situations while a student begins to use a money-card or numberline strategy.) |

## SKILL CLUSTER II: MONEY-CARD STRATEGY

This skill cluster involves the use of money cards for frequently purchased items. Each card contains a symbol of the desired item and the price (in some cases the price is rounded up so that the card will apply to more than one brand of an item and to cover sales tax). Next to the symbol of the item, a configuration of coins/bills is presented. Coin configuration could be represented with pictures or indentations such as those in coin collectors' booklets.

| Single-item purchase | Multiple-item purchase | Decision points and suggestions for implementation |
| --- | --- | --- |
| ___ A. Matches a single coin/bill to a money card to complete a transaction<br>___ B. Matches different combinations of coins/bills to a money card to complete a transaction | (This strategy parallels the one used for single-item purchases. Students should be proficient in the money-card strategy for single items prior to beginning instruction on multiple items.)<br>___ A. Matches a single coin/bill to a money card corresponding with each item desired and pools the money to cover the cost of all items<br>___ B. Matches quarters, dimes, nickels and bills in different combinations to a money card corresponding with each item desired; then pools the money to cover the cost of all items | Money cards may be organized in a variety of ways. The cards can be carried in a 3″ × 5″ binder and grouped by environment (e.g., a set for restaurants, grocery stores, work) and/or by cost (e.g., a set of items that can be purchased for less than $1.00). Students could be taught to examine their daily schedules and identify which money cards are needed. They could then place those particular money cards in their wallets.<br>*Decision point:* After a student has mastered the use of money cards with *any* coins/bills, he or she should move to Skill Cluster III—particularly if mastery occurred within a reasonably short time period (1 month to 1 year). |

## SKILL CLUSTER III: USING A NUMBERLINE STRATEGY FOR A SINGLE-ITEM PURCHASE AND A CALCULATOR FOR A MULTIPLE-ITEM PURCHASE

This skill cluster involves *calculating* whether an item(s) can be purchased or not. To purchase a single item, the student is taught to use a numberline strategy. Determinations of "enough" and "not enough" are based on an understanding of the relative positions of two numbers on the numberline: 1) the number representing the price of an item, and 2) the number representing the money to be spent. A student first learns to determine affordability by using a numberline marked from 1¢ to 10¢. After demonstrating mastery of the strategy with this basic numberline, he or she is taught to transfer the strategy to a more complex version that is marked by 10s to $1.00.

To purchase more than one item, a calculator subtraction system is used to determine the affordability. This system was first described by Wheeler, Ford, Nietupski, Loomis, and Brown (1980). Students who learn this system perform the following steps: 1) count the money to be spent; 2) enter amount into calculator, disregarding decimals; 3) press the minus sign and the price of the item; and 4) repeat step three unless the display shows a minus sign, which means that there is "not enough" money to purchase the last item subtracted. More sophisticated uses of the calculator are taught once the basic system is mastered.

| Skills | Decision points and suggestions for implementation |
|---|---|

### SINGLE-ITEM PURCHASE

___ A. Determines affordability of an item by using the numberline and *pennies to 10¢*

    ___ 1. Counts pennies to 10¢

At this point a numberline may be used to facilitate learning to count. The numberline should be gradually faded before moving on to the next skill.

| 1 | 2 | 3 | 4 | 5 | 6 | 7 | 8 | 9 | 10 |
|---|---|---|---|---|---|---|---|---|---|
| o | o | o | o | o | o | o | o | o | o |

    ___ 2. Counts out the following sums when given a greater number of pennies (e.g. the student is given 8¢ and asked to count out the 3¢ necessary to purchase gum)

From this point, and throughout the remaining sequence, a few coins other than the targeted denomination should be included in the sum of money with which the student is working.

        ___ 2¢ ___ 5¢ ___ 8¢
        ___ 3¢ ___ 6¢ ___ 9¢
        ___ 4¢ ___ 7¢ ___ 10¢

    ___ 3. When given 10 pennies or less and an item with a price from 1¢ to 10¢:
        a. locates position of price on the numberline
        b. counts out "just enough money"

Realistic purchasing situations with pennies are very limited. Nonetheless it is important that the items and prices used approximate the *real* world. Items that normally cost more than 10¢ should not be used.

| Skills | Decision points and suggestions for implementation |
|---|---|
| ___ 4. When given pennies and an item:<br>   a. with a price that is less than amount given (1¢–9¢), counts out "enough money"<br>   b. with a price that is more than amount given (2¢–9¢), indicates "not enough money" | Possible environments within which to teach and reinforce these objectives might be a store that sells penny candy or has a gumball machine and a school store that sells pencils and paper.<br>  A visual aid such as a moveable clip may be needed in order for the student to remember where the price of an item falls on the numberline (before comparing the price to the amount of available money). Again, this numberline is gradually faded before moving on to the next skill. The numberline may be reintroduced when teaching a new skill. |

An example of "just enough money"

An example of "not enough money"

| | |
|---|---|
| ___ B. Determines affordability of an item by using a numberline and *a dime*<br>  ___ 1. When given more than 10 pennies and presented with a dime, counts out 10 pennies to demonstrate equivalency<br>  ___ 2. When given a dime and an item that contains a 10¢ price tag:<br>    a. locates position of price on the numberline<br>    b. indicates "just enough money"<br>  ___ 3. When given a dime and an item:<br>    a. with a price that is less than 10¢, indicates "enough money"<br>    b. with a price that is 11¢–19¢, indicates "not enough money" | *Decision point:* The progress made by a student up until this point in the sequence should be carefully considered. If the student has a solid understanding of the numberline strategy, he or she should be able to make the transition from pennies to dimes without great difficulty. The "enough/not enough" strategy is essentially the same. From this point forward, however, the coin combinations and the prices get more difficult. If you have spent 1–2 years on Step A, and the student is having difficulty with determinations of "enough/not enough," it may be unwise to con- |

| Skills | Decision points and suggestions for implementation |
|---|---|
| | tinue with this sequence. This is particularly true for an older student. This student might benefit from just learning the calculator system (for both single- and multiple-item purchases). |
| ___ C. Determines affordability of an item by using a numberline and *dimes to $1.00* | |
|    ___ 1. Counts dimes to $1.00 | At this point, a new numberline is introduced that is organized in multiples of 10. |
|    ___ 2. Counts dimes from a larger sum:<br>     ___ 20¢<br>     ___ 30¢<br>     ___ 40¢<br>     ___ 50¢<br>     ___ 60¢<br>     ___ 70¢<br>     ___ 80¢<br>     ___ 90¢<br>     ___ $1.00 | Some possible environments within which to teach and reinforce these skills include: school cafeterias, public transportation, vending machines, stores, and restaurants. |
|    ___ 3. When given 10 dimes or less and an item priced in a multiple of 10 (to $1.00):<br>     a. locates position of price on numberline<br>     b. counts out "just enough money" | At this point the problem of sales tax should be presented. Example: "You have just enough for this candy bar, but what if there is tax? Can you buy it? No, you need a little extra money." The problem of sales tax, and needing a little extra money, should be incorporated into all instruction beyond this point.<br>   For some students, it may be appropriate to teach the distinction between taxable and nontaxable items. |
|    ___ 4. When given dimes and an item:<br>     a. with a price that is less than amount given (in multiples of 10), counts out "enough money"<br>     b. with a price that is more than the amount given (in multiples of 10), indicates "not enough money" | |
|    ___ 5. When given an item with a price from 1¢ to 99¢:<br>     a. locates approximate position of the price on the numberline | For the first time, a student will be asked to *approximate* where the price falls on the numberline |

| Skills | Decision points and suggestions for implementation |
|---|---|
| (e.g., the price is 34¢, and the student marks the numberline between 30 and 40) | *Price = 64¢* |

"next 10 = 70¢"

    b. indicates what the "next 10" is, or how much would be enough (e.g., 34¢ = price; "next 10" = 40¢; 40¢ is enough)

\_\_ 6. When given 10 dimes or less and an item:
    a. with a price that is less than amount given (not in multiples of 10), counts out "enough money"
    b. with a price that is more than amount given (not in multiples of 10), indicates "not enough money"

\_\_ D. Determines affordability of an item by using the numberline and *quarters to $1.00*
    \_\_ 1. Counts quarters to $1.00

At this point, the denominations of 25¢ can be added into the existing numberline.

    \_\_ 2. Counts quarters from a larger sum:
        \_\_ 25¢
        \_\_ 50¢
        \_\_ 75¢
        \_\_ $1.00
    \_\_ 3. When given four quarters or less and an item:
        a. with a price that is less than amount given, counts out "enough money"
        b. with a price that is more than amount given, indicates "not enough money"

\_\_ E. Determines affordability of an item by using a numberline and *two quarters plus dimes to $1.00*
    \_\_ 1. Counts out two quarters plus dimes from a larger sum (beginning with quarters):
        \_\_ 60¢ (two quarters plus one dime)
        \_\_ 70¢ (two quarters plus two dimes)
        \_\_ 80¢ (two quarters plus three dimes)

| Skills | Decision points and suggestions for implementation |
|---|---|

_____ 90¢ (two quarters plus four
       dimes)

_____ $1.00 (two quarters plus five
       dimes)

_____ 2. When given two quarters plus
       dimes, and an item:

    a. with a price that is less than
       amount given, counts out
       "enough money"

    b. with a price that is more than
       amount given, indicates "not
       enough money"

_____ F. Determines affordability of an item by using
       the numberline and *nickels to $1.00*

    _____ 1. Counts nickels to $1.00

Since nickels are not represented on the sample numberline, a new numberline may be needed at this point.

    _____ 2. Counts out the following sums of
       nickels from a larger sum:

| | | | |
|---|---|---|---|
| _____ | 5¢ | _____ | 55¢ |
| _____ | 10¢ | _____ | 60¢ |
| _____ | 15¢ | _____ | 65¢ |
| _____ | 20¢ | _____ | 70¢ |
| _____ | 25¢ | _____ | 75¢ |
| _____ | 30¢ | _____ | 80¢ |
| _____ | 35¢ | _____ | 85¢ |
| _____ | 40¢ | _____ | 90¢ |
| _____ | 45¢ | _____ | 95¢ |
| _____ | 50¢ | _____ | $1.00 |

    _____ 3. When given 20 nickels or less and
       an item:

    a. with a price that is less than
       amount given, counts out
       "enough money"

    b. with a price that is more than
       amount given, indicates "not
       enough money"

_____ G. Determines affordability of an item by
       using the numberline and *quarters plus
       nickels to $1.00*

    _____ 1. Counts out quarters plus nickels
       from a larger sum (beginning with
       quarters):

    _____ 30¢, 35¢, 40¢, etc.
       (one quarter and nickels)

| Skills | Decision points and suggestions for implementation |
|---|---|

    —— 55¢, 60¢, 65¢, etc.
(two quarters and nickels)
    —— 80¢, 85¢, 90¢, etc.
(three quarters and nickels)

—— 2. When given quarters and nickels (to $1.00) and an item:

    a. with a price that is less than amount given, counts out "enough money"

    b. with a price that is more than amount given, indicates "not enough money"

—— H. Determines affordability of an item by using the numberline and *dimes plus nickels to $1.00*

    —— 1. Counts out dimes plus nickels from a larger sum (beginning with dimes):

      —— 15¢, 20¢, 25¢, etc.
(one dime and nickels)
      —— 25¢, 30¢, 35¢, etc.
(two dimes and nickels)
      —— 35¢, 40¢, 45¢, etc.
(three dimes and nickels)
      —— 45¢, 50¢, 55¢, etc.
(four dimes and nickels)
      —— 55¢, 60¢, 65¢, etc.
(five dimes and nickels)
      —— 65¢, 70¢, 75¢, etc.
(six dimes and nickels)
      —— 75¢, 80¢, 85¢, etc.
(seven dimes and nickels)
      —— 85¢, 90¢, 95¢, etc.
(eight dimes and nickels)
      —— 95¢, $1.00
(nine dimes and nickels)

    —— 2. When given dimes and nickels (to $1.00) and an item:

    a. with a price that is less than amount given, counts out "enough money"

    b. with a price that is more than amount given, indicates "not enough money"

—— I. Determines affordability of an item using the numberline and *quarters plus dimes to $1.00*

| Skills | Decision points and suggestions for implementation |
|---|---|

___ 1. Counts out quarters plus dimes
from a larger sum:
   ___ 60¢, 70¢, 80¢, etc.
   (two quarters and dimes)
   ___ 35¢, 45¢, 55¢, etc.
   (one quarter and dimes)
   ___ 85¢, 95¢
   (three quarters and dimes)
___ 2. When given quarters and dimes (to
$1.00) and an item:
  a. with a price that is less than
amount given, counts out
"enough money"
  b. with a price that is more than
amount given, indicates "not
enough money"

___ J. Determines affordability of an item using
the numberline and *quarters, dimes, and
nickels to $1.00*
  ___ 1. Counts out quarters, dimes, and
nickels from a larger sum (begins
with quarters, then dimes, then
nickels):
  ___ 2. When given quarters, dimes, and
nickels (to $1.00) and an item:
    a. with a price that is less than
amount given, counts out
"enough money"
    b. with a price that is more than
amount given, determines "not
enough money"

___ K. Determines affordability of an item by
using a numberline and *singles to $10.00*
  ___ 1. Counts singles to $10.00
  ___ 2. Counts out specified amount from a
larger sum of singles:
    ___ $ 2.00
    ___ $ 3.00
    ___ $ 4.00
    ___ $ 5.00
    ___ $ 6.00
    ___ $ 7.00
    ___ $ 8.00
    ___ $ 9.00
    ___ $10.00

| Skills | Decision points and suggestions for implementation |
|---|---|
| ____ 3. When given 10 singles or less, and an item with a price tag from $1.00 to $20.00 (no cents):<br>a. locates the position of price on the numberline | Again, it is important to use realistic prices and price tags through the sequence. |
| b. counts out "just enough money" | A new numberline is constructed that contains dollar values. |

$$/ \ / \ / \quad 100 \quad / \ / \ / \quad 200 \quad / \ / \ / \quad 300$$

"just enough money"

Note: It is important to stress continually the need to carry extra change for sales tax.

| Skills | Decision points and suggestions for implementation |
|---|---|
| ____ 4. When given 10 singles or less, and an item:<br>a. with a price that is less than the amount given (no cents), indicates "enough money"<br>b. with a price that is more than the amount given (no cents), indicates "not enough money" | |
| ____ 5. When given an item with a price from $1.00 to $20.00 (now including cents):<br>a. locates the approximate position on the numberline (e.g., the price is $2.49, and the student marks the numberline between "200" and "300")<br>b. indicates what the "next dollar" is, or how much would be enough (e.g., $2.49 = price; "next dollar" = $3.00; therefore $3.00 is enough) | Students should use the numberline to locate the approximate position of the price. A paper clip might be attached to the numberline and moved to the position that best *approximates* the price:<br>"Enough" (the dollar is "more than" the price; or the dollar "is past the price") |

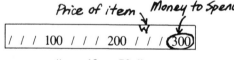

"next 10 = 70¢"

"Not enough" (the dollar is "less than" the price; or the dollar "is not past the price")

| Skills |  |
|---|---|
| ____ 6. When given 10 singles or less, and an item:<br>a. with a price that is less than amount given (including cents values), counts out "enough" money<br>b. with a price that is more than amount given (including cents), indicates "not enough" money | |

When teaching the interpretation of the price tag, the dollar place value

| Skills | Decision points and suggestions for implementation |
|---|---|
| | should be accentuated and the cents values made incidental (e.g., $5.39; the 5 is exaggerated and the 39 is downplayed). |

___ L. Determines affordability of an item by using the numberline and *a $5 bill and singles to $20.00*

    ___ 1. Counts singles to $20.00

___ 2. Counts out singles from a larger sum:

    ___ $11.00    ___ $16.00
    ___ $12.00    ___ $17.00
    ___ $13.00    ___ $18.00
    ___ $14.00    ___ $19.00
    ___ $15.00    ___ $20.00

___ 3. When given singles to $20.00 and an item:

    a. with a price that is less than amount given, counts out "enough money"

    b. with a price that is more than amount given, indicates "not enough money"

___ 4. Counts two $5 bills to $10.00

___ 5. Counts one $5 bill plus singles to $10.00

___ 6. Counts out $5 bills plus singles from a larger sum:

    ___ $5 bill plus one single
    ___ $5 bill plus two singles
    ___ $5 bill plus three singles
    ___ $5 bill plus four singles
    ___ $5 bill plus five singles

___ 7. When given a $5 bill plus singles, and an item:

    a. with a price that is less than amount given, counts out "enough money"

    b. with a price that is more than amount given, indicates "not enough" money

___ 8. Counts $5 bills to $20.00

___ 9. Counts out $5 bills from a larger amount

    ___ $ 5.00
    ___ $10.00
    ___ $15.00

| Skills | Decision points and suggestions for implementation |
|---|---|

\_\_\_ 10. Counts out $5 bills plus singles to
$20.00 (beginning with $5 bills):
- \_\_\_ $5+5+1+1+1+1+1+1+1+1+1+1$
- \_\_\_ $5+5+1+1+1+1+1+1+1+1+1$
- \_\_\_ $5+5+1+1+1+1+1+1+1+1$
- \_\_\_ etc.
- \_\_\_ $5+5+5+1+1+1+1+1$
- \_\_\_ $5+5+5+1+1+1+1$
- \_\_\_ $5+5+5+1+1+1$
- \_\_\_ etc.

\_\_\_ 11. When given $5 bills and singles to
$20.00, and an item:
- a. with a price that is less than
amount given, counts out
"enough money"
- b. with a price that is more than
amount given, indicates "not
enough money"

\_\_\_ M. Determines affordability of an item by
using a numberline and *$10 bills and
singles to $20.00*

     \_\_\_ 1. Counts outs $10 bills and singles
from a larger sum (beginning with
$10 bills):
- \_\_\_ $10 + $10
- \_\_\_ $10 + 1+1+1+1+1+1+1+1+1+1+1$
- \_\_\_ $10 + 1+1+1+1+1+1+1+1+1$
- \_\_\_ $10 + 1+1+1+1+1+1+1+1$
- \_\_\_ etc.

     \_\_\_ 2. When given $10 bills and singles,
and an item:
- a. with a price that is less than the
amount given, counts out
"enough money"
- b. with a price that is more than
the amount given, indicates "not
enough money"

\_\_\_ N. Determines affordability of an item using a
numberline and *$10 bills, $5 bills, and
singles to $20.00*

     \_\_\_ 1. Counts out $10 bills, $5 bills, and
singles from a larger sum:
- \_\_\_ $10 + 5 + 5
- \_\_\_ $10 + 5 + 1+1+1+1+1$
- \_\_\_ $10 + 5 + 1+1+1+1$
- \_\_\_ $10 + 5 + 1+1+1$
- \_\_\_ etc.

| Skills | Decision points and suggestions for implementation |
|---|---|
| ___ 2. When given a $10 bill, $5 bills, and singles, and an item: <br> a. with a price that is less than the amount given, counts out "enough money" <br> b. with a price that is more than the amount given, indicates "not enough" money | Students who reach this point should be taught to combine bills and coins (e.g., counts three singles and two quarters for a $3.50 total). The same procedure should be followed for determining affordability. |

## MULTIPLE-ITEM PURCHASE

A. Uses a calculator with bills and price subtraction system to determine affordability. Gradually increases the number of bills handled and the number of items purchased.

The focus of this step is to teach the basic subtraction system. Careful attention should be paid to the instructional term used. The basic procedure is illustrated below with suggested terminology.

| Bills | Items |
|---|---|
| ___ $1.00 | ___ one item |
| ___ $2.00 | ___ two items |
| ___ $3.00 | ___ three items |
| ___ $4.00 | |
| ___ $5.00–$10.00 (singles) | |
| ___ $5 bill plus singles to $10.00, etc. | |

1. I "count the money" that I have to spend. (counts $1.00)
2. I "enter 100" into the calculator. (disregarding decimals, 1-0-0 is entered into calculator.)

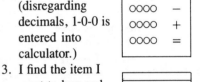

3. I find the item I want to buy and press "take away" button.
4. I find the "price" and "enter it into the calculator." (This is a basic match-to-sample task. The student need not be able to interpret the value of the price.)

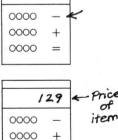

Price of item

5. I "check the display" to make sure that I entered the "right price."
6. I "press equal."

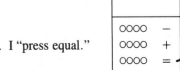

| Skills | Decision points and suggestions for implementation |
|---|---|

_"not enough"_

| | | |
|---|---|---|
| | | −29 |
| oooo | − |
| oooo | + |
| oooo | = |

7. I "check display" to see if I have "enough."

 Here, the student should look at the display to see if a "minus" sign has appeared. The student will learn the basic rule that: (a) "if there is a minus sign, I do not have enough money for that item"; or (b) "if no minus sign, I have enough!"

 a. Replace the item (or, if in restaurant, don't order item) when a minus sign appears on the display.

 b. Put item in cart (or, if in restaurant, plan to order the item) and continue purchasing additional items.

\_\_\_ B. Uses a calculator with bills, price subtraction system, and tax table. Subtracts tax "off the top" (from the amount entered):

 \_\_\_ 1. uses tax table to subtract taxes on $1.00

 \_\_\_ 2. uses tax table to subtract taxes on $2.00

 \_\_\_ 3. uses tax table to subtract taxes on $3.00

 \_\_\_ 4. uses tax table to subtract taxes on $4.00–$10.00

New York State has a 7% sales tax. To account for this tax, students learn to subtract it off the top of their spending amount. Thus, if a student has $3 to spend, he or she will subtract 21¢ prior to making any purchases. A tax table such as the one presented below can be taped to the back of the calculator or inserted in the pocket of the calculator.

| $ | TAX |
|---|---|
| 1000 | − 70 |
| 900 | − 63 |
| 800 | − 56 |
| 700 | − 49 |
| 600 | − 42 |
| 500 | − 35 |
| 400 | − 28 |
| 300 | − 21 |
| 200 | − 14 |
| 100 | − 7 |

|                                          | Decision points and<br>suggestions for implementation |
| Skills                                   |                                                        |

___ C. Uses a calculator with bills and coins (added into calculator), price subtraction system, and tax table.

With the new step of adding coins plus bills into the calculator, the student will need to: enter bills and add coins into calculator (e.g., enters 200 then adds in "25" for a quarter and "10" for a dime—totaling 235); rounds up to the "next dollar" to determine tax (e.g., the "next dollar" is 300 and the tax is 21¢); subtracts tax and prices of items; determines affordability.

Bills and coins: Rounding up to next dollar

| ___ three to four coins of same denomination | ___ next $ = $1.00 |
| | ___ next $ = $2.00 |
| | ___ next $ = $3.00 |
| ___ one to two coins of different denominations | ___ next $ = $4.00 |
| | ___ next $ = $5.00– |
| | $10.00 |
| ___ three to four coins of different denominations | |

In the previous steps the student learned to enter bills into the calculator. What happens when the student has a lot of coins to spend but doesn't know how to count them proficiently? The solution we offer is adding the value of the coins into the calculator. First he or she enters the dollar amount, then coin-by-coin the values are entered (e.g., +25, +25, +5—for two quarters and a nickel). The student presses an "equal" sign after the last coin has been added. Pennies are excluded since every additional entry increases the risk of an error occurring.

Students who are unable to remember the value of coins may use a card inserted into the calculator case that shows actual size representations of the coins and corresponding values. For example:

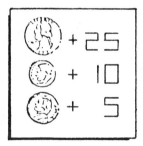

In the previous step, a student learned to use the tax table when he or she had exact dollar amounts (e.g., 100, 200, 300). Now, because coins will be added to the dollar amounts the entry will not be an exact figure (e.g., 135, 255, 375). To determine tax the student will need to learn to round up to the next dollar amount.

This "next dollar" strategy will be useful in other situations as well.

| Skills | Decision points and suggestions for implementation |
| --- | --- |
| | For example, when making a single-item purchase the student rounds up to the next dollar. At a restaurant when the student gets a check, he or she rounds up to the next dollar to figure out how much to pay. |

# CHAPTER 9

# Time Management

*Alison Ford, Jim Black, Linda Davern,*
*and Roberta Schnorr*

The outcomes of math programs will vary considerably given the range of learners attending today's schools. Many students will be able to graduate from high school with marked proficiency in advanced reasoning and problem-solving skills; others will be challenged by learning the basic math application skills necessary to function in everyday life. This chapter is devoted to one of these basic math application areas—time management.

The underlying rationale for providing instruction in time-management skills is to assist individuals in *understanding, predicting,* and *preparing for* events that occur in their lives. Consider that in our daily lives, most of us understand what comes next in our schedule of activities. Furthermore, we often use our ability to interpret clocks and watches to predict and prepare for upcoming transitions and activities. We "get ready" for sleep, work, lunch, travel, leisure time, and social activities. Certainly, for many of us, the mastery of time-management competencies has been a meaningful outcome of education because it has enabled us to be better organized and more efficient in our behavior.

Many individuals with moderate and severe handicaps have not achieved functional time-management outcomes. For these individuals, the sequence of daily events in their lives may not be understandable. They are often unable to predict and prepare for upcoming activities, resulting in an increased need for supervision and assistance. Other individuals may have mastered the "mechanics" of telling time (e.g., "the little hand means hours"), but are unable to use these isolated skills in their daily lives. With systematic instruction guided by appropriate decision making, many students can achieve a more sophisticated time-management outcome. For example:

- Kevin is 15 years old. He is now in his 10th year of time-management instruction. During the past 10 years, he has progressed steadily through a streamlined academic skill sequence. By the time he was 6, he could indicate "what's next" by pointing to a pictorial schedule. He learned to manage time to the hour at age 10 and was able to use these skills in school and at home. Currently, he is working on telling time at 15-minute intervals. Kevin is making steady progress toward the projected outcome of managing time to the minute by reading and interpreting clock faces.
- Janice is 10 years old. To date, she has received systematic time-management instruction within the context of following her daily schedule. When she first received time-management instruction, the focus was on her learning to change activities according to familiar environmental cues. For example, when nearby

classrooms emptied out, she learned to recognize that it was "time for lunch."
Now, she has expanded her repertoire to include referring to simple and familiar
pictures to determine "what's next." Future time-management objectives will
focus on expanding her ability to use more complex picture-symbol schedules,
natural cues, and adaptive timers.

This chapter outlines possible instructional approaches for teaching essential
time-management skills. As in each of the other functional academic areas, we discuss a range of approaches that should be considered when determining which time-
management skills to teach.

## SCOPE AND SEQUENCE

The time-management scope and sequence chart (Chart 9.1) is organized in a format
similar to the other functional academic areas. It consists of four basic approaches:

- *Regular:* The teacher uses the scope and sequence that is outlined in the math
  program adopted by the school or school district.
- *Regular–adapted:* The teacher modifies the regular math program by placing
  greater emphasis on essential skills and concepts and ensures application to everyday life.
- *Functional– Time-Management Sequence:* The teacher develops or adopts a functional, easy-to-hard sequence that leads to the interpretation of clock time to
  monitor daily activity.
- *Functional–Embedded Time-Management Skills:* The teacher identifies ways for
  a student to be aware of and manage a daily schedule as the need arises.

For the purposes of this guide, we are concerned with those students who would
probably not become proficient "time managers" if they were only exposed to the
"regular" math curriculum (even in its adapted form). Thus, we use this section to
describe the functional approaches included in Chart 9.1.

Perhaps the most preferred outcome in the time-management area would be student mastery of the interpretation of clock faces. This learner outcome is preferred
because it provides the student with a powerful and flexible tool with which to manage time. With generalized mastery of this skill, a student is capable of interpreting
clocks and watches to predict and prepare for daily events. A brief description of this
approach to time management is presented below:

- *Interpreting clocks and watches to tell time:* Telling time by interpreting the relative position of the hour and minute hands on a watch or clock face is the strategy
  used by most nonhandicapped adults in our society. This strategy requires the
  understanding and mastery of a number of concepts and skills if it is to be functional in daily living. Time tellers must discriminate between the hands on a clock
  face, and recognize the numbers 1 to 12 and their relative positions. Additionally,
  individuals using this strategy must understand the movement of the minute hand
  in relation to the hour hand, and use it to anticipate and predict upcoming events.

Even with carefully planned sequences, not all students with moderate and severe disabilities will progress sufficiently to achieve this proficient outcome. However, other functional strategies for managing time should be considered, including:

Chart 9.1.  Scope and sequence for time management

| | | Age-level goals | | | |
| | | Elementary school | | Middle and high school (by age 18) | Outcome upon graduation (by age 21) |
| Approach | | Primary (by age 8) | Intermediate (by age 12) | | |
|---|---|---|---|---|---|
| Regular<br>The teacher uses the scope and sequence that is outlined in the math program adopted by the school district. | Math concepts and operations | • Has developed an understanding of numbers, place value, numeration, and basic operations of adding and subtracting and multiplying (at approximately the 2nd-grade level). | • Has developed the math concepts and operations necessary to approach problems requiring adding and subtracting (with regrouping), multiplying, dividing, estimation, graphing, measurement, and time (at least 5th-grade mastery level.) | • Has developed math concepts and operations beyond the 5th-grade mastery level. | • Uses a 5th--12th+ grade math level to question, estimate, explore, and solve problems as a means of developing advanced reasoning skills and furthering educational/career options; is able to apply basic math concepts and operations to everyday time-management needs. |
| Regular–adapted<br>The teacher modifies the regular math program by placing greater emphasis on essential skills and concepts and ensures application to everyday life. | Basic math concepts and operations | • Has developed an understanding of sets or classification, one-to-one correspondence, ordinality, rational counting (symbol association), place value (compare value of sets, numerals), combining sets (basic addition), and the inverse of addition (subtraction). | • Has developed an understanding of numbers, place value, numeration, and basic operation of adding and subtracting and multiplying. | • Has developed the math concepts and operations necessary to approach problems requiring adding and subtracting (with regrouping), multiplying, dividing, estimation, graphing, measurement, and time (at least 5th-grade mastery level). | • Uses at least a 5th-grade math ability to approach problems requiring adding, subtracting, multiplying, dividing, estimation, graphing, measurement, and time. |
| | Time application | • Uses clock time on the hour and half-hour to comment on the time, estimate time needs, and solve real-life problems. | • Uses face and digital clocks at all intervals (hour, half-hour, 15 minutes, 5 minutes, minute) to comment on the time, estimate time needs, and solve real-life problems. | | • Applies time and measurement skills to estimating time needs, reading schedules (bus schedules, TV programs), using calendar, interpreting time from face and digital clocks. |

*(continued)*

Chart 9.1.  (continued)

| Approach | | Age-level goals | | | |
| --- | --- | --- | --- | --- | --- |
| | | Elementary school | | Middle and high school (by age 18) | Outcome upon graduation (by age 21) |
| | | Primary (by age 8) | Intermediate (by age 12) | | |
| Functional–time management sequence<br>The teacher develops or adopts a functional, easy-to-hard sequence that leads to the interpretation of clock time to monitor daily activity. | Clock time | • Uses a picture-symbol schedule to manage daily activities and responds to a familiar hand position on a clock as a cue for a specific event. | • Uses face and digital clocks at all intervals (hour, half-hour, 15 minutes, 5 minutes, minute) to comment on the time, estimate time needs, and solve real-life problems. | | • Uses clocks and watches to understand time, predict, and prepare for events. |
| Functional–embedded time-management skills<br>The teacher identifies ways for a student to be aware of and manage a daily schedule as the need arises. | Picture-symbol schedule | • Uses a picture-symbol schedule to manage daily activities. | | | • Uses a picture-symbol schedule to manage daily activities. |
| | Environmental cues | • Uses increasing numbers of environmental cues to signal the onset of routine events. | | | • Uses environmental cues to signal the onset of routine events. |

- *Picture-symbol schedule strategy:* In order to manage daily routines, students can learn to follow a sequenced series of pictures, symbols, and/or words that represent their daily schedules. For example, Missy follows a daily schedule consisting of a series of six simple line drawings that represent her school and community activities. Students may need to rely on some type of cue that signals that they should check their schedules and move on to the next activity. Options to consider when pairing cues with picture-symbol schedules include: the natural environmental cues (e.g., the school bell system, a factory whistle), or adapted cues (e.g., electronic watches or timers—there are timers available that can be programmed for up to four different alarm intervals at one time).
- *Environmental-cue strategy:* Students who learn to use the environmental-cue strategy will respond to natural and adaptive cues to understand and predict their daily schedules. Environmental cues available within the home, school, or community environments can be highlighted, enhanced, adapted, or created to facilitate an individual's awareness of transitions in his or her routine. For example, John is taught to respond to his classmates' departure as the cue for lunchtime. For Cynthia, these natural cues were not sufficient to indicate breaktime at her job site. Therefore her teacher set her electronic watch to "beep" just before break. Environmental-cue strategies are very context specific, and are typically used to signal specific prioritized transitions within an individual's schedule.

Thus, when specifying meaningful outcomes within the time-management area, at least three possible outcomes might be considered: interpreting clock faces, using picture-symbol schedules and using environmental cues. Achieving meaningful outcomes in time management will require systematically identifying and teaching students the skills and adaptations that are functional in their daily lives, and that build toward the mastery of more sophisticated and flexible strategies. Within this framework all students, including those with the most severe disabilities, can achieve some functional ability to manage time.

## OPPORTUNITIES TO USE TIME-MANAGEMENT SKILLS

A common frustration reported by teachers who provide time management instruction is that, "The students don't use their skills when they really need them!" Consider some of these complaints: 1) "I know Sarah can tell time to the hour, but yesterday when she was supposed to go to the nurse's office at 11:00 I had to tell her when to leave." 2) "Joe can interpret his picture schedule when we review it during homeroom, but he doesn't use it correctly throughout the day." and 3) "Harriet wears a watch every day but I have never seen her look at it." These complaints underpin the need to ensure that time-management skills are taught in the actual problem-solving contexts in which they are needed.

To ensure the actual use of time-management skills, the teacher must, first, identify the opportunities that exist during the day to teach or reinforce particular skills. We have included a table that will help you identify some of these opportunities (see Table 9.1). Then, the teacher must remain consciously aware of these opportunities and draw students' attention to them as they arise. For example, knowing that Sarah needs to go to the nurse at 11:00, the teacher might remind her of this fact before the class begins. If necessary, the teacher might provide a minute or two of instruction on

Table 9.1.  Time-management opportunities

| Elementary school | Middle and high school |
| --- | --- |
| Responds to bells or other cues for arrival and departure | Responds to bells or other cues for passage between classes |
| Uses class calendar to determine which day it is, what activities are planned, and so forth | Uses personal calendar to keep track of birthdates and other special dates, events that are planned, and so forth |
| Follows classroom schedule of daily activities | Follows personal schedule of classes for day and week |
| Uses wall clock and/or watch to manage time throughout day | Uses wall clock and/or watch to manage time throughout day |
| | Uses timer during home economics class to monitor cooking activities |
| | Manages time card at job site |
| | Manages time as needed in community situations (e.g., bus use, arrival, breaktime, and departure from job site) |

what the clock looks like when it is 11:00 or almost 11:00 (using real materials of course). Then, once or twice during the lesson, Sarah would be encouraged to check the clock (helping her to judge the passage of time). At 10:55, the teacher would teach Sarah to recognize that it is "almost 11:00" and ensure that she is ready to leave at the designated time.

## DETERMINING THE TIME-MANAGEMENT PROGRAM FOR A PARTICULAR STUDENT

The decision-making process described here closely parallels that described in the money-handling chapter (Chapter 8). The first two steps in the time-management decision process seek to understand the student's existing math repertoire and the nature of his or her past programs. You will notice that this is essentially the same information that was gathered for a money-handling program, except for the inclusion of information that pertains directly to time management skills. The remaining steps help you determine which approach is best suited to a particular student and what skills to target for instruction.

### Step 1: Gain an understanding of the student's existing repertoire in math—and, specifically, time management.

Information gathered through cumulative records, direct observation, basic math skill inventories, and student/family input will help you to construct a profile of the student's existing math repertoire, including time-management skills. Since the guiding questions listed in the previous chapter also apply here (see Step 1 in Chapter 8), they are not reiterated. Instead, we pose a single question about time management.

1.  How would you describe the student's present math performance in terms of time management? Does the student demonstrate an understanding of basic language associated with time (e.g., soon, now, later, tomorrow, after, before, long time ago)? Does the student use environmental cues to determine what to do next? Can the student follow a schedule of events? How does the student use the calendar? Does the student relate clock time to the daily schedule? Can the student tell time on a clock face to the hour, half-hour, quarter-hour, and so forth?

> *Mary Z.:* After following a predictable schedule for a month or so, she is able to anticipate what major activity is next. For example, after lunch she will initiate going to the restroom located next to the cafeteria. When she leaves the restroom she will go to the library. As of yet, she has not had any experience following a picture schedule.

## Step 2: Consider the chronological age of the student and other important factors such as learning style, extent of progress in previous math or time programs, and the integrity of previous programs. Use this information when determining the instructional approach best suited for the student.

After completing Step 1 you should have an understanding of the student's repertoire in time management and other basic math skills. Before determining which approach to use with a particular student, however, you will want to consider other factors such as chronological age and success in past programs:

1. What is the student's *chronological age*?

   > *Mary Z.:* Mary is 14 years old.

2. How would you describe his or her learning style (particularly as it may influence the development of time-management skills)?

   > *Mary Z.:* Some of Mary's frustration seems to stem from her inability to predict which activities are next. She is often "led" to a class or activity without any acknowledgment from her that she knows where she is going. A high priority would be for her to learn to follow a picture-symbol schedule (or to use representational objects such as being handed her gym suit to signify that she is about to go to physical education class) so that she can better predict and orient to events in her day.

3. What was the rate of progress in previous time-management or math programs?

   > *Mary Z.:* Mary has not received any instruction on time-management techniques.

4. What is the integrity of the previous time-management or math programs?

   > *Mary Z.:* No systematic efforts have been made to teach Mary how to manage time.

## Step 3: Review the scope and sequence chart and specify which approach should be used with a particular student.

The information you collected in Steps 1 and 2 should help you decide which approach is best suited for a student. If your team is debating between two approaches, it is generally better to select the more sophisticated approach rather than take the risk of underchallenging the student.

> *Mary Z.:* Based on Mary's chronological age and performance repertoire, a picture-symbol schedule approach will be used. Instruction will be embedded throughout the day so that Mary learns to rely on her schedule of line drawings to determine what happens next. The schedule will be arranged in a flip-chart fashion so that only one line drawing is displayed at a time. When the activity is completed, Mary will flip to the next line drawing to determine the next event. Initially it may be necessary to pair objects with the line drawings (e.g., a gym suit with the line drawing representing physical education).

## Step 4: Develop or adopt a program or skill sequence to match the specified approach.

If you plan to use a regular or regular–adapted math approach, you will probably be using many of the same materials used by the students without special needs. For older students using an adapted approach, you might want to consult with your colleagues about appropriate consumer math materials.

The functional time–management sequence and functional–embedded approaches will also require systematic planning and careful attention to the sequence of learning experiences structured for a particular student. In the appendix at the end of this chapter, we have included a sequence that was designed to correspond with these functional approaches. As with all sequences, it is important that you review it thoroughly and determine how to modify it to meet your particular needs.

## Step 5: Estimate where to place the student in the program or skill sequence and conduct a detailed assessment to establish baseline performance.

The procedures outlined for the other functional academic chapters also apply here (see Step 5 in Chapter 7). By this point in the decision process you have probably secured enough information to estimate where to place a student in a sequence or program. Then you would use the actual skill sequence as a tool to conduct a more detailed assessment of the student's performance. This assessment should lead to a precise determination of which skills will be targeted for instruction.

*Mary Z.:* The skill sequence contained in the appendix at the end of this chapter was modified and used to assess Mary's time-management repertoire. Anecdotal data were also gathered to record how she anticipated events in her daily schedule.

## WRITING GOALS AND OBJECTIVES

The step-by-step process outlined above should lead to determinations about instructional priorities in the time-management area. An embedded approach will be taken with Mary Z.'s program. Thus, it logically follows that the objectives written into her individualized education program (IEP) should be embedded into other major content areas. Below are some examples.

---

### Goals and Objectives for Mary Z.

#### Goal

Mary will look at symbols on a picture schedule to follow a prescribed routine at the hospital work site, including breaktime.

#### Objective

When presented with a horizontal display of three work activities, Mary will look at the symbol for the next scheduled activity as pointed to by a co-worker or teacher.

#### Goal

Mary will follow a picture schedule throughout each day to prepare belongings for transitions to activities in school and community settings.

#### Objectives

- At the end of each period or activity, Mary will point (in response to a request) to the symbol on her picture schedule for the current activity and look at the symbol to the right for the next scheduled activity (successfully, throughout the day, for 5 consecutive days).
- After orienting to the next activity on her picture schedule, Mary will participate in gathering the appropriate belongings or items as needed.

---

## MONITORING ACADEMIC PROGRESS AND MAKING DECISIONS FOR DEPARTURE TO ALTERNATIVE SEQUENCES

As we have discussed in the other functional academic chapters, the pace at which a student progresses through a sequence must be monitored carefully to ensure that he or she reaches the greatest degree of proficiency in time management. The outcomes and paces at which they are achieved will undoubtedly vary from student to student. Consider the examples illustrated below:

| Three Students' Pace in Acquiring Time-Management Skills | | |
|---|---|---|
| age 5 | age 10 | age 21 |
| Kevin | Regular–Adapted | Functional–Time-Management Sequence |
| Missy | Picture-Symbol Schedule | Clock Time | Picture-Symbol Schedule |
| Cynthia | Environmental Cues | |

Kevin, the student discussed in the introduction to this chapter, is an example of an individual who is appropriately making progress in a functional–time-management sequence. During his first 3 years of school the instructional approach used fell within the regular–adapted category. In third grade, a departure was made to include a functional–time-management approach. Currently, at age 15, he is working on telling time at 15-minute intervals.

Missy, however, has moved through the sequences at a different pace. She had progressed to the point of using picture-symbol schedules by age 10. After some unsuccessful teaching of interpreting clock faces, a decision was made to return to the picture-symbol strategy and expand its use.

Cynthia, the third student represented in the illustration, was not able to use symbols effectively enough for time management purposes. Therefore, at age 18 she is continuing to progress on an instructional path emphasizing her use of a few environmental cues to signal routine events.

As Kevin, Missy, and Cynthia illustrate, the achievement of meaningful and functional academic outcomes is possible for all students. In the time-management skill area, our ultimate goal remains—to provide students with some method of understanding, predicting, and preparing for the demands of their environment.

## QUESTIONS AND ANSWERS

Q: Sally will be learning to interpret clock time. Should I encourage her (and her family) to purchase a digital watch when she is ready to own and wear a watch?

A: Interpretation of digital time pieces is sometimes offered as a time-telling strategy. However, this requires a student to understand the relationship between the progression of minute digits (1–59) and the change of hour digits (1–12). Without the visual image of a standard clock face, many students have difficulty interpreting digital time in a functional manner.

If a student or his or her family is interested in purchasing a watch, an analog watch is highly preferable. Watches come in numerous face designs—displaying hours as roman numerals, simple slashes, and highly decorative numbers. For a student who may find time telling a complex and challenging task, a display that is simple and clear will most likely lead to a more rapid achievement of functional skills.

Q:  There are many commercially available materials that are designed to help students learn time-telling skills. Should I be using these materials?

A:  It is true that there are many time-telling materials that can be purchased from catalogs. At some point, most of us have come across cardboard clocks, clock-face rubber stamps, worksheet packets, and computer software programs. The usefulness of these materials, however, is highly questionable. All too often we see students who can complete the worksheets correctly and tell time on the cardboard clock, but cannot interpret time on the real clock. Since the ultimate goal is to have the student interpret time in *natural contexts* with *naturally available materials,* these materials (real clocks and watches) should be used for instruction.

## READINGS AND RESOURCES

Browder, D., & Snell, M. (1987). Functional academics. In M. Snell (Ed.), *Systematic instruction of persons with severe handicaps* (pp. 436–468). Columbus, OH: Charles E. Merrill.

Peterson, D. (1973). *Functional mathematics for the mentally retarded.* Columbus, OH: Charles E. Merrill.

Resnick, L.B., Wang, M.C., & Kaplan, J. (1973). Task analysis in curriculum design: A hierarchically sequenced introductory mathematics curriculum. *Journal of Applied Behavioral Analysis, 6,* 697–710.

Smeets, P.M., Lancioni, G.E., & Van Lieshout, R.W. (1985). Teaching mentally retarded children to use an experimental device for telling time and meeting appointments. *Applied Research in Mental Retardation, 6,* 51–70.

# APPENDIX: TIME-MANAGEMENT SKILL SEQUENCE

The following pages contain guidelines and a suggested sequence for teaching time-management skills for each of the three approaches included in the functional section of the scope and sequence chart: using an environmental-cue strategy, using a picture-symbol strategy, and interpreting clock time. The proposed skill sequence was developed with the assumption that from the onset of instruction in elementary school (or whenever a student begins with the sequence) the concepts, strategies, and mechanics of time management are taught within, or referenced to a student's daily experiences. Consequently, each of these skill clusters, in itself, might represent a meaningful outcome for an individual student. Additionally, mastery of each skill cluster should lead to a more difficult (and more proficient) skill cluster. Finally, the skill sequence includes decision points to help you evaluate a student's progress and determine whether a departure to an alternative approach should be made.

## An overview of the time-management sequence

| Approach | Skill cluster |
|---|---|
| Embedded–environmental cues | I. Using environmental cues to signal routine activities |
| Embedded–picture-symbol schedule | II. Using picture-symbol schedules to manage daily activities |
| Functional–time-management sequence | III. Interpreting clocks and watches to tell time: |
| |     A. By responding to familiar hand positions on a clock |
| |     B. To the hour |
| |     C. At 30 minutes past the hour |
| |     D. At 15 minutes past the hour |
| |     E. At 15 minutes before the hour |
| |     F. At 45 minutes past the hour |
| |     G. At 5 minutes past the hour |
| |     H. At 5 minutes before the hour |
| |     I. To the minute |

## SKILL CLUSTER I: AN ENVIRONMENTAL-CUE STRATEGY

In this skill cluster, students will learn to respond to the natural and adaptive cues within their environment as a basic strategy for managing time. Select events will be used to signal the need to change activities. Some examples include:

- Students passing in the hallway may signal the student to move on to the next activity in his or her schedule
- Students throwing away their lunch trays may indicate to the student that lunchtime is coming to an end.
- Students lining up at the door might signal that recess is over.
- A timer that goes off at the job site might indicate that it is time for a break.

| Skills | Decision points and suggestions for implementation |
|---|---|
| ____ A. Demonstrates behavior specific to certain contexts (e.g., when the student enters the gym, he or she indicates a desire to transfer from the wheelchair to the exercise mat.) | Progress is greatly enhanced by the provision of regular, consistent, and predictable daily routines and activities. The appropriate environmental cues (e.g., school bell) may need to be accentuated for students. |
| ____ B. Attends to environmental cues related to transitions in familiar environments | This skill addresses *awareness* of transitions. Instructionally, students would be prompted to demonstrate awareness (e.g., by looking, listening) of transition activities. For example, a teacher might draw a student's attention to peers who are taking out their lunches before going to the cafeteria. |
| ____ C. Goes to next activity scheduled using environmental cues | Students should do this for several different transition periods before moving on to Skill Cluster II. |

## SKILL CLUSTER II: USING PICTURE-SYMBOL SCHEDULES

This skill cluster introduces a more complex strategy for managing a daily schedule through the use of picture symbols that represent activities in a student's daily routine. Students will learn to follow a sequence of pictures, line drawings, and/or words.

| Skills | Decision points and suggestions for implementation |
|---|---|
| ___ A. Identifies the picture symbol that represents the activity in which the student is engaged | Frequent review and reference to predictable written/pictorial classroom schedules will facilitate mastery of this skill cluster. |
| ___ B. Identifies the picture symbol of the *next* activity | Sets of selected line drawings are commercially available, or may be teacher made. |
| ___ C. Sequences symbols of at least three activities as they are to occur in a daily routine | |
| ___ D. Refers to a written and/or pictorial schedule to determine "what comes next" | |

## SKILL CLUSTER III: USING CLOCKS AND WATCHES TO TELL TIME

In this skill cluster, students learn to interpret the relative position of the hands on clock faces to manage time. Students should be encouraged to own and wear nondigital watches.

| Skills | Decision points and suggestions for implementation |
|---|---|

____ A. Demonstrates ability to respond to a familiar hand position on a clock as a cue for a specific event (e.g., 11:35 = lunch)

____ B. Telling time at the hour

    ____ 1. Indicates time on the hour:

        1:00 ("one o'clock")

        2:00

        3:00

        4:00

        5:00

        6:00

        7:00

        8:00

        9:00

        10:00

        11:00

        12:00 ("twelve o'clock")

 = Lunch

 = "One o'clock; it's time for music"

A variety of *real* clocks and watches should be used in small group sessions. These instructional sessions may provide extra practice toward mastery of basic time-telling "mechanics." At this point, students need to make discriminations about parts and functions of items on a clock face:

1. Identifies the "hour hand"
2. Indicates the direction that the hour hand moves in (movement of the minute hand is regarded as an irrelevant cue)
3. Indicates the number that the hour hand points to (1 to 12)
4. Identifies the "minute hand"
5. Identifies the "o'clock" position of the minute hand (at 12)

Instruction should reference meaningful situations, through simulation/role play (e.g., "The scout meeting begins at 7:00. . . Adjust time on real clock. . . "Is it 7:00?").

In addition to regularly scheduled instructional sessions, there are many informal opportunities to practice time-telling skills throughout the day. For example:

1. Ask a student for the time when filling out a hall pass.

| Skills | Decision points and suggestions for implementation |
|--------|---------------------------------------------------|

2. Ask a student to monitor the time (e.g., "We need to go to the library at 11:00. Let us know when it is time to go.").

___ 2. Indicates that it is "past ___ o'clock" with the minute hand no more than 10 minutes after the hour (e.g., 10:04)

___ 3. Indicates that it is "almost ___ o'clock" when the minute hand is no more than 10 minutes before the hour (e.g., 10:51)

"Past three o'clock"     "Before three o'clock"

___ 4. Initiates a specific action at the correct hourly time (e.g., puts away materials for lunchtime at 12:00)

___ 5. Interprets written and digital time (on the hour) by pairing it with the correct positions of the hands on a clock face

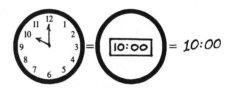

Mastery of this skill is not required before moving ahead in the sequence.

___ 6. Estimates the time of day based on contextual cues (e.g., "We just returned from Phys.Ed., so it must be about 11 o'clock.")

___ 7. Discriminates activities that take "about an hour" from activities that take "a few minutes" (e.g., cooking class takes "about an hour," but getting a drink of water only takes "a few minutes")

___ 8. Uses hour intervals to solve practical problems:
  a. uses present time *plus* an hourly interval to plan an action (e.g., "It is 1:00. The next bus will be here in an hour. What time do we need to catch the bus?"—"2:00.")

"It is one o'clock now. I have to leave in an hour. It will be two o'clock."

| Skills | Decision points and suggestions for implementation |
|---|---|

b. uses present time and the time of a future event or action to determine the (hourly) interval period in between (e.g., "It is 1:00. We need to catch the bus at 2:00. How much time do we have before we catch the bus?"—"1 hour.")

 = 1 hour "It is one o'clock now. I have to catch the bus at two o'clock. I have to wait an hour."

Mastery of these two problem-solving situations is not required before moving on in the sequence.

____ C. Telling time at 30 minutes past the hour
    ____ 1. Indicates that it is 30 minutes past the hour:
        1:30 ("One thirty")
        2:30
        3:30
        4:30
        5:30
        6:30
        7:30
        8:30
        9:30
        10:30
        11:30
        12:30 ("Twelve thirty")

At this point, students are introduced to the "30-minute unit" of time.

We suggest that students learn to think about time in "units." To introduce this concept, the teacher might show how an hour equals a 60-minute unit—"When the minute hand moves 60 times, an hour has gone by." This concept should be taught and reinforced throughout the sequence. For example, the teacher might begin a time session by saying:

"Remember, when the minute hand moves 60 times, an hour has gone by. For practice, please count the 60 minutes as I move the minute hand. It is 11:00 now. Let's count the minutes until 12:00." The teacher uses a real clock and moves the minute hand. Students count from 1 to 60 as the hand is moved. Not all students will be able to count to 60. Counting is not the goal, only the association between a whole hour and a 60-minute unit of time. This concept will serve as a foundation for later units of time:

 = 60 minutes

| Skills | Decision points and suggestions for implementation |
|---|---|

 = 30 minutes

 = 15 minutes

___ 2. Indicates a specific action at "30 minutes past the hour":
   a. when given an appointment at 30 minutes past the hour, initiates the necessary actions just before the appointment in order to avoid being late
   b. when given an appointment at 30 minutes past the hour, acknowledges that it is "just past" the time of the appointment and initiates the necessary actions in order to avoid further tardiness

___ 3. Interprets written and digital time (30 minutes past the hour) by pairing them with the correct positions of the hands on a clock face

Mastery is not required to move on.

___ 4. Uses 30-minute intervals to solve practical problems:
   a. uses present time *plus* a 30-minute interval to plan an action or activity (e.g., "It is 11:30. Lunch is 30 minutes long. What time will you be back from lunch?"— "12:00.")
   b. uses future time *minus* a 30-minute interval to plan an action or activity (e.g., "You need to be back from lunch at 12:00. It takes 30 minutes to eat lunch. What time should you leave for lunch?"— "11:30.")

Understanding of these problems at this point should enhance learning and performance in later problems. Mastery is not required, however, before moving on.

| Skills | Decision points and suggestions for implementation |
|---|---|

c. uses present time and the time of a future event or action to determine the 30-minute interval period in between (e.g., "It is 11:30 now. You have to be back in the room at 12:00. How much time do you have for lunch?"—"30 minutes.")

___ D. Telling time at 15 minutes past the hour:

   ___ 1. Indicates 15 minutes past the hour: 1:15 ("one fifteen") 2:15 3:15 4:15 5:15 6:15 7:15 8:15 9:15 10:15 11:15 12:15 ("twelve fifteen")

Students are introduced to the "15-minute unit" of time, which is positioned past the hour:

   ___ 2. Initiates a specific action at "15 minutes past the hour"

   ___ 3. Interprets written and digital time 15 minutes past the hour) by pairing them with the correct positions of the hands on a clock face

Mastery of this skill is not required before moving ahead in the skill sequence.

   ___ 4. Uses 15-minute time intervals to solve practical problems

Refer to skill C-4 for problem-solving formats.

___ E. Telling time at 15 minutes before the hour

   ___ 1. Indicates 15 minutes before the hour: 15 minutes before one o'clock 15 minutes before two o'clock 15 minutes before three o'clock (Continuing until 15 minutes before twelve o'clock)

Students learn that the 15-minute unit of time can also be positioned "before the hour"

   ___ 2. Initiates a specific action at "15-minute intervals before the hour"

___ F. Telling time at 45 minutes past the hour

| Skills | Decision points and suggestions for implementation |
|--------|---------------------------------------------------|
| ___ 1. Indicates 45 minutes past the hour:<br>1:45 ("one forty-five")<br>2:45<br>3:45<br>4:45<br>5:45<br>6:45<br>7:45<br>8:45<br>9:45<br>10:45<br>11:45<br>12:45 ("twelve forty-five") | Here, the student should be made aware of the relationship between "45 minutes past the hour" and "15 minutes before the hour":<br> |
| ___ 2. Initiates a specific action at "45 minutes past the hour" | |
| ___ 3. Interprets written and digital time (___ o'clock, ___:15, ___:45) by pairing them with the correct positions of the hands on a clock face | Mastery of this skill is not required before moving ahead in the skill sequence. |
| ___ G. Telling time at 5-minute intervals past the hour | |
| ___ 1. Indicates that it is 5 minutes past the hour:<br>1:05 ("5 minutes past one")<br>2:05<br>3:05<br>etc. | Students are introduced to the 5-minute unit of time, which is positioned "past the hour."<br> |
| ___ 2. Indicates 5-minute intervals past the hour to 55:<br>a. 12:05, 12:10 . . . 12:55<br>b. 1:05, 1:10 . . . 1:55<br>c. 2:05, 2:10 . . . 2:55<br>(Continue 5-minute intervals through 11:55) | |
| ___ 3. Initiates a specific action at an interval of 5 minutes after the hour (e.g., 10:20) | |
| ___ 4. Interprets written and digital time (___:05 to ___:55) by pairing them with the correct positions of the hands on a clock face | Mastery of this skill is not required before moving ahead in the skill sequence. |

| Skills | Decision points and suggestions for implementation |
|---|---|
| ___ 5. Uses 5-minute intervals to solve practical problems | Refer to skill C-4 for problem-solving formats. |
| ___ H. Telling time at 5-minute intervals before the hour | |
| ___ 1. Indicates that it is 5 minutes before the hour:<br>5 minutes before one o'clock<br>5 minutes before two o'clock<br>5 minutes before three o'clock<br>5 minutes before . . . | Students learn that the 5-minute unit also can be positioned before the hour: |
| ___ 2. Indicates 5-minute intervals before the hour:<br>25 minutes before two o'clock<br>20 minutes before two o'clock<br>15 minutes before two o'clock<br>10 minutes before two o'clock<br>25 minutes before three o'clock<br>20 minutes before three o'clock<br>15 minutes before three o'clock<br>10 minutes before three o'clock<br>(Continue in 5-minute intervals through twelve o'clock) | |
| ___ 3. Initiates a specific action at "5-minute intervals before the hour" | |
| ___ 4. Interprets written and digital time (in 5-minute intervals "before the hour") by pairing them with the correct positions of the hands on a clock face | Mastery of this skill is not required before moving ahead in the skill sequence.<br>    For many students, telling time at 5-minute intervals will represent the functional attainment of "interpreting clock faces." |
| ___ I. Telling time to the minute | |
| ___ 1. Indicates the correct time to the minute "after the hour" | |
| ___ 2. Indicates the correct time to the minute "before the hour" | |
| ___ 3. Follows a written and/or pictorial schedule with activities changing at any time interval | |
| ___ 4. Interprets written and digital time (any time) by pairing them with the correct positions of the hands on a clock face | |
| ___ 5. Uses any time intervals to solve practical problems | Refer to skill C-4 for problem-solving formats. |

# SECTION V

# Embedded Social, Communication, and Motor Skills

A student's individualized education program (IEP) may consist of activities selected from a wide variety of content areas including math, language arts, science, social studies, physical education, fine arts, vocational, and community living. Almost all of these activities will require the performance of social, communication, and motor skills. For example, embedded in the activity "checking out a book from the library" are the skills "removing a book from the shelf and turning its pages" (motor), and "showing it to a friend" and "waiting for it to be stamped by the librarian" (social and communication). For some students, these social, communication, and motor skills may be acquired with considerable ease. For others, however, they may be difficult or impossible to acquire unless we find an alternative way to perform them.

The scope and sequence charts included in this section of the *Guide* are called "skill functions charts" and are designed to give you some ideas about the many alternative ways students can perform social, motor, and communication skills. If we concentrate on only one established way of performing a skill—for example, the way most nondisabled students use the school cafeteria—many students with severe disabilities will have difficulty meeting these expectations. Will the student be able to say "I'll have pizza today," as the others do when they are asked which of the two entrees they prefer? Will she or he be able to walk through the cafeteria line? Finally, will the student who has no eyesight and no speech be able to invite a friend to join him or her for lunch in the same way that others do? Perhaps not. If, however, we focus our attention on the *functions* that these skills serve, then many more avenues for participation exist. The function of the statement "I'll have pizza today" is to *request an object or action*. As you will see in the communication skill functions chart, there are numerous ways to address this function. A request can be made by pointing one's finger, using an eye gaze, presenting a picture card, and so forth. Using a similar analysis, we can see how the skill of walking serves the function of *traveling from one location to another*. As is discussed in the motor skills section, there are many ways to travel besides walking, including driving a wheelchair or being pushed in a wheelchair. Social skills can also be categorized under the functions they serve. For example, one function of social behavior is *to initiate*. Certainly, there is more than one way to initiate contact with a friend whose lunch company is desired. This function can be met by calling out to the friend once she or he has arrived in the cafeteria or by simply having a shared understanding that Thursdays are reserved for each other.

The charts should give you a framework from which to consider the social, communication, and motor skills (and functions) that might be included in a student's IEP—but, by no means do they stand alone in the decision-making process. For each embedded area, you are asked, first, to consider the *opportunities* available to use these important skills. Of what good is learning how to maneuver a wheelchair if there is no place to wheel to? Or, why should a student learn how to use a picture communication board if the only communication partners available are the teacher and a few classmates who are not able to meaningfully interpret the picture symbols? The environments, activities, and people making up our day-to-day existence not only help to define the richness of our lives, but also dramatically affect our desire to learn new skills. If a student has relatively few places to go, few meaningful activities in which to engage, few people with whom to communicate, and few, if any, friends, then it seems logical to begin the planning process by creating opportunities that are lacking in the repertoire of that individual.

The planning process for each of the embedded skills chapters begins with the step of examining the opportunities available to a student and ends with the writing of goals and objectives. Although there is some variation among the three chapters, they share the following major steps:

- *First*: Review information on the student's opportunities to use social, motor and communication skills and the strength of his or her repertoire in each of these areas. Identify ways to increase and enrich opportunities, if necessary.
- *Second*: Refer to the skill functions chart to gain an understanding of the range of skill functions that should be considered when designing a student's program.
- *Third*: Use a team process to select priority skills and functions.

The general guidelines contained in the following chapters in this section are intended to facilitate a *team* planning process around the areas of social, communication, and motor functioning. It should be evident from these guidelines that no one person can assume full responsibility for a particular domain. That is, the communication domain cannot become the sole responsibility of the speech and language therapist; nor can the motor domain be "doled out" to the physical or occupational therapist. This isolated approach works against the goal of embedding and teaching these skills within the natural activities and routines in which they occur.

# CHAPTER 10

# Social Skills

*Susan M. St. Peter, Barbara J. Ayres,*
*Luanna Meyer, and Seunghee Park-Lee*

Performing a task such as buying groceries requires that we learn to do many different behaviors in some systematic sequence. Being successful at "buying groceries" surely must involve returning home with the purchases we needed. But does being successful in such an activity depend upon only this criterion? Doesn't some measure of our success in "buying groceries" come from the social competence we display while performing the task?

Almost everything we do, it seems, involves either interacting with other persons or inhibiting interactions with other persons. If we fail to follow the often unspoken rules about these interactions, the consequences will be clear: Others will judge us to be socially incompetent. Thus, understanding these social rules can be as critical to someone's success as mastering other aspects such as the motor responses involved in putting groceries in the cart or the academic skills of counting money in order to pay for them.

Although most people cannot define social competence, they are nevertheless able to perceive its presence or absence. The difficulty that many of us have in developing social competence probably stems from the complexity of many social decisions. Obviously it is not enough to know how to do some "social" behavior, such as saying, "thank you" or making eye contact. A person must also know the rules for the many circumstances in which it is acceptable *or* unacceptable to do so. Does it do a person any good to learn to repeat "please" when that person doesn't learn to use this new word in response to natural cues? Is it really appropriate for teenagers to walk up to a visitor in their high school class and introduce themselves? Is it appropriate to repeat "Hello!" a second time, only a few minutes later? We would argue that these are not consistent with the social rules followed by nondisabled teenagers, and a little bit of social skill may be as damaging to judgments of social competence as none at all!

Just like the many other skills discussed throughout this guide, social skills must be learned and practiced in the various natural situations and environments in which they will be used. Further, they will be different at different age levels. Therefore, in this chapter, we begin by providing a context within which to address social skills: We present a rationale for stressing the importance of the environments, activities, and relationships that make up each individual's social network. Second, we provide a chart of social skill functions and their levels of sophistication as demonstrated at various ages. Third, we describe a process for selecting social skills for instruction.

The writing of this manuscript was supported in part by Grant #G008530254 and Grant #G008530151 from Special Education Programs, U.S. Department of Education, to Syracuse University, Division of Special Education and Rehabilitation. This manuscript does not necessarily reflect the position or policies of the U.S. Department of Education, and no official endorsement should be inferred.

Fourth, we describe how to write social skill objectives in an embedded format. Fifth, we discuss the facilitation of interactions and friendships between students who have disabilities and those who do not. We conclude the discussion with questions and answers relating to social skills development. Finally, we provide a list of references and suggested readings.

## UNDERSTANDING SOCIAL NETWORKS:
## ENVIRONMENTS, ACTIVITIES, AND RELATIONSHIPS

It is critical to acknowledge that opportunities to learn and practice new skills must be available if students are to develop social competence. It would be impossible for a teacher or even a parent to teach a child all the social skills he or she needs to function successfully in the community: Direct instruction and one-to-one interactions between the adult and that child would never be enough, nor would this be desirable. Our society generally accepts that the social development of children depends to a great extent on their many formal and informal interactions with peers, family, and others both in school and in the community. Social development may hinge on the range of opportunities afforded an individual by his or her complex networks of interactions with people, environments, and activities. And yet, children with disabilities often do not have social networks that are similar to those experienced by their nondisabled peers. These limited social networks are often accepted without question. Children with disabilities seem to be set up for even greater difficulty in developing social competence than their disabilities alone would have created!

A comparison of the social interaction opportunities of four pairs of individuals is presented in Table 10.1. For each pair, one student with no disability is matched to a same-age student with moderate or severe disabilities. Information is provided showing examples of what, where, how often, and with whom each student spends some unstructured time. Each case identifies three common activities often experienced by students at the four respective ages during the following times in their schedules: 1) weekday morning routines are described for 8-year-old Jennifer and Amy, 2) afterschool routines are described for 13-year-old Mark and Jeff, 3) weekend activities are listed for 17-year-old Dan and Craig, and 4) after-school activities are listed for 19-year-old Anna and Karen.

These comparisons—based upon the experiences of students whom we know—reveal significant discrepancies between interactions available to nondisabled students versus those available to students with disabilities. What are the consequences when some people, namely students with disabilities, are excluded from the kinds of experiences enjoyed by their typical peers? We can only conclude that, logically, these students may not develop socially to the best of their abilities when they are not given opportunities that are at least comparable to those taken for granted by nondisabled individuals. Thus, although we spend some time in this chapter describing strategies for planning direct instruction of social skills to meet the needs of individual students, instruction alone is not enough. We want to emphasize that such efforts will be futile unless the student has a chance to practice and use these skills in a wide range of activities and environments with friends, relatives, and the many other people with whom she or he must ultimately come into contact. Persons with moderate and severe disabilities typically need assistance with enriching and strengthening their social networks to ensure them an equitable range of opportunities to learn and practice social skills in natural contexts.

Table 10.1. Comparison of social interaction opportunities of students with and without disabilities

| Age levels | Names | Typical, age-appropriate activities | | |
|---|---|---|---|---|
| Elementary school students (8-year-olds) | Jennifer (nondisabled) | Waits for school bus with neighborhood friends. Sits on bus with best friend. | Goes into school with friends. Greets students in halls and in class. | Eats in middle of cafeteria with classmates. Sits with friends of choice. |
| | Amy (has severe disability) | Waits for van at home and walks to van with mother. Sits with adult van assistant. | Met at van and taken into school (holding hands) by special education teacher or assistant. Greets no peers. | Eats at end of cafeteria with other students with disabilities. Sits with educational assistant or teacher. |
| Middle school students (13-year-olds) | Mark (nondisabled) | Attends drama practice with classmates three times per week. Uses weight room with two friends, three times per week. | Walks home from school with two friends. | Goes to friend's house three to four times per week, to pizza place/movie with friends two times per week. |
| | Jeff (has severe disability) | Intramurals for 4 weeks with nondisabled peers and coach, two times per week. | Rides a special bus even though he lives within walking distance. | Goes home to have snack with mother; to community center with adult—plays and swims with typical peers, two times per week. |
| High school students (17-year-olds) | Dan (nondisabled) | Goes to malls with one to four friends on rainy weekends to "hang out" and meet kids from other schools. | Goes to theater of choice with one to four friends once per week. | Goes skateboarding in city streets with several friends on sunny weekends to meet kids from other schools. |
| | Craig (has severe disability) | Goes to grocery store with group-home staff person to buy groceries. | Goes to movie with group-home staff and residents about once every 2 months. | Goes for ride in group-home van, to ice cream store, with two staff members and six other residents once per week. |
| Young adults (19-year-olds) | Anna (nondisabled) | Watches soap operas with one to six friends in dorm, from 2:00 to 4:00, Monday through Friday. | Plays football, soccer, volleyball, softball, or broomball approximately one or two times per week. | Eats in dorm cafeteria or local restaurant with 8–10 friends (19-year-olds) nightly. |
| | Karen (has severe disability) | Watches T.V. alone most afternoons. | Goes skiing or bowling (5 weeks of each sport) with nondisabled peer helpers and disabled classmates two times per week. | Eats at home with parents. |

173

This brings us to an important point: Social interaction with other people is the basis of our friendships. Most of us have friends with whom we share common interests and experiences. The value and nature of these friendships is widely varied and often complex, but mutual acceptance and respect as well as informal networks of interdependent support are usually inherent to them. Strully and Strully (1984) wrote about the value of their daughter Shawntell's friendship with a nondisabled child her own age as perhaps *the* critical factor in determining her future. Strully (1988) reported that Shawntell has many nondisabled friends in her high school and that they go to concerts, movies, and shopping malls together just as do teenagers all over the country. Further, they accept and lend support to each other. With assistance, all persons with severe disabilities should be able to experience the range of social interactions that leads to the development of that kind of camaraderie. The task confronting educators is to design services that do not compromise the building of friendships as essential components of our quality of life (Meyer, in press).

What can a teacher do to facilitate the growth and strengthening of these social networks within which friendships and other relationships develop? First, we must realize that tolerating the continuation of flimsy social networks amounts to tolerating social deprivation. Then, using the characteristics of typical same-age peers' social networks as guiding criteria, we must create chances for students with disabilities to: 1) experience the same or similar range of environments, 2) interact with the same or similar range of other people, and 3) engage in the same or similar range of activities.

For example, referring to Table 10.1, Amy's teacher might arrange for some nondisabled peers to meet Amy's van, walk Amy to her classroom and to the cafeteria, eat breakfast with her, and spend time interacting with her during other activities throughout the school day. Ideally—if Amy attends the same school as the other children in her neighborhood—some of these nondisabled friends could wait for and ride the school bus with her and spend some nonschool leisure time with her as well. Similarly, consider the opportunities experienced regularly by Jeff, Craig, and Karen. How could their teachers and parents increase those opportunities?

So far we have addressed the importance of providing opportunities within activities and environments where relationships may develop. However, while these opportunities are necessary, simply providing such opportunities may not be sufficient to support the development of social competence. In the next section of this chapter, we provide a framework that should be helpful when planning social skills instruction.

## SOCIAL SKILL FUNCTIONS

Just as there is a scope and sequence for each of the primary domains in this guide, there is a related conceptual framework for social skills. However, since social skills are embedded in virtually every activity, environment, and domain it would be impossible to list them within a single chart. Instead, we provide a list of 11 social skill functions (the "scope") previously identified by Meyer and her colleagues (1985) on the social skills function chart (Chart 10.1). This chart also includes brief definitions of the functions and examples of each as they typically occur in selected activities throughout early childhood, elementary school, and middle/high school.

The examples provided are intended to do the following:

- Clarify the functions' definitions as they relate to social purposes rather than any specific skills or behaviors

Chart 10.1. Social skill functions and examples at various school levels

| Social skill functions[a] | Examples: Early childhood | Examples: Elementary school | Examples: Middle/high school |
|---|---|---|---|
| Initiate: Joins an ongoing interaction or starts a new one | Get attention<br>a. Vocalizes/cries to gain attention<br>b. Moves toward or reaches out to gain attention<br>c. Calls out to specific person | Greeting<br>a. Says "hi" or gestures greeting repeatedly during interaction<br>b. Greets friends for specific purpose (e.g., playing game, eating lunch together)<br>c. Invites friend to sleep over, after sleeping over at his or her house | Hanging out/free time<br>a. Stands close to peer activity<br>b. Shares object or activity with peer<br>c. Joins group of close friends during lunch |
| Self-regulate: Manages own behavior without instruction from others | Toileting<br>a. Cries when diaper is wet<br>b. When wet, gets clean diaper and takes to caregiver<br>c. Uses toilet appropriately | Snack<br>a. Gets chair to sit on during snacktime<br>b. Follows simple menu<br>c. Checks appearance independently after snack | Shop class<br>a. Puts on eye/ear protectors when appropriate<br>b. Checks off steps completed on class project<br>c. Resists peer pressure to skip class |
| Follow rules: Follows rules, guidelines, and routines of activities | Bedtime routine<br>a. Falls asleep when put into crib with blanket<br>b. Requests bedtime story each night<br>c. Selects pajamas appropriate for temperature | Board game<br>a. Follows step-by-step instructions given by teacher<br>b. Follows rules without teacher assistance<br>c. Makes adaptation in game so that everyone can play | Eating out<br>a. Indicates hunger at same times every day<br>b. Follows restaurant signs such as "Enter," "Place Order," "Pick-up Order," etc.<br>c. Uses fingers to eat chicken or pizza; uses knife and fork to eat messy sandwich |
| Provide positive feedback: Provides positive feedback and reinforcement to others | Eating<br>a. Smiles when given liked food<br>b. Says "Thank you" when given preferred food<br>c. Shares preferred food with another person | Group academic activity<br>a. Smiles when teacher calls his or her name<br>b. Smiles and talks quietly to friend but waits until after class for louder behavior<br>c. Helps peer complete his or her portion of group project | Job site<br>a. Joins familiar co-workers in break room, but not strangers<br>b. Compliments co-worker(s) on appearance or work<br>c. Helps co-worker with nonpreferred task prior to taking break together |

(continued)

175

Chart 10.1. (continued)

| Social skill functions[a] | Examples: Early childhood | Examples: Elementary school | Examples: Middle/high school |
|---|---|---|---|
| Provide negative feedback: Provides negative feedback and consequates others | Shopping<br>a. Makes faces or cries to indicate discomfort or boredom<br>b. Says or gestures "no!" to discourage adult from entering additional stores<br>c. Pleasantly rejects help from parent while trying on shoes | Household chores<br>a. Says or gestures "no" when presented with nonpreferred task<br>b. Renegotiates household duties to avoid disliked tasks<br>c. Politely turns down offer of assistance with task she or he prefers to do alone | Interacting with friends<br>a. When approached by disliked peer, turns or moves away to avoid contact<br>b. Ignores inappropriate behaviors of friends in school cafeteria<br>c. Can disagree with friend without becoming upset |
| Obtain cues: Obtains and responds to relevant situational cues | Grooming<br>a. Glances briefly at hairbrush when adult picks it up<br>b. Holds toothbrush by its handle rather than its bristles<br>c. Closes eye when parent applies shampoo | Restaurant<br>a. Turns to face waitress when she asks for order<br>b. Follows hostess to table and sits down<br>c. Selects choices from menu | Going to a movie<br>a. Watches screen during movie<br>b. Uses available signs to locate restrooms, snack bar, etc.<br>c. Consults friend and newspaper to consider options (i.e., movies, times, locations) |
| Provides information/offers assistance: Provides information and offers assistance to others | Chores<br>a. Vocalizes/gestures to show adult that he is returning toy to toy box<br>b. Takes adult to correct closet when asked where broom is<br>c. Holds dustpan for adult who is sweeping | Work in library<br>a. Gets librarian when someone asks for help<br>b. Shows young student how to use tape player rather than doing it for him or her<br>c. Watches another student looking for book and offers help when needed | Cooperative home economics project<br>a. After stirring cake mix shows it to classmate<br>b. Holds oven door open while classmate puts cake into oven<br>c. When classmate spills something, continues to offer possible solutions until mess is cleaned up |
| Request/accept assistance: Requests and accepts assistance from others | Dressing<br>a. Allows others to help put on clothes<br>b. Communicates "help me" when trying to zip coat<br>c. Asks for help unbuttoning sleeves | Academic activity<br>a. When having difficulty with task allows others to help<br>b. Asks same classmate to study for spelling quiz every week<br>c. Raises hand in class for clarification on assignment | Shopping<br>a. When in need of help, approaches store employee<br>b. Seeks out store employee when bottle of juice breaks on floor<br>c. Asks for elaboration when first response is unclear (e.g., "Where is aisle 4?") |

| Function | Example | Example | Example |
|---|---|---|---|
| Indicate preference: Makes choices from among available and possible alternatives | Toys<br>a. Pays more attention to some toys than to others<br>b. Seeks out favorite toy<br>c. When offered one or two toys, requests another toy that is not present but might be available | Recess<br>a. Watches new person or activity on playground<br>b. Asks specific peer to play<br>c. Participates in disliked activity to remain with close friend | Planning wardrobe<br>a. Pays more attention to blue clothes than to brown clothes<br>b. Wears certain outfit more frequently than others<br>c. Explains why one outfit is preferred to another (e.g., style, fabric, color) |
| Cope with negatives: Exhibits alternative strategies to cope with negative situations | Injures self<br>a. Cries when injured<br>b. Goes to parent when hurt<br>c. Avoids situation that caused injury in the past | Shopping<br>a. When tired, becomes irritable<br>b. Quits tugging on person when told to stop<br>c. Walks next to adult when told to stop running | Household chores<br>a. Complains when asked to complete household chores<br>b. When asked to stop vacuuming so someone can watch T.V., dusts instead<br>c. Asks for directions before attempting task that has been criticized previously |
| Terminate: Terminates or withdraws from an interaction and/or activity | Eating<br>a. Suddenly stops eating and leaves table<br>b. Says "All done" and leaves table even if others are still eating<br>c. Asks for permission to leave table when finished eating | Bike riding<br>a. Abandons bicycle on driveway when finished riding<br>b. Puts bike away in anticipation of dinner<br>c. When bike riding with friends, suggests taking break before they become bored | Work<br>a. Stops in middle of task to take break<br>b. Politely ends interaction at break when it is time to return to work<br>c. Leaves job for more challenging position |

[a]The functions were selected from *Assessment of Social Competence: A Scale of Social Competence Functions* (Meyer et al., 1985). For each function, examples of increasingly sophisticated social skills are provided for each age level, from less sophisticated (a), to more sophisticated (c), involving age-appropriate accomplishment of that particular function regardless of level of functioning.

- Illustrate the functions as they apply to everyday life at different age levels for children and youth who do not have disabilities
- Show some variations in the levels of sophistication with which people exhibit these functions at each age level; that is, in each activity, examples a, b, and c represent a hierarchy of increasing sophistication.

This chart is by no means an exhaustive list of opportunities for using social skills: It is intended only as a guide for establishing a mindset and should not be used as a source of social skill goals and objectives. In order to use this chart when developing individualized social skill objectives, consider all examples of all functions as they are illustrated at all ages. Such thinking should help you acquire a broad view of social skill functions as they occur in everyday life. Also, it should help you see unlimited possibilities for enhancing your students' social competence by teaching the social skill functions that are critical to each student's priority activity goals.

Chart 10.1 identifies social behaviors of nondisabled individuals. In the event you have difficulty seeing any relationship between the skills listed and your student who is moderately, severely, or even multiply disabled, we have provided some samples of the many possible adaptations (see Table 10.2). The challenge to each teacher is to create adaptations for each individual so as to bridge the gap between the way in which the function is typically accomplished and the range of the particular individual's abilities.

Building on the foundation provided by appreciating the importance of social networks as well as social skill functions, you should be ready to plan for social skill instruction for individual students.

## SELECTING SOCIAL SKILLS FOR INSTRUCTION

In the following paragraphs we outline the steps a teacher might follow when: 1) gathering information about a student, 2) gaining an understanding of social skills and functions, and 3) prioritizing social skills for instruction. We illustrate this process by providing examples of social skill selection with Mary Z., the student whose IEP was being developed in the previous chapters of this guide.

### Step 1: Gather information on the student's social opportunities/repertoire.

As you work to determine priority activities for an individual student, it will be helpful to ask some open-ended questions. All team members, especially the parents, should be interviewed. Through this process you will not only gain information on activities requiring instruction, but learn how the presence or absence of appropriate social skills influences the student's participation in the activities. The questions should focus on identifying: 1) in *what* activities the person currently engages, 2) *where* these activities occur, and 3) *with whom* they participate. Three sets of questions that could be asked of team members follow (if you have used the community living chapters of this guide, you have probably already gathered information for the first two sets of questions):

1. In *what* types of activities does the student currently participate at home, in the community, at work, and for recreation? How well does he or she do in these activities? What other activities would you like to see the student experience? How could his or her participation in these activities be increased or expanded?

Table 10.2. Illustrations of adaptations for skills serving social functions

| Social function | As performed by a nondisabled child | As performed by a child with disabilities |
| --- | --- | --- |
| Initiate | Gets attention by approaching another person | Gets attention by pressing buzzer on wheelchair |
| Self-regulate | Follows written directions | Follows directions by using picture prompt booklet |
| Follows rules | Locates own school locker by its number | Locates own school locker by using color-coded symbol |
| Request assistance | Verbally asks store clerk for location of desired item | Asks store clerk for location of desired item by showing picture card or coupon |
| Indicate preference | Chooses to play with certain video game during leisure time | Communicates choice of leisure activity by using eye gaze |

What do you feel are the most important activities in which the student should participate both now and in the future?

2. *Where* does the student go on a regular basis within the community? How often does he or she participate in these settings? How well does he or she do in these community environments? What other places would you like for the student to experience? How could his or her opportunities be increased? What do you feel are the most important community environments for the student to access both now and in the future?

3. With *whom* does the student spend his or her time (parents, siblings, teachers, staff, friends)? How often does he or she participate in activities with non-disabled peers and friends? How could we help the student get to know other people? What do you think are the most important relationship or interaction skills for the student to learn both now and in the future?

Through the answers elicited by these questions, the team will be able to enrich the individualized education program (IEP) and, ultimately, improve the student's social repertoire and all embedded skills (i.e., social, motor, and communication) within priority activities.

*Mary Z.:* Consider the following examples of comments made by Mary's parents and home economics teacher regarding her participation in activities:

Parents: "The worst thing is that she seems pretty lonely. She doesn't usually have anyone to do things with except us. We try to take her out a lot but parents can not substitute for friends her own age."

Home economics teacher: "Mary is pretty good in home ec. class, especially since the teaching assistant is usually with her and does a lot of the work for her. I have noticed that when Mary works too long or has to do too much by herself she seems to get frustrated. The other kids in the class don't seem to pay much attention to her one way or the other. She is mostly with the assistant. Maybe Mary and the other kids could learn to make sandwiches or simple meals together without the assistant."

The discussions that stem from open-ended questions can lead to the identification of interactions that require the team's attention. In the above example, Mary's home economics teacher recognized the need to restructure the grouping pattern so that Mary would spend less time with the assistant and more time with her peers. We also learned that Mary's parents are concerned about her isolated social life. Here, the team might brainstorm ways to help Mary become involved with her peers during after-school hours.

Another way to gain insights into the gaps that exist in a student's social repertoire is to complete a social opportunities/repertoire worksheet (Table 10.3). When completing this worksheet, the following procedures could be used:

1.   On the left side, fill in the social opportunities (i.e., doing what? with whom?) common to typical, nondisabled students at your school.
2.   Complete the next two columns based on the information you have about the particular student's opportunities and skills and those of a student with no disabilities.
3.   Discuss with team members the relative importance of the discrepancies between the two middle columns.
4.   In the far right column, note the teaching decisions that will increase the particular student's social opportunities and promote interactions with others.

Table 10.3 reveals the daily social opportunities available to Mary Z. as compared to those experienced by Lisa, a nondisabled student at Mary's school. It provides a means of examining current situations and proposing changes that could serve to enhance the quality of a student's school experiences, and of course, carry over to nonschool environments and activities. A teacher should set target dates for accomplishing the various changes.

## Step 2: Gain an understanding of the social skills and functions embedded within priority activities.

Once you have identified priority activities for a student you can begin to focus on the embedded social skills. Earlier, we described 11 social skill functions. As you develop a task sequence for a specific activity, consider the social skills typically included as people complete the activity. Remember to include the simple greetings that people often exchange. At this point you should not be concerned about identifying priority social skills, just with recognizing the social skills that are embedded within the activity. Although this step is not one you would do for every activity, it will help create a mindset for team members and illustrate that all activities include social skills.

*Mary Z.:* This process led to the identification of the following social skills (and many others) required in home economics class at Mary Z.'s school: wash and dry hands (follow rules), choose type of sandwich (indicate preferences), prepare sandwich (follow rules/request and accept assistance), serve beverage to peers (initiate interactions/offer assistance), chew with lips closed (self-regulate), and take drink without spilling (self-regulate).

## Step 3: Identify priority social skills for an individual.

This step requires certain considerations that pertain to the specific social skill requirements of the activity and team priorities based on the student's social skill repertoire. After consulting the information gathered through the open-ended questions and the social opportunities/repertoire worksheet, you should be in a better position

Table 10.3.    Social opportunities/repertoire worksheet

| Social opportunities | Repertoire of Lisa (who has no disability) | Repertoire of Mary Z. (who has a severe disability) | Teaching decisions |
|---|---|---|---|
| Before school | Walks to school with two friends. Talks with friends. Plays games in front of school. Shares homework papers. Shares Walkman/ tapes. | Rides to school on special wheelchair bus. Waits outside of building with teaching assistant. | Recruit students to walk to school with Mary and to engage her in activities before school. Teach Mary to initiate interactions with her peers. |
| Homeroom | Sits at desk near two friends. Shares papers/books. Talks with friends. | Does not attend homeroom with nondisabled peers. | Arrange for Mary to attend homeroom with her peers. Provide adult assistance initially, but work to estab-lish a group of stu-dents who will support and involve Mary in homeroom activities. |
| Class change | Walks with two to three friends. Gets drink of water. Goes to locker. Greets many peers. | Is wheeled to class by teaching assistant. Looks down while traveling. Greets no peers. | Assign Mary a locker in an area with her nondisabled peers' lockers. Recruit students in Mary's classes to walk with Mary. Teach Mary to greet peers and respond when they initiate interactions. |
| Art class | Talks with friends. Shares art materials. Asks friends for help. | Sits at table with non-disabled classmates but does not interact. Responds when teacher tells her what to do. | Structure cooperative activities for Mary and her classmates. Teach Mary to initiate interactions with classmates and to ask them for assistance when necessary. |
| Science class | Listens to lectures. Watches films. Participates in small group science experiments. Works with friend on homework. Talks with classmates. | Does not attend science class. | Arrange for Mary to attend science class. Teach her classmates to include her in small group activities. |

*(continued)*

Table 10.3.　　(continued)

| Social opportunities | Repertoire of Lisa (who has no disability) | Repertoire of Mary Z. (who has a severe disability) | Teaching decisions |
|---|---|---|---|
| Lunch | Walks to cafeteria with three to four friends. Talks to friends. Shares food. Goes outside or into hall with friends after eating. | Goes to cafeteria with peers from special class. Sits with teaching assistant and classmates. Eats quietly. | Arrange for Mary to sit with non-disabled peers. Teach Mary and her peers to initiate/ maintain interactions with each other. |
| Home economics class | Sits and talks with friends. Works in small groups. Shares materials. Asks friends for help. | Sits at table with teaching assistant. Follows instructions from adult. Does not interact with her class-mates. | Teach Mary's class-mates to work with her on projects. Fade the adult's assistance. Teach Mary to initiate interactions with her peers. Teach Mary to request help from her peers. |
| After school | Attends drama practice. Uses computer room with friends. Uses weight room with friends. Attends intramurals. Walks home with friends. | Goes home alone. Attended intramurals for 1 month. | Arrange for Mary to participate in intra-murals on a regular basis. Recruit students from Mary's neighbor-hood to go home with her. |

to identify priority social skills. To narrow down the number of skills to include in an IEP, you might consider the following:

1. Does this skill represent a critical step in performing a priority activity?
2. Will this skill strengthen peer relationships?
3. Is this skill required in several settings and activities?
4. Will this skill enable a student to move to a more competent form of social behavior?
5. Does this skill enhance the student's ability to gain access to future settings?

The selection of a social skill that satisfies these criteria is undeniably functional and could be critical to a student's success in integrated school and community settings.

*Mary Z.:* Several team members noted how Mary becomes easily frustrated with an activity. Perhaps a priority social skill objective would be to teach Mary to *request assistance* before she gets frustrated. In addition, the home economics teacher stated that the students don't pay much attention to Mary. Another priority social skill objective within the home economics activity could be to assist Mary in *initiating* and maintaining interactions with her nondisabled classmates.

After the selection of priority social skills within activities has been completed, the student should be assessed for his or her level of competence within that social skill function. Now, the goal is to design a program to increase the social competence of the student. For example, in home economics class, Mary Z. currently makes noises when she gets frustrated with an activity. Our goal would be to teach Mary to request assistance *before* she becomes frustrated (which would demonstrate a higher level of competence in requesting assistance).

## WRITING GOALS AND OBJECTIVES

The IEP should reflect the fact that social skills are naturally embedded within activities. Just as goals and objectives are written to teach specific task steps within priority activities, so should they be written to teach the social skills embedded within those activities. The social skill goals and objectives should then be included within the activity goals on the student's IEP. We would discourage the practice of writing all social skill objectives on a separate page of the IEP. Below, we have illustrated a method for embedding social skill objectives within priority activities from the self-management/home living section of Mary Z.'s IEP:

---

### Goals and Objectives for Mary Z.

#### Goal

When positioned at her school locker (approximately four to five times daily), Mary will remove or replace her outer clothing and gather belongings to prepare for the next scheduled activity.

#### Objectives

- Mary will request help opening her locker by gesturing to a familiar classmate.
- When positioned at her locker before homeroom, Mary will greet familiar students nearby by smiling at them.

#### Goal

During daily situations that involve eating (e.g., home economics, lunch), Mary will increase her mealtime skills.

#### Objectives

- When given a gestural prompt (pointing), Mary will look at peers at her table.

#### Goal

During home economics class (3 days/week), Mary will increase her participation in the preparation of snacks and meals with one to four classmates.

#### Objectives

- When stirring ingredients, Mary will allow peer/instructor to assist her using a hand-over-hand method.
- Mary will request help to open a container by holding the container out to a classmate in the kitchen.

---

## FACILITATING INTERACTIONS AND FRIENDSHIPS

Providing opportunities for interactions and increasing the social competence of students with severe disabilities does not guarantee peer interactions and friendships. We now discuss how teachers can facilitate the development of friendships between students with disabilities and their nondisabled peers.

Many nondisabled students have had little or no experience interacting with peers who have severe disabilities. Since these students may have difficulty initiating and maintaining social interactions and developing friendships with each other, there is a need to assist students in developing these relationships.

How can we promote peer interactions that may develop into friendships between students with severe disabilities and their nondisabled peers? The following is a short list of strategies teachers should consider when providing ongoing support for the development of friendships between students:

- Provide positive information to nondisabled students about students with disabilities so they can understand similarities and dissimilarities and feel more comfortable with their peers with disabilities. This information should explain any adaptations such as wheelchairs and communication systems (Ayres et al., 1986; Stainback & Stainback, 1985). But it should *not* focus upon stereotypes or clinical descriptions of diagnoses or labels (Voeltz, 1984).
- Teach nondisabled students and adults how to interact with students who have disabilities. When the teacher models positive and respectful attitudes and actions toward students with disabilities, these behaviors can be observed and imitated by others (Gaylord-Ross, Haring, Breen, & Pitts-Conway, 1982; Voeltz et al., 1983).
- Use cooperative activities to promote interdependence between students with disabilities and those without. Activities that stress cooperation yield more positive interactions between students than those that encourage students to compete with one another (Eichinger, 1988; Johnson & Johnson, 1984, 1986; Rynders, Johnson, Johnson, & Schmidt, 1980).
- Involve students in interactive rather than isolated activities. Select activities that are age appropriate and will be enjoyed by all of the students (Gaylord-Ross et al., 1982; Stainback & Stainback, 1985).
- Establish ongoing rather than episodic interaction opportunities for students (Voeltz, 1984). Students are more likely to become comfortable and spontaneous with each other if they spend time together regularly (Forest, 1987).

## CONCLUSION

No cookbook approach to social skills instruction could meet the widely varied needs of students with moderate and severe disabilities. Rather, we have provided some guidelines for thinking about social skills in general as well as for planning specific social skills programs. We hope that this chapter fosters an approach that emphasizes education as a means of enhancing rather than compromising the quality of each individual's life. We encourage you to follow that line of thinking as you read the following questions and answers pertaining to social skills and as you plan for each student's social skill instruction.

## QUESTIONS AND ANSWERS

Q: What if my student doesn't have *any* social skills and doesn't even seem to like interacting with other students or adults? Shouldn't I start by teaching eye contact?

A: No, please don't! First of all, everyone has some social skills. The first step might be to find out under what circumstances your student does want attention (or help) from someone, and when he or she prefers to be left alone. By also knowing what kinds of things the student likes, you could pair those things with special interactions with a potential friend, for example. After all, sharing positive experiences is how most people prefer to spend time together—not simply looking at one another's eyes—and your student is no exception.

Q: Tommy won't do what he's supposed to do—he's *so* noncompliant. Isn't it important for him to learn how to do what's expected of him?

A: Well, yes, but perhaps "what's expected" could be re-evaluated. If Tommy is *very* noncompliant, something must be wrong. Does he have any control over his daily activities? Does he understand what is happening and will happen to him throughout the school day? Can he be given the opportunity to make some choices (you might have to teach him how to do this), or to signal when the task is too hard or too boring, or when something is bothering him?

Q: But I can't let Tommy have his way all the time! I understand why choices are important, but some things just have to be done, and I can't give in to unreasonable demands. After all, the real world won't give in, right?

A: That's true, but the point is that Tommy needs to learn both the new skill to tell you things *and* how to use that skill in a reasonable way. If you expect it all at once, your program will not work.

Q: Can you give me an example?

A: Let's say that Tommy typically works for only 5 minutes or so—no matter what the task—and then he might leave his seat, throw things, or even hit someone. If we stop the task, he seems content to be left alone. First, Tommy needs to learn a way to ask for a break, and you would prompt him to ask for a break after 4 minutes—before he loses control—and give him a few minutes off. When he begins initiating a request for a break (he's learned the new communication skill!), you can then gradually increase the amount of time he's expected to wait before he gets a break. You might tell him, "Yes, you can have a break in just a minute, but please do this one thing first." Then give him a break a minute later. It will take some systematic instruction and time, but eventually Tommy will be able to meet more reasonable expectations. But like anything else, you have to do things systematically and in stages—not all at once.

Q: I have a student, Monique, who is 15 and doesn't really have any age-appropriate activities to engage in during free time. In fact, she really loves to spend her time playing with a "See and Say" toy. Wouldn't it be okay to use this toy to get her to interact with a nonhandicapped peer, as long as the peer doesn't mind? After all, isn't it more important for Monique to be with her peers rather than worrying about what she does?

A: You need to think about the probable consequences of using the "See and Say" toy this way. First, as the toy is designed for preschool-age children, the peer is not really going to be enthused about this shared experience, and the interaction will be totally dependent upon his or her willingness to continue what is clearly not a particularly enjoyable activity. Wouldn't it be better if *both* teenagers got pleasure from the activity? Second, if other teenagers see Monique and her friend playing with this toy, what will they think? Will this enhance Monique's image, and would it encourage other peers to become involved with Monique? Or would it reinforce negative stereotypes? And, in the long run, doesn't Monique need to expand her enjoyment of other activities? You can use the features of this toy to help you identify something more age appropriate that she might learn to like, such as video games. And wouldn't video games be far more likely to increase Monique's interactions with her peers over the long run?

Q: It seems to me that students need to learn things like standing in line, taking turns, and saying "please" and "thank you." Society expects these things. At what age should students who are severely retarded begin to learn things like this?

A: These are certainly the kinds of social skills that most people use a great deal of the time. Rather than thinking about age or developmental level in deciding when to identify something as a social skill objective for the IEP, use the priority activity goals you have already identified as your starting point. For example, suppose you have a student who is learning to shop at the grocery store as a priority activity goal in the community domain. Standing in line is part of the "steps" needed to purchase items in many different environments. If this seems like a reasonable goal for your student, then you have an excellent opportunity for him or her to acquire this particular social skill. But the important thing to remember is that "standing in line" is taught because it is part of an activity goal—grocery shopping—that has already been identified as a priority. You will want to avoid teaching social skills in isolation from natural environments and interactions with other people—it really can't be done any other way!

Q: Several of my students have severe multiple handicaps, are nonambulatory, and have severe to profound mental retardation. They also don't talk. I'm trying to get my assistants to talk to them more and just generally socially interact with them, but the students don't seem very interested and it's difficult to keep things going. What can I do?

A: It's obvious that your students are going to be very dependent upon initiations from others: They need other children to approach them and play with them! It's critical that your students have opportunities to interact with their nonhandicapped peers often throughout the day, and in their neighborhoods after school and on weekends. As their teacher, you can encourage such interactions by inviting students who are the same age to be "buddies" for different activities, and you can join with teachers in regular education to plan such activities together. We've found that very soon—as long as the children do indeed live in the same neighborhood and *can* do this—there will be invitations back and forth for after-school and weekend play together. Remember that all the adult attention in the world can't replace the need for friends your own age!

Q: How can I help my students make friends? I feel uncomfortable asking non-disabled students to spend time with my students.

A: Many nondisabled students do not know how to interact with their peers with disabilities. Sometimes they just need an invitation to do something fun with your students. Teachers are often surprised at the number of typical peers who want to interact with the disabled students when they are given the opportunity and some encouragement. Remember, you are the model: When you interact naturally and positively with your students, others will be encouraged to do the same.

# REFERENCES

Ayres, B., Bramman, H., Mitchell, B., Savage, M., Nietupski, J., & Hamre-Nietupski, S. (1986). *Project infusion: Infusing information and activities related to disabilities into the general education curriculum.* Des Moines: Iowa Department of Education.

Eichinger, J. (1988). *The effects of cooperative versus individualistic goal-structured activities upon social interaction behavior between severely disabled and nondisabled students.* Unpublished doctoral dissertation, Syracuse University, Syracuse, NY.

Forest, M. (Ed.). (1987). *More education/integration: A further collection of readings in the integration of children with mental handicaps into regular systems.* Downsview, Ontario: Roeher Institute.

Gaylord-Ross, R., Haring, T., Breen, C., & Pitts-Conway, V. (1982). The training and generalization of social interaction skills with autistic youth. In R. Gaylord-Ross, T. Haring, C. Breen, & V. Pitts-Conway (Eds.), *The social integration of autistic and severely handicapped students.* San Francisco: San Francisco State University.

Johnson, D.W., & Johnson, R.T. (1984). Classroom learning structures and attitudes toward handicapped students in mainstream settings: A theoretical model and research evidence. In R. Jones (Ed.), *Special education in transition: Attitudes toward the handicapped.* Reston, VA: Council for Exceptional Children, ERIC Clearinghouse on Handicapped and Gifted Children.

Johnson, D.W., & Johnson, R.T. (1986). Mainstreaming and cooperative learning strategies. *Exceptional Children, 52*(6), 553–561.

Meyer, L.H. (in press). An essay on friendships. In L.H. Meyer, C. Peck, & L. Brown (Eds.), *Critical issues in the lives of people with severe disabilities.* Baltimore: Paul H. Brookes Publishing Co.

Meyer, L.H., Reichle, J., McQuarter, R., Cole, D., Vandercook, T., Evans, I., Neel, R., & Kishi, G. (1985). *Assessment of social competence (ASC): A scale of social competence functions.* Minneapolis: University of Minnesota Consortium Institute for the Education of Severely Handicapped Learners.

Rynders, J., Johnson, R., Johnson, D.W., & Schmidt, B. (1980). Effects of cooperative goal structuring in producing positive interactions between Down's Syndrome and nonhandicapped teenagers: Implications for mainstreaming. *American Journal of Mental Deficiency, 85*, 268–273.

Stainback, S., & Stainback, W. (1985). *Integration of students with severe handicaps into regular schools.* Reston, VA: Council for Exceptional Children, ERIC Clearinghouse on Handicapped and Gifted Children.

Strully, J. (1988, June). *Building friendships, achieving school integration, creating desirable futures, and other issues affecting the lives of children and adults with severe disabilities: An evening for parents and professionals.* Syracuse, NY.

Strully, J., & Strully, C. (1984). Shawntell and Tanya: A story of friendship. *Exceptional Parent, 41*(2), 35–40.

Voeltz, L.H. (1984). Program and curriculum innovations to prepare children for integration. In N. Certo, N. Haring, & R. York (Eds.), *Public school integration: Rational issues and progressive alternatives* (pp. 155–184). Baltimore: Paul H. Brookes Publishing Co.

Voeltz, L.M., Hemphill, N.M., Brown, S., Kishi, G., Klein, R., Fruehling, R., Collie, J., Levy, G., & Kube, C. (1983). *The special friends program: A trainer's manual for integrated settings* (rev. ed.). Honolulu: University of Hawaii, Department of Special Education.

## ADDITIONAL READINGS AND RESOURCES

Certo, N., & Kohl, F. L. (1984). A strategy for developing interpersonal interaction instructional content for severely handicapped students. In N. Certo, N. Haring, & R. York (Eds.), *Public school integration of severely handicapped students: Rational issues and progressive alternatives* (pp. 221–244). Baltimore: Paul H. Brookes Publishing Co.

Gaylord-Ross, R., Stremel-Campbell, K., & Storey, K. (1986). Social skill training in natural contexts. In R. H. Horner, L.H. Meyer, & H.D.B. Fredericks (Eds.), *Education of learners with severe handicaps: Exemplary service strategies* (pp. 161–187). Baltimore: Paul H. Brookes Publishing Co.

Gresham, F. M. (1981). Social skills training with handicapped children: A review. *Review of Educational Research, 51*(1), 139–176.

Johnson, D. W., Johnson, R. T., Holubec, E., & Roy, P. (1984). *Circles of learning: Cooperation in the classroom.* Alexandria, VA: Association for Supervision and Curriculum Development.

Lehr, S., & Taylor, S.J. (1987). *Teaching social skills to youngsters with disabilities: A manual for parents.* Boston: Technical Assistance for Parent Programs (TAPP) Project.

McGinnis, E., Goldstein, A.P., Sprafkin, R.P., & Overshaw, N.J. (1984). *Skill-streaming the elementary school child: A guide for teaching social skills.* Champaign, IL: Research Press.

Meyer, L.H., Cole, D.A., McQuarter, R., & Reichle, J. (1988). *Validation of a measure of social competence in children and young adults with mental retardation and other disabilities.* Syracuse, NY: Syracuse University. Division of Special Education and Rehabilitation.

O'Brien, J. (1987). A guide to life-style planning: Using *The Activities Catalog* to integrate services and natural support systems. In B. Wilcox & G. T. Bellamy, *A comprehensive guide to The Activities Catalog: An alternative curriculum for youth and adults with severe disabilities* (pp. 175–189). Baltimore: Paul H. Brookes Publishing Co.

Schutz, R.P., Williams, W., Iverson, G.S., & Duncan, D. (1984). Social integration of severely handicapped students. In N. Certo, N. Haring, & R. York (Eds.), *Public school integration of severely handicapped students: Rational issues and progressive alternatives* (pp. 15–42). Baltimore: Paul H. Brookes Publishing Co.

Strully, J., & Strully, C. (1985). Friendship and our children. *Journal of The Association for Persons with Severe Handicaps, 10*, 224–227.

Walker, H.M., McConnell, S., Holmes, D., Todis, B., Walker, J., & Golden, N. (1983). *The Walker social skills curriculum: The accepts program.* Austin, TX: PRO-ED.

# CHAPTER 11

# Communication Skills

*Pat Mirenda and Marsha Smith-Lewis*

Many of the tasks that a student must perform on a regular basis require the ability to communicate with both familiar and unfamiliar partners, including family members, friends, teachers, shopkeepers, bus drivers, and other persons. Such communication skills include the ability to make requests for assistance, communicate choices, offer rejections, make comments, and so forth (Light, McNaughton, & Parnes, 1986). Depending on the context of the interaction, one or more of these may predominate. Thus, it is important to identify the communication requirements of specific tasks in order to ensure that students have the means to fulfill as many of the communication requirements as possible, either through natural and/or adapted means. For example, one obvious communication skill required for the activity "eating in a restaurant" is that of communicating one's order to the waiter. This can be accomplished through the use of natural speech or an adapted communication display that depicts the menu choices available. Another requirement for "eating out" is to be able to engage in social etiquette routines (e.g., saying "hello" and "thank you"). This might involve a different technique than that used to order food; for example, the student might be taught to smile at the waiter at the appropriate times. An equally important, but perhaps less obvious, communication need in this context is that of maintaining social closeness with one's partner. After all, for most of us "eating out" is more likely to fulfill a social need than any other need. To maintain "social closeness" the student must have one or more ways to engage in casual interactions—for example, the ability to tell a partner a joke, communicate about past and current events, or gain a friend's attention. Many different communication techniques may be used to accomplish this, including facial expressions, gestures, signing, symbol systems, and other means. What is important here is that those involved in educational planning must acknowledge that *all* students have communication needs that go beyond the obvious one of making requests for desired items. In addition, a successful plan should acknowledge that a student will invariably use different communication techniques depending on the partners involved in the interaction and where the interaction takes place.

## OPPORTUNITIES FOR COMMUNICATION

Communication opportunities are directly related to the environments and activities in which a student participates and the partner(s) with whom a student interacts. Some activities and environments require a minimal amount of communication, while others require more. For example, a student may have little opportunity to communicate freely in the school library but may be expected to be more interactive in the lunchroom or during "free time" between classes or before school. Similarly, some communication partners are more demanding than others. Family members and familiar teachers may learn to anticipate a student's needs to the extent that a subtle gesture or expression takes the place of a more formal means of communication. However, when the student interacts with partners who are less familiar and less able to interpret unique communication techniques, communication breakdowns may occur. An understanding of communication opportunities—that is, the day-to-day situations in which a student will be expected to communicate—is basic to planning development of a communication system. The following questions are designed to help you identify some of the opportunity barriers that can have a negative impact on communication effectiveness.

- *Are there scheduling problems that restrict access to communication partners?* If a student is, for instance, scheduled to ride a different school bus, eat in the classroom as opposed to the school lunchroom, or spend most of his or her time in an instructional group comprising three or four classmates, opportunities to communicate will be unduly limited.
- *Are the student's physical disabilities leading to modifications that limit involvement with peers?* For example, consider a student, dependent on someone for mobility, who is pushed to the rear of the school lunchroom, is positioned with his back to the crowd, and is assisted with feeding. These practices may limit the student's access to peers and make him completely dependent on others for appropriate interaction opportunities.
- *Are there unduly restrictive rules in certain places?* For example, the rules in a particular classroom might require that children be "quiet" at all times and that they raise their hands to get an adult's attention. If these rules are not flexible enough to allow a student who needs to rely on vocalizing or other modes (e.g., battery-generated buzzer) for the same purpose, unnecessary barriers to communication will lead to communication breakdowns.
- *Are ongoing decisions being made for the student, rather than encouraging his or her involvement?* It is often the case that choices that could be made *by* the student are made *for* the student; such choices might include what clothing to wear to school, what to have for breakfast, whom to sit next to on the school bus, whom to play with during recess, and when to terminate an activity, to name a few. If such opportunities are not provided throughout the day, many students learn to assume a passive role or engage in "inappropriate" behaviors in an attempt to become more active participants.
- *Is insufficient information provided to the student's communication partner?* For example, a student may be using a hand-waving motion to indicate "it is time to stop" an activity, but the communication partner may be unaware of the meaning of such a gesture. If the student becomes angry and frustrated and resorts to knocking the table over when repeating the request, using this technique was not effective. In addition, partners might not know how to manage other aspects of the exchange. For example, a partner may need to learn to pause at key points in an exchange, so that the student knows that a turn is expected and has sufficient time to take a turn. Failure to teach partners such techniques often result in limited student participation.

## A COMMUNICATION SYSTEM

To enhance the student's communication functioning, we must attend to the various components of the student's system. The term "communication system" refers to the integrated network of *messages*, *techniques*, and *symbols* that an individual uses to communicate. Many students with moderate to severe disabilities rely on augmentative communication systems. *Augmentative* is used to describe adaptations used to help a student's communication ability by *supplementing* (not replacing) natural gestures, speech, vocalizations, facial expressions, and other means the student may have to express messages. Figure 11.1 illustrates the range of messages, techniques, and symbol systems available to the student.

A message can be described in terms of both the *function* or purpose it serves and the *form* or vocabulary used to express it. A single form can often have a number of functions, depending on the context; for example, in one context a hand wave (the form) could be a greeting (function); in another context, a request for attention (function); and in a third context, a gesture of protest (function). Similarly, the same function can be communicated through a number of forms; a student might, for example, indicate that he wants a particular item by pointing to it, by grabbing it, or by using a manual sign. Generally, the form that the student finds to be the most efficient and effective will be the one used most frequently. In the communication skill functions chart (Chart 11.1) we have listed some of the most common communicative functions along with some examples of the forms that may be used by students of various school levels.

For students who are unable to communicate successfully through the use of natural gestures or speech, there are a number of adapted techniques that might be used to supplement more commonly used techniques. Depending on the student's capabilities in a number of areas that are discussed later in this chapter, the adapted or "augmentative" communication techniques can require the use of either a device (aided technique) or the body itself (unaided technique). Some examples of the most common unaided and aided augmentative communication techniques are listed below:

1. Unaided
   a. Vocalizing
   b. Verbalizing
   c. Using facial and body movements
   d. Gesturing
   e. Manual signing
   f. Pantomiming
2. Aided
   a. Using a symbol board/booklet
   b. Using a pencil and paper
   c. Using electronic aids and computers
   d. Using symbols displayed in specific locations

The final component of a communication system is the symbol system used to represent the message. Unaided symbol systems (i.e., those expressed with a part of the body) include the use of various types of manual signs as well as easily understood natural gestures, vocalizations, and speech. They are listed below, along with

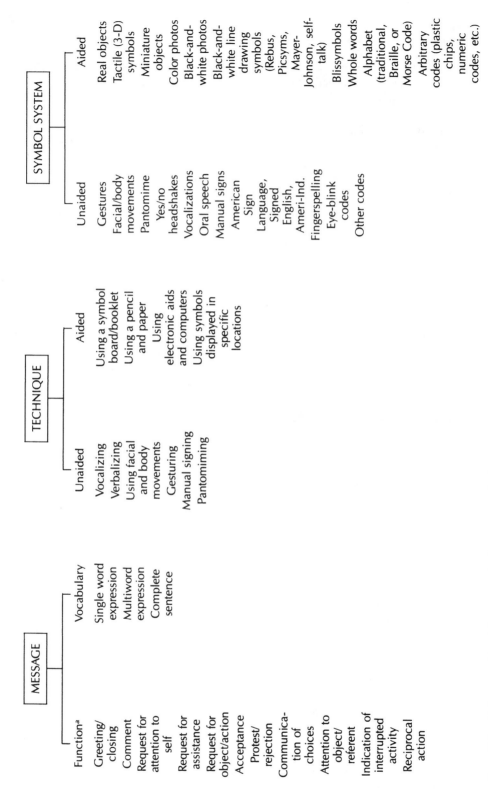

Figure 11.1. Major components of a communication system. ([a]The functions were adapted from Light, McNaughton, and Parnes [1986].)

Chart 11.1. Communication skill functions and examples at various school levels

| Communication functions[a] | Examples: Early childhood | Examples: Elementary school | Examples: Middle/high school |
|---|---|---|---|
| *Greeting/closing:* Acts or utterances that acknowledge the partner's arrival or departure | Waves to peer at end of recess<br>Greets familiar adult or child with smile or hug<br>Displays positive affect when preferred person enters the room<br>Displays negative affect when preferred person leaves the room | Shakes hands with unfamiliar people when greeting or closing<br>Uses different behaviors directed toward peers than familiar adults | Approaches unfamiliar co-worker and offers hand in greeting<br>Smiles at and greets waitress when approached for order in restaurant<br>Vocalizes in response to bus driver's greeting or departure statement<br>Discriminates familiar from unfamiliar people and changes behavior when greeting or closing accordingly |
| *Comment:* Acts or utterances that label, describe, or provide information about a person, event, or object either within or outside of the immediate environment | Responds to questions or spontaneously provides information about familiar people, events, or objects<br>Uses some means to provide information about completed activity (e.g., weekend activity)<br>Answers yes/no questions related to preferences, activities, or information (e.g., "Did you go to the store? to the park?")<br>Uses some means to indicate recognition of familiar person's absence | Uses some means to report activities during community instruction to peer or adult who did not participate in instruction<br>Uses some means to indicate awareness of next event in daily schedule<br>Remembers to pass note from school to home and vice versa | Uses some means to answer survival questions such as "What is your name?" "Where do you live?", and, "What is your phone number?"<br>Manages daily schedule and reports significant events with minimal assistance<br>Answers specific question related to food order in restaurant (e.g., "Small or large fries?", "With or without catsup?") |
| *Request for attention to self:* Acts or utterances that serve to secure the partner's attention but do not direct the partner to a specific referent; attention may be for some general social purpose or as a preface to another communicative function (e.g., a request for an object or action) | Makes noises or cries to get attention<br>Positions self in front of partner and gives eye contact prior to initiating manual sign<br>Uses battery-operated call buzzer to attract peer's attention | Taps peer on shoulder to get attention prior to requesting turn during jump-rope activity<br>Raises hand in class before responding to question<br>Uses some means to call attention to self when teacher asks group of students, "Who wants x?" | Politely gets clerk's attention prior to asking for assistance to locate correct size in clothing store<br>Gets attention during unstructured activity through humor or joking<br>Approaches employer, waits until unoccupied, and gives eye contact prior to making request |
| *Request for assistance:* Acts or utterances that attempt to direct the partner to provide physical assistance | Cries or vocalizes when hungry or when diaper needs to be changed<br>Approaches adult when needs help with clothing<br>Uses some means to ask for help when unable to complete or continue art project | Asks parents for assistance in locating restroom when at store<br>Raises hand or uses call buzzer during class to request assistance from teacher or peer<br>Enlists assistance of appropriate adult when lost in unfamiliar environment (e.g., shopping mall) | Requests assistance from clerk in grocery store when unable to locate item<br>Requests assistance during vocational activity when difficulty is encountered<br>Accepts assistance from co-worker or peer when offered |

*(continued)*

193

Chart 11.1. (continued)

| Communication functions[a] | Examples: Early childhood | Examples: Elementary school | Examples: Middle/high school |
|---|---|---|---|
| *Request for object/action:* Attempts to direct the partner to provide an object or activity either within or outside of the immediate environment | Uses eye gaze, vocalization, or gesture to request "more" when partner pauses during favorite interactive game (e.g., peek-a-boo) or song (e.g., "Row, row, row your boat")<br>Brings coat to parent to request walk to park<br>Uses some means to request toy that is visible but out of reach on shelf | Uses some means to indicate desire to listen to music in music area<br>Orders food in restaurant by pointing to picture of desired food in communication book<br>Leads peer to cupboard containing desired game and places peer's hand on cupboard door | Indicates need for missing supplies at work site<br>Taps partner on shoulder and points to desired item during expedition to shopping mall |
| *Acceptance:* Acts or utterances that indicate acceptance of an object or partner's offer of an object | Quiets when distressed if physical care needs are met<br>Reaches toward preferred object or food when offered<br>Uses eye gaze, vocalization, or gesture to answer, "Yes" when preferred item is offered and partner asks, "Do you want x?" during snacktime<br>Displays positive affect (smile, gesture) when favorite person or parent approaches | Indicates that some types of music are preferred over others during peer activity<br>Expresses pleasure during routine that signals favorite activity is imminent (e.g., putting on a coat before going outside for recess)<br>Attends better to preferred than to nonpreferred activity | Indicates pleasure when it is breaktime at the vocational site<br>Performs actions that indicate enjoyment during after-school recreational activity with peer |
| *Protest/rejection:* Acts or utterances that serve to place or return a nonpreferred activity or item into the possession of another or that indicate objection to or refusal of an activity or item | Cries or fusses when distressed<br>Uses eye gaze, vocalization, or gesture to indicate "no" when nonpreferred item is offered and partner asks, "Do you want x?" during free-play time<br>Indicates displeasure when preferred activity (e.g., water play) is discontinued | Performs actions that indicate dislike of activity or food when offered (actions may include excess behavior)<br>When being read to, closes book to indicate desire for termination of activity<br>Brings dishes to sink to signal termination of cooking activity<br>Pushes away materials related to activity that is disliked | Uses some means to protest when usual routine is interrupted (e.g., when bus is late after school)<br>Displays negative but appropriate affect when unfamiliar or nonpreferred person approaches<br>Expresses annoyance if request is not fulfilled by partner |
| *Communication of choices:* Indicates preference between two or more referents | Uses eye gaze, vocalization, or gesture to choose preferred over nonpreferred item when offered both and asked "What do you want?" during snack time | Chooses desired item from vending machine, restaurant menu, or other display containing two or more choices<br>Can differentiate and choose between items that are relevant and irrelevant | Chooses peer to sit next to during pep rally<br>Chooses food from cafeteria line using gestures or communication adaptation |

194

| | | | |
|---|---|---|---|
| | Makes choices between two or more items offered during circle-time activity | to activity (e.g., choose grooming items over recreation/leisure items prior to grooming activity)<br>Indicates preferences for peer partners during activity | Communicates preferences from range of options related to long-term vocational plans<br>Chooses to discontinue participation in optional after-school activity because of lack of interest<br>Chooses peer to accompany to school dance or prom |
| *Attention to object/referent:* Physical and/or visual orientation to partner, partner's action(s), and/or referents indicated by the partner | Looks toward door when new person enters room<br>Orients head or body in direction of familiar partner's voice<br>Interrupts activity and looks around to locate source of sudden, loud noise<br>Changes affect in response to distress vocalizations by peer<br>Follows movement of remote-control car operated by microswitch<br>Indicates awareness of leader's actions during "Simon Says" game by visual orientation or imitation | Orients in direction of waitress when asked for order at restaurant<br>Attends to clerk in grocery store when payment is requested or change provided<br>Follows movement of familiar adult or peer in classroom<br>Watches cooking demonstration by partner<br>Looks in direction toward which partner is pointing when crossing street | Attends to action during basketball game in gym<br>Locates telephone when it rings<br>Locates and orients toward public bus as it approaches bus stop<br>Orients to task at work site |
| *Indication of interrupted activity:* Indicates that the student is aware that the partner is the controlling agent in an interrupted shared activity | Vocalizes or moves when being fed if food is not immediately forthcoming<br>Cries or fusses to continue diapering routine if partner pauses or is interrupted<br>Performs action to continue routine during dressing/undressing activity after pause | Appears to notice when partner pauses during routine walk to grocery store or restaurant<br>Vocalizes or moves if partner pauses during familiar cooking routine that requires physical prompting (e.g., stirring batter)<br>During recess, reacts when peer stops pushing him or her on swing | Vocalizes or gestures to continue routine during shaving or showering activity<br>Uses eye gaze, vocalization, or gesture when partner pauses during predictable calisthenic routine<br>Anticipates next step in familiar job performed with peer |
| *Reciprocal action:* Acts or utterances directed toward another that serve to participate in a mutual activity in which the participants take repeated turns | Indicates awareness of turn during beanbag toss game with another peer<br>Imitates partner's pounding action with hammer during turn-taking activity in free-play time | Takes turn during game of "catch"<br>Waits for turn and acknowledges when turn has come in line at store<br>Accepts and passes food from adjacent partner during meal or snack served family-style | Indicates desire for "turn" at video arcade<br>Takes and relinquishes turn during game of Yahtzee or card game<br>Accepts one plate at a time from peer partner and dries plate during joint dishwashing activity at domestic site |

[a]Categories adapted from Light, McNaughton, and Parnes (1986).

195

aided symbol systems that range from real objects to pictorial symbols to written words:

1. Unaided symbol systems
   a. Gestures
   b. Facial/body movements
   c. Pantomime
   d. Yes/no headshakes
   e. Vocalizataions
   f. Oral speech
   g. Manual signs
   h. American Sign Language, Signed English, Ameri-Ind., etc.
   i. Fingerspelling
   j. Eye-blink codes
   k. Other codes
2. Aided symbol systems
   a. Real objects
   b. Tactile (3-D) symbols
   c. Miniature objects
   d. Color photos
   e. Black-and-white photos
   f. Black-and-white line drawing symbols (Rebus, Picsyms, Mayer-Johnson, Self-talk)
   g. Blissymbols
   h. Whole words
   i. Alphabet (traditional, Braille, or Morse Code)
   j. Arbitrary codes (plastic chips, numeric codes, etc.)

The list of aided symbol systems is arranged according to the level of difficulty researchers suggest may exist for learning and/or recognizing what the symbol represents. Of course, this easy-to-difficult sequence should only be used as a guide in addition to other critical information regarding the student, such as whether his or her visual discrimination and symbol-referent matching abilities are similar to those required to successfully use a particular symbol system. (The reader who is interested in descriptions and illustrations of many of these techniques and symbol systems should see the references and additional readings listed at the end of this chapter.)

## DEVELOPING AN AUGMENTATIVE COMMUNICATION SYSTEM AND SELECTING SKILLS FOR INSTRUCTION

The question to be addressed at this point is: What communication adaptations/devices provide the "best match" between the student's communication needs and opportunities available, the student's ability profile, the requirements of the system/device, and any constraints that may be associated with the selection of a particular system/device? Certainly, this decision is complex in nature, and should never be made hastily or arbitrarily (e.g., based on a limited professional knowledge base, or based on professional biases). All of the specific factors that might lead toward one decision versus another cannot be detailed here; however, a few of the most important considerations are incorporated within the planning process described below. As in earlier chapters, the example of 14-year-old Mary Z. is used throughout the discussion.

## Step 1: Review the opportunities that exist to use communication skills and identify ways to remedy any barriers that exist.

It is important to identify and remediate as many of these opportunity barriers as possible. Some remedies might require changes in the schedule—such as adding new environments that are more "communicatively rich." Other remedies might require taking a close look at a particular environment where communication problems exist. This observation should reveal which communication partner(s) needs specific instruction, direction, and/or practice in order to make communication exchanges more successful. The need for interventions related to the opportunity barriers must be identified and addressed as part of both the initial and the ongoing planning process.

*Mary Z.:* After reviewing Mary's current schedule and sharing observations, team members highlighted two opportunity barriers as being responsible for some of Mary's communication breakdowns. One of these was related to scheduling problems that prevented her from eating lunch at the same time as the peers she knew best; the result was that Mary was essentially isolated from social contact during the lunch hour. The other opportunity barrier was related to the gestures Mary used to communicate. Some of her gestures, such as picking up and showing items to adults in her environment, had multiple meanings depending on the context. For example, if she picked up and showed an item to an adult, it could mean "May I have this?" or, "What is this called?" or, "Look what I have!" or, "This is for you." If her listener did not interpret her gesture correctly and provide the appropriate, related response ("Yes/no, you may/may not have that." or "That's an *x*." or "Yes, I see what you have!" or "Thank you for giving that to me.") a communication breakdown and concomitant behavior problems were likely to occur.

In order to resolve the scheduling problem, Mary's lunch time was moved forward 30 minutes, which afforded her the opportunity to spend time with her friends during each lunch period. In addition, plans were made to teach her to communicate and socialize with unfamiliar peers in the cafeteria by using teen magazines around which informational interactions could be structured. The barrier related to misinterpretation of Mary's natural gestures was resolved after considerable observation of Mary in various settings. Based on these observations, it was possible to firm up the meanings that each gesture had. This information was compiled by the communication therapist and shared among the staff and key students. This educational solution was sufficient to remove the opportunity barrier that was causing Mary's natural gestures to be misinterpreted.

## Step 2: Gain an understanding of the range of communicative functions (and their forms), techniques, and symbol systems that should be considered when designing a student's program.

The team members familiarized themselves with the communication options currently available for nonreading, nonwriting students such as Mary who have adequate use of their hands by reviewing relevant resource books in this regard (see the references listed at the end of this chapter). They also reviewed the communications skills functions chart (Chart 11.1).

*Mary Z.:* The input of Mary's family members was given considerable weight during the team discussion. Mary's parents and sister did not like the sound of the synthetic speech in computerized devices, saying that they thought it sounded too masculine for a young girl, "too much like a robot," and was hard to understand. They also wanted to be sure that her communication system did not preclude the use of her natural gestures and vocalizations, which adequately met her communication needs at home much of the time. Finally, everyone agreed that transportability was a major factor that needed to be considered in selecting a system, since Mary was experiencing more and more school and community settings.

## Step 3: When expanding and changing an augmentative communication system, conduct a more thorough assessment to determine which communication adaptations/devices are the "best matches" for the student of concern.

In order for a communication assessment to be successful, it is critical that a team of individuals including a teacher, parent, speech/language pathologist, occupational therapist, and physical therapist be involved throughout the process. In addition, input from the student, his or her friends, and current or future employer(s) is also essential. One of the initial assessment steps involves determining the student's current status related to mobility and positioning, manipulation (fine motor) skills, sensory/perceptual skills, communication, and cognitive/language skills. It is not critical that exhaustive assessments be undertaken in all of these areas; rather, what is important is to gather information that is directly related to a student's ability to access various communication techniques and symbol systems. A summary of the critical assessment questions that should be addressed in each of the five areas is provided below.

### Mobility/Positioning

- If the student is ambulatory, what restrictions (if any) exist that might limit the type of communication system recommended? For example, are there balance and/or gait problems? Can one or both hands be used to carry a device? Is there a limit to the amount of weight that can be carried? Can a device be carried on a shoulder strap? on a handle? on a belt or in a pocket?
- If the student is not ambulatory, what is the current method of mobility? For example, does the current method of mobility, such as a wheelchair, provide adequate head, trunk, arm, pelvic, and foot supports without unnecessarily restricting movement? Does it allow for independent mobility, such as a power wheelchair? If not, is powered mobility a possibility for the student either now or in the future? When during the day does the student use equipment other than that required for mobility (e.g., prone stander, kneeler, side-lier)?

*Mary Z.:* Mary uses a one-arm drive wheelchair for mobility purposes. The chair was recently purchased so that she could learn to maneuver her own chair for short distances. She is just beginning to wheel the chair and is able to push herself forward several feet.

### Manipulation (Fine Motor) Skills

For students without overt motor difficulties, assessment will not be required in all of these areas. However, students with physical or sensory handicaps will generally require assessment related to the use of one or more of these techniques as part of the decision-making process. The following questions are intended to be general guides to the complex process of determining the best method of motor access. Assistance from a physical or occupational therapist with expertise in this area will be critically important in order to make these determinations for students with extensive physical impairments.

- How well can the student use his or her hands? For example, what does he or she do to gesture? to write? to use a conventional keyboard? Can the student use an adapted keyboard? Can he or she form manual signs or point to a symbol of what he or she wants? What is the accuracy, rate and efficiency, and level of student fatigue? If pictorial symbol use seems viable, what size symbol is required for accurate pointing (either with a finger, the fist, or the whole hand)? How far apart do symbols need to be for accuracy? Is the range of motion of the upper extremities restricted to a particular area for pointing?

- If the student does not have efficient use of the hands/arms for one of the above techniques, can he or she use a headstick or mouthstick for pointing? What about a light pointer mounted on the head?
- If one of the above options is not viable in terms of efficiency, accuracy, and so forth, how well can the student use eye gaze (also known as eye pointing) for communication purposes? How many items can the student scan and still be accurate and readable using eye gaze? How large do the items need to be, how far apart, and so forth?
- Can the student activate a microswitch accurately and efficiently with any body part? A microswitch assessment should include evaluation of multiple potential microswitch sites, including the head (front, back, both sides), arms, hands, knees, legs, feet, and other sites as necessary (e.g., chin, tongue, eyebrow).

*Mary Z.:* Mary uses her hands to make a variety of gestures, including greeting and pointing. She is unable to handwrite, though she can motorically access a conventional typewriter or computer keyboard. She has difficulty forming simple manual signs, such as "cookie," "bathroom," and "juice," and appears to be quite manually uncoordinated. She is able to point to pictures that are as small as 3 inches in size with accuracy and efficiency. She prefers to use her right hand for most manual activities. She can activate a microswitch easily with either hand with as much accuracy and efficiency as direct pointing. Since her hand and arm use were sufficient to permit use of this access technique for communication, assessment of other options was not indicated.

### Sensory/Perceptual Abilities

- How well does the student see? Is there double vision? tunnel vision? If vision is restricted, what is the smallest size object or picture the student can accurately identify? Would glasses or a change in prescription at least partially improve the vision? What are the student's visual scanning abilities; that is, what is the maximum number of objects or pictures the student can visually scan at one time and still make accurate choices? Does the student have problems with figure-ground discrimination; that is, can he or she see dark pictures on a light background and/or vice versa?
- How well does the student hear? Does he or she seem to hear natural speech in a quiet room? in a noisy room? Does he or she seem to hear and understand synthetic speech in a quiet room? in a noisy room?

*Mary Z.:* A recent vision examination indicated that Mary has 20/60 vision, and glasses have been prescribed in this regard. She can identify pictures as small as 3 inches in size with her glasses on, but accuracy decreases when she is presented with an array of more than three pictures horizontally.

### Communication

- How does the student currently communicate? For example, does he or she have any speech? How intelligible is it to familiar people? to unfamiliar people? A thorough description of the current communication system as well as those that have been attempted in the past should be compiled through interviews with significant people in the student's life and observations in a variety of familiar and unfamiliar contexts. In this respect, it is also important to at least estimate the extent to which the student's communications are apparently purposeful (i.e., the extent to which the student seems to be able to predict the effect of his or her communicative acts on the communication partner/environment).

- About what does the student currently communicate?(Some examples of the major communicative functions and how they might be conveyed are presented in Chart 11.1.) A thorough description of the range of messages conveyed through each of the means delineated should be compiled through observations and interviews.

- Who are the student's current and potential communication partners? This question is critically important in order to avoid making communication system decisions that will unnecessarily restrict the number of people with whom the student can independently interact. Often, a comprehensive assessment of the current and potential communication partners reveals that the student will need to use several different communication modes across different persons and settings. For example, a student might use manual signing with family members, teachers, classmates, and close friends and resort to a communication booklet when interacting with other less familiar individuals.

- How motivated is the student to communicate? With whom or under what circumstances is the student most motivated? least motivated? Does the student initiate interactions? with whom? How does he or she do so?

*Mary Z.:* Mary currently communicates through gestures and vocalizations, but has no intelligible speech. She has never had a formal alternative communication system, though manual sign instruction was attempted when she was in elementary school, with little progress noted. She answers "no" questions fairly accurately with head shakes, gets other persons' attention and initiates interactions either by vocalizing or waving her hands, and terminates an activity by pushing an item away. She is learning to respond to greetings with a handshake or smile and to wave goodbye. Mary can make choices from an array of three horizontal items by pointing; and indicates her desire for an object, food, or activity (including assistance) by pointing or grabbing. However, she has no way of requesting an item that is not in the immediate environment. She has no viable way to say "Thank you," "Please," or other social amenities. She enjoys communicating with her family, peers, and familiar adults, but is hesitant to interact with others. She does best in environments where there are clear expectations and a predictable flow of activities. She is particularly motivated to interact in the context of enjoyable activities.

## Cognitive/Language Skills

- What is the student's receptive language ability at the present time? A variety of assessment procedures can be used to gather this information. The speech therapist might be one team member who could provide such information after conducting observations of the student and interviews with people who know the student.

- What are the results of formalized testing procedures designed to measure cognitive ability? It is critical to note that the results of such procedures (e.g., IQ or mental age scores) should *never* be used as criteria for communication "readiness." Rather, the student's performance on the subscales used in such measures may provide important information about learning style, rate, and current level of general performance.

- What is the student's representational ability at the present time? A thorough assessment of the student's ability to recognize various types of symbols to represent messages is critically important in order to design an appropriate communication system. (A summary of the types of symbols that might be considered was presented earlier in this chapter.) Procedures for determining the appropriate symbol level for an individual student can be found elsewhere (Keogh & Reichle, 1985; Mirenda & Locke, in press).

- What are the student's abilities related to literacy? Specifically, does the student read, and at what grade level? Does the student recognize single words in functional contexts? how many and which words? Can the student spontaneously spell words from memory? how many and which words?

*Mary Z.:* Informal and formal assessments revealed that Mary is able to identify approximately 20 frequently used objects when presented with verbal labels in a meaningful context. She understands simple one- or two-step commands in familiar contexts and learns routines after a few weeks of daily practice. Recent formal test results place her in the severe to profound range of intellectual disability and indicate that her strengths lie in the area of visual-spatial skills. She is able to recognize simple black-and-white line drawings when repeatedly paired with a frequently used (and desired) object. She is not able to read, write, or spell, and she does not recognize single words in context. She demonstrates clear understanding of cause-and-effect relationships for both people and objects, and anticipates regularly scheduled events based on common cues. For example, she can anticipate the activities of the day when a picture schedule is provided. She understands the notion of turn taking, but has difficulty waiting for her turn in game situations. She appears to remember where items in the classroom and in other areas at school are stored from one day to the next and can retrieve them when requested.

## Step 4: Determine priorities and finalize team recommendations.

The information obtained during assessment must be summarized by the team involved and compared with the requirements of a number of potential communication devices and systems.

*Mary Z.:* Because Mary, at age 14, had no speech, it was felt that interventions designed to build her natural ability in this area were inappropriate. However, the decision was made to encourage her to use the natural gestures and vocalizations she had already developed as part of her overall system. Manual signs were not an option because of manual dexterity problems. However, since there was a clear advantage to the use of an alternative technique that could be attached to her wheelchair, the team's attention focused on a number of flexible communication boards that could accommodate the use of small (3 inch) black-and-white symbols to represent messages.

A number of both low-tech (e.g., communication boards) and high-tech devices (e.g., lightweight computers with synthetic speech output) were considered. The assessment indicated that Mary's unmet communication needs largely occurred in community or group settings. In such settings, she experienced difficulty understanding synthetic speech; in addition, she did not seem particularly motivated by this form of output. Furthermore, one of the constraints identified during the assessment process was that Mary's parents and sister did not like the synthetic speech available in most devices at the time. Based on these combined factors, the decision was made not to pursue a voice output device for Mary at the present time. However, the team recommended that this decision be reassessed in 1–2 years time.

The team decided to have a portable plexiglass communication board constructed that could be attached to the lap tray of her wheelchair. Different sheets of communication symbols would slide under the board so that Mary could continuously expand the number of vocabulary items. It was also decided that Mary's initial communication board should contain only three symbols per sheet (three in a horizontal display), since Mary's visual scanning accuracy decreased as more symbols were added. The symbols were to be arranged by environment for each access (which meant that symbols for frequently occurring messages were included in more than one section), and the vocabulary was determined to correspond to the activities of concern (e.g., playing Yahtzee, ordering food at the restaurant) as well as generic needs such as that for requesting objects outside of the immediate environment. Those symbols that were used in only one particular setting were not included on the board or symbol sheets that traveled with her. Instead they remained in the setting in which they were used (e.g., in art class she had a separate sheet of symbols that were used).

## WRITING GOALS AND OBJECTIVES

As is the case with other embedded skill areas, the goals and objectives related to communication will generally not be written separately from the activities in which they are used. For example, in the recreation/leisure section of this guide there are a number of goals and objectives for Mary Z., several of which include the embedded skill area of communication. Some of these goals are related to expressive communication, while others are related to receptive understanding of labels, directions, and so forth.

### Goals and Objectives for Mary Z.

#### Goal

While participating daily in Art 8, Mary will express herself creatively by contributing to the completion of individual and group projects.

#### Objectives

- Mary will greet classmates who share her table by seeking eye contact and smiling.
- When a supply or assistance is needed, Mary will gesture to a classmate or point to her communication board to request help.

#### Goal

Mary will increase her participation when using a cassette tape player in the school library when selected as a free-time activity during daily oportunities.

#### Objectives

- Mary will greet the librarian and request headphones by pointing to her communication board, and thank her by smiling (four of five trials in 1 week).
- Mary will indicate her preference by pointing to one of three tapes, and will gesture to a peer when a change in tapes or activity is desired.

#### Goal

When using the computer room during the school day or in after-school computer club (twice a week), Mary will participate in computer games with another student.

**Objectives**

- Upon entering the computer room, Mary will approach a familiar student and point to a symbol on her board to show interest in playing a computer game (within 3 minutes, for 3 consecutive days).
- When playing a computer game with a friend, Mary will respond to his or her reminder of her turn by pressing the keyboard.

The IEP could not possibly contain all of the embedded communication skills that should be addressed in Mary's school day. Instead it will only highlight relatively few. It is important to recognize, however, that every opportunity should be used to enhance a student's communication—regardless of whether it is in the IEP. There are numerous "teachable moments" that occur throughout the day, and conscious efforts must be made to take advantage of them.

## TEACHING IN MEANINGFUL CONTEXTS

Most students will require ongoing instruction related to use of their systems in the natural contexts selected to communicate messages to a variety of persons. Since communication is an embedded skill area, it is anticipated that most, if not all, of the instruction will occur in the environments and activities included in the student's daily schedule. The integrated team will need to continue to function as a unit to provide communication instruction related to their specialty areas. For example, the physical therapist may need to periodically accompany the student in the community to assess and make adjustments to the system in terms of motor access. The speech/language therapist will need to work closely with teachers to keep the vocabulary current, institute instructional programs to facilitate use of the system, and coach listeners (teachers, employers, and peers) to interact appropriately with the student. These ongoing instructional needs are just as important as is the initial assessment and decision-making process.

The success of a communication system should not be taken for granted. Ongoing evaluation must be undertaken to determine the student's ability to use the system in relation to his or her communication needs. If the identified needs are being met, a mechanism for ongoing monitoring and follow-up should be devised and implemented. It is critical that this mechanism include a process for making future changes in the system through the integrated team approach, so that unilateral and/or arbitrary decisions are not made based on individual professional preferences. The primary purpose of the follow-up mechanism should be to provide a structured way for the team to be responsive to changing student needs and abilities; the communication system generally should *not* be changed except in relation to these two issues. If the current needs are not met by the intervention, reassessment of opportunity and/or access barriers to participation will be required.

Let's go back to the example of Mary Z. and examine how instructional and evaluation strategies were designed and implemented to teach her to use the communication system selected. First, a mechanism was set up to compile the vocabulary items to be contained on her board through input from Mary's family and school staff, using a vocabulary inventory form adapted from Carlson (1981). A decision was

made that, since Mary was most motivated to communicate during enjoyable activities with familiar peers, initial instruction would be provided during group recrea-
tion/leisure activities such as Yahtzee and browsing in stores. Other activities would
be added once Mary was familiar with the device. Mary's parents and younger sister
were supportive of the decisions made and indicated that they would be willing to use
the board at home when appropriate. However, they felt that Mary should not be
required to use the symbol board for communication in areas where her natural gestures and vocalizations were currently adequate; the professionals on the team whole-
heartedly supported this approach.

Finally, the members of the team divided up the responsibilities for designing
and constructing Mary's board (occupational therapist and teacher, with family input
and assistance), providing instruction in the natural contexts identified (teacher, with
speech/language pathologist to accompany Mary to the community), and evaluating
progress (all team members). Regular meetings were set up for the team to evaluate
the data collected as part of her overall instructional program and to make decisions,
as necessary, for modifications to the system and instructional plan.

## QUESTIONS AND ANSWERS

Q:   I work with students who have profound mental retardation and multiple handi-
     caps. They don't communicate at all, and would not be able to use a communica-
     tion adaptation. Shouldn't the emphasis be placed on sensory stimulation and
     positioning for these students, rather than on communication?

A:   First of all, let's examine the assumption that students such as those you describe
     don't communicate at all. What you probably mean is that they don't communi-
     cate *intentionally*, or that they don't use sophisticated forms to communicate.
     This means that the goal for initial communication interventions will be to teach
     your students that they can control what happens to them through gestures, vo-
     calizations, and other body movements. In order for this to occur, their com-
     munication partners will need to learn to respond to what may be unintentional
     behaviors in consistent, meaningful ways. For example, if a student cries or
     seems distressed, you probably approach him or her and try to figure out what's
     wrong. If you do this consistently, the student will eventually learn that crying is
     a way to say "I want some attention." Later on, the student will begin to cry,
     fuss, or move in certain ways when he or she is hungry (message: "I want to
     eat") and in other ways when bored (message: "I want something to do"), or in
     pain (message: "I'm uncomfortable"). When you respond sensitively to these
     messages, which may initially be unintentional, you're teaching communica-
     tion! While this may not seem very sophisticated, it may be an appropriate first
     step in communication instruction for students such as you describe.

Q:   Marcy is a 15-year-old student in my class who has a lot of inappropriate be-
     haviors. Shouldn't I focus on decreasing these behaviors before worrying about
     communication instruction?

A:   But what if her inappropriate behaviors are actually the result of her not having
     "better" communication strategies? Perhaps Marcy uses most, if not all, of her
     "inappropriate behaviors" to communicate some message. Generally, initiation
     of a communication system should be a high priority goal for students who ex-
     hibit a lot of excess behavior, in order to give them a better way to communicate
     the message(s) currently conveyed through the behavior(s) of concern. For ex-

ample, a student may throw a tantrum as a way of saying "I don't want to do this activity" or "I've done this long enough; I want to stop now." If you think that Marcy is acting out to ask that an activity be terminated, you might supply her with a card to hold up instead of throwing a tantrum when she wants to finish. At the first slight sign that she is beginning to get restless, go over to her and physically prompt her to hold up the card. Then immediately respond by saying "Oh, you're finished" and give her a short break. Gradually, if your analysis of the function of the tantrum was correct, Marcy should begin to hold up the card on her own, and the tantrums should decrease at the same time. In this way, you have not only decreased a problematic behavior, but have also taught her a communication skill to replace it.

Q: Three of the students in my class have communication books, but they almost never use them unless I prompt them to do so. I'm getting really frustrated! What should I do?

A: This is a common problem, and usually occurs for one of several reasons. The first reason may be that the vocabulary items contained in the book do not meet the student's needs. The items may not be motivating, or the items may have to do with wants and needs that are met automatically for the student, so that he or she doesn't really have to ask for them. A second reason may be that the vocabulary is appropriate but the symbol level is too abstract for the student to understand. It will be difficult for students to use their systems if they don't know what the symbols mean! Careful evaluation of the student's symbol level may be necessary in order to determine if this is part of the problem. Third, the students may not be using their books because sufficient time is not provided for them to do so. This is particularly a problem in classrooms where activities are very tightly scheduled, so that students are expected to move from one thing to the next very rapidly. Students with motor impairments or students just learning to use their systems may need the schedule to be readjusted to a slower pace so that they have ample time to produce and convey the desired message. A fourth reason for students' failure to use their systems is instructional in nature: maybe they don't understand *how* to use them. There are a number of instructional techniques designed for students who experience such problems; in particular, the "interrupted behavior chain" and the "verbal prompt-free" strategies referenced in the "Additional Readings and Resources" section at the end of this chapter may be useful in this regard.

Q: Darin is a boy in my class who uses gestures to communicate a lot of his messages. For example, he nods or shakes his head for "yes" or "no," even though those messages are on his communication board. Or, he points to what he wants rather than using the pictures on his board. What should I do to get Darin to use his board to communicate these messages?

A: Nothing! It is quite acceptable for students to use gestures or other natural means to communicate messages that are easily conveyed in this manner. Remember, the goal is *communication*; the form a student uses to accomplish this is less important than overall efficiency and accuracy. Students should never be forced to use their communication displays to communicate messages that are readily and acceptably conveyed through other means.

Q: Thomas is an 18-year-old student with severe physical problems in addition to communication needs. He has had five different communication systems in the past 6 years, since each new speech-language pathologist who sees him seems to have a preference for a different approach. The latest recommendation is for an electronic device that will cost over $2,500. I'm really worried that this isn't the right thing for him either, and that all that money will be spent for nothing. What should I do about this?

A:  The situation you describe illustrates one of the reasons that an integrated team approach is so critically important in dealing with students who have the need for communication adaptations. Decisions about communication interventions should never be made based on preferences or input from one person alone. An article listed in the "Additional Readings and Resources–General Information" section written by Smith-Lewis and Ford (1987) describes how these kinds of decisions can have an impact on the life of a consumer. Team members should be encouraged to read this article before final considerations for changing Thomas' communication system are made.

Q:  What are some sources available for funding of expensive communication devices?

A:  A variety of funding sources have been used successfully. These include private insurance companies; Medicaid; and philanthropic organizations such as the Rotary Club, Lions, Kiwanis, Sertoma Club, and others. The process of securing funding is quite complicated, and you should consult with someone who has had some experience in this regard to find out the "do's" and "don't's" involved before trying it yourself the first time. An excellent resource in this regard is a newsletter called *The Many Faces of Funding*, which is distributed by subscription through Phonic Ear, Inc., of Mill Valley, CA (see the "Additional Readings and Resources–General Information" section at the end of this chapter). Anna Hoffman, who authors the newsletter, will be happy to provide you with information related to your particular circumstances.

Q:  Is there anywhere I can call to find out about augmentative communication resources in my area of the country?

A:  Yes! In 1988, a service was started by Sarah Blackstone, who ran an augmentative communication project for the American Speech-Language-Hearing Association. The service consists of a quarterly newsletter called *Augmentative Communication News* (see the "Additional Readings and Resources–General Information" section at the end of this chapter), plus a "hotline" available to all subscribers. Through the hotline, you can call and access information about any issue of concern related to this area.

# REFERENCES

Carlson, F.L. (1981). A format for selecting vocabulary for the nonspeaking child. *Language, Speech and Hearing Services in Schools, 12*, 240–245.

Keogh, W.J., & Reichle, J. (1985). Communication intervention for the "difficult-to-teach" severely handicapped. In S.F. Warren & A.K. Rogers-Warren (Eds.), *Teaching functional language* (pp. 157–194). Austin, TX: PRO-ED.

Light, J., McNaughton, D., & Parnes, P. (1986). *A protocol for the assessment of the communicative interaction skills of nonspeaking severely handicapped adults and their facilitators.* Toronto: Augmentative Communication Service, Hugh MacMillan Medical Centre.

Mirenda, P., & Locke, P. (in press). A comparison of symbol transparency in nonspeaking persons with intellectual disabilities. *Journal of Speech and Language Disorders.*

Reichle, J., Williams, W., & Ryan, S. (1981). Selecting signs for the formulation of an augmentative communication modality. *Journal of The Association for the Severely Handicapped*, *6*, 48–56.

## ADDITIONAL READINGS AND RESOURCES

### General Information

*Augmentative and Alternative Communication* [quarterly professional journal]. (Available from Williams & Wilkins, 428 East Preston Street, Baltimore, MD 21202)

*Augmentative Communication News* [Periodical]. (Available from One Surf Way, Suite #215, Monterey, CA 93940)

*Communication Outlook* [Periodical]. (Available from Artificial Language Laboratory, Michigan State University, East Lansing, MI 40824-1042)

Hoffman, A.C. (Ed.). *The many faces of funding* [book and periodical]. (Available from Phonic Ear, Inc., 250 Camino Alto, Mill Valley, CA 94941)

International Society for Augmentative and Alternative Communication (ISAAC) [Organization for professionals, parents, and consumers.], P.O. Box 1762, Station R, Toronto, Ontario M4G 4A3, CANADA.

Musselwhite, C.R., & St. Louis, K.W. (1988). *Communication programming for persons with severe handicaps* (2nd ed.). Boston: College-Hill.

National Association for Hearing and Speech Action. (1987). *Augmentative Communication Introductory Booklets* [series of five booklets aimed at each of: the general public, consumers and their families, the medical community, special education administrators, and teachers]. (Available from NAHSA, 10801 Rockville Pike, Rockville, MD 20852)

Reichle, J., & Keogh, W.J. (1986). Communication instruction for learners with severe handicaps: Some unresolved issues. In R.H. Horner, L.H. Meyer, & H.D.B. Fredericks (Eds.), *Education of learners with severe handicaps: Exemplary service strategies* (pp. 189–220). Baltimore: Paul H. Brookes Publishing Co.

Smith-Lewis, M., & Ford, A. (1987). A user's perspective on augmentative communications. *Augmentative and Alternative Communication*, *3*(1), 12–17.

Warren, S.F., & Rogers-Warren, A.K. (Eds.). (1985). *Teaching functional language*. Austin, TX: PRO-ED.

### Assessment

Blackstone, S.W. (Ed.). (1987). *Augmentative communication: An introduction*. Rockville, MD: American Speech-Language-Hearing Association.

Coggins, T., & Carpenter, R. (1981). The communication intention inventory: A system for observing and coding children's early intentional communication. *Applied Psycholinguistics*, *2*, 235–251.

Donnellan, A.M., Mirenda, P.L., Mesaros, R.A., & Fassbender, L.L. (1984). Analyzing the communicative functions of aberrant behavior. *Journal of The Association for Persons with Severe Handicaps*, *9*, 201–212.

Musselwhite, C.R., & St. Louis, K.W. (1988). *Communication programming for persons with severe handicaps* (2nd ed.). Boston: College-Hill.

Schuler, A.L., & Baldwin, M. (1981). Non-speech communication and childhood autism. *Language, Speech, and Hearing Services in Schools*, *12*, 245–257.

### Symbols and Symbol Selection

Blackstone, S.W. (Ed.). (1987). *Augmentative communication: An introduction*. Rockville, MD: American Speech-Language-Hearing Association.

Blissymbolics Communication Institute. (1984). *A supplement to Blissymbolics for use*. Toronto: Author.

Carlson, F. (1985). *Picsyms categorical dictionary*. Lawrence, KS: Baggeboda Press.

Claark, C.R., Davies, C.O., & Woodcock, R.W. (1974). *Standard Rebus glossary*. Circles Pines, MN: American Guidance Service.

Hehner, B. (1980). *Blissymbols for use*. Toronto: Blissymbolics Communication Institute.

Johnson, J. (1986). *Self-talk: Communication boards for children and adults*. Tucson, AZ: Communication Skill Builders.

Karlan, G., & Lloyd, L. (1983). Considerations in the planning of communication intervention: Selecting a lexicon. *Journal of The Association for the Severely Handicapped, 8*, 13–25.

Landman, C., & Schaeffler, C. (1986). Object communication boards. *Communication Outlook, 8*(1), 7–8.

Mayer-Johnson Co. (1986). *The picture communication symbols, Book I*. (Available from Mayer-Johnson Co., P.O. Box AD, Solana Beach, CA 92075).

Musselwhite, C.R., & St. Louis, K.W. (1988). *Communication programming for persons with severe handicaps*. Boston: College-Hill.

## Communication Systems and Devices

Adaptive Communication Systems, Box 12440, Pittsburgh, PA 15231.

Beukelman, D.R., Yorkston, K.M., & Dowden, P.A. (1985). *Communication augmentation: A casebook of clinical management*. San Diego: College-Hill Press.

Blackstone, S.W. (Ed.). (1987). *Augmentative communication: An introduction*. Rockville, MD: American Speech-Language-Hearing Association.

Brandenburg, S.A., & Vanderheiden, G.C. (1987). *Communication, control, and computer access for disabled & elderly individuals (Resource Book I, Communication aids; Resource Book II, Switches and environmental controls; Resource Book III, Hardware and software)*. Boston: College-Hill.

Fristoe, M., & Lloyd, L. (1980). Planning an initial expressive sign lexicon for persons with severe communication impairment. *Journal of Speech and Hearing Disorders, 45*, 170–180.

Don Johnston Developmental Equipment, Inc., 900 Winnetka Terrace, Lake Zurich, IL 60047.

Mirenda, P. (1985). Designing pictoral communication systems for physically able-bodied students with severe handicaps. *Augmentative and Alternative Communication, 1*, 58–64.

Musselwhite, C.R., & St. Louis, K.W. (1988). *Communication programming for persons with severe handicaps* (2nd ed.). Boston: College-Hill.

## Instructional Techniques

Blackstone, S.W. (Ed.). (1987). *Augmentative communication: An introduction*. Rockville, MD: American Speech-Language-Hearing Association.

Halle, J. (1982). Teaching functional language to the handicapped: An integrative model of natural environment teaching techniques. *Journal of The Association for the Severely Handicapped, 7*, 29–37.

Hunt, P., Goetz, L., Alwell, M., & Sailor, W. (1986). Using an interrupted behavior chain strategy to teach generalized communication responses. *Journal of The Association for Persons with Severe Handicaps, 11*, 196–204.

Locke, P.A., & Mirenda, P. (1988). A computer-supported communication approach for a nonspeaking child with severe visual and cognitive impairments: A case study. *Augmentative and Alternative Communication, 4*, 15–22.

Mirenda, P., & Dattilo, J. (1987). Instructional techniques in alternative communication for students with severe intellectual handicaps. *Augmentative and Alternative Communication, 3*, 143–152.

Mirenda, P., & Santogrossi, J. (1985). A prompt-free strategy to teach pictoral communication system use. *Augmentative and Alternative Communication, 1*, 143–150.

Musselwhite, C.R. (1986). *Adaptive play for special needs children: Strategies to enhance communication and learning*. Boston: College-Hill.

Musselwhite, C.R., & St. Louis, K.W. (1988). *Communication programming for persons with severe handicaps* (2nd ed.). Boston: College-Hill.

Peck, C.A. (1985). Increasing opportunities for social control by children with autism and severe handicaps: Effects on student behavior and perceived classroom climate. *Journal of The Association for Persons with Severe Handicaps, 10*, 183–193.

Reichle, J., & Keogh, W.J. (1986). Communication instruction for learners with severe handicaps: Some unresolved issues. In R.H. Horner, L.H. Meyer, & H.D.B. Fredericks (Eds.),

*Education of learners with severe handicaps: Exemplary service strategies* (pp. 189–220). Baltimore: Paul H. Brookes Publishing Co.

Snyder-McLean, L.K., Solomonson, B., McLean, J.E., & Sack, S. (1984). Structuring joint action routines: A strategy for facilitating language and communication development in the classroom. *Seminars in Speech and Language*, *5*, 159–170.

Yoder, D., & Calculator, S. (1981). Some perspectives on intervention strategies for persons with developmental disorders. *Journal of Autism and Developmental Disorders*, *11*, 107–123.

# CHAPTER 12

# Motor Skills

*Beverly Rainforth, Mike Giangreco and Ruth Dennis*

It is hard to imagine any functional routine that does not involve some motor activity. Whether playing a game at home with friends, dining in a restaurant, or stapling newsletters in an office, participation involves numerous motor skills. Although motor skills traditionally have been viewed in relation to the normal motor development of a young child, it is useful to consider the functions that motor skills serve. For example, in the routines we just listed, people use motor skills to travel from one geographic location to another. This may involve walking, climbing the steps of a bus, or driving a car. Once at the home, restaurant, or office, the participants use mobility skills to walk between rooms and between areas within rooms. Then they assume and maintain positions that are functional for the activity. They probably sit to eat, but might sit or stand to staple. The functional positioning for the game depends upon whether they are playing cards, croquet, or Twister. Finally, they participate in the core of the activity, which requires motor skills to visually scan and gaze at materials, to manipulate materials, and to eat. Even performing the simplest of the embedded social and communication skills involves some type of motor skills (e.g., smiling when greeted, pointing to a choice).

When we think about the ways we typically perform these functional routines, it seems that participation requires an extensive repertoire of sophisticated motor skills. If we concentrate on the functions that motor skills serve in the activities, however, we can see many more possibilities. We know that the mobility function of walking can be fulfilled by crawling or driving a wheelchair. We know that positioning can be assisted through a variety of adapted equipment. And we know that participation can be elicited through systematic prompts, partial participation, and adaptations. Focusing on the functions of motor skills allows us to see how students with even the most severe physical disabilities can participate in activities. This does not suggest that students do not need to learn or improve motor skills. Generally, walking is faster and more versatile than crawling or driving a wheelchair. Assuming, maintaining, and changing positions independently, and as personal comfort or preference dictate, are preferable to having another person expend time and energy lifting and positioning in costly adapted equipment according to a schedule. And performing at least parts of a routine independently reduces reliance upon personal assistance and adaptations, which are not always available. Therefore, individualized education programs (IEPs) need to achieve a balance between assisting students to fulfill the motor functions that will maximize participation today, and teaching students the motor skills that will increase their independence in the future.

Many children with moderate and severe disabilities achieve the typical "motor milestones" at a slower rate, but follow the normal sequences. It is fairly common for these children to receive motor skills instruction incidentally and in functional contexts. Other children have more severe or multiple physical disabilities, including cerebral palsy, in which motor development is disorganized as well as delayed. Spasticity, hypotonia, and primitive reflex patterns interfere with experiencing and practicing normal movement, and hinder motor skill development. Unfortunately, therapists and teachers tend to exclude children with severe and multiple physical disabilities from activities in which they could develop motor skills, because the children do not already perform the motor skills that constitute the activity. Such circular reasoning can produce three outcomes. First, children and adults with severe and multiple physical disabilities receive instruction in "prerequisite" movements and motor skills in isolated and nonfunctional contexts where there is no clear purpose for performing the tasks. Second, instruction is episodic, so they do not have enough practice to learn the motor skills. Third, they rarely reach the criterion skill levels, so they never "earn" the right to participate actively in integrated community environments. There is evidence that children with physical disabilities become more interested in activities when they are given a means to participate actively, and when they achieve some control over their environment (Hulme, Poor, Schulein, & Pezzino, 1983). Therefore, whether a student has moderate motor skill deficits or severe and multiple physical disabilities, it is essential that teachers and therapists provide frequent opportunities for him or her to learn and practice functional motor skills through meaningful activities in normal environments.

## OPPORTUNITIES TO USE MOTOR SKILLS

While motor sequences help determine which motor skills the student can realistically achieve, and in what order, natural routines and the functions of motor skills help to define the scope of the curriculum. The routines that occur in the home, for example, present endless opportunities to teach motor skills. When arising in the morning, a person rolls out of bed, assumes an upright position, travels to the bathroom, assumes some functional position in front of the sink, and manipulates faucets, washcloth, soap, toothbrush, toothpaste tube, and other implements. The person travels back to the bedroom, opens and closes drawers and closet doors, removes sleepwear, and puts on clothing for the day. Breakfast may entail cooking, setting the table, and cleaning up, as well as eating. The motor functions of positioning, mobility, manipulation, vision, and eating are clear in these routines.

Family members are important in defining the motor curriculum, since they can describe how motor functions are fulfilled at home, which ways are satisfactory, and whether proposed alternatives will be acceptable. The means used to fulfill motor functions at home may be different from those used in the community. For example, York (1987) found that adults with physical disabilities typically walked (if they could) when in or near their home, but used a wheelchair to travel in the community. The same people often crawled on the floor in their home, especially in the bedroom and bathroom, because crawling was safer and more functional. Parents remind us that adapted mobility and positioning equipment sometimes does not fit the space or atmosphere of a home. Parents also can identify the routines where teaching the child functional motor skills would be most beneficial, and when family members have time to teach. Keeping a log of 2 or 3 days' activities is an effective way for a family to identify their priorities and time constraints (Rainforth & Salisbury, 1988). As the child grows older, the family can provide important information about the motor skills the child has used in the past, and about the methods and adaptations that have been tried.

In community environments and activities, every routine should be examined for opportunities to use or teach motor functions. How does the child travel to the school, workplace, or other community environment? How does the child travel through the building, and within rooms in the building? Is the child encouraged to use or develop independent mobility? What positions does the child use when participating in the activities? Is the child encouraged to use and improve postural control? Would other positions improve the quality of participation? How does the child participate in the activity itself, and in the set up and clean up? Is the child encouraged to use or improve manipulation, eating, and vision skills? Could/should the activity or materials be adapted to increase participation?

## MOTOR SKILL FUNCTIONS

Development of motor skills is considered to follow certain sequences. There are specific skill sequences that delineate the many steps from developing head control to learning to walk, and from grasping objects with a fisted hand to writing with a pencil. These sequences are often analyzed or described in terms of more general patterns of development, which are thought to follow certain progressions: head to foot, gross to fine, weightbearing to nonweightbearing, and proximal to distal (near the body to farther from the body). The "head to foot" pattern reflects the progression of control from the head, to the trunk, and finally to the legs. The "gross to fine" pattern reflects the development of large body movements, such as walking, before refined movements, such as buttoning and writing. The "weightbearing to nonweightbearing" pattern describes that children learn to prop up on their arms before they become skilled at reach and grasp. The "proximal to distal" pattern reflects development of control at the shoulders and hips before control at the hands and feet, as illustrated in the other examples above.

Because the skill sequences in motor development have been studied so extensively, many therapists and teachers now consider the sequences to be prescriptive, with earlier skills in the sequences viewed as prerequisites for teaching later skills. For typical children, however, great variations in the rate and sequence of motor development are considered normal (e.g., learning to walk without ever crawling). Furthermore, motor development does not always follow even the general patterns described above (Horowitz & Sharby, 1988; Loria, 1980). Loria found that children simultaneously worked on proximal and distal, weightbearing and nonweightbearing, and gross and fine motor development in the arm and hand. She also found that children achieved the corresponding motor skills in varying sequences. Although the sequences and patterns that typically occur still provide useful guidelines, such research findings of variations in motor development support motor skills instruction for children with physical disabilities that can and should focus on many areas and levels of development simultaneously.

Although we caution against letting "normal" motor development sequences dictate prerequisites for teaching other motor skills, there are other types of prerequisites to which therapists and teachers need to attend. For example, locomotion, eating, looking, and handling objects all require stabilization of some body parts while coordinating movement of other body parts. If there is insufficient stabilization of body parts or coordination of movement, the student will be unsuccessful in performing the motor components of the task. In this sense, stabilization and coordination are prerequisites to the task. One way to view motor development sequences is that they reflect progressive improvements in stabilization and coordinated movement, which tend to follow the patterns described above. Positioning, handling, and prompting augment the child's internal motor control, and are faded as the child learns to stabilize and coordinate various body parts. The motor skill functions chart (Chart 12.1) reflects a combination of this stabilization-coordination orientation and the "normal" sequences of motor development. It is organized into these major functions: positioning, mobility, manipulation, oral motor functions, and visual functions.

The motor skill functions chart includes only basic information about motor skill development. Other considerations, such as strength, speed, rate, power, and stamina, are not covered here. Factors such as range of motion, muscle tone, and primitive reflexes, which may limit acquisition of motor skills, have been discussed only briefly. For more extensive information and methods, consult with the physical or occupational therapist assigned to your team or school district.

## SELECTING EMBEDDED MOTOR SKILLS

Most activities present far more opportunities for teaching functional motor skills than time and resources allow teachers to address. Of course, your team must first decide whether motor development is even an instructional priority. Not all students need to have goals and objectives identified for this particular area. If it is determined that specific attention should be given to motor skills development, it will be necessary to set priorities for instruction. Where do we begin in the selection process? How do we select priority skills to include in a student's IEP? The following steps are designed to assist you and your team in the selection process. As in previous chapters, the example of Mary Z. is continued.

### Step 1: Review the number and type of opportunities available to the student to practice and further develop motor skills.

This step involves determining in *what* activities the student will engage, *where* these activities will occur, and *with whom* the student will participate. If a parent has been keeping a log of routines, time constraints, and other pertinent data be sure to include that information in the review process. From this discussion, the team might identify ways to enrich the opportunities available to use motor skills.

*Mary Z.:* Mary Z., who has cerebral palsy, in addition to severe cognitive deficits, is involved in many activities including: shopping in the grocery store with peers; using the school library to select, use, and borrow talking books with peers; using the school cafeteria or a restaurant with friends; and packaging and labeling equipment at the central supply area of a hospital. Note that three of the four activities are activities that Mary might also do with family members (i.e., using library, grocery store, and restaurant). These activities are included in Mary's IEP because her family identified needs related to her participation. Even though these are family priorities, the educational team provides the majority of *instruction;* the family provides opportunities for practice, maintenance, and generalization.

### Step 2: Review the motor functions and motor skills the student can currently perform.

This step involves determining the mobility the student uses to travel to and within the area where the activity occurs, the positions the student uses when performing the

Chart 12.1. Motor skill functions

A. Positioning
Functions:
1. Assume and maintain positions for participation (consider typical position for task, environment, opportunities for social interaction, student age, and motor skills)
2. Maintain health, by alternating positions (consider optimal position for safety, respiration, digestion, preventing deformity and pressure sores)
3. Maintain and improve postural control

| Skill sequence | Stabilization/coordination | Adaptations (examples) |
|---|---|---|
| Head upright<br>Trunk upright<br>Trunk slightly reclined<br>Lying on stomach, propped on arms | Stabilize at head, trunk, all other body parts; fade as child gains internal control, leans on arms to stabilize head<br>Stabilize as needed when child eats, uses hands | Chair with head, forearm, and trunk supports<br>Supine stander<br>Wedge or roll |
| Sitting<br>Side sitting<br>Indian or ring sitting<br>Long sitting<br>(avoid "W" sitting) | Stabilize around shoulders for child to prop on arms<br>Prompt at trunk/hips to push up to side sit from stomach<br>Stabilize at trunk/hips to sit without arm support<br>Fade control (shoulders to trunk to hips) as child gains internal control<br>Stabilize as needed when child reaches, uses hands | Regular chair<br>Adapted chair<br>Corner sitter<br>Bolster chair<br>  (above may have tray and must support feet and thighs)<br>Body jacket |
| Hands and knees | Prompt at hips/shoulders to push up from side sit, to maintain position<br>Fade control (shoulders to hips) as child gains internal control | Bolster<br>Low stool |
| Kneeling | Prompt and stabilize at hips/shoulders to rise up to kneel, to remain kneeling<br>Child uses hands/arms to push/pull up, hold position<br>Fade (trunk to hips) as child gains internal control | Table/counter<br>Kneeling box |
| Standing | Prompt and stabilize at hips/knees/ankles to half-kneel then stand, to remain standing<br>Child uses hands/arms to pull up, hold position<br>Fade where possible as child gains internal control | Prone stander<br>Supine stander<br>Parapodium stand<br>Standing box<br>Railing<br>Ankle splints |

(continued)

215

Chart 12.1. *(continued)*

B. Mobility
Functions:
1. Travel from one location to another (consider typical mobility for activity and environment, student age and motor skills, efficiency)
2. Maintain health through exercise

| Skill sequence | Stabilization/coordination | Adaptations (examples) |
|---|---|---|
| Rolling<br>Without trunk rotation<br>With trunk rotation | Prompt at head/shoulders/hips/knees; stabilize as needed to limit flexion/extension<br>Fade as child coordinates limbs, trunk rotation | Inclined surface |
| Crawling on stomach (commando crawling) with reciprocal arm and leg movement | Prompt around elbows/knees for reciprocal crawling<br>Fade as child coordinates reciprocal pattern | Scooter board |
| *Note:* Dragging arms/legs interferes with further skill development; if unable to prompt reciprocal movement, consider alternative forms of mobility | | |
| Creeping on hands and knees with reciprocal movement | Prompt at forehead/chest to maintain position<br>Prompt at elbows/knees for reciprocal creeping | Low stool with wheels |
| *Note:* "Bunny-hopping" interferes with further skill development; if unable to prompt reciprocal movement (or prevent hopping by holding the ankles), consider alternative forms of mobility | | |
| Kneewalking | Stabilize at chest/hips<br>Prompt at knees to step<br>Child may use hands for support/balance<br>Fade as child gains coordination, balance | Low walker<br>Stool with wheels<br>Kneepads |
| Walking | Prompt at shoulders/hips/knees for trunk rotation, reciprocal gait<br>Child may use hands for support/balance<br>Fade where/when possible | Walker with hip/trunk support<br>Walker/rollator<br>Crutches<br>Ankle splints<br>Parapodium |
| Climbing stairs<br>Up, step to step, step over step<br>Down, step to step, step over step | Prompt at knees to step, at shoulders/hips to shift weight<br>Child may hold rail for support/balance | Elevator<br>At home, may sit on step and scoot up/down |
| Alternative forms of mobility<br>Pushing a wheelchair | Prompt at elbows to wheel | Extension knobs on wheel<br>One-arm drive |
| Driving a wheelchair | Prompt varies with switches | Switches: toggle leaf, eyeblink, sip-and-puff, hand/foot tread |
| Riding a bicycle or tricycle | Prompt at knees to pedal, at elbows to steer | Trunk support<br>Foot straps<br>Training wheels |

216

C. Manipulation

| Skill sequence | Stabilization/coordination | Functions | Adaptations |
|---|---|---|---|
| Reach | Stabilize shoulder: prompt above/below elbows to reach; at wrist to open hand | Contact materials for manipulation | Friction-free or inclined surface |
| Prop on arms Push | Prompt at shoulders/elbows to reach at wrists to position hand open and flat | Stabilize/support other body parts Move grocery cart, vacuum cleaner, push toy | Motor power Switches Adapted handle |
| Retrieve Pull (+/− grasp) | Prompt at elbows to pull, at wrists to maintain hold (also see "Grasp") | Bring cup to mouth Pick up telephone Open refrigerator Pull cart | |
| Grasp (see types) | Stabilize shoulder/elbow; prevent wrist flexion; prompt at wrist and fingers; traction of object on fingers | Hold materials for manipulation | Wrist splint (functional position) |
| Gross/palmar (+/− thumb) | Prompt at base of thumb if thumb in palm | Hold handle, hammer, broom, can, knife Squeeze sponge | Change size/direction of cylinder Grasping mitt Universal cuff |
| Lateral | Prompt at thumb and first finger Support ulnar side of hand to stabilize, isolate fingers | Hold coins Turn toothpaste cap | |
| Three-finger | Hold palm open Prompt at thumb and first/second/third fingers | Hold sandwich, spoon, pencil Turn jar cover | Add cylinder (sandwich holder) |
| Pincer | Hold palm open Prompt at thumb and first/second finger | Hold buttons, coins, small finger foods, jewelry, needle | Splint to hold palm open |
| Point | Stabilize to shoulder Prompt gross grasp, isolate one finger | Dial telephone Push button on elevator, copier, vending machine | Hold cylinder Use fist Head pointer |
| Release | Stabilize to shoulder Stabilize arm/wrist Prompt wrist flexion to open fingers | Place materials Throw ball Alternate grasps as manipulate | |
| Twist | Stabilize, prompt as to grasp and release Prompt at wrist to rotate forearm | Turn doorknob, screwdriver, key | Add cylinder at right angle to push/pull Add lever |

Note: External stabilization (handling and/or adapted positioning equipment) may be needed at the head/trunk to concentrate on task performance

*(continued)*

Chart 12.1. (continued)

## D. Oral motor functions

| Skill sequence | Stabilization/coordination | Functions | Adaptations |
|---|---|---|---|
| Swallowing | Position upright<br>Stabilize at head with chin tucked<br>Prompt intermittent closure at jaw, lower lip<br>Wait for swallow; do not try to prompt | Ingest liquids, foods | Intravenous or tube feeding |
| Drinking (sucking or sipping) | Position upright, stabilize jaw<br>Prompt tongue inside by nipple on tongue/cup on lower lip, or wait for retraction | Hydration<br>Socialization | Orthodonture (for jaw closure) |
| From cup | Stabilize mouth by cup rim on lower lip<br>Prompt by tipping small amount liquid from cup | | Cut-out cup |
| From straw | Prompt by placing straw on tongue, squeezing small sips from bottle | | Sports bottle<br>Pump cup |
| Eating | Position upright, stabilize head/mouth with jaw control | Nutrition<br>Socialization<br>Reciprocal interaction | |
| Spoon eating | Place spoon on center of tongue; give jaw control (intermittent) | | |
| Biting | Prompt by pressing food down on lower incisors | Remove edible-size piece of food | Grind food<br>Cut food |
| Chewing | Prompt by pressing food down on lower molars and waiting<br>May prompt rotary | Grind food to size/consistency to swallow easily | Select soft foods<br>Grind food |
| Speaking | Promote by teaching effective eating/drinking/respiration patterns | Communication<br>Socialization | Augmentative communication |

Note: Eating and drinking always occur in an upright position, unless there are compelling reasons to use alternative positions; external stabilization (handling and/or adapted positioning equipment) may be needed at the head/trunk to concentrate on task performance; self-feeding combines oral motor and manipulation skills

## E. Visual functions

| Skill sequence | Stabilization/coordination | Functions | Adaptations |
|---|---|---|---|
| Fixing gaze | Stabilize at head and trunk | Receive information<br>Monitor own manipulation of materials<br>Communicate choices | Illuminate object<br>Use contrast<br>Use other senses |
| Orienting, shifting gaze, scanning | Stabilize at head and trunk<br>Prompt by turning head | Find people, places, materials in environment<br>Find obstacles in environment<br>View selection of choices | Enter line of vision<br>Redirect line with mirror |
| Tracking | Stabilize at head and trunk<br>Prompt by turning head/preventing turning | Follow activity (e.g., ball game)<br>Reading | Turn head |

activity, and how the student participates in the activity, which may include manipulation of materials, oral motor functions, and/or vision functions. This information is acquired through direct observation, which may be followed by diagnostic assessment. Initially team members observe the student in the actual activities and environments where participation is desired. Observation may include some aspects of intervention, to determine the amount and type of assistance the student may need to perform the various functions in a more normalized way. An important consideration when conducting a motor assessment in public environments is to maintain the student's dignity. Arranging a follow-up "diagnostic" assessment responds to this concern for dignity, and also provides additional opportunities for occupational and physical therapists to incorporate their expertise. The follow-up diagnostic assessment allows therapists to look more closely at factors such as motor development, integration of primitive reflexes, muscle tone, strength, coordination, and range of motion—*as these factors relate to participation in priority activities and environments.*

*Mary Z.:* The team may observe that Mary sits during most activities; they think standing would be more appropriate. The physical therapist (PT) conducts a follow-up assessment to determine whether standing is a realistic expectation for Mary, which motoric factors interfere, how to reduce that interference, which of Mary's current activities are most compatible (motorically) with standing, what equipment may be necessary to position Mary, and how to prompt Mary to assume and maintain a standing position. The PT would observe Mary in the natural environments and conduct the diagnostic assessment there as much as possible. The follow-up assessment would focus on collecting the remaining information needed to answer questions about standing and other motor skills, as needed for the team to make programmatic decisions. In other words, the assessment is carried out with a specific purpose in mind.

At this point in the assessment process, teachers and therapists may find that norm-referenced motor development assessment instruments have some utility. These instruments typically include items that occur in the course of normal gross, fine, and oral motor development, and reflect increasing levels of motor control in populations of children with no known handicapping condition. Therefore, they provide frameworks for assessing large numbers of related skills and for sequencing instructional objectives. The tools might best be used to guide and record a therapist's observations in natural environments, or an assessment interview with family members. This will help you assess the motor component (e.g., note grasping patterns even if item is not performed "correctly") while ensuring that the assessment materials are functional to the student (e.g., grasp spoon rather than grasp rattle).

*Mary Z.:* An assessment of Mary's motor skills was conducted in natural settings. A sample of the information gathered in various settings is provided below:

**Shopping in Grocery Store**   *Positioning:* Mary sits in her adapted wheelchair; postural control is sufficient for all tasks. *Manipulation:* She grasps, places in shopping basket, and releases items that are less than 2 inches in diameter; movement is shaky, she does better with stabilization at wrist/arm/elbow; she points to items she can't reach; she opens purse and handles money only with hand-over-hand assistance. *Visual functions:* Mary looks at designated picture in shopping list, looks at shelves, and looks/points when companion points to object on shelf; she does not scan with visual or physical prompts. (Performance in other activities was consistent; follow-up assessment indicated that she can track horizontally, but has greater difficulty vertically or diagonally.)

**Using the School Cafeteria**   *Mobility:* A friend wheels her through line; she will wheel 3 feet to table with repeated physical prompts, much encouragement, and meal on table. *Oral motor functions:* Mary drinks, eats mashed/ground foods without difficulty; she swallows whole foods without chewing.

**Packaging and Labeling Equipment in Central Supply Department of Hospital** *Positioning:* Mary sits in her adapted wheelchair. (Follow-up assessment indicated that she could stand in a parapodium stander for about 10 minutes before tiring; she still can package and label in this position; the PT will work on a simplified standing adaptation to use in the central supply department at the hospital.) *Manipulation:* She grasps and places towelette packets in counting jig with verbal prompts; to label bag, she needs hand over hand prompts to use thumb-fingertip (versus gross) grasp to slide the bag under the electric stamping/labeling machine.

The above represent just a few of the motor functions and skills that would occur during Mary's activities. Since Mary has multiple handicaps, each activity in her weekly schedule presents far more needs and opportunities than could possibly be addressed, which brings us to the next step.

### Step 3: Determine the priority motor functions and skills that will be included in the IEP.

We recommend that consideration be given to at least three major criteria: 1) maintaining health, 2) increasing immediate participation in integrated environments, and 3) increasing future participation in integrated environments.

### Maintaining Health

Bricker and Campbell (1980) described "surviving and thriving" factors that may be critical to any student's health, and therefore his or her ability to benefit from instruction. Important areas for assessment and intervention include growth, cardiac and respiratory function, nutrition and hydration, seizure control, and medication levels. Although these may be viewed as medical management concerns, educators have important roles in assessment and program implementation. First, teachers assist with assessment through ongoing data collection and communication of findings to medical personnel. Second, educators may assume major responsibilities for implementing health management plans on a day-to-day basis. At a minimum, this would involve monitoring a student and calling the school nurse or therapist when certain signs are noticed, or taking the student to the nursing office for routine services. Frequently, teachers participate more directly by dispensing medication, performing postural drainage, positioning, feeding by mouth or tube, toileting and changing diapers, performing intermittent catheterization, and managing a variety of seizures. Even when these management activities do not include instruction, they need to assume high priority in the daily routine because they allow students to benefit from instruction.

Finally, given that maintaining health is such a high priority, it is appropriate to incorporate instruction into health routines. Whenever possible, students should be taught to monitor their own schedules, travel to health offices, and perform other aspects of the routine independently. Because students with severe physical disabilities tend to have extensive health care needs, determining when and how to incorporate instruction may be challenging. For example, some students are unable to change their own position, but need to be repositioned regularly to prevent deformity and pressure sores. In this routine, instruction might focus on the student moving his or her head, arms, or other body parts in the direction of the move, holding onto the teacher, supporting his or her own weight, or maintaining normal tone (rather than shooting into extension) during the move. Similarly, routines such as changing pant liners offer opportunities to increase range of motion, normalize tone, encourage active arm and leg movement for dressing, roll and push up to sit, and so on. McCormick, Cooper, and Goldman (1979) found that incorporating instruction into caregiving routines increased the amount of instruction received by students with severe handicaps by as much as 50%.

### Increasing Immediate Participation in Integrated Environments

After maintaining health, the primary criterion for selecting instructional priorities is that acquisition of the motor skill would increase participation in typical home, school, and community environments. If a child has multiple disabilities, it is appropriate for objectives to address the entire scope of needs. Questions to help identify priorities include the following:

- Will the skill increase participation in a priority activity or environment?
- Will the skill allow participation in a new activity or environment?
- Will the skill provide the student with (more appropriate) control over the environment?
- Will the skill enhance the student's social integration?
- Is the skill appropriate for the activity and environment where its use is intended, and for the age of the student?
- Will the skill apply to many functional activities and/or environments?
- Will the student have opportunities for repeated practice of the skill in his or her daily routine?

### Increasing Future Participation in Integrated Environments

While most objectives will focus on achieving participation immediately, it is also appropriate to identify and teach motor skills that are foundations for greater independence in the future. For example, a child may be able to participate in activities as long as she is fully supported by her adapted wheelchair. Although the adaptation allows her to participate now, it does not encourage her to use the bit of head and trunk control she has or to further develop that control. Improvement in head and trunk control would allow the child to use a greater variety of positions and to use her hands for functions other than trunk support. It might also promote independence in mobility and better ocular control (as for scanning and gazing at choices).

Another child may eat ground-up food independently with a spoon, which can be arranged even in restaurants through selection of food or use of a hand-operated food mill. Future independence, acceptance, health, and quality of life would be increased if the child could eat whole foods. Initially, however, the child will probably resist whole foods, and may gag at the feeling of solid food in his mouth. It may be necessary to teach him to chew, which often requires an adult to hold or move food between the child's molars. If these changes and procedures are introduced, the child will lose independence temporarily. You might also have some concerns about whether instruction of this sort should take place in some integrated environments (e.g., the school cafeteria) for fear that it would compromise the child's dignity. One strategy is to start teaching the child to eat whole foods during a snacktime in a more private location. The child would continue to eat other meals independently in the cafeteria, with a systematic plan to introduce whole foods in this location as essential criteria are met.

Choosing between immediate participation and eventual independence is a difficult decision, since much depends upon the accuracy of long-term predictions. Fortunately, there are few all-or-nothing decisions. Even so, this area is likely to arouse conflict between team members with developmental and functional orientations. Decision making will be assisted by considering the following questions:

- Is the skill part of a valid sequence to achieve independence in the future?
- Will the motor skill apply to many motor functions, activities, and/or environments?
- Does achievement seem likely when the student's age, current motor skills, and prior responses to systematic instruction are considered?
- Can instruction be incorporated into or coordinated with current activities?
- Are restrictive conditions required to teach the skill? If so, is there a less restrictive way to achieve the goal?

*Mary Z.:* Using the criteria above, the team agreed that the following motor functions and skills were priorities for Mary's IEP.

*Positioning:* Improve ability to stand. (Mary sits for most activities, so preventing contractures is a concern; standing is appropriate for many environments and activities; participation will be enhanced as standing ability improves; feasibility at her work site is being investigated.)

*Mobility:* Wheel own chair for short distances. (This will increase independence; it will also improve strength/coordination in her arms, which may generalize to manipulation functions.)

*Manipulation:* Use pincer grasp. (This will allow more sophisticated participation in many activities; while learning this grasp, however, physical prompting will decrease independence.)

*Oral motor functions:* Chew food. (Health, participation , and social acceptance are all concerns; to protect privacy, instruction will occur at a separate snack time, rather than in the cafeteria at lunchtime.)

*Visual functions:* Scan choices in a horizontal display. (This will allow Mary to locate desired objects in her environment, as well as to use her communication board more successfully.)

The considerations noted above suggest that the team will teach some motor skills directly, but they will use alternative strategies to fulfill other functions.

## Step 4: Create adaptations that will enhance participation.

When a student has severe physical disabilities, it is appropriate to consider providing adaptations that will enhance participation, rather than teach all the motor skills required for an activity. When evaluating this option, considerations include the following:

- Will the adaptation fulfill the intended motor function?
- How will the adaptation influence other motor functions and further development of motor skills?
- Will the appearance of the adaptation influence social interactions?
- Is the adaptation simple enough so most people in the student's environment can set it up and provide instruction in its use?
- How much instruction will the student need to use the adaptation?
- What are the costs to buy, maintain, repair, and replace the adaptation?
- Is the adaptation available on loan for an evaluation period?
- Is this adaptation the most beneficial and cost-effective way to achieve participation? (That is, could time and money be spent better by teaching the actual motor skill or by using another adaptation?)

*Mary Z.:* The team considered two adaptations that would allow Mary to perform priority motor functions prior to developing the associated motor skills. The adaptations also seemed to be less restrictive than physical prompting. Finally, each adaptation increased opportunities to practice the desired motor skills, and could be faded systematically to promote skill acquisition.

*Pincer grasp:* A small plastic splint was made to hold Mary's hand open while allowing her to oppose her fingers; it can be applied easily, and is barely noticeable.

*Standing:* At home and in some school locations, a parapodium stander will be used; a stander cannot be supplied or transported to the work site, so a belt for hip support was attached to the table in the central supply area where she works; utility and durability of this adaptation will be assessed.

Mary also uses the adaptation of partial participation extensively. For example, a priority is for Mary to wheel her own chair for short distances, but a companion usually pushes her when longer distances, greater speed, and steering are required.

## WRITING GOALS AND OBJECTIVES

The process of selecting embedded motor skills began with identification of activities and environments where motor skills were required for participation. To ensure that motor skills instruction remains relevant, it is recommended that goals address these more general aspects of participation. That is, goals will specify the contexts in which the desired motor skills will be used, and the functional outcome of achieving the motor skill. Goals also need to specify observable learner behavior and describe the direction or type of change that is desired.

Objectives will focus on the priority motor functions and skills that will improve learner performance. Motor objectives, like other behavioral objectives, include three primary components: student behavior, conditions under which the behavior occurs, and criteria for achievement. Each of these components presents particular challenges when writing motor skill objectives. The student's *behavior* is defined in observable and measurable terms. Therapists may find it difficult to define their qualitative concerns related to "normal postures" and "coordination." Refocusing on what the student will be able to do when coordination improves is one way to deal with this problem. The objective includes those *conditions* for performance that are considered crucial or unique. For motor skills, important conditions might include special materials, positioning, manual stabilization of body parts, physical prompts, or procedures intended to prepare the student for participation (e.g., oral facilitation, tone normalization). It is not necessary to include every condition, however, since related information can be included in the instructional procedure. The *criteria* specify the quality or quantity of acceptable performance, and may be stated in terms of latency, duration, frequency, rate, and so forth. For motor skills, it may be appropriate to include a qualitative criterion (e.g., will roll without arching). Criteria include a second component that specifies the stability of performance over time for competence to be confirmed. The considerations described above are reflected in the following goals and objectives for Mary Z..

### Goals and Objectives for Mary Z.

#### Goal

Using the cafeteria at lunchtime, Mary will increase the rate and distance she wheels her chair to travel through the cafeteria line.

#### Objective

When positioned in her wheelchair 5 feet from her table, and prompted at the elbows, Mary will push her chair to the table (within 2 minutes, for 5 consecutive days).

**Goal**

When packaging and labeling items in the central supply department of Mercy Hospital 2 afternoons per week, Mary will increase her rate and accuracy.

**Objectives**

- When positioned standing with a belt supporting her hips, Mary will stand with her knees straight (for 12 minutes per hour, during 2 hours each day, for 3 out of 3 days).
- After wearing a palmar splint for 20 minutes of packaging, Mary will maintain use of a pincer grasp (for the next two opportunities, three of four trials per day, for 2 days).

**Goal**

During daily situations that involve eating and drinking, (snack) Mary will increase her mealtime skills.

**Objective**

- When Mary is assisted to place a chewable food between her molars, she will close her mouth and chew (for 10 seconds before attempting to remove or swallow the food, during 8 of 10 trials, for 3 consecutive days). (Chewable foods will be licorice, fruit strips, or beef jerky.)

**Goal**

Mary will purchase two or three familiar items during weekly trips to the grocery store.

**Objective**

- When given physical assistance to stabilize her head and a moving finger to track, Mary will scan items on a grocery shelf (for a distance of 3 feet, on four of five trials, during two trips to the grocery store).

## TEACHING IN MEANINGFUL CONTEXTS

Traditionally, students considered to have physical disabilities or delayed motor development have received physical therapy, occupational therapy, and/or adapted physical education services to remediate motor skill deficits. Often, students were removed from the natural environments where they needed to use motor skills, and were taught motor skills in isolated therapy rooms or the "special" gym. They learned to climb steps to nowhere, but not the school-bus steps; they learned to put pegs in a board, but not straws in their milk cartons. More recently, we have started to realize that the most important motor skills to teach are those that occur in students' natural environments and routines. Furthermore, natural environments and routines provide ample opportunities to teach a variety of new and meaningful motor skills.

The value of learning motor skills is directly related to an individual's ability to apply the targeted motor skills to activities and places that are meaningful to them and perceived as meaningful by others. Thus, the appropriateness of an "isolated therapy model" is being challenged on logical grounds. First, the isolated model is based on a "train and hope" approach (Stokes & Baer, 1977). In this approach, students receive instruction and/or therapy related to motor skills in isolated contexts while staff "hope" that the student will be able to apply the motor skill in functional situations. If isolated intervention takes place, there are three general outcomes: 1) the student will not learn the skill; 2) the student will learn the skill, but not generalize it to functional use; or 3) the student will learn the skill and be able to generalize its use to functional acitivites. Two of these three outcomes are clearly undesirable and the third is based on generalization occurring.

It may be difficult for students, especially those with severe cognitive impairments, to see the value in "climbing stairs that lead to nowhere." Isolated approaches detract from the development and implementation of shared goals and limit opportunities of the exchange of information among adults that would be necessary to facilitate improved functioning. When students are removed from typical school routines, valuable time may be wasted and students may be unduly stigmatized by the experience. Immediately moving students into isolated learning environments is not consistent with providing service in the least restrictive environment. These are some of the primary reasons why teachers, parents, and therapists are increasingly advocating alternatives to traditional isolated approaches to teaching motor skills.

The term "integrated therapy" was introduced by Sternat, Messina, Nietupski, Lyon, and Brown (1977) to describe a variation of transdisciplinary service delivery where students learn motor skills and receive the input of occupational and physical therapists in the contexts of functional activities in natural environments. Integrated therapy refers to the incorporation of educational and therapeutic techniques employed *cooperatively* to assess, plan, implement, evaluate, and report progress on common needs and goals (Giangreco, 1986). In recent years there have been a number of research studies supporting the efficacy of integrated therapy (Campbell, McInerney, & Cooper, 1984; Giangreco, 1986). Integrated therapy has logical appeal because: 1) students learn motor skills within functional routines, thus eliminating the danger of not generalizing the skill; 2) the motor skill is used in appropriate contexts, thus making it easier for the student to understand the purpose of the activity and making it inherently more motivating; 3) time can be used efficiently by combining the teaching of skills from various curricular domains; 4) parents, peers, and staff have enhanced opportunities to learn from each other, share knowledge and skills, and become released from their traditional roles; and 5) students are allowed and encouraged to remain part of the typical school routine while motor skill training methods are applied in ways that attempt to minimize any stigma associated with specialized services.

Decisions about how and where to deliver motor skills instruction will require individualized decision making. While there may be occasions when separation from the class is appropriate for reasons such as privacy or distractibility, isolated intervention should be considered the last resort, and if implemented, plans should be set forth to reintroduce the student to the natural environment. The importance and potential impact of teaching motor skills within meaningful activities and contexts cannot be overstated. By pursuing this approach parents and professionals can minimize risks to students and simultaneously offer enhanced opportunities for learning and participation.

## QUESTIONS AND ANSWERS

Q:  The therapist has recommended sensory stimulation for one student. The daily regime includes massage and a variety of tactile and vestibular stimulation. The student remains passive, and I'm not sure how I should measure progress. How can I determine when the program should be changed or when it can be discontinued?

A:  The sensory stimulation is meant to help the student organize his motor performance and prepare for functional activities. As a result, the student should tolerate handling or actively engage in some activity more successfully. Positive results might be indicated by improvements in head control, visual fixation, or ability to hold or manipulate objects. Another positive effect might be improved tolerance to handling and movement during self-care or transition routines, such as eating or changing positions. Ask the therapist what the desired effects are for this particular student, and how the stimulation is intended to improve participation in functional routines. Then identify one or two functional activities where positive effects are desired, and measure progress or effectiveness of the sensory stimulation program in relation to these activities.

Q:  One of my students requires physical prompting for many activities where he uses his hands, especially eating with a spoon. I had planned to use the prompting hierarchy that progresses from hand-over-hand guidance, to physical assistance, to verbal and/or visual prompts, to independence. But when I give hand-over-hand guidance, the student pulls his hand away. Now where do I start?

A:  The physical prompting hierarchy you described is not appropriate for all students. You need to see what type and sequence of prompts work best for your student. The hands are very sensitive, and some students find it irritating to have their hands touched; they may be especially sensitive to light touch. Ask your therapist to help identify other ways and places to prompt this student. He may be able to tolerate the situation better if he touches the object before you touch him. At lunch, try placing the spoon in his hand without touching him, and guiding movement from a less sensitive body part, such as the elbow or upper arm. Holding the spoon near your student's hand and allowing him to initiate the contact may also help him tolerate touch, since he gains some control over when and how the touch occurs.

Q:  One of my students has been working on head control over a wedge for years and there is no consistent evidence of progress. Our therapist recommends that we continue to work on head control in this position because it is a prerequisite to other motor skills. What should I do?

A:  In a developmental model, head control in prone lying and supported sitting is a skill that is practiced and achieved within the first 6 months of life. It usually comes before other gross motor and functional hand-use skills, so it has been viewed as a prerequisite for further motor development. When a child has difficulty achieving head control, however, it becomes important to look at alternative positions and/or positioning adaptations. Ask your therapist to help you identify other positions where your student can work on head control. Also ask the therapist to select or develop positioning adaptations that minimize the need for head control, so your student can practice "higher level" motor skills in functional routines. Although normal development is a useful guide, many children do not develop motor skills in the "normal" sequence. You do not have to wait for your student to master one skill in the developmental sequence before starting to teach skills at higher levels.

Q:   Where can I find task analyses of functional motor skills?

A:   You can write them, based on your own performance or your observation of others. If you will use the task analysis with young children, observe a young child perform the task. Once you have devised your task analysis, you can ask your occupational or physical therapist to help identify the critical elements of a specific movement or motor activity for use in assessment or teaching.

Q:   One of my students uses a wheelchair, a scooter board, a bean-bag chair, and a prone stander during the school day. He has been placed full time in a regular fifth-grade class, but because of his equipment, he is usually off to the side away from the other students. How can I get him more involved in group activities?

A:   Find out what the purpose of each piece of equipment is and which pieces really need to be used in the fifth grade classroom. Some equipment might be used more appropriately in other locations at school or at home. Some equipment may not be necessary at all. See if you can meet the student's positioning needs by adapting regular classroom chairs, desks, and work areas. Make every effort to have the student use materials and equipment that are unobtrusive and accessible to other students in the fifth grade. Consider age-appropriate colors and accessories to make the adaptations less noticeable.

Q:   Our educational team has worked to embed motor objectives into functional goals in the domain areas. The parents of one of my students have asked that we add 30 minutes of daily physical therapy (PT) to their son's education program. What should we do?

A:   There are several things to consider. First, consider the outcomes that parents may want when they make this type of request. Discuss the parents' priorities that they hope to achieve through the PT program. These outcomes need to be addressed. You may need to demonstrate how these concerns are or can be addressed in the context of instruction in functional activities. Show the parents how their child will have more opportunities to practice the skill in functional routines than if only practiced in therapy. Devise ways to show that the possible opportunities do actually occur, and make regular progress reports to the parents. Second, sometimes parents don't know what they want their child to achieve in PT, but they know that their physician recommended it. They are concerned that their child may have permanent damage or lose a critical opportunity if therapy is not received. Their concerns may be real. It is up to you to help the parents determine which of the child's many needs are priorities, and how those priorities might best be addressed. This will require communication with all others who are involved in the care of the child, and must go beyond the school-based team. More frequent communication and informal education may be needed. In particular, be prepared to assist parents in articulating the philosophy and methods of embedding motor skills within functional daily routines.

Finally, you may agree that PT is needed, but you think it should be carried out at home; there are only so many things that can be done during the school day. However, many parents have been implementing PT programs since their children were babies. There comes a time when both parent and child need to be relieved of this relationship, so other more appropriate life roles can develop in the family. Give the parents opportunities to become involved in other aspects of their child's program, and assure them that their child's motor needs will be addressed.

## REFERENCES

Bricker, W.A., & Campbell, P.H. (1980). Interdisciplinary assessment and programming for multihandicapped students. In W. Sailor, B. Wilcox, & L. Brown (Eds.), *Methods of instruction for severely handicapped students* (pp. 3–45). Baltimore: Paul H. Brookes Publishing Co.

Campbell, P., McInerney, W., & Cooper, M. (1984). Therapeutic programming for students with severe handicaps. *American Journal of Occupational Therapy, 38*(9), 594–602.

Giangreco, M. (1986). Effects of integrated therapy: A pilot study. *Journal of The Association for Persons with Severe Handicaps, 11*, 205–208.

Horowitz, L., & Sharby, N. (1988). Development of prone extension postures in healthy infants. *Physical Therapy, 68*(1), 32–36.

Hulme, J.B., Poor, R., Schulein, M., & Pezzino, J. (1983). Perceived behavioral changes observed with adaptive seating devices and training programs for multihandicapped, developmentally disabled individuals. *Physical Therapy, 63*(2), 204–208.

Loria, C. (1980). Relationship of proximal and distal function in motor development. *Physical Therapy, 60*(2), 167–172.

McCormick, L., Cooper, M., & Goldman, R. (1979). Training teachers to maximize instructional time provided to severely and profoundly handicapped children. *AAESPH Review, 4*(3), 301–310.

Rainforth, B., & Salisbury, C. (1988). Functional home programs: A model for therapists. *Topics in Early Childhood Special Education, 7*(4), 33–45.

Sternat, J., Messina, R., Nietupski, J., Lyon, S., & Brown, L. (1977). Occupational and physical therapy services for severely handicapped students: Toward a naturalized public school service delivery model. In E. Sontag, J. Smith, & N. Certo (Eds.), *Educational programming for the severely and profoundly handicapped* (pp. 263–278). Reston, VA: Council for Exceptional Children, Division on Mental Retardation.

Stokes, T., & Baer, D. (1977). An implicit technology of generalization. *Journal of Applied Behavior Analysis, 10*(2), 349–367.

York, J. (1987). *Mobility methods used and their effectiveness in home and community environments for individuals with physical disabilities.* Unpublished doctoral dissertation, University of Wisconsin, Madison.

## ADDITIONAL READINGS AND RESOURCES

Baumgart, D., Brown, L., Pumpian, I., Nisbet, J., Ford, A., Sweet, M., Messina, R., & Schroeder, J. (1982). Principle of partial participation and individualized adaptations in educational programs for severely handicapped students. *Journal of The Association for the Severely Handicapped, 7*(2), 17–27.

Bigge, J. (Ed.). (1982). *Teaching individuals with physical and multiple disabilities.* Columbus, OH: Charles E. Merrill.

Campbell, P. (1987a). Integrated programming for students with multiple handicaps. In L. Goetz., D. Guess, & K. Stremel-Campbell (Eds.), *Innovative program design for individuals with dual sensory impairments* (pp. 159–188). Baltimore: Paul H. Brookes Publishing Co.

Campbell, P. (1987b). The integrated programming team: An approach for coordinating professionals of various disciplines in programs for students with severe and multiple handicaps. *Journal of The Association for Persons with Severe Handicaps, 12*, 107–116.

Campbell, P. (1987c). Physical handling and management procedures with students with severe movement dysfunction. In M. Snell (Ed.), *Systematic instruction of persons with severe handicaps* (3rd ed., pp. 188–211). Columbus, OH: Charles E. Merrill.

Campbell, P., & Stewart, B. (1986). Measuring changes in movement skills with infants and young children with handicaps. *Journal of the Association for Persons with Severe Handicaps, 11*, 153–161.

Cohen, M., & Gross, P. (1979). *The developmental resource: Behavioral sequences for assessment and program planning* (Vol. 1). New York: Grune & Stratton.

Connor, F., Williamson, B., & Seipp, J. (1978). *Program guide for infants and toddlers with neuromotor and other developmental disabilities.* New York: Columbia University–Teachers' College Press.

Dennis, R., Reichle, J., Williams, W., & Vogelsberg, T. (1982). Motor factors influencing the selection of vocabulary for sign production programs. *Journal of The Association for the Severely Handicapped, 7*(1), 20–32.

Donnellan, A. (1984). The criterion of the least dangerous assumption. *Behavioral Disorders, 9*(2), 141–150.

Erhardt, R.P. (1975). Sequential levels in development of prehension. *American Journal of Occupational Therapy, 8*(10), 592–597.

Erhardt, R.P. (1982). *Developmental hand dysfunction: Theory, assessment, treatment.* Laurel, MD: RAMSCO.

Erhardt, R.P. (1987). Sequential levels in the visual-motor development of a child with cerebral palsy. *American Journal of Occupational Therapy, 41*(1), 43–49.

Erhardt, R.P., Beattie, P.A., & Hertsgaard, D. (1981). A prehension assessment for handicapped children. *American Journal of Occupational Therapy, 35*(4), 237–242.

Finnie, N. (1975). *Handling the young cerebral palsied child at home* (2nd ed.) New York: E.P. Dutton.

Fraser, B.A., & Hensinger, R.N. (1983). *Managing physical handicaps. A practical guide for parents, care providers, and educators.* Baltimore: Paul H. Brookes Publishing Co.

Gilfoyle, E., Grady, A., & Moore, J. (1981). *Children adapt.* Thoroughfare, NJ: Charles B. Slack.

Goetz, L., & Gee, K. (1987). Functional vision programming: A model for teaching visual behaviors in natural contexts. In L. Goetz., D. Guess, & K. Stremel-Campbell (Eds.), *Innovative program design for students with dual sensory impairments* (pp. 77–97). Baltimore: Paul H. Brookes Publishing Co.

Guess, D., & Helmstetter, E. (1986). Skill cluster instruction and the individualized curriculum sequencing model. In R.H. Horner, L.H. Meyer, & H.D.B. Fredericks (Eds.), *Education of learners with severe handicaps: Exemplary service strategies* (pp. 221–248). Baltimore: Paul H. Brookes Publishing Co.

Hansen, M., & Harris, S. (1986). *Teaching the young child with motor delays: A guide for parents and professionals.* Austin, TX: PRO-ED.

Leavitt, S. (1982). *Treatment of cerebral palsy and motor delay* (2nd ed.). Boston: Blackwell Scientific Publications.

Levin, J., & Scherfenberg, L. (1986). *Breaking barriers. How children and adults with severe handicaps can access the world through simple technology.* Minneapolis: Ablenet.

Levin, J., & Scherfenberg, L. (1987). *Selection and use of simple technology in home, school, work, and community settings.* Minneapolis: Ablenet.

Lyon, S., & Lyon, G. (1980). Team functioning and staff development: A role release approach to providing integrated educational services for severely handicapped students. *Journal of The Association for the Severely Handicapped, 5*(3), 250–263.

McCormick, L., Cooper, M., & Goldman, R. (1979). Training teachers to maximize instructional time provided to severely and profoundly handicapped children. *AAESPH Review, 4*(3), 301–310.

Morris, S., & Klein, M. (1987). *Pre-feeding skills: A comprehensive resource for feeding development.* Tucson, AZ: Therapy Skill Builders.

Orelove, F., & Hanley, C. (1979). Modifying school buildings for the severely handicapped: A school accessibility survey. *AAESPH Review, 4*(3), 219–236.

Orelove, F.P., & Sobsey, F. (1987). Sensory impairments. In F.P. Orelove & D. Sobsey, *Educating children with multiple disabilities: A transdisciplinary approach* (pp. 105–128). Baltimore: Paul H. Brookes Publishing Co.

Rainforth, B., & York, J. (1987a). Handling and positioning. In F.P. Orelove & D. Sobsey, *Educating students with multiple disabilities: A transdisciplinary approach* (pp. 67–103). Baltimore: Paul H. Brookes Publishing Co.

Rainforth, B., & York, J. (1987b). Integrating related services in community instruction. *Journal of The Association for Persons with Severe Handicaps, 12*, 190–198.

Sobsey, D., & Ludlow, B. (1984). Guidelines for setting instructional criteria. *Education and Treatment of Children, 7*, 157–165.

York, J., & Rainforth, B. (1987). Developing instructional adaptations. In F.P. Orelove & D. Sobsey, *Educating students with multiple disabilities: A transdisciplinary approach* (pp. 183–217). Baltimore: Paul H. Brookes Publishing Co.

# SECTION VI

# Implementation Strategies

In previous sections of this guide we focused on *what* activities and skills could be included in a student's educational program from the community-referenced curriculum. In this section, we shift our attention to "how" to implement the curriculum. There are many implementation strategies that could be covered. We could include lengthy discussions on the topics of student motivation, learning styles, lesson planning, record keeping, classroom dynamics, peer tutoring, and so forth. However, in order to make this section manageable, we narrowed down the strategies to those that seem to have the greatest impact on implementing community-referenced curricula and have presented them within Chapters 13–16: "Developing Individualized Education Programs" (IEPs), "Scheduling," "Managing Classroom Operations," and "Planning and Implementing Activity-Based Lessons." We recognize that teachers will (and should) use these recommended strategies selectively, based on their own experiences, knowledge, students' needs, classroom needs, and other program development variables.

The first chapter in this section concerns developing IEPs. It is likely that you and your district have already developed an approach to writing IEPs. Perhaps some of the new dimensions that this chapter offers are: 1) ways to write IEPs that not only articulate students' needs in the community-living areas, but also clearly establish their involvement in other areas of the typical school program; 2) a process for actively involving parents and students in the IEP decision-making process; and 3) ways for the team leader to secure and manage input from a variety of sources.

The chapter on scheduling takes you through a step-by-step process for designing a weekly schedule that reflects the individual needs of each student on your class-list. This process is illustrated through two case examples; one at the elementary school level, and the other at the secondary level. The next chapter deals with managing classroom operations. It includes strategies for working with paraprofessionals, enhancing integration, organizing instructional sessions for a diverse group of learners, and managing logistical constraints (e.g., policy limitations, limited funds, transportation problems). The final chapter outlines strategies for planning and implementing activity-based lessons.

# CHAPTER 13

# Developing Individualized Education Programs

*Roberta Schnorr and Alison Ford*

An individualized education program (IEP) is required for all students who are identified as having a handicapping condition and who are receiving special education services. The IEP should include the following information:

- Student's current performance
- Long- and short-term educational goals
- Special education and related services to be provided
- Timelines for initiation and completion of services
- Percentage of time and activity in regular and special education
- Extent to which the learner will participate in activities with nonhandicapped peers
- Means for evaluating student progress

Parent participation is essential to the IEP process. Parents have a wealth of information about their children that can provide an important foundation from which to develop the IEP. They have knowledge about their child's preferences, skills and routines, the way leisure time is spent, relationships with family and friends, and other pertinent information that is likely to influence their child's program.

A successful IEP process will not only enlist the active participation of parents, but will ensure the meaningful participation of each member of a student's team. In addition to parents and the primary teacher(s), the team might include a speech/language therapist, a physical therapist, an occupational therapist, a vocational teacher (for older students), and the student.

## THE IEP PROCESS

There are many approaches used to develop IEPs. We have identified eight key steps in the IEP process. These steps are: 1) review current information, 2) secure parental involvement, 3) evaluate the most recent IEP and outline ideas for revision, 4) prepare for the IEP conference, 5) conduct the IEP conference, 6) write the formal IEP, 7) secure parent signatures, and 8) update the IEP.

### Step 1: Review current information.

There are many sources of information available to you as you begin the IEP process. It is essential to review all available information to gain a general understanding of the learner's acquired skills, learning style, and needs. Some sources of information you may rely upon to gain this understanding include:

1. **Key documents from the cumulative folder:** Cumulative folders should contain IEPs, progress reports, medical histories, and other documents. In some cases, these documents provide extremely useful information about the learner. Unfortunately, in other cases, these documents offer little information that relates to constructive programming. Nonetheless, they should be examined to gain an understanding of the student's previous learning opportunities and services.

2. **Direct observation and interaction with student across a variety of settings:** Of course, it would not be possible to design a meaningful IEP without the input of the student. Some students may not be able to provide information through interviews or other verbal exchanges. Thus, to become more fully acquainted with a student, direct observation and regular contact in both school and non-school situations are essential. Observation should help the teacher answer questions that might not be answered through other sources. Some examples of these questions are:

   a. To what extent does the student participate in routines at home?

   b. With whom does he or she spend leisure time during after-school hours?

   c. How does the student express himself or herself at home, in school, and in the community?

   d. How does the student participate in activities outside of home or school?

   e. To what extent has he or she developed relationships with nonhandicapped peers?

3. **Home-school collaboration:** As previously mentioned, parents have a wealth of information about their children. By maintaining regular communication with families, teachers will develop a more comprehensive and accurate understanding of a student's abilities, learning styles, needs, and behavior.

4. **Up-to-date curriculum materials:** Curriculum materials that reflect the most promising educational practices can be useful sources of information. Well-constructed guides enhance the probability that decisions will be made within a longitudinal framework. A district-wide curriculum fosters planning and preparation as part of the overall program, with an emphasis on getting individuals ready for each major transition.

Completion of Step 1 should provide the teacher with an initial summary and hypotheses regarding each of the following:

- Learner's most recent education program and goals; clues to his or her learning style
- Related services that the student received in the past
- Formal evaluation results from past assessments
- Learner's level of participation in various settings (including home) and the strength of his or her social network
- Interests and preferences of the learner

### Step 2: Secure parental involvement.

Active home-school collaboration often depends on a certain amount of preparedness. Teachers and parents can facilitate the IEP process by organizing their contributions and priorities according to a similar structure. Teachers may want to gather information in a more open-ended manner by posing general questions to parents during a telephone conversation in the week preceding the IEP planning conference.

Review of the forms provided in Appendix A at the end of this guide may help teachers to organize their thoughts about the kinds of general questions they might ask to learn about parents' priorities for the student's school program. Consider the conversation that took place when Mary Z.'s teacher called Mrs. Z. prior to the IEP conference:

*Mary Z.:* Mary's teacher began the conversation by saying, "Mrs. Z., in order to be better prepared for the upcoming IEP conference, I thought I would get some ideas from you regarding Mary's needs. How are you feeling, generally, about the kinds of activities that are on Mary's IEP? Should I be thinking about some areas that you would like to see changed . . . added?"

Mrs. Z. talked about how Mary seems to get along fine in most activities—her morning routine, getting up and ready for school, mealtimes, wheeling around the neighborhood with her sister or brother, watching TV in the evening with the family, getting ready for bed, and so forth. While Mary needs assistance with most routines, one of the only really difficult times reported was shampooing—she often acts angry and uncooperative at this time. Mrs. Z. mentioned that the most trying times in general were weekends and school vacations—that it was difficult to help Mary fill the hours when there was a lot of free time.

After listening and taking notes about these concerns, Mary's teacher responded, "I see what you're saying. I'll be sure to schedule some time at the planning meeting to see how we can work on some of these things as part of her school program. It sounds like Mary spends most of her time with you and other family members. Does she do things in the community with you— like shopping and going out to eat?"

Mrs. Z. talked about Mary going to the mall—that's something she likes a lot. She doesn't go with her mother to the grocery store often, because it's difficult to shop with her unless an additional person is available to help. Mary loves to go to restaurants, especially fast-food places like McDonald's and Burger King.

Mary's teacher asked a few general questions throughout the conversation to try and get a picture of how Mary participates in these different settings and how people assist her. He also reminded Mrs. Z. about a previous conversation that they had about Mary's participation in community-based vocational training. Based on this conversation, he promised to schedule time on the planning conference agenda to discuss Mary's needs for free time, as well as ideas for her first "work site." He offered to share copies of the "Student Preference" and "Parent Input on Recreation/Leisure" forms (from Appendix A) to help Mrs. Z. identify more specific free-time needs that might be addressed in the IEP. Mrs. Z. asked him to send these copies home to review before the conference, although she wasn't sure she would have time to fill them out. He also made a note to consider school-day opportunities to work on shampooing with Mary.

Some parents and teachers find it helpful to use a parent input form to structure information in a way that will lead directly to developing IEP goals. (Sample forms are included in Appendix A at the end of this guide.) Of course, any parent input form should be used in a flexible manner, and consideration should be given to the timing of its use. Certain forms might only be used at particular points of a student's career, or for situations that are of special concern to parents. For example, the vocational form may be most helpful when a student is entering middle school (and beginning community-based vocational training), and later as he or she approaches transition from school to work. Parents would rarely be asked to complete the entire set of forms, and even if this were the case, they would certainly not be expected to repeat this task every year. There may be times when the forms would not be sent home at all. Some parents may prefer to go through the inventory items over the phone, or during an informal meeting with the teacher at home or school.

Completion of Step 2 should lead to:

- Information from parents regarding their child's functioning during nonschool hours
- Identification of parent concerns and priorities to include in the agenda for the upcoming IEP planning conference

### Step 3: Evaluate the most recent IEP and outline ideas for revision.

Unless a student has just been referred for special education, there should be an IEP from last year's program or one developed for the current year. Even if the dates on the IEP are current (for this school year), it should be reviewed and evaluated. As you evaluate the IEP, you will undoubtedly come up with ideas for revising it. Below are some steps that may be useful in this initial revision process.

1. Evaluate the previous IEP and reorganize headings to reflect priority content areas. For example:

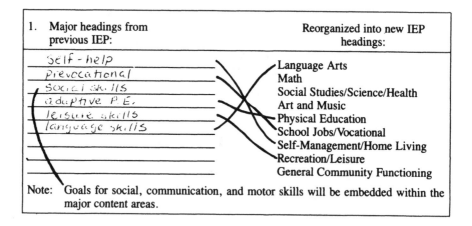

| 1. Major headings from previous IEP: | Reorganized into new IEP headings: |
|---|---|
| Self-help | Language Arts |
| Prevocational | Math |
| Social skills | Social Studies/Science/Health |
| Adaptive P.E. | Art and Music |
| Leisure skills | Physical Education |
| Language skills | School Jobs/Vocational |
| | Self-Management/Home Living |
| | Recreation/Leisure |
| | General Community Functioning |

Note: Goals for social, communication, and motor skills will be embedded within the major content areas.

2. List activities from the previous IEP that should be retained. Use the IEP *Conference Planning Form* (Form 13.1) to complete this step.
3. List possible new activities on the IEP *Conference Planning Form*.
4. Share the outline of possible activities with other teachers and therapists who will be working with the learner. Ask them to augment activities to reflect their specific intervention concerns.
5. Parents would also have an opportunity to complete their own *Conference Planning Forms* as a part of Step 2. Student preferences should also be noted. A friend, parent and/or teacher could help the student indicate preferences. If the student is not able to reveal preferences in this manner, the worksheet could be completed by asking the following questions: 1) "Do we know of any preferences that Mary has in this area (e.g., recreation/leisure)?", and 2) "What are they?" (e.g., "She enjoys music, likes to be with other teenagers"), and 3) "How do we know that she feels this way?" (e.g., "She gets very excited when music is played and when others are around. She shows signs of pleasure in general body language and facial expression.").

Conference Planning Form: IEP Priorities

Student: _Mary Z._          Teacher: _Doug L._          Date: _Sept. 22, 1989_

Parent: _____          Others: _____

| Content areas: | Activities to retain: | New priorities | | | Team decisions about IEP activities |
|---|---|---|---|---|---|
| | | Parent | Student | Teacher/ therapist | |
| Language arts | | | | | |
| Math | Continue to address math skills within daily routines. | | | Money handling | |
| Social studies/science/health | | | | | |
| Art and music | Art class? | | | | |
| Physical education | Swimming? | | | | |
| School jobs/ vocational | | | Opportunities for interactions with co-workers new tasks? | | |
| Self-management/ home living | Eating Snack and meal prep | | Hall locker Home Ec 8? Follow picture schedule | | |
| Recreation/leisure | Using cassette player | | Art 8 Use public library Check extracurric. options | | |

Conference Planning Form: IEP Priorities (continued)

Student: _Mary Z._                Teacher: _Doug L._                Date: _Sept. 22, 1989_

Parent: _____        Others: _____

| Content areas: | Activities to retain: | New priorities | | | Team decisions about IEP activities |
| | | Parent | Student | Teacher/ therapist | |
|---|---|---|---|---|---|
| General community functioning | Choose foods- school cafeteria | | | Grocery shopping | |
| Social | | | | Initiate and maintain contact with peers | |
| Embedded — Communication | | | | | |
| Motor | | | | | |

Completion of Step 3 should lead to:

- Tentative outline of possible activities (continued and new) that can serve as a framework for discussion at the IEP conference (list may change considerably at the conference, where parents and other team members will be asked for further input about their priorities)
- Incorporation of related services

### Step 4: Prepare for the IEP conference.

Because of their key role in developing the IEP, conference arrangements should be made in consultation with parents. The form entitled *The IEP Conference: Participants and Meeting Arrangements* (see Appendix A at the end of this guide) asks parents to indicate their preferences with regard to the following questions:

1. **Who will attend the planning conference?** Either the parents or the school district may invite others to the conference. Parents may wish to bring a relative or friend for support; or, they may want to invite others who interact with the learner in nonschool settings (recreation staff, child care providers, etc.). A friend of the student might be invited to participate in the session. (The *McGill Action Plan-*

*ning System [MAPS]* is a process developed by Marsha Forest and Judith Snow [1986] that relies heavily on peer input.) Efforts should be made to include a manageable number of people. Also, attempts should be made to avoid turning the meeting into a "reporting session," where one professional after another reports on the progress of a student, leaving very little time for actual planning.

2. **When will the conference be held?** A date and time should be selected according to parent availability. Be sure to allow enough time and give parents an idea of how long the conference may take. Try to allow flexibility regarding the ending time. (Avoid scheduling back-to-back conferences.)

3. **Where will the conference be held?** School, home, or other options may be considered.

4. **What special arrangements are needed?** Make every effort to assist parents in making arrangements for child care or transportation that will ensure their participation.

When the conference is held, use the time wisely. To ensure that key issues are addressed, the teacher should prepare an agenda and planning worksheet. Since time will not allow for each content area to be discussed in detail, the agenda should note the *priority* areas that will have time reserved for discussion. These might include areas of concern to the parents (e.g., Mary—leisure-time needs) as well as teacher concerns (e.g., reserving time to talk about a new component, such as community vocational training).

It is recommended that all participants (e.g., parents, therapists, teachers) receive a copy of the agenda at least several days before the conference. An example conference agenda is provided in Form 13.2.

---

FORM 13.2

### IEP Planning Conference Agenda

Student: _Mary Z._   Meeting Place: _____

Date of Conference: _September 22_   Time: _2:30 - 4:00_

Planning Committee:

| | |
|---|---|
| Mrs Z. (parent) | Anna G. (vice principal) |
| Mary Z. (student) | Cheri L. (speech & language therapist) |
| Linda T. (friend - 8th grader) | Roseann B. (teacher) |
| Doug L. (teacher) | Tom B. (physical therapist) |

1. Introductions and review agenda (5 minutes)
2. Explain IEP planning form (3 minutes)
3. Which activities do we want to keep from last IEP? (10 minutes)
4. What new activities should be included?
   a. List parent priorities for each content area (5 minutes)—this should be a sufficient time allotment since you are only listing items; discussion will occur during item #5 of the agenda.
   b. List student priorities (5 minutes)
   c. List teacher and therapist priorities (5 minutes)
5. Review lists; identify highest priorities and discuss them (40 minutes)
   a. _Leisure activities_
   b. _Community-based vocational training_
   c. _____
   d. _____
6. Identify and briefly discuss any remaining new activities (15 minutes)
7. Summary of activities to be addressed in new IEP (5 minutes)
8. Conclude meeting and discuss steps to come (5 minutes)

Completion of Step 4 should lead to:

- Confirmed IEP conference appointment
- Identification of who will attend the conference
- Written agenda for the conference, which has been sent to each participant

## Step 5: Conduct the IEP conference.

The teacher may lead the group through the planning process. A suggested step-by-step procedure for leading an IEP conference is outlined below.

1. **Open meeting (5 minutes):** Pass out copies of the agenda. Introduce all participants and describe their roles. Review the purpose of the conference and go over the agenda, including the time alloted for each task. Determine whether any changes are needed in the agenda.
2. **Explain *Conference Planning Form* (3 minutes):** Pass out blank copies of the *Conference Planning Form*, which will be used to summarize the information discussed during the conference. This form is organized into content area headings that will be reflected in the IEP. Explain each heading briefly, especially if they are different from those in previous IEPs. One person should be identified as the primary recorder of information.
3. **Determine activities to be retained from previous IEP (10 minutes):** Review the activities to be retained from the previous IEP. Gain a consensus of group members for each area that has a continued activity.
4. **List parent priorities (5 minutes):** Go through each content area and list priorities as shared by parents (hold discussion until all lists are shared).
5. **List student priorities (5 minutes):** Go through each content area and list student priorities (hold discussion at this time).
6. **List teacher and therapist priorities (5 minutes):** Go through each content area and list professional members' priorities (hold discussion at this time).
7. **Identify and discuss high-priority content areas (40 minutes):** Discuss student needs and activities for the areas that were identified on the agenda as being of highest priority, as determined by preliminary contacts with parents and professionals. For example, Mary Z.'s mother was most concerned about her needs during free time. Her teacher felt a need to discuss community vocational training—a new area. If any other priorities arise during the meeting—and if time permits—discuss them. If there isn't sufficient time, indicate the need to schedule another meeting to discuss these additional priorities. The discussion should end with a list of new activities (including settings) that the group recommends for addressing these priority areas.
8. **Identify and briefly discuss new activities for remaining content areas (15 minutes):** Discuss and list new activities (including settings) for each remaining content area.
9. **Summarize all activities to be addressed in the IEP (5 minutes):** Review each content area and briefly summarize the team decisions.
10. **Conclude the meeting (5 minutes):** Identify any follow-up responsibilities (writing objectives, scheduling an additional meeting, etc.). Give parents and other team members a legible copy of today's conference form to take with them. Thank all for their valuable participation.

Completion of Step 5 should lead to:

- Identification and written copy of priority activities for goals based upon parent, student, and professional input
- Identification of those responsible for preparing the formal version of the IEP

## Step 6: Write the formal IEP.

Typically, the teacher assumes responsibility for developing the formal draft of the IEP. Other personnel (related services providers, other teachers) may write the objectives for any goals for which they are responsible.

It is very important that parents and other planners recognize their input in the formal IEP. Items from the *Conference Planning Form* (Form 13.3) should be clearly related to the content of the IEP. (A complete listing of IEP goals and objectives for Mary Z. is presented in Appendix E at the end of the *Guide.*)

1. **Review the IEP for quality:** Review the written draft of the IEP. Does the IEP:
   a. reflect parent concerns and priorities?
   b. reflect the student's interests?
   c. reflect chronological age appropriateness?
   d. indicate the settings and situations in which skills will be learned?
   e. include objectives that involve the participation of nonhandicapped peers?
   f. have an appropriate balance between school and community goals?
   g. clearly state the accomplishments expected of the student—no matter how severely disabled?
   h. contain an appropriate number of objectives?
   i. closely resemble the outline of goals developed at the planning conference?
   j. contain language that is understandable—jargon-free?
2. **Revise IEP if necessary:** Make final changes if needed.

Completion of Step 6 should lead to:

- IEP that has been written to reflect the input of participants in the planning process

## Step 7: Secure parent signatures.

Once the IEP has been written, parents and other planners must sign the formal copy as evidence of their participation in its development. Here again, parents may differ in how they wish to complete this step. Some parents may desire another conference to review the formal IEP in detail with the teacher. Others may find it more convenient to review a copy at home with an opportunity to discuss comments or questions by phone. This review may prompt a request for additions or modifications. A copy of the IEP should be readily available to all staff members and, of course, parents should receive a personal copy for their records.

Completion of Step 7 should result in:

- Copies of the signed IEP being distributed to parents and others who will implement its components

## Step 8: Update the IEP.

The IEP process must be responsive to the ongoing needs of the student. At any point during the year, amendments to the IEP in the form of modifications, addenda, and so

Conference Planning Form: IEP Priorities

Student: **Mary Z.**　　Teacher: **Doug L.**　　Date: **Sept. 22, 1989**

Parent: **Mrs W. Z.**　　Others: **Linda T., Anna G., Cheri L., Roseann B., Tom B.**

| Content areas: | Activities to retain: | New priorities | | | Team decisions about IEP activities |
|---|---|---|---|---|---|
| | | Parent | Student | Teacher/therapist | |
| Language arts | Listening to stories | | Likes the school library. Likes looking at photos. | | Listening to stories / Looking at books and magazines / Developing a photo journal |
| Math | Continue to address math skills within daily routines | | | Money handling | Making daily purchases (school & community) / Follow picture schedule for transitions |
| Social studies/science/health | | | | | |
| Art and music | Art class | Schedule with non-handicapped students | | | Art 8 / IA 9 (Industrial Arts - Wood) |
| Physical education | Swimming | | Swimming | | PE 8 - swimming |
| School jobs/vocational | | Office setting? | Quiet environment | Opportunities for interactions w/co-workers, new tasks? | Develop community job site (office? packaging at hospital) / Train work-related skills |
| Self-management/home living | Eating / Snack & meal prep. / Dressing & undressing / Using the toilet | Simple breakfasts / Shampooing | | Use hall locker / Home Ec 8? / Follow picture schedule | Eating / Home Ec snack/food prep / Use picture schedule / Use restrooms (school, community) / shampoo & dress (swimming) / Hall locker - w/partner |
| Recreation/leisure | Using cassette tape player / Swimming / Art | Activities for after-school and weekends, expand number of activities | Enjoys computer games | Art 8 / Use public library / Check extracurricular options | Computer Club / Tape player / Swimming (PE 8) & Art 8 / Use public library / Table games (2nd semester Pictionary) / Determine other preferences |

FORM 13.3

Conference Planning Form: IEP Priorities *(continued)*

Student: Mary Z.  Teacher: Doug L.  Date: Sept. 22, 1989

Parent: Mrs. W.Z.  Others: Linda T., AnnaG., CheriL., Roseann B., Tom B.

| Content areas: | Activities to retain: | New priorities | | | Team decisions about IEP activities |
|---|---|---|---|---|---|
| | | Parent | Student | Teacher/ therapist | |
| General community functioning | Choose foods – school cafeteria | | Likes fast-food restaurants | Grocery shopping | School cafeteria Grocery shopping (1x week) Fast-food restaurant (1x week) |
| Embedded — Social | Requesting assistance Using acceptable manners | Maintain contact with circle of friends | To keep peers involved | Initiate and maintain contact with peers | Address these social skills priorities within above activities |
| Embedded — Communication | Using gestures to to express desires | Use more gestures (to tell when she wants to "stop") | | Use picture symbol board & booklets; make requests, acknowledge – what's next?" | Address these communication skills within above activities |
| Embedded — Motor | Refine grasp for efficiency Increase mobility (wheelchair) | | Help achieve comfortable positions | Weight-bearing (use standing frame) | Address these motor skills within above activities |

forth, may occur. These changes may be initiated by either the parent or one of the instructors. Some reasons for updating the IEP may be: 1) progress is not evident, indicating the need for change in instructional objectives; and 2) new priority goals are identified. Amendments to the IEP should be documented on formal copies of the IEP and reviewed with parents. Updated signatures should be obtained for these changes.

Completion of Step 8 should result in:

- Timely revisions of the IEP, based upon learner progress and changing needs

## Final Remarks

The eight steps described in the IEP process are provided as guidelines for teachers and parents as they develop individualized programs that include community-referenced curriculum goals. Just as each student will have a unique, individual plan, the process for developing that plan will also vary somewhat from family to family and teacher to teacher. It is anticipated that the preceding eight steps will be modified for individual use, according to the needs of participants. However, it is important to acknowledge that the parent-teacher partnership conveyed in this step-by-step process is fundamental to the successful development of an IEP.

## QUESTIONS AND ANSWERS

Q:  I think IEP conferences are important, but only a few of my students' parents come to the meetings. How can I encourage parents to come to these meetings?

A:  First of all, you need to give careful consideration to how conferences are scheduled. Are all parents expected to come in during the school-day, before 3:00? Is the school the only location where the meetings can be held? Try to get information from individual parents about when they would be available before you begin to schedule conference appointments. If transportation is a problem, you might offer to have the conference at their home, or at a location in their neighborhood (e.g., another school, a community center, a conference room of the public library). If child care is a problem, can someone be recruited to provide such services?

Q:  During the planning conference, I always take time to explain each goal so the parents will understand the IEP before I ask them to sign it. But they hardly ever have anything to contribute to the IEP. The meetings take a lot of time, and sometimes I think I might as well send the IEP home for them to read and sign. Is that an acceptable alternative?

A:  No. The "planning" conference time should be used for that purpose—to "plan" the IEP with the active participation of all team members, *including* parents. To conduct a conference after the IEP (or a "draft") has already been written puts parents (and other team members) in a poor position for anything beyond token participation.

Q:  Since the goal of my program is to prepare students for active participation in the community, I have organized my IEPs according to the following headings: domestic, general community, leisure, and vocational. However, many of the parents I've met with are very concerned about this. They are complaining about a lack of academics, although I've included academic goals as they relate to the headings just listed. How can I explain to them that this is the right way to think about their child's school program?

A:  This isn't necessarily the "right" way, or the only way to organize IEPs. What is important is that the parents (and other team members) can make sense of the way the IEP is structured so they can contribute in a meaningful way. While the community living areas are important, they only represent a portion of the entire scope of a student's school program. Familiar headings such as language arts, math, social studies, art, and music should be included even if a child's goals in these areas are different from the traditional academic classroom activities. Language arts goals might include learning to read picture symbols, or practicing communication skills. Math could address goals for handling money in purchasing situations, or time management. It might be helpful to list these more familiar headings first, and then the relevant community living areas. This kind of organization would better reflect the balance of activities that is important for each student.

Q:  It seems that many of my students do not achieve a large proportion of their IEP objectives within a given school year. The result is that some objectives are repeated during successive school years. What can I do to help prevent this when writing IEP objectives?

A:   Perhaps more attention needs to be given to the *criteria* noted for each objective. Criteria should answer the following question: "When will I know that the student has mastered this objective—that I can now move on to a more sophisticated objective for this skill or teach a new skill?" Examples of performance criteria that could be included to address this question are statements related to latency (e.g., "within one minute"), frequency (e.g., "four times"), and duration (e.g., "for three minutes"). For example, Mary Z. is using a predetermined-amount strategy to make purchases. One of her shopping objectives may state that she will hand over the correct amount of money when positioned in front of the cashier *within 5 seconds of the clerk's request, for three consecutive opportunities*. After Mary has demonstrated the behavior at the stated criteria, a new or revised objective should replace this one.

## REFERENCE

Forest, M., & Snow, J. (1986). *McGill action planning system (MAPS)*. Toronto: Center for Integration, Frontier College.

## ADDITIONAL READINGS AND RESOURCES

Cutler, B. (1981). *Unraveling the special education maze: An action guide for parents*. Champaign, IL: Research Press.

Forest, M. (Producer). (1988). *With a little help from my friends* [Video]. Toronto: Center for Integration, Frontier College.

Turnbull, A., Strickland, B., & Brantley, J. (1978). *Developing and implementing individualized education programs*. Columbus, OH: Charles E. Merrill.

# Scheduling

### *Linda Davern and Alison Ford*

Designing and implementing an effective schedule may be one of the most challenging tasks faced by teachers. The many decisions that are made during the scheduling process can be directed by a set of guidelines based on both practical and philosophical concerns. This chapter presents such guidelines as well as a step-by-step process that can be used in designing a schedule.

## SCHEDULING GUIDELINES

The hypothetical example[1] presented in the following paragraphs illustrates how various factors related to scheduling can influence the quality of a student's experience:

> Sarah, age 9, was met at the bus and wheeled toward her class. A friend tried to stop her in the hall to show her his new game, but the teacher wheeling Sarah only stopped for a brief moment. Sarah was pushed to her locker where her jacket was removed for her and placed on a hook. The bag attached to the back of her wheelchair was emptied by the teacher; this included a change of clothing and a notebook that was passed daily between the teacher and Sarah's parents.
>
> Sarah was wheeled to her classroom and sat near the doorway while the teacher read the notes and placed her extra clothing in the changing room. She continued to wait while the assistant and teacher went to help other classmates. Finally, another third grader, who noticed Sarah's situation, came over, greeted her, and asked her if she wanted to go into the classroom.
>
> A short while later she was wheeled to the bathroom. She was lifted and placed on a toilet specially adapted for her. The teacher left to assist another student in the hall and returned a few minutes later. Sometimes Sarah was expected to participate in washing her hands, but on this day the teacher must have been in a hurry because she quickly washed Sarah's hands, without expecting her to initiate any movements.
>
> Back in her classroom, Sarah was wheeled to the computer for an instructional session with a teaching assistant who was assigned to work one-to-one with her. Another child came over to join them but was asked not to interrupt the instruction. After this activity, Sarah was pulled from class for a speech therapy session down the hall. When she returned, her classmates had already left for art class. She joined them midway through the class.
>
> Upon returning from art class, Sarah was scheduled to practice skills related to zipping and unzipping. She was asked to grasp a large ring fastened to a zipper

_____

[1]Adapted from Ford et al. (1982).

mounted on a board. In order to practice this, Sarah was positioned in the back corner of the room with a teaching assistant. After this, the teacher asked the teaching assistant to help Sarah with her photo journal during the writing session in which all students worked on their journals. The teaching assistant had never been involved in this activity before, and was given no guidance. The teacher usually expected Sarah to perform specific steps related to recalling yesterday's photos and deciding on today's, but the assistant, unaware of the targeted steps, neglected to ask her to perform them, and introduced new ones instead. By this time, Sarah was rather confused by the events of the day. She had no idea what to expect next. She also wondered if she would have any chance to be with friends today. It seemed like she spent all her time with adults.

The problems associated with Sarah's schedule can help us identify a set of guidelines to use when developing a student's schedule.

### Take advantage of natural times to provide instruction.

Sarah was pushed to her locker where her jacket was removed for her and placed on a hook.

Even though Sarah had self-management/home living goals related to zippering and motor goals related to the use of her upper body, she was not expected to participate in the removal of her jacket upon arrival at school. She sat passively as her jacket was removed and placed in her locker. The teacher assisting her was in a rush to get her to the classroom where the "real" instruction would take place. Yet, later that day, she was expected to practice zipping and unzipping at a time and in a place that didn't make sense to her and with an adaptation (a large ring) that was not available when she actually needed it! Routine activities encountered by Sarah throughout her school day were not targeted as opportunities for instruction. To avoid this situation, time needs to be set aside during the day to provide instruction in particular activities when they *naturally* occur rather than creating an artificial instructional session.

While many "natural" times are very obvious and occur on a routine basis (e.g., teaching eating skills in the cafeteria, recreation skills during recess or free time, money-handling skills when paying for lunch), other "teachable moments" occur spontaneously throughout the school day and are just as valuable as those represented on a classroom schedule. One such moment might have occurred when a student approached Sarah while she was using the computer. Sarah had been learning how to use a picture symbol board attached to her wheelchair. This may have been an opportunity to monitor whether she attempted any response to the boy's question with her communication board, or perhaps to provide her with some additional instruction in the use of this system.

### Maximize the use of instruction in groups that include students with a range of skills.

. . . Sarah was wheeled to the computer for an instructional session with a teaching assistant who was assigned to work one-to-one with her.

Unfortunately, a common pattern that occurs for students with severe handicaps is the overuse of one-to-one teaching sessions. In the example above, Sarah was scheduled to learn how to play a computer game with a teaching assistant. Sarah's interest, motivation, and ability to learn from the actions of others may have been significantly increased if she were learning how to play the game with a group of other children.

Instead, another child who showed interest was asked *not to interrupt* the instructional session. Although there are undoubtedly times when a one-to-one learning session is appropriate, teachers must be careful that this way of organizing instruction does not dominate a student's school day.

When group instruction is used, students with handicaps are often grouped together on the basis of similar levels of functioning. The negative consequences of this type of grouping arrangement include: limited role models; limited student-to-student learning interactions; social isolation; staffing difficulties, and so forth.

Emerging models that emphasize a high degree of student-to-student interaction (e.g., cooperative learning) hold great promise for planning instruction that allows children of varying characteristics to learn together while still being involved in a manner that is meaningful for each student. Later in this chapter we discuss ways to organize instruction in patterns other than one-to-one or ability grouping.

## Minimize the extent of "pull-out" activities.

> . . . Sarah was pulled from class for a speech therapy session . . . . When she returned, her classmates had already left for art class.

Sarah missed the beginning of her art class because she was removed from class to receive speech/language services in a therapy room. Her daily activities with other students were often interrupted by "pull out" sessions (e.g., speech/language therapy, physical therapy, occupational therapy). While the purpose of related services is to help a child benefit from his or her educational program, for many students these services fragment their daily schedules rather than facilitate their educational success. Thus, many teachers and related services providers are exploring ways to minimize the amount of time a student is pulled out for services. Models for doing this include: therapists working as consultants with all the staff rather than (or in addition to) providing direct services (Giangreco, 1986), and therapists becoming involved in small group instruction in the classroom or other settings (Rainforth & York, 1987).

Sarah's teacher also scheduled many activities when Sarah would be positioned at the rear of the room to work with a teaching assistant, separate from other students in the class. As noted above, efforts should be made to minimize the time a student is isolated from her or his peers.

## Schedule a predictable flow of activities.

> By this time, Sarah was rather confused by the events of the day. She had no idea what to expect next.

Sarah could not anticipate which skills were expected of her at any given moment. Some days she was expected to perform particular steps in developing her photo journal; other days she was not. Some days she was expected to initiate several of the steps related to washing her hands; other days she was not.

If the goal for a student is to retain skills and know when to use them, a predictable flow of activities is desirable. Having "routines" allows students to develop and demonstrate competence in daily activities. If students always need to depend on another person to tell them how and when to act, they are at a great disadvantage. Instruction that is sporadic and unpredictable is not likely to teach a student to initiate the steps in a given routine or develop the degree of independence that may be within her or his potential.

Of course, this guideline does not mean that a schedule should be viewed as a rigid plan from which no variation is allowed. Many opportunities for learning within the school day occur spontaneously or through a planned departure from the typical routine. These experiences can be valuable for all students. The point of this guideline is that if we expect to see growth in a particular skill or in the degree of participation within an activity, students need consistent and predictable opportunities to practice.

### Schedule enough time for an activity.

. . . but on this day the teacher must have been in a hurry because the teacher quickly washed Sarah's hands, without expecting her to initiate any movements.

Although partial participation in "washing her hands" after using the toilet was a targeted educational goal for Sarah, on many days the person assisting her was too rushed to have her participate. If, on a regular basis, a teacher feels rushed during an instructional activity, this may indicate that too many objectives have been targeted for the particular activity, or that too little time has been allocated for instruction. If washing her hands is an important goal for Sarah, adequate time should be scheduled for it. Unusual circumstances will occasionally interfere with instructional plans, but frequent disruptions in the daily routine may indicate the need for an adjustment in the overall schedule.

### Make staff-to-student assignments that are consistent over time for an activity.

The teaching assistant had never been involved in this [photo-journal] activity before . . . [and] unaware of the targeted steps, neglected to ask her [Sarah] to perform them, and introduced new ones instead.

Since the teaching assistant wasn't familiar with the photo-journal routine, she didn't have Sarah perform many of the skills usually expected. While it is important that a student be involved with many other students and adults, it is wise to establish some consistency in the staff-to-student teaching assignments. This does not mean that a student should spend a majority of her or his day with a particular adult, but rather that, to whatever extent possible, the same adults are consistently involved in particular activities. For example, at 10:00 every day, Sarah is expected to participate in the "journal-writing" activity. If different personnel are assigned to assist Sarah—oftentimes on an impromptu basis—they will undoubtedly have different expectations for Sarah's level of involvement. Consequently, her ability to gain more independence in this activity will be compromised. When variation in staff assignments can not be avoided, communication between personnel is critical.

### Appreciate the value of daily social routines.

A friend tried to stop her in the hall to show her his new game, but the teacher wheeling Sarah only stopped for a brief moment.

Regular social routines (arrival, recess, transitions, homerooms, doing class jobs together, recess, library time) should not be viewed as "down time" to be sacrificed during the scheduling process. These are opportunities for students to get to know each other, enjoy each other, and learn from each other. In fact, as many teachers will attest, students are often more attentive to each other than to adults. For students with handicaps, for whom the development of age-appropriate social skills is critical, these times should be recognized as valuable learning times.

## Allow students to be together without the unnecessary interference of adults.

> She [Sarah] also wondered if she would have any chance to be with friends today. It seemed like she spent all her time with adults.

Often students who require a lot of assistance in their daily activities are constantly attended to by adults who mediate nearly every experience for them. While students should receive an appropriate level of support to learn and participate, they should also be allowed the educational opportunities that arise from being with others their age, free from the unnecessary interference of adults. Personnel who are assigned to assist a student should develop a sensitivity as to when monitoring a situation from a distance may be more appropriate.

### Final Remarks

Although these scheduling guidelines are focused on the needs of the student, each has benefits for the personnel involved with students as well. Personnel who know with whom they will be assigned to work, what activity they will be doing, and how to provide systematic instruction are more likely to grow in feelings of personal competence and job satisfaction.

With these guidelines as a basis for decision making, the process of developing a schedule can begin. We realize that many factors affect the design of a classroom schedule—some of which are within the control of the teacher(s), and others of which are not. Nonetheless, following a structured process is much more likely to result in an effective daily schedule.

## DESIGNING THE WEEKLY SCHEDULE

### Step-by-Step Process

The following process is outlined for the person(s) responsible for designing students' schedules. It comprises the following four major steps (much of this process was influenced by Chapter 7 "Managing Classroom Operations," in Wilcox & Bellamy, 1982):

- Step 1: Create a master list that contains the major instructional goal areas and activities for each student.
- Step 2: Determine the availability of staff, volunteers, and other personnel resources.
- Step 3: Using a weekly format, schedule integrated regular class sessions as well as the unstructured parts of the school day (e.g., arrival, recess, lunch). Many functional activities can be incorporated at "natural times." Determine staff assignments where needed.
- Step 4: Schedule remaining functional activities in ways that optimize the use of heterogeneous groups of students; determine/finalize which personnel will assist in particular activities and groupings.

To demonstrate the use of this process, two examples are provided (in the appendix at the end of this chapter). One example is of a fully integrated fifth-grade class taught by Ms. Frank. Ms. Frank has a teaching assistant, and a special education teacher allocates a portion of his time to this classroom. Ms. Frank will use the process described above to determine how best to incorporate activities from the community living areas into her weekly schedule as they are needed for a particular student with severe handicaps.

Mr. Lane, who teaches at a middle school, is our second example. When he began teaching 2 years ago, he was assigned to a special class with six students considered as either moderately or severely handicapped, with one full-time teaching assistant and one half-time teaching assistant. There was little precedent at this particular school for integrating his students into regular classes. During his first 2 years he worked closely with the administration and other teachers to create integrated learning opportunities for his students. His goal is to eliminate the use of special classes and spaces for his students and move toward a more fully integrated model. You should also notice that Mr. Lane has Mary Z. in his class—the student who has been discussed throughout each section of this guide.

Although their situations are quite different, both teachers can benefit from using a similar process to determine how best to incorporate the goals and activities listed on each student's individualized education program (IEP) into a weekly schedule for all students in the class. If you are a teacher in a high school setting, the middle school process can be readily adapted to your situation. If you are an elementary school teacher with a "self-contained" special class, you may have difficulty applying the process used by Ms. Frank, the fifth-grade teacher. In this case, you might find that the middle school example is more similar to the process that you would use (i.e., your students are based in a special class and you work with other teachers to involve them in age-appropriate regular classes). Of course, the challenges involved in designing a hypothetical schedule are minimal compared to the substantial problems and roadblocks that teachers face daily. It is our hope that this scheduling process can be of benefit to you, even if your final schedule reflects some compromises due to the nature of your particular setting.

## Managing the Range of Instructional Goals

A scheduling process must account for the great diversity of instructional goals that may occur among the students on a class list—yet, remain a manageable system. To help us understand the relationship between the goals for the students with IEPs (in each content area) and the goals for their nondisabled classmates, a designation is noted. It is important to note that modification and individualization may also be necessary for other students in a given class who do not have IEPs. (For example, the range of reading ability in a class may be quite great.)

- *Regular*: The student participates in the regular curriculum—that is, the goals and objectives are drawn directly from the regular curriculum at the same grade level as other classmates (without IEPs). The teacher may modify the curriculum for the student—but these modifications are made on a *lesson-by-lesson* basis as needed. For example, Sharon, a fifth grader, may have goals and objectives in the social studies area that are similar to those of her nonhandicapped peers. There may be modifications made if a particular lesson is based on extensive reading of fifth grade materials. These modifications may include having a student from the seventh grade tape sections of the text or using cooperative models where other group members could read aloud. The information that Sharon is expected to master may not be at the same level of detail as compared to other classmates.

- *Regular–adapted*: The student participates in the regular curriculum (possibly at a different level), however, substantial adaptations are made that require systematic, advanced planning to ensure that a student is mastering essential skills and concepts. For example, the goals and objectives for Peter's math program are drawn from the regular math curriculum although at a level below that of most of his classmates. In order to ensure that instruction is meaningful and that he progresses at as rapid a pace as possible, a systematic plan is put in place. His teacher plans on "streamlining" the content that Peter is expected to master—that is, essential skills will be highlighted and instruction will be highly individualized or tailored to his needs. The "regular–adapted" designation is most appropriate to content areas that are based on the mastering of a set of skills that are hierarchical (e.g., reading and math), but other content areas may also require substantial advance planning to ensure meaningful involvement.
- *Embedded*: The student participates in many activities that may be drawn from the regular curriculum. The goal, however, is not so much to master the skills/concepts from a particular subject area, but rather to afford the student the opportunity to participate in group instruction and further develop embedded social, motor, and communication skills. For example, the goals and objectives for Tom's involvement in some fifth-grade social studies classes will be related to improving his ability to communicate with peers, and use appropriate social skills. A typical activity-based lesson might be the design and construction of a bulletin board whose theme is related to the civil rights movement. Tom's involvement may include helping to gather resources (with assistance), cut out pictures, and assist in the actual construction of the board. He is not expected to master the social studies content as will most of his peers—but he will be expected to be learning individualized social and communication skills as a result of his involvement.
- *Functional*: The *primary* goals and objectives are not drawn from the regular curriculum, but are skills that have an immediate use in the student's daily experience both in and out of school. For example, Ted is learning to use a predetermined amount of money to make purchases at the school store and at the grocery store. He is also learning to manage time by using a picture-symbol system to follow his daily schedule.

It is important to keep in mind that the above designations are *not* presented as a basis for grouping students for instruction. The main function of the designations is to clarify how the primary goals and objectives delineated on an IEP are related to both the regular curriculum content areas and community-referenced curricular components.

## CONCLUSION

Designing the schedule is one task; making it work is quite another. If you are an experienced teacher, you are probably familiar with the *challenges* involved in making the schedule work. You have learned to tolerate (and actually plan for) a certain amount of unpredictability during the first weeks of school: a new student suddenly appears during week 2; the art teacher hasn't been hired yet; the community vocational teacher is unable to firm up times until several other teachers have been contacted; and, the teaching assistant decided to make a career change in week 3. Piece-by-piece, however, you manage to design a schedule that reflects a variety of interest-

ing classes and activities in which students are able to learn and develop together—
with all students being full members of their school.

## QUESTIONS AND ANSWERS

Q: I am trying to implement an effective schedule, but my students are constantly
being pulled out of class to receive physical therapy or speech and language
services. How can I influence the related services providers to consider a more
integrated therapy model?

A: The service delivery models that many therapists implement are, of course, related to those they are exposed to in their own preparation programs. Many preparation programs emphasize an isolated therapy model. You may want to consider offering the therapists on your team resource materials that state both the
rationale and implementation ideas for integrated models (particularly for students with more extensive needs). Perhaps you could obtain information about
other school districts that may be effectively implementing such models and
arrange visits for both yourself and your team members. As with other change
efforts, reluctant providers may need reassurance that they are not expected to
alter their delivery models overnight, but can develop a plan to gradually modify
their services over a period of time as they become comfortable with the new
approach.

Q: A step-by-step process to developing a schedule sounds great, but there are so
many changes in the first month of school, it seems unworkable. Is it better to
wait until things "settle down" to develop a written schedule?

A: Changes are inevitable, particularly in the first few weeks of the school year. It
may be wise to begin with the components of the schedule that seem most likely
to remain stable, and work in changes in activities, personnel, and students as
they arise. The disadvantage to postponing the development of a clear, up-to-
date schedule is that the teacher does not have a good idea of how proposed
changes will affect existing elements in the schedule. Even if changes occur
daily, the teacher is in a far better position to assess the impact of the change if
she or he is maintaining some semblance of a workable schedule.

## REFERENCES

Ford, A., Davis, J., Messina, R., Ranieri, L., Nisbet, J., & Sweet, M. (1982). Arranging
instruction to ensure the active participation of severely multiply handicapped students. In
L. Brown, J. Nisbet, A. Ford, M. Sweet, B. Shiraga, & L. Gruenewald (Eds.), *Educational
programs for severely handicapped students, Volume XII* (pp. 31–80). Madison, WI: Madison Metropolitan School District.
Giangreco, M. (1986). Delivery of therapeutic services in special education programs for
learners with severe handicaps. *Physical & Occupational Therapy*, 6(2), 5–13.
Rainforth, B., & York, J. (1987). Integrated related services in community instruction. *Journal
of The Association for Persons with Severe Handicaps*, *12* 190–198.
Wilcox, B., & Bellamy, G. T. (1982). *Design of high school programs for severely handicapped students*. Baltimore: Paul H. Brookes Publishing Co.

## ADDITIONAL READINGS AND RESOURCES

Orelove, F. P., & Sobsey, D. (1987). *Educating children with multiple disabilities: A transdisciplinary approach*. Baltimore: Paul H. Brookes Publishing Co.

Sailor, W., Halvorsen, A., Anderson, J., Goetz, L., Gee, K., Doering, K., & Hunt, P. (1986). Community intensive instruction. In R.H. Horner, L.H. Meyer, & H. D. B. Fredericks (Eds.), *Education of learners with severe handicaps: Exemplary service strategies* (pp. 251–288). Baltimore: Paul H. Brookes Publishing Co.

# APPENDIX: EXAMPLES OF
# STEP-BY-STEP SCHEDULING PROCESS

## FIFTH-GRADE EXAMPLE

The step-by-step process was used to design a fifth-grade schedule. The charts included in this example show each of these steps and how the needs of the *entire* class are addressed. In addition, we have outlined a typical day for one of the students included in the fifth-grade schedule. We have selected "TC" for this purpose since he is a student who has many activities drawn from the community living areas. The following is an overview of a typical Monday for TC:

- 8:20—*Arrival*   TC arrives at school. He walks into the building with friends. A teaching assistant meets him at his locker and assists him with taking off his coat and organizing his belongings. There are a few minutes before class begins to socialize in the hallways.
- 8:30—*Announcements*   TC listens to announcements and organizes and reviews his picture schedule with assistance.
- 8:40—*Language Arts*   While students rotate between reading groups and individual or partner activities, TC looks at books with a partner for 20 minutes. Then he joins other students who will be using the computer and finishing assignments at learning centers. Two examples of assignments TC would do at a learning center include: looking for pictures he will use for his journal later in the afternoon; and gathering the appropriate picture cards for purchases he will make at the grocery store, and mounting them in the small notebook that he takes with him. When activities are more cooperative or activity based, he is included— with an emphasis on motor, communication, and social skills. An example of such an activity might be helping to gather the resources for his group (e.g., dictionary, paper, reference books), or contributing ideas for themes for special writing projects (by pointing at pictures).
- 10:00—*Snack Preparation*   Each day a student is chosen to be a partner to TC as he makes a mid-morning snack. The partner is a child who has already mastered the material being presented during math class. TC is learning some basic snack preparation skills such as slicing cheese for crackers, cleaning and cutting fruit, and making a peanut butter sandwich.
- 10:30—*Attendance Slips*   TC picks up the attendance slips from other fifth-grade classrooms and brings them to the office.
- 11:00—*Recess*   TC joins his classmates in recess activities and engages in a variety of activities with classmates.
- 11:15—*Art*   TC joins his classmates in various art projects with adaptations and assistance provided as needed. Activities include drawing, painting, printmaking, claywork, and so forth.
- 12:00—*Lunch*   Some assistance is needed by TC in the cafeteria lunch line and with eating. He joins friends at lunch and an adult assisting him positions herself in a manner that does not interfere with peer interaction. The assistant is teaching TC to eat with a spoon. TC is learning to request help from his peers for some of the other steps in the routine (if needed) such as opening his milk carton and gathering his trash to throw away.
- 12:30—*Science/Health*   Many of Mr. Frank's science/health lessons are activity based. TC's small group has been given the task of planning how to convince consumers to recycle many things they normally throw out. TC will collect pictures of paper, glass, and plastic objects that will be displayed as part of the project.
- 1:30—*Silent Reading*   TC looks at a book from the library or the classroom collection.
- 1:45—*Grocery Store*   Three classmates join TC for a trip to the grocery store. Since this occurs during choice time and journal time, there is little risk of students missing important information that would affect their academic development. TC is learning how to cross streets and use a shopping list to find and purchase two items at the store. His classmates

will be expected to demonstrate the application of several math and health/science concepts when questions are presented by the teacher at the store.

- 2:45—*Dismissal*  TC gathers his belongings, puts on his outerwear, and heads home for the day.

**Step 1:**   *Create a master list that contains the major instructional goal areas and activities for each student.*

Notice from the master list on the next three pages that Ms. Frank has 24 students in her fifth-grade class. Three of the students receive special education services and have IEPs (initials: PL, SG, and TC). One student (TC) has activities specified on his IEP that are drawn from the community living areas.

The goal areas and activities listed for the students without IEPs are drawn from the grade-level curricula and guidelines in use by the school district. Those shown on this chart are only a partial listing due to limitations in space. We are not necessarily suggesting that you write in all of this information for students within the regular curricula. However, your district may have a condensed chart such as this already prepared so that you can see the full curriculum at a glance.

The goal areas, activities, and modifications listed for PL, SG, and TC are drawn from their IEPs. As revealed in the master list, PL and SG do not need direct instruction in the community living areas, but do need adaptations in the curriculum in order to succeed. TC has significant discrepancies in his achievement and performance. (This student would be considered severely handicapped.) Many of the activities that fall under the community living areas are appropriate for him.

There may be more than one designation given for a particular student in a specific content area: For example, TC has both a "functional" approach *and* a "regular–embedded" approach listed under mathematics. This means that he may occasionally be involved in activity-based lessons that address the content area of mathematics, but his involvement would center on the acquisition of embedded skills as opposed to the mathematical processes being targeted. He will also be involved in activities that have a focus on the development of functional math skills in the areas of money use and time management. And of course, opportunities to develop embedded communication, motor, and social skills are inherent in any activity regardless of whether they are specified as the primary emphasis in a given content area.

Finally, please note that the master list does not contain separate headings for social, motor, and communication skills since these *embedded* areas do not require the scheduling of a specific segment of time.

Step 1. Master list for Ms. Frank's fifth-grade class

| Students' Initials | Language Arts | Mathematics | Science |
|---|---|---|---|
| GA<br>SA<br>PB<br>AD<br>TD<br>FJ<br>BF<br>RG<br>SJ<br>RL<br>TL<br>RM<br>CN<br>BN<br>GO<br>BS<br>ST<br>DT<br>JV<br>GW<br>AW<br>(students without IEPs) | Decoding (syllabication)<br>Vocabulary skills<br>• antonyms<br>• synonyms (etc.)<br>Comprehension skills<br>• main idea<br>• sequence<br>• cause/effect (etc.)<br>Study skills<br>• dictionary use<br>• library use<br>Speaking<br>• asking questions<br>• reporting<br>• expressing<br>• intonation (etc.)<br>Writing<br>• stories of several<br>    paragraphs<br>• topics in outline form<br>• proofing and editing (etc.)<br>GO,CN,RM—6B<br>GA,RL,SJ,GW,JV,AW,BF—<br>    5B<br>SA,PB,FJ,RG,BS,ST—5A<br>BN,TL—4B<br>AD,TD—4A<br>DT—3A | Writing/reading numbers to<br>    100,000,000<br>Addition (3 and 4 digit)<br>Subtraction (4 digit with<br>    renaming)<br>Division (2 digit)<br>Factoring<br>Multiples of numerals up<br>    to 24<br>Word problems with +, −,<br>    ÷, ×<br>Decimals<br>• equivalent fractions<br>• rounding +, −, × ·<br>Fractions<br>• addition<br>• multiplication<br>• subtraction<br>Geometry<br>• terms of plane figures<br>• perimeter<br>• area (etc.)<br>AD,TL,DT—Streamlined<br>    3rd | Physical health<br>• nutrition<br>• dental care<br>• symptoms of disease<br>• nervous, muscular, and<br>    skeletal systems<br>• sense organs and functions<br>Sociological health<br>    problems<br>• drugs<br>• alcohol<br>• smoking<br>Survival education<br>• fire prevention<br>• consumer safety<br>Emotional growth<br>• stress<br>• real-life problems; con-<br>    sequences; alternatives<br>Environment<br>• pollution<br>• citizen responsibility (etc.) |
| PL<br>(student with IEP) | Regular–adapted<br>Streamlined 2nd-grade read-<br>    ing series<br>Supplementary phonics | Regular–adapted<br>Streamlined 3rd-grade math<br>    series | Regular; modifications on a<br>    lesson-by-lesson basis as<br>    needed |
| SG<br>(student with IEP) | Regular–adapted<br>Streamlined 1st grade read-<br>    ing series (high interest)<br>Supplementary phonics | Regular–adapted<br>Streamlined 3rd-grade math<br>    series | Regular; modifications on a<br>    lesson-by-lesson basis as<br>    needed |
| TC<br>(student with IEP) | Functional<br>• picture-symbol approach<br>• listens to stories<br>• looks at books and<br>    magazines<br>Regular–embedded; em-<br>    phasis on social, motor,<br>    and communication skills | Functional<br>• money handling (in<br>    context); predetermined<br>    amount<br>• time management; pic-<br>    ture-symbol approach<br>Regular–embedded; em-<br>    phasis on social, motor,<br>    and communication skills | Regular–embedded;<br>    emphasis on embedded<br>    social, motor, and com-<br>    munication skills |

*See additional content areas on next page.*

Step 1.   Master List *(continued)*

| Students' Initials | Social Studies | Arts | | Physical Education |
| | | Visual Arts | Music | |
|---|---|---|---|---|
| GA<br>SA<br>PB<br>AD<br>TD<br>FJ<br>BF<br>RG<br>SJ<br>RL<br>TL<br>RM<br>CN<br>BN<br>GO<br>BS<br>ST<br>DT<br>JV<br>GW<br>AW<br>(students<br>without<br>IEPs) | Geography<br>• terms and<br>  directons<br>• map use<br>• hemispheres<br>History<br>• colonization<br>• Native Americans<br>• colonial leaders<br>• Revolutionary War<br>• Civil War, etc.<br>Political Science<br>• states and capitals<br>• Declaration of<br>  Independence<br>• Constitution and<br>  Bill of Rights (etc.)<br>Economics<br>• resources<br>• interdependence<br>Sociology<br>• ethnic groups<br>• social changes<br>  (etc.) | Art concepts<br>• expression<br>• perception<br>• discrimination<br>• manipulation<br>Growth in concepts<br>  developed<br>  through:<br>• drawing<br>• painting<br>• printmaking<br>• constructing forms<br>  (paper, clay,<br>  wood, papier-mâ-<br>  che, weaving,<br>  collage, mosaic,<br>  plastic, batik,<br>  etc.) | Creative expression<br>• uses rhythm<br>  instruments<br>Instrumental<br>• distinguishes<br>  among families of<br>  instruments<br>Listening skills<br>• major and minor<br>  tonality<br>Movement skills<br>• original movement<br>  to songs<br>Music reading<br>• reads notes of sim-<br>  ple songs<br>Rhythm<br>• reads rhythms by<br>  clapping<br>Singing<br>• sings two-part<br>  harmony | Aerobics<br>Organized games/<br>  team sports<br>• basketball<br>• field hockey<br>• floor hockey<br>• football<br>• lacrosse<br>• softball<br>• volleyball<br>• soccer<br>• tennis<br>Individual sports/<br>  activities<br>• jogging<br>• gymnastics<br>• swimming<br>Rhythm and dance<br>Track-and-field<br>  activities |
| PL<br>(student<br>with IEP) | Regular; modifica-<br>tions on a lesson-<br>by-lesson basis as<br>needed | Regular; modifica-<br>tions on a lesson-<br>by-lesson basis as<br>needed | Regular; modifica-<br>tions on a lesson-<br>by-lesson basis as<br>needed | Regular; modifica-<br>tions on a lesson-<br>by-lesson basis as<br>needed |
| SG<br>(student<br>with IEP) | Regular; modifica-<br>tions on a lesson-<br>by-lesson basis as<br>needed | Regular; modifica-<br>tions on a lesson-<br>by-lesson basis as<br>needed | Regular; modifica-<br>tions on a lesson-<br>by-lesson basis as<br>needed | Regular; modifica-<br>tions on a lesson-<br>by-lesson basis as<br>needed |
| TC<br>(student<br>with IEP) | Regular—embedded;<br>emphasis on em-<br>bedded social,<br>motor, and com-<br>munication skills | Regular—adapted | Regular—adapted | Regular—adapted |

*See additional content areas on next page.*

Step 1. Master list *(continued)*

| Students' Initials | Community Living Areas | | | |
|---|---|---|---|---|
| | School Jobs/Routines | Self-Management/ Home Living | General Community Functioning | Recreation/Leisure |
| GA SA PB AD TD FJ BF RG SJ RL TL RM CN BN GO BS ST DT JV GW AW (students without IEPs) | Rotation of various class/school jobs • attendance slips • erase boards • pass out papers (etc.) | | Settings in community used as a context for application and integration of skills in content areas | Settings (choice time; recess) used as a context for the development of prosocial skills for all students |
| PL (student with IEP) | Rotation of various class/school jobs | | Functional • using caution with strangers (reminders on field trips and outings) | |
| SG (student with IEP) | Rotation of various class/school jobs | | | |
| TC (student with IEP) | Rotation of various class/school jobs | Functional • eating • snack preparation (5 days) • toileting • dressing • combing hair | Functional • buying a snack at school store (twice/week) grocery store (once/week) • crossing streets | Functional • looking at books and magazines • Connect Four • computer games • other preferences to be determined |

**Step 2:**  *Determine the availability of staff, volunteers, and other personnel resources.*

Using a weekly format, like the one on the next page, the times that different personnel are available are noted. Ms. Frank (T) and her teaching assistant (TA) will be with the class on a full-time basis. In addition, a special education teacher (SET) has allocated a portion of his time to the class since there are three students with special needs enrolled. The special education teacher will serve two roles: 1) to be responsible for teaching a section of language arts (when the groups go to the learning centers), and 2) to be available to assist with adapting the curriculum and making other instructional modifications.

The times that the fifth grade is scheduled into special area classes are noted. The involved personnel include the art teacher (AT), music teacher (MT), librarian (L), and physical education teacher (PET). Since TC receives related services, the speech/language therapist (ST) and physical therapist (PT) are also included on the schedule. Both of these therapists realize the limitations of "pull-out" sessions. For this reason they have tried to schedule themselves into class activities that will offer the best opportunities to integrate their expertise (e.g., the PT will work with the PET to maximize TC's participation in that class). In addition, they want to keep some of their time flexible so that they can observe TC in his interactions with others, consult with the staff who work with TC, and provide guidance within the flow of the school day.

Step 2. Availability of staff at elementary school

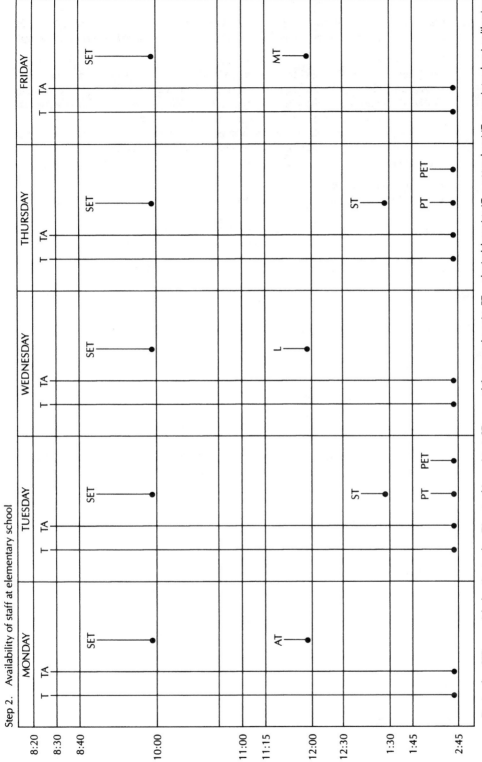

T = teacher; SET = special education teacher; TA = teaching assistant; ST = speech/language therapist; PT = physical therapist; AT = art teacher; MT = music teacher; L = librarian; PET = physical education teacher

263

**Step 3:** *Using a weekly schedule format, schedule regular class sessions as well as the unstructured parts of the school day (e.g., arrival, recess, and lunch). Many functional activities can be incorporated at "natural" times.*

The general class schedule has been constructed by Ms. Frank. As you may recall, many of the goals and activities for the three students with IEPs will be drawn from the regular curriculum and thus do not require special scheduling consideration. But, what about the activities that fall under the "functional" category? TC's IEP contains many of these activities.

When outlining the schedule on the next page, Ms. Frank was aware of how many of TC's functional activities could be incorporated within the natural flow of the school day. For example:

- Arrival: removing outerwear
- Use of Restroom: grooming and toilet use
- Lunch: eating
- Physical Education class: dressing and undressing; grooming
- Library, Recess, Choice Time, Silent Reading: recreation/leisure activities
- School Store: money-use skills
- Dismissal: putting on outerwear

Step 3. Schedule the regular classroom sessions

| | MONDAY | TUESDAY | WEDNESDAY | THURSDAY | FRIDAY |
|---|---|---|---|---|---|
| 8:20 | Arrival → | | | | |
| 8:30 | Announcements → | | | | |
| 8:40 | Language Arts | Language Arts | Language Arts | Language Arts | Language Arts |
| 10:00 | Math | Math | Math | Math | Math |
| | School store (students can use 1–2x/week) → | | | | |
| 11:00 | Recess | Recess | Recess | Recess | Recess |
| 11:15 | Art | Group Projects; integrating content areas | Library | Group Projects; integrating content areas | Music |
| 12:00 | Lunch | Lunch | Lunch | Lunch | Lunch |
| 12:30 | Science/Health | Social Studies | Science/Health | Social Studies | Science/Health |
| 1:30 | Silent Reading | Silent Reading | Silent Reading | Silent Reading | Silent Reading |
| 1:45 | Choice Time | Physical Education | Choice Time | Physical Education | Choice Time |
| | Journal | | Journal | | Journal |
| 2:45 | Dismissal → | | | | |

**Step 4:** *Schedule remaining instructional activities in ways that optimize the use of heterogeneous groups of students, and determine/finalize which personnel will assist in particular activities and groupings.*

At this point, Ms. Frank will determine a schedule of in-school activities. Following this she will determine how best to incorporate the remainder of activities from the community living areas: street crossing and buying a snack at the grocery store. She has chosen the choice-time and journal periods on Monday for small group instruction at the grocery store. Each Monday, different students are rotated through a group that goes to the grocery store. TC is a member of the group each week. Three students (without handicaps) in the group use the store as a context for the application and integration of skills from various content areas (e.g., math, science, health), while TC is learning how to cross streets, locate items in a store, and handle money.

Ms. Frank wants TC to have more than one opportunity during the week to learn to cross streets. On Friday morning, she has scheduled a small group to mail letters that the students compose during language arts. Different students are rotated through this small group, but TC is a member each week.

It should be obvious that Ms. Frank has examined her weekly schedule and attempted to determine how she could structure learning activities for TC that allow him to learn with and from a variety of his classmates. Although either she or her teaching assistant are scheduled to be with TC for the majority of the school day, this pattern should not be confused with one-to-one instruction. TC is often involved with small groups of students engaged in various activities with one adult monitoring as needed. Blanks indicate times when students will rotate through a particular activity with TC (such as snack preparation and reviewing a pictorial schedule).

For special area classes, the teacher or teaching assistant is assisting the special area instructor with the entire class. Sometimes the teacher will be assisting TC, and other times the special area teacher or another student assists. Classes may be organized in a variety of ways—partners, small groups, or large groups.

Step 4.  Schedule remaining functional activities and determine teaching assignments

| | MONDAY | TUESDAY | WEDNESDAY | THURSDAY | FRIDAY | |
|---|---|---|---|---|---|---|
| 8:20 | Arrival: (TA) removing outerwear; (TC) locker use; socializing) → | | | | | |
| 8:30 | Announcements: (TA) reviewing picto-(TC) rial schedule → | | | | | |
| 8:40 | Language Arts<br>CA,PB,AD,  SA,TO, (SET)<br>JF,BF,RG,CN  GO,SJ,RL,TC<br>PL,BK,AW (TA)  GW,JV,BN<br>SG,ST  PT,ST<br>(T) —, —, —<br>Writing and other language activities in small groups | Language Arts<br>→<br>→<br>→ | Language Arts | Language Arts | Language Arts<br><br>(TC, (TA) Mail letters in neighborhood (street crossing) | |
| 10:00 | Math<br>large/small (TA) snack preparation →<br>group instruction (TA) attendance slips →<br>(T) small group practi- (TC)<br>cal application<br>School store (students can use 1–2x/week) | Math<br>School store (buying item; handling money)<br>(T) TC, —, — (TA) | Math | Math<br>(buying item; handling money)<br>(T) TC, —, — (TA) | Math | (TA) lunch break |
| 11:00 | Recess (T) | Recess (TA) | Recess (T) | Recess (TA) | Recess (T) | |
| 11:15 | Art (AT, T)<br>grouping patterns vary<br>(T) looking at books and magazines<br>TC, — Grocery Store (street crossing; shopping skills; money handling) | Group Projects<br>(integrating content areas)<br>grouping patterns vary (T) | Library (looking at books and magazines)<br>grouping patterns vary (L) | Group Projects<br>(integrating content areas)<br>grouping patterns vary | Music (MT, T)<br>grouping patterns vary | (T) lunch break |
| 12:00 | Lunch (TA) eating skills; money (TC) handling | Lunch (TA) (TC) | Lunch (TA) (TC) | Lunch | Lunch | (TA) break |
| 12:30 | Science/Health (TA)<br>grouping patterns vary | Social Studies (T, TA, ST)<br>grouping patterns vary | Science/Health (T, TA)<br>grouping patterns vary | Social Studies (T, TA, ST)<br>grouping patterns vary | Science/Health (T, TA)<br>grouping patterns vary | (T)+(TA) planning period on Tuesday + Thursday |
| 1:30 | Silent Reading (T) | Silent Reading (T) | Silent Reading | Silent Reading* | Silent Reading | |
| 1:45 | Choice Time (TA)<br>Journal (TA) | Physical Education (PET, PT) | Choice Time (T, TA) (Recreation/Leisure activities)<br>Journal (T)(TC) —, Monitoring Journals<br>(T, TA) Large group journal sharing | Physical Education* (PET, PT) | Choice Time (T, TA) (Recreation/Leisure activities)<br>Journal (T)(TC) —, — Monitoring Journals<br>(T, TA) Large group journal sharing | |
| 2:45 | Dismissal (TA) dressing; locker use; (TC) socializing → | | | | | |

T = teacher, TA = teaching assistant, SET = special education teacher, AT = art teacher, L = librarian, MT = music teacher, ST = speech/language therapist, PET = physical education teacher, PT = physical therapist (other initials [i.e., TC, GA, PB] are those of students in Ms. Frank's class).

267

## MIDDLE SCHOOL EXAMPLE

Mr. Lane, Mary Z.'s teacher, has used the step-by-step process to construct a schedule. Yet he is not entirely satisfied with the schedule he has in place. It represents some compromises. He is still using a special education classroom for part of the school day (e.g., for some recreation/leisure activities, and preparing for outings into the community). Even though he has arranged for other students to join his students for recreational activities, he still feels that the space tends to stigmatize his students and is exploring options for using study halls or other spaces for these purposes. The administration is also investigating what alternative uses could be made for the classroom space so that different groups of students could be using it at different times.

Mr. Lane hopes to include students who are not handicapped into some of the community experiences as the school year progresses. This is more problematic in middle school than in elementary school, given students' regular education schedules. Mr. Lane sees his school moving toward a more fully integrated model. As this evolves, he sees himself becoming a resource to regular educators and a coordinator of the instruction that takes place in community settings. For now, he has done his best to devise a schedule that accounts for the diverse needs of the students on his classlist.

If we just focused on Mary Z. and followed her movement through the schedule (school day), we would get an indication of how her IEP goals are being met throughout the day. The following is an overview of a typical Tuesday for Mary Z.:

- 7:50—*Arrival*   Mary arrives at Johnson Middle School. She enters the school with two friends, one of whom pushes her wheelchair. They spend a few minutes in the halls with other students before proceeding to Mary's locker. At Mary's locker, one of the students works the combination and lifts the handle. She encourages Mary to pull the door open. Mary is also encouraged to take off her own hat and gloves. After her friends help her gather her things for homeroom, she proceeds to Mr. Taylor's room.

- 8:07—*Homeroom*   After Mr. Taylor takes attendance, students are able to talk, look at magazines, or use the computer while waiting for the bell to ring. Mary joins in these activities. Students are also expected to listen to the announcements. Just before the bell rings for first period, a teaching assistant or a friend asks Mary to point to the symbol on her picture schedule for homeroom, and then scan to the right to orient herself to which class is coming up next. (These symbols were prearranged in the correct order for Tuesdays.)

- 8:28—*English*   Students in Ms. Shafer's English class are expected to devote part of one class each week to their journals. During this time, Mary constructs a photo journal with assistance from another student while a teaching assistant monitors as needed. Mary has several photos from a recent school dance that she is inserting into her journal. During the latter half of class, she uses the school library to check out a book of her choice. With assistance, she will also check out a reference book needed by several classmates for an English project.

- 9:17—*Physical Education*   Mary proceeds to the locker room to prepare for swimming class. She is learning to locate her locker and gesture to a classmate for help with her locker. She participates in several steps of changing into her bathing suit with help from a teaching assistant. Today's activity is water polo. While supported by an adapted innertube, Mary is learning to watch the ball and push it toward a classmate when it comes near her. After changing her clothes, she proceeds to third period.

- 10:06—*Art*   Mary is encouraged to greet the classmates who share her table in art class by looking at them in response to their greetings. This week's project is printmaking. She is learning to indicate the need for help by making a gesture and, if necessary, pointing to the appropriate symbol on her communication board.

- 10:54—*Lunch*   Mary proceeds to lunch. The teacher accompanying her helps Mary find John's table. Mary usually joins John and his friends for lunch. Mary knows these students from computer club. She is learning to participate more actively in several mealtime skills such as using her napkin and using utensils. The teacher thought it would be a good idea for

Mary to bring her photo journal to lunch to show the pictures from the dance to the students at her table.

- 11:30—*Vocational Training*  Two afternoons a week, Mary travels to the central supply department at Mercy Hospital. She is learning some of the steps involved in packaging supplies. Mary takes a break at mid-afternoon and purchases a snack in the cafeteria where she joins other employees from her department. After break, she returns to work until 1:40.
- 2:00—*Dismissal and Extracurricular Activities*  Mary returns to Johnson Middle School. With help from a teaching assistant, Mary prearranges the sequence of class symbols that will be appropriate for the following day and then proceeds to the computer club, which meets after school every Tuesday. Mary is learning to activate several single-switch computer games. Different club members join her in these games. At 3:15 she returns to her locker and prepares to go home.

**Step 1:**  *Create a master list that contains the major instructional goal areas and activities for each student.*

The goal areas and activities on this master list are drawn from the IEPs of each of the six students at this middle school. The activities shown on the master list on the next three pages represent what teachers, parents, and students propose to be a desirable plan of goals and activities for each student. It is recognized that some compromises may be necessary when the list is transposed into an actual schedule.

Prior to the start of the school year, a determination will be made as to in which classes a particular individual should enroll. As with any student, it is not expected that the student will participate in a class for each corresponding content area during a given semester, but may enroll in classes based on several factors including: student interest, classes attended during the previous year, and so forth. There also may be designations under the content areas of language arts and math that may not necessarily result in attending a class devoted to that content area. For example, SP will not be enrolled in an English class this semester, but he will be using pictures and symbols throughout his school day—a form of interpreting symbols that is related to the content area of language arts.

It should be noted that the activities listed under the community living areas are individualized—even for students who have very similar learning characteristics. For example, "shampooing hair" is listed for Mary Z. Her parents have difficulty gaining her cooperation with this task and have requested that she be given instruction after gym class; shopping is not a targeted activity for BL since he shops quite often with his family, and they feel it is not a priority in his educational plan.

Step 1.  Master list for six students at Johnson Middle School

| Students' Initials | Language Arts | Mathematics | Science |
|---|---|---|---|
| Mary Z. (age 14) | Functional • picture-symbol approach Regular–embedded; emphasis on social, motor, and communication skills | Functional • money handling (in context); predetermined amount • time telling; picture-symbol approach | |
| BL (age 14) | Functional • experiential reading/writing approach | Functional • money handling (calculator use; numberline strategy) • time telling (clock/watch use) | |
| SP (age 13) | Functional • picture-symbol approach (in context) | Functional • money handling (in context); predetermined amount • time telling (in context); environmental cues | |
| LT (age 13) | Regular–adapted • streamlined basal series | Functional • money handling (calculator use; numberline strategy) • time telling; (clock/watch use) | Regular–adapted |
| KG (age 13) | Functional • experiential reading/writing approach | Functional • money handling (calculator use; money-card strategy) | Regular–adapted |
| JS (age 12) | Functional • experiential reading/writing approach | Functional • money handling (calculator use; numberline strategy) • time telling (clock/watch use) | Regular–adapted |

*See additional content areas on next page.*

Step 1.   Master list *(continued)*

| Students' Initials | Social Studies | Art and Music | Industrial Arts | Home Economics | Physical Education |
|---|---|---|---|---|---|
| Mary Z. (age 14) | | Art 8 Regular– adapted | IA 9 Regular– adapted | Functional • snack/meal preparation Regular– adapted | Regular– adapted (integration of physical therapy exercises) |
| BL (age 14) | | Music 8 Regular– adapted | | Functional • snack/meal preparation Regular– adapted | Regular– adapted |
| SP (age 13) | Regular– embedded; emphasis on social, motor, and commu- nication skills | Music 7 Regular– adapted | IA 9 Regular– adapted | Functional • snack/meal preparation Regular– adapted | Regular– adapted (integration of physical therapy exercises) |
| LT (aged 13) | | Art 8 Regular– adapted | | | Regular– adapted |
| KG (age 13) | | Music 7 Regular– adapted | | Functional • snack/meal preparation Regular– adapted | Regular– adapted |
| JS (age 12) | Regular– adapted | Music 7 Regular– adapted | | Functional • snack/meal preparation Regular– adapted | Regular– adapted |

*See additional content areas on next page.*

Step 1. Master list *(continued)*

| Students' Initials | Community Living Areas | | | |
| --- | --- | --- | --- | --- |
| | Vocational/Career Education | Self-Management/ Home Living | General Community Functioning | Recreation/Leisure |
| Mary Z. (age 14) | Community site (2x/week) | Eating<br>Snack/meal prep-<br>  aration; home<br>  economics class<br>  (2–3x/week)<br>Dressing/undressing<br>Shampooing<br>Toilet use | Shopping (1x/week)<br>Restaurant use<br>  (1x/week) | Tape player<br>Other preferences to<br>  be determined<br>Extracurricular<br>• computer club |
| BL (age 14) | Community site (2x/week) | Snack/meal prep-<br>  aration; home<br>  economics<br>  (2–3x/week)<br>Maintaining<br>  appearance | Street crossing<br>Restaurant use<br>  (1x/week)<br>Using caution with<br>  strangers<br>City bus | Cards<br>• rummy<br>Computer games<br>Extracurricular<br>• ski club |
| SP (age 13) | School-based job; library (2x/week) | Eating<br>Snack/meal prep-<br>  aration; home<br>  economics class<br>  (3–4x/week)<br>Maintaining<br>  appearance<br>Dressing<br>Brushing teeth<br>Toilet use | Orienting to traffic<br>Shopping (1x/week)<br>Restaurant use<br>  (1x/week)<br>City bus | Single-switch com-<br>  puter games<br>Swimming<br>Tape player<br>Looking at books/<br>  magazines |
| LT (age 13) | School-based job; a.v. equipment (2x/week) | Maintaining<br>  appearance | Street crossing<br>Shopping (1x/week)<br>Restaurant use<br>  (1x/week)<br>City Bus | Swimming<br>Cards<br>• rummy<br>Extracurricular<br>• ski club<br>Other preferences to<br>  be determined |
| KG (age 13) | School-based job; a.v. equipment (2x/week) | Eating<br>Snack/meal prep-<br>  aration; home<br>  economics class<br>  (2x/week)<br>Maintaining<br>  appearance | Street crossing<br>Shopping (1x/week)<br>Restaurant use<br>  (1x/week)<br>City bus | Tape player<br>Board game<br>Other preferences to<br>  be determined |
| JS (age 12) | School-based job; library (2x/week) | Eating<br>Snack/meal prep-<br>  aration; home<br>  economics class<br>  (2x/week)<br>Maintaining<br>  appearance | Street crossing<br>Shopping (1x/week)<br>Restaurant use<br>  (1x/week)<br>City bus | Swimming<br>Computer games<br>Looking at books/<br>  magazines<br>Extracurricular<br>• jogging |

**Step 2.** *Determine the availability of staff, volunteers, and other personnel resources.*

There is one full-time teaching assistant and one half-time teaching assistant assigned to assist the six students at Johnson Middle School. There are two reasons why these assistants are assigned to a relatively small group of students. *First,* the six students assigned to Mr. Lane represent a very heterogeneous group. Two students, Mary Z. and SP, require a substantial amount of support. Rather than assigning Mary and SP to a school where they are grouped with other students who have similar characteristics, Mr. Lane's district has these two students attend their local middle school. Mr. Lane serves fewer students with a wide range of learning characteristics, as opposed to a larger homogeneous group (e.g., a special class of 10 students considered moderately handicapped). *Second,* Mr. Lane's role is *not* to teach these six students as a self-contained group. Rather, his role is to teach and support them in regular, age-appropriate classes and in the community. This district has recognized that to effectively support students in regular classes and in the community, greater staff-to-student ratios are needed.

Several of the six students receive related services. The optimal times for the therapists to be present will be determined at a later step—after the students' classes are scheduled.

A community vocational teacher will provide vocational instruction to the two oldest students. At the time of constructing the schedule, Mr. Lane knows that the sites have been determined and that the vocational teacher will be available on Tuesday and Thursday afternoons to provide instruction.

Step 2. Availability of staff at Johnson Middle School

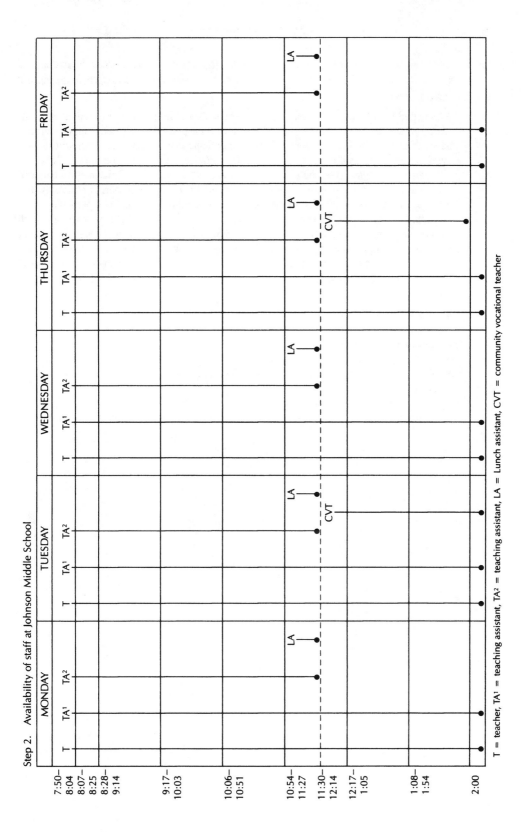

T = teacher, TA¹ = teaching assistant, TA² = teaching assistant, LA = Lunch assistant, CVT = community vocational teacher

275

**Step 3.** *Using a weekly schedule format, schedule the integrated regular class sessions as well as the unstructured parts of the school day (e.g., arrival, homeroom, lunch). Many functional activities can be incorporated at "natural" times.*

As noted in Step 1, several factors influence which class a particular student will attend. Mr. Lane has listed the target classes from information off the school's master list of classes and has begun to determine which students will attend particular classes and which staff will support them as needed. Even if class scheduling is still tentative, he will pencil it in at this time.

Mr. Lane is limited by the number of adults available to support students in integrated classes at this time, so he is very conscious of using his personnel resources efficiently. If a teacher or paraprofessional is scheduled to assist a student (or students) in a particular class, this could lead to several patterns of organizing instruction. The staff person may team teach with the regular education teacher, assist the teacher with adaptations in curriculum, monitor students' work, or provide more direct assistance to the student with special needs in the class.

As with the elementary school example, Mr. Lane is aware that many of the functional activities targeted for students will be incorporated within the natural flow of the school day. For example:

- Arrival: removing outerwear
- Use of Restroom: grooming and toilet use
- Lunch: eating, cafeteria use, money-use
- Home Economics class: snack/meal preparation
- Physical Education class: dressing and undressing, grooming
- School Store: money-use skills
- Dismissal: putting on outerwear
- Extracurricular: swimming, skiing, jogging, using computers, playing team sports

Step 3. Schedule the regular classroom sessions

| | MONDAY | TUESDAY | WEDNESDAY | THURSDAY | FRIDAY |
|---|---|---|---|---|---|
| 7:50–8:04 | Arrival Routine (removing outerwear; locker use; socializing) | | | | |
| 8:07–8:25 | Homerooms (preparing for daily events; socializing) | | | | |
| 8:28–9:14 | Phys.Ed. 7 (TA¹) JS KG LT   Social Studies 7 (TA²) SP   English 8 (T) BL MZ | | | | |
| 9:17–10:03 | Phys.Ed. 8 (TA²) MZ BL SP   Science 7 (TA³) KG JS   Reading Lab (T) LT | | | | |
| 10:06–10:51 | Home Ec. 7 (T) KG JS SP   Music 8 (TA¹) BL   Art 8 (TA³) MZ LT | | | | |
| | Lunch (10:54–11:27) 4th period (11:30–12:14) | | | | |
| | 4th period (10:54–11:27) Lunch (11:30–12:14) | | | | |
| 12:17–1:05 | Industrial Arts 8 (TA¹) MZ SP   Math Lab (T) LT KG BL JS | | | | |
| 1:08–1:54 | Home Ec. 8 (TA¹) MZ BL   Music 7 (T) KG JS SP   English 8 (T) LT | | | | |
| 2:00 | Dismissal and Extracurricular activities (dressing; locker use; socializing) | | | | |

T = teacher, TA¹ = teaching assistant, TA² = teaching assistant, TA³ = teaching assistant

277

**Step 4:** *Schedule remaining instructional activities in ways that optimize the use of heterogeneous groups of students, and finalize which personnel will assist in particular activities and groupings.*

After Mr. Lane has a tentative schedule of classes for each student, he will determine how best to incorporate the remainder of activities from the community living and vocational areas. He will attempt to do this in a way that is least disruptive to a particular student's schedule of classes. At this point, therapists will determine the optimal way in which to integrate their services into a student's schedule (e.g., physical therapist assists MZ, BL, and SP during physical education class; speech/language therapist accompanies MZ, SP, and KG to the grocery store).

The last step in this process is to finalize which personnel will be assigned to a particular class or activity. Mr. Lane has arranged to provide assistance to some content area teachers a few days a week, and have the student attend without the additional assistance the remaining days (e.g., LT in English 8; KG bringing independent work to the math lab on Wednesday).

**Step 4.** Schedule remaining functional activities and finalize teaching assignments

| Time | MONDAY | TUESDAY | WEDNESDAY | THURSDAY | FRIDAY |
|---|---|---|---|---|---|
| 7:50–8:04 | Arrival routines (removing outerwear; locker use; socializing) → | | | | |
| 8:07–8:25 | Homerooms (preparing for daily events; socializing) → | | | (TA¹) MZ SP / (TA²) SP MZ | |
| 8:28–9:14 | English 8 (↑) BL MZ; Social Studies 7 (TA¹) SP; Phys.Ed. 7 (TA¹) JS KG LT | | | | Reading Lab (TA¹) LT; Sci. 7 JS |
| 9:17–10:03 | Reading Lab (↑) LT; Science 7 (TA) KG JS; Phys.Ed. 8 (TA)+PT MZ BL SP | | | | Phys. Ed. 8 (TA²)+PT BL; Restaurant (snack); Grocery Store (T+ST) MZ SP KG |
| 10:06–10:51 | Art 8 (TA) MZ LT; Music 8 (TA) BL; Home Ec. 7 (T) KG JS SP | | | | Home Ec. 7 (TA²) JS; Music 8 (TA) BL; Art 8 LT |
| 10:54–11:27 | (TA) JS SP Library; Recreation/Leisure (TA) LT KG; Lunch (LA) BL MZ | (TA) JS SP School Job; (TA) LT KG School Job; Lunch (LA) BL MZ | (TA²) SP Recreation/Leisure; (TA) KG MZ Library; Lunch (LA) MZ | (TA¹) LT KG School Job; Lunch (LA) BL MZ; Lunch (LA) JS KG | (TA¹) Lunch — Break on Friday only; (TA²) KG SP Recreation/Leisure; Grocery (TA¹) LT JS |
| 11:30–12:14 | BL Recreation/Leisure MZ; Math Lab (T) LT KG BL JS; Lunch (LA) SP JS KG | Vocational Training (CVT) MZ BL; Math Lab (T) LT KG JS; Industrial Arts 8 (TA) SP; Lunch (LA) SP JS KG | Restaurant Use (T) BL LT JS; Math Lab (T) KG; Recreation/Leisure; Industrial Arts 8 (TA¹ ST) SP MZ; Lunch (ST) SP KG | (TA²) JS SP School Job; Vocational Training (CVT) MZ BL; Math Lab (T) LT KG JS; Industrial Arts 8 (TA²) SP; Lunch (LA) MZ LT JS | (T) BL MZ Recreation/Leisure; Library; Lunch (LA) SP KG MZ |
| 12:17–1:05 | Industrial Arts 8 (TA) MZ SP | Music 7 (T) KG JS SP; English 8 (TA¹) LT | Home Ec. 8 (TA¹) MZ BL; Music 7 (T) KG JS SP; English 8 LT | Music 7 (T) KG JS SP; English 8 (TA¹) LT | Math Lab (T) KG BL; Industrial Arts 8 (T) SP MZ |
| 1:08–1:54 | Home Ec. 8 (TA¹) MZ BL; Music 7 (T) KG JS SP; English 8 LT | | | | Home Ec. 8 (TA¹) MZ BL; Music 7 (T) MZ KG JS; English 8 LT |
| 2:00 | Dismissal and Extracurricular activities (dressing; locker use; socializing) | | | | |

Notes: (T) Lunch break on Friday only; (TA¹) Lunch break (except Fri.)

T = teacher, TA¹ = teaching assistant, TA² = teaching assistant, LA = lunch assistant, CVT = community vocational teacher, ST = speech/language therapist, PT = physical therapist (other initials [i.e., MZ, KG, JS] are those of students).

# CHAPTER 15

# Managing Classroom Operations

## Linda Davern and Alison Ford

When educating a diverse group of students, careful attention must be given to the management skills of the teacher. For example, the teacher must be skilled in working with other team members (e.g., paraprofessionals, related service providers), supporting students in regular classes, and managing the logistics of community-based instruction. We have selected several of what we consider to be the most challenging aspects of classroom operations for discussion:

- Teamwork: working successfully with professional and paraprofessional staff
- Alternative methods of organizing instructional sessions
- Considerations in determining the physical layout of a classroom
- Handling logistical concerns related to providing instruction in the community
- Moving forward with integration

## TEAMWORK: WORKING SUCCESSFULLY WITH PROFESSIONAL AND PARAPROFESSIONAL STAFF

Models of providing educational services for students with moderate and severe handicaps often include the presence of more than one adult in the classroom (e.g., the presence of paraprofessionals; team teaching arrangements). The success of such classrooms often depends on the ability of adults to work collaboratively on a daily basis—that is, effective teamwork. Effective teamwork is also necessary for implementing integrated therapy services and participating on grade-level planning teams. Successful teams can be characterized by the following: commitment to a shared philosophy, respect for the contributions of each team member; consensus on roles and responsibilities; use of ongoing forums for communication, and use of collaborative problem-solving skills. You and your team members might review your team's performance in relation to the following five questions.

### Do you have a commitment to a shared philosophy?

The success of your team will be influenced by each member's philosophy toward education and students with handicaps. The development of a shared philosophy can be seen as a developmental process. Professionals and paraprofessionals who compose a newly formed team, or join an already existing team, come to their roles with various histories, attitudes and expectations. This may be frustrating for other team members who have strongly held convictions regarding adherence to educational principles such as the right to receive instruction with peers who are not handicapped, age appropriateness, respect for the dignity of individuals; the validity of partial participation as an educational outcome; and the importance of home-school collaboration. It is important in such situations to realize that attitudes change over time—particularly in the presence of strong, patient, and articulate role models. It is important at the beginning of a team-building process to clarify (and attempt to reach consensus on) which philosophical principles will undergird the work of the team.

There are several aspects of being an effective leader and model that will have a substantial effect on the development of a shared philosophy, as well as the day-to-day atmosphere in the classroom. Provencal (1987) brings attention to the importance of leaders setting the tone for others (robust as opposed to "whiney"), elevating displays of ingenuity, and refraining from hoarding the credit for successes. Effective leaders present their successes as an outcome of what *we* have accomplished, as opposed to *I*.

### Is there respect for the contributions of each team member?

Members will contribute to the success of the team to the extent that they feel that their participation and contributions are valued. This is particularly true of paraprofessionals. It is not unusual for paraprofessionals to feel that the important role they play in the educational experience of students is not fully appreciated. An appreciation for their contribution can be demonstrated by both teachers and administrators, through actions such as verbal acknowledgment of their skills and commitment, seeking information on the performance of students, and inclusion in the decision making that accompanies classroom planning.

### Is there consensus on roles and responsibilities?

A team is much more likely to function effectively if members have a clear understanding of their roles and responsibilities. It may be useful at the beginning of the school year to make a list of the major responsibilities and who will carry them out. This listing may evolve over the year, and certain duties may rotate. Many teachers feel that it is important to rotate duties so that each team member is aware of the nature of various tasks, and particular team members do not feel that less desirable duties (e.g., clerical tasks) are always delegated to them because of their position in the hierarchy.

### Are there ongoing forums for communication?

While there may be opportunities throughout the school day to share information about students and other aspects of classroom operations, it is important that team members have an opportunity to meet on a frequent and regular basis. This ensures that a member with a concern or suggestion will have the chance to bring it to the attention of all other team members. Meetings serve as a forum for solving problems as well as an opportunity to share successes and pleasant anecdotes. This contributes to each member's sense of commitment to the group goal of providing the best possible learning environment for students.

One useful practice is keeping an ongoing list of agenda items. As concerns arise throughout the week, they are added to the agenda. Meeting time can also serve as an opportunity to use a collaborative problem-solving process.

### Do you use a collaborative problem-solving process?

Planning and implementing educational programs requires a tremendous amount of decision making and problem solving. A process for "collaborative problem-solving" can be used on either a formal or informal basis. The following six steps are recommended when a team is attempting to reach consensus on the best approach to a given problem (Bolton, 1979):

1. Define the problem in terms of needs, not solutions. ("What do we need?")
2. Brainstorm possible solutions. (List possible solutions, don't evaluate.)
3. Select which solutions seem best, and discuss the consequences of each.
4. Plan who will do "what," as well as "where" and "when" they will do it.
5. Implement the plan.
6. Evaluate the group's problem-solving process, and later, how the plan has worked out.

The advantage to a collaborative problem-solving process is that members are encouraged to refrain from immediately vetoing original or unique ideas. Team members are allowed to express their ideas. Evaluation is left until all ideas have been contributed. This open stance toward team members' contributions often leads to more and better ideas, but also to a greater sense of commitment by all to whichever plan of action is ultimately chosen.

When a teacher has the dual goal of making optimal classroom decisions, as well as including other adults such as paraprofessionals in the decision-making process, it may be important to engage in "hierarchy collapsing"—that is, seeking to reach consensus on a decision, rather than simply imposing it on other team members (Doyle & Strauss, 1976). This means that problems are discussed with other team members, and the team seeks a "win/win" solution—that is, a solution or plan that all members can accept. Ultimately, if a plan that is acceptable to all members cannot be made, the teacher may need to make the decision since she or he is ultimately responsible for the educational program. In such a case, however, other team members will have more information and understanding of the rationale for the teacher's decision, and thus will be more likely to implement the decision effectively since they were involved in the process. An example of how this process can be used to resolve a classroom issue is presented in Table 15.1.

## ALTERNATIVE METHODS OF STRUCTURING INSTRUCTIONAL SESSIONS

The ways in which classroom activities are structured has significant influence on the quality of students' experiences. Alternative methods of organizing learning experiences can facilitate the inclusion of students with moderate or severe handicaps with other students. Examples of alternative methods include cooperative learning strategies, activity-based sessions with individualized objectives, large group lessons with individualized objectives for a particular student, tutoring relationships, and community-based instruction with a heterogeneous group of students. A brief discussion of such alternatives with examples of implementation follows.

### Cooperative Learning Strategies

As noted by Johnson, Johnson, Holubec, and Roy (1984), lessons in school are structured in one of three ways: individualistically, competitively, or cooperatively. The predominant structures used in classrooms today are competitive and individualistic in nature. In classrooms with a heterogeneous grouping of students, an emphasis on competitive activities is not appropriate since students bring different resources to the classroom (Stainback & Stainback, 1989). A day that is structured around individu-

Table 15.1.    Team problem-solving process

The following is an example of a collaborative problem-solving process being used to address the issue of "determining teacher assistant (TA) responsibilities and evaluation plans":

Step 1: Define the problem. What do we need?
  1.  Way to determine responsibility for teaching tasks
  2.  Way to determine responsibility for nonteaching duties (materials development, hall duty, etc.)
  3.  Plan for describing/modeling methods of instruction
  4.  Plan for discussing implementation on an ongoing basis
  5.  Way to evaluate implementation on an ongoing basis
  6.  Scheduled time to review lesson plans
  7.  _____
  8.  _____

Step 2: Brainstorm possible solutions. (Don't evaluate yet—just list ideas.)
  1.  Way to determine responsibility for teaching tasks
      a.  Teacher is responsible for a particular content area and assigns tasks for TAs during that class period
      b.  During team meetings TAs are asked: "What are you good at?" and "What areas do you enjoy teaching?"—this input is used to identify teaching areas
      c.  _____
      d.  _____

  2.  Way to determine responsibility for nonteaching duties
      a.  List of duties is generated each week—TAs and teachers sign up for the responsibilities on a weekly basis
      b.  List of duties is generated for the month and team members are assigned on a rotating basis
      c.  Some duties may be permanent if there is mutual agreement
      d.  _____
      e.  _____

  3.  Plan for describing/modeling methods of instruction
      a.  TA observes teacher with small group for first two to three sessions
      b.  TA co-teaches lesson with teacher for first week
      c.  TA and teacher observe videotape of model lesson
      d.  TA and teacher review a written description of lesson
      e.  _____
      f.  _____

  4.  Plan for discussing implementation on an ongoing basis
      a.  Use a notebook or clipboard to log concerns—go over each item at the weekly team meeting
      b.  Set aside two morning sessions a week (15–20 minutes) for team meetings (this would be in addition to the weekly meeting)
      c.  Encourage TA to raise questions during or directly after a lesson if the situation permits; hold extended discussion for after school or meeting time
      d.  _____
      e.  _____

  5.  Way to evaluate implementation on an ongoing basis
      a.  Observe lesson frequently in beginning stages
      b.  Observe lesson and offer feedback every 2–3 weeks
      c.  Develop a form where the TA can make notations about lesson and evaluate his or her own performance
      d.  _____
      e.  _____

(continued)

Table 15.1.   (*continued*)

6.   Scheduled time to review lesson plans
   a.   Schedule time so that written plans can be reviewed at the beginning of each day or end of each day
   b.   If extra time is needed on a particular day for a team meeting, arrange for "comp time" for a TA on another day
   c.   _____
   d.   _____

Step 3: Select solutions that seem best. Discuss the consequences. Formulate a plan.

Step 4: Plan who will do "what," and "where" and "when" they will do it.

Step 5: Implement the plan.

Step 6: Review and evaluate plan on a monthly basis, or as needed, and revise accordingly. Evaluate the problem-solving process.

alistic learning experiences does not take advantage of the numerous benefits that result from student-to-student interactions. The third structure, cooperative learning, holds very exciting potential for realizing these benefits. (Resources on cooperative learning methods are listed in the "References" and "Additional Readings and Resources" sections at the end of this chapter.)

Johnson et al. (1984) describe four components to cooperative learning: positive interdependence (each student's success is linked with the success of other group members), individual accountability (ensuring that each student learns), face-to-face interactions, and teaching cooperative group skills. Cooperative learning methods are gaining prominence due to outcomes such as higher academic achievement, more positive heterogeneous relationships, and higher levels of student motivation (Johnson & Johnson, 1986). Greater use of these models, as opposed to more traditional lecture and seatwork formats, will provide more opportunities to include students with moderate or severe handicaps in instructional activities with their peers.

In a heterogeneous classroom it is possible for a student who is handicapped to participate in a cooperative lesson in a modified way if necessary. Consider the following example where each student contributes something different to the group goal:

Five students are given the group goal of constructing a salt-and-flour relief map depicting the geographic features of Africa. John's assignment is to go with a friend to pick up a reference book at the library, join the group of five, assist with mixing the ingredients, and pass the mixture to group members as needed.

### Activity-Based Sessions with Individualized Objectives

Often an activity can serve as a basis for working on different objectives for students within the same small group:

Every day in math time, Shawn and Jerry were assigned to The Hot Chocolate Business—a classroom fundraising project. Other groups of students—four at a time—were assigned to the Hot Chocolate Business on a rotating basis. During this time students would graph how much hot chocolate was sold at lunch the previous day and make estimations and plans regarding future sales and use of profits. They would also prepare to purchase needed supplies. While the objectives targeted for the four rotating students included the application of math concepts drawn from the regular fourth-grade curriculum, Jerry was learning how to count money and use a calculator and Shawn was learning to match coins to pictures on money cards. One day a week, Jerry, Shawn, and two other students traveled to the store to replenish supplies for the project, giving them an opportunity to practice street-crossing, money-use, and grocery-shopping skills. (For a complete discussion of this activity, see Ford & Davern [1989, pp. 13–17].)[1]

## Large Group Lessons with Objectives Individualized for Particular Student(s)

It is often possible to structure a large group lesson while still individualizing the objectives for a given student. Consider the following:

A group of 20 students is involved in a health lesson related to nutrition. One of the members of the group is a 12-year-old student who is learning (with a partner) to use an adapted switch to operate a blender to prepare a snack. The activity of preparing a yogurt and fruit snack for the class will serve as a backdrop for a discussion of diet and its effects on health.

## Tutoring Relationships

Tutoring by children from upper grades can benefit any young child. Consider the following:

Students from a fifth-grade class spend 30 minutes a week with children in the second grade. Their assignment is to choose a book with the second grader and sit as partners while the second grader reads. They are encouraged to give each child assistance if needed, and respond to her or his questions. Jennifer is being read to by a fifth grader, and is learning to look at the pictures, turn the pages, and attend to the older students.

## Community-Based Instruction with Heterogeneous Group of Students

Similar to activity-based sessions, it is possible to design community-based instruction so that it is relevant to students with and without handicaps. The following example presented by Ford and Black (1989) illustrates the wide range of educational opportunities that can be addressed with community-based instruction.

On Monday, Tuesday, and Wednesday afternoons, Mr. Clift supervises community-internship experiences for a small group of juniors from Maxwell High School. His group includes Frank, Becky, Montez, Carol, and Sam. Becky experiences a severe disability. The other students in the group have more typical learning styles. This semester the members of the group are interning at Terrace Labs, where they are learning science as well as career/vocational skills. Montez is in the top 5 percent of his class in his academic standing. Becky is described in her school records as profoundly mentally retarded and functions within the lowest 1 percent of the population based on most standardized measures. The educational needs of both students are met within a real community work environment. As a strong science student, Montez leans toward a career in chemistry or mathematics. At Terrace, he learns and applies principles of chemistry as they pertain to the production of pharmaceutical products. As an research assistant to his mentor he assists with the research and production activities of the plant. Becky assists with the sterilization of test tubes and lab equipment under the supervision of a job coach. For Becky, this assignment is the most challenging of her placements so far. She is increasing her social interaction skills as well as her work endurance. (pp. 162–163)

---

[1]This activity was adapted from an instructional program developed by David Smukler while he was completing an internship at Ed Smith Elementary School in Syracuse, New York.

## CONSIDERATIONS IN DETERMINING PHYSICAL LAYOUT OF A CLASSROOM

When alternative methods of organizing instruction are utilized, changes are usually made in the physical layout of the classroom. The following questions might be asked when considering an optimal classroom layout (ideas were generated by staff members of Salem Hyde Elementary School during a workshop in August, 1988):

- Look around the room—are your spaces well defined (e.g., a space for silent reading, for computer usage, for leisure, for large and small group work)?
- Do you have areas that can be used for various group sizes (e.g., for the entire class, for one or two students, for a group of 10 students)?
- Have you arranged seating so that the students with disabilities are interspersed with their nondisabled peers?
- Have you done careful matching of students/partners to promote positive relationships and friendship development?
- Does your room communicate a sense of cooperation (e.g., students' desks are clustered in groups versus long rows of desks facing the teacher)?
- Have you organized materials on shelves so that the students can gain access to material independently?
- Have you explored other spaces in the building that can be incorporated into your schedule for small group instruction (e.g., library, cafeteria, math lab)?
- Are there any spaces that you tend to use only with a student(s) with disabilities? How can you avoid this?
- Do you have a space where each student can put his or her personal belongings? Do you have a mail box (or in/out basket) for each student to manage the flow of communication that goes between home and school?

For a more detailed discussion of structuring a classroom for diversity, see Stainback and Stainback (1989) in the "References" section at the end of this chapter.

A teacher who has students who are involved in activities drawn from the community living areas may face logistical concerns beyond those associated with in-school student groupings and the physical layout of the classroom. Concerns that are related to providing instruction in the community are addressed below.

## HANDLING LOGISTICAL CONCERNS RELATED TO PROVIDING INSTRUCTION IN THE COMMUNITY

Teachers often face logistical barriers that make it difficult to fully implement the weekly schedule. The school district may have a policy that prohibits teaching assistants from teaching in community settings unless accompanied by a teacher. There may be no system for acquiring "petty cash" for purchasing grocery items for snack preparation or providing instruction at a restaurant. A town may not have a public bus system and teachers may not be allowed to transport students in their cars. On a short-term basis, the most any teacher can do is utilize the available resources as effectively and efficiently as possible.

On a long-term basis, it will be important to advocate for changes in district policies and practices that impede classroom operation. In Table 15.2 we have listed some common concerns encountered by teachers and the short-term temporary strategies that have been used to address them.

Table 15.2.    Common logistical concerns and short-term strategies

| Logistical concerns | Temporary strategies |
| --- | --- |
| **Paraprofessionals**<br>• Teacher assistant may only carry out instructional plans in the presence of a certified teacher. | • The teacher could provide community-based instruction to a small group of students while remaining students receive instruction from a paraprofessional at school in the presence of a different teacher.<br>• Select community sites that can accommodate a larger number of students so that both a teacher and teacher assistant can provide instruction at the same time in the same basic location (e.g., different tables in a restaurant, different sections of a large store, adjacent stores in a mall). This is the least desirable strategy since a large number of students in one setting has a potentially negative effect on how they are perceived. |
| **Money**<br>• Cash is not available for: making purchases in stores, eating in restaurants, paying bus fares, and so forth. | • Students could practice skills by making purchases for another person (e.g., buying grocery items for the home economics teacher, buying items for the student's family with money from home).<br>• Parents may give their son or daughter a small allowance for a weekly purchase of a drink or snack at a restaurant. |
| **Transportation**<br>• Transportation to community sites is not available. | • Investigate sites that are within walking distance or are on a public transportation route.<br>• Seek permission for staff to transport students (check on insurance and liability issues).<br>• Identify times when school buses may be available and arrange your schedule to provide community instruction at those times (e.g., Tues./Thurs. between 10:00 A.M. and 1:00 P.M.).<br>• Arrange instructional sites that are close to one another so that several small groups of students can be transported by the same bus (e.g., a vocational site and a shopping site on the same side of town are utilized for two different student groups on the same days). |
| **Staff**<br>• Not enough staff. | • Schedule fewer instructional sessions in the community (e.g., all students receive instruction in community settings, but less frequently to keep group size small).<br>• Identify other staff that might provide community instruction for some students (e.g., speech therapist provides language instruction to several students in a restaurant setting). |

(continued)

Table 15.2.   *(continued)*

| Logistical concerns | Temporary strategies |
| --- | --- |
| **Assigned Student Groupings**<br>• A homogeneous group of students with severe disabilities. | • Create a small instructional group of students that is more heterogeneous by teaming with another teacher and regrouping students from both classes throughout the school day. Strive to include students without handicaps in community instruction. |

Adapted from Schnorr, Ford, Davern, Park-Lee, and Meyer (1989).

## MOVING FORWARD WITH INTEGRATION

Many of the examples given earlier in this chapter emphasize the importance of children being able to learn together. Many teachers believe that integration is important but face obstacles in their particular school settings. Although many students with moderate and severe handicaps now receive their education in public schools, the daily experience for many of these students is quite varied—ranging from full integration in regular classes to defacto segregation within special classes with little or no opportunity to learn from or develop relationships with other students. Regardless of in which situation students are placed, there are important steps to take in moving forward with integration in a particular school or school district. The following situations are representative of those commonly faced by teachers.

**Situation: A teacher believes that her students should be participating in integrated classes, but there is no precedent at her school for doing so. She is wondering where she should start.**

Often, there is no precedent at a particular school for including students with moderate or severe handicaps in classes with nonhandicapped students. The thought of attempting to negotiate these arrangements in addition to an already overwhelming list of responsibilities may be discouraging. Progress may seem slow at times, but each step toward a more fully integrated school day for students is an important accomplishment. Some suggestions teachers have made with regard to facilitating integration include:

1.  Be prepared to help educators understand why it is important for the student to be involved in the particular class. Your rationale should address both social and curricular needs.
2.  Be prepared to describe how the student(s) will be involved in the class and the level of support you or other school personnel plan to provide. This may range from consultation in adapting curriculum to having a staff person assist in class.
3.  Build ongoing relationships with administrators and educators to pave the way for future integration efforts. To do this you might:
    a.  elicit administrative support for measures such as reducing class sizes for teachers who will have students on their classlists who need extensive support
    b.  establish an ongoing system of communication with cooperating teachers and express a willingness to assist with any problems that arise
    c.  acknowledge the contributions of the cooperating teachers toward achieving a school community that is truly inclusive of all students

4. Support parents who seek to expand the opportunities available to their children.
5. Integrate yourself. Visit the teachers' lounge regularly. Attend staff meetings. Show interest in the issues that affect the entire school. Become a coach, a club leader, a union representative, and so forth.

### Situation: The students at Dalton Elementary School are already placed in regular classes. How does "moving forward with school integration" apply to these teachers?

Achieving "physical" integration is a necessary prerequisite to achieving *social* integration—but often it is not enough. Although a student may be placed in regular classes, he or she may need assistance in becoming part of a network of friends. This assistance can range from less to more formal actions, such as the following:

1. Rewarding students (in a natural, subtle way) for showing an interest in the student of concern.
2. Using students' interest in you as a bridge to getting to know a particular student (e.g., bringing attention to common interests).
3. Arranging instruction in a manner that increases the likelihood of children developing positive attitudes about each other (e.g., using cooperative rather than competitive structuring of activities).
4. Creating a classroom atmosphere that rewards prosocial behaviors such as the acceptance of individual differences and the valuing of the unique character of each child.
5. Instituting, if necessary, a more formal plan for addressing the problem of social isolation, such as the *McGill Action Planning System* (Forest & Snow, 1986). Such a plan recruits and organizes a group of students (a "circle of friends") to assist a student socially. The goal of such a plan is eventually to withdraw the formal aspect and let the emerging relationships develop in a more natural fashion.

### Situation: The teacher at Fairfield High School has worked hard to schedule his students into regular classes. Both he and a teaching assistant will be providing "support" to certain students in particular classes. How do they best provide this support?

Supporting a student with severe disabilities in a regular high school class requires thoughtful planning. You will want to ensure that the student is an active learner in the class—whether the goals are to master some essential component of the regular curriculum or to develop related functional or embedded skills. You will also want to ensure that the student becomes *a part of* the class and the social networks that exist in that setting. The following ideas may be helpful in performing this role. (Many of these ideas were generated by the following individuals who have had the experience of supporting students in regular junior and senior high school classes and in community job sites: Jim Cashen, Carol Ann Donnellan, Jean Delmonico, Maureen Blake, and Kim Kaiser.):

1. Establish rapport with the classroom teacher and try to understand his or her perspective on the student's involvement.
   a. Do not assume that teachers have information about students or appreciate why integration is important (for both the individual and other students in the class). Be prepared to provide a rationale for teachers in response to concerns such as: "Does she really belong here?" or "What is he getting out of it?" Also

be prepared to explain concepts such as partial participation in a way that is easily understood.

    b. Give background information on the student such as what types of skills he or she has, or what the student enjoys doing (ideas related to motivation). You might develop a one-page profile to share with teachers.

    c. Show interest in the particular content area and learn as much as you can about the curriculum.

    d. Relate positive anecdotes about how the student feels about the class.

    e. Try to understand attitudes that may be less than welcoming. For example, a teacher who is normally the only adult in the class may feel uneasy about your presence, especially in the beginning. A teacher may be apprehensive about issues such as curricular adaptation, grading, and so forth. Alleviate these concerns, to the extent possible, and emphasize the benefits accruing to all students.

    f. Be aware of the politics of a particular situation. For example, did the teacher have a bad experience in the past with having students placed in his or her class without adequate support or planning? Knowledge of this and other factors will affect your approach.

2. Plan for the students' involvement.

    a. Have empathy for the demands on the teacher's time. Realize that, given the large number of students for which a secondary-level teacher is often responsible, you may need to be rather informal in your meeting time (e.g., catching the teacher before and after class). You will need to continuously judge the level of involvement a teacher is willing to have with planning, adapting curriculum, and so forth.

    b. View your role as an assistant or co-teacher in the class. This means that you will assist other students in addition to the student with handicaps. Attempt to gradually fade your direct assistance to the student with handicaps while establishing or reinforcing peer support.

    c. Demonstrate the respect you have for the student. For example, do not talk about the student in his or her presence without including the student in the conversation—"Isn't that right, Kate?"; use age-appropriate language and intonation patterns.

    d. Comment positively in a natural, unobtrusive way on the social interactions that occur between students with handicaps and those without.

    e. If a student is not "connecting" with his or her classmates, receive a commitment from several students in the class to become a part of a support group. Help these students to understand and appreciate their unique roles in ensuring that the student is actively involved in the class activities.

3. Always remain sensitive to the needs of the student.

    a. Acknowledge when a situation is not benefiting a student and investigate a different class or teacher. There are times when a student and teacher are simply incompatible. It is important to recognize this and make the necessary changes.

## Final Remarks

Regardless of in which state of integration a particular school or district is, there will always be work to do in helping students become a more integral part of the school community. For some schools in beginning stages, this work will involve taking basic first steps in breaking patterns of isolated, segregated service models. For other schools who have achieved physical integration, the challenge will be that of creating the conditions that will allow each child to be a fully accepted and valued member of the regular class and school.

## SUMMARY

Each of the elements discussed in this chapter make an important contribution to the quality of a student's educational experience:

- Utilizing an effective team of adults that is committed to providing the best educational environment possible
- Developing an openness to investigating alternative methods of organizing learning experiences
- Designing an appropriate classroom physical layout
- Implementing short-term strategies to overcome logistical barriers to instruction in the community, while continuing to work for long-term changes in policies and practices
- Maintaining an awareness that an integrated educational program is never fully developed, but is always in a dynamic state of change with the goal of continued improvement and refinement

## QUESTIONS AND ANSWERS

Q:  I am interested in implementing some cooperative learning activities and activity-based lessons in order to better include my students with special needs, but where do I start?

A:  Teacher centers and city and university libraries may have collections of lesson plan ideas and other resources. (Also, see the "Suggested Readings and Resources" section at the end of this and other chapters of the *Guide*). Often the most effective way of starting is by visiting teachers who have experience with such methods. This allows you the opportunity not only to see how such lessons are organized and what sorts of materials are used, but also to talk with teachers who have surmounted the obstacles that are inevitable in the early stages of implementation. It is important to note that a teacher need not completely transform his or her methods of organizing lessons overnight. It may be wise to start with one aspect of the program, and gradually transform others as desired. Oftentimes staff development personnel will survey teachers about their inservice interests. This would be an opportunity for you to express an interest in classes or workshops on cooperative learning models.

Q:  I am interested in implementing a collaborative problem-solving process with the related services providers, a parent volunteer who spends a great deal of time in the classroom, and the teaching assistant in my classroom. How can I cope with the added time demands of such a decision-making process as well as people's negative attitudes about meetings?

A:  Group decision making often entails an additional time commitment on the part of team members. But in terms of the benefits realized in motivation, creativity, and shared ownership, it is well worth the investment. It may be wise to try to establish a regular time for members to meet to avoid the logistical constraints of trying to organize last-minute meetings. It may also be possible to arrange for an assistant to work 30 minutes later 1 day per week in exchange for a later starting time.

It will be important for the teacher to sort out which matters are best addressed by the group, and which can be resolved solely by the teacher. Several variables to consider include: 1) Does the issue under discussion have direct consequences for other group members? 2) Is there enough time for a group decision? 3) Is information needed from the group? 4) Is group ownership an important variable? and 5) Does the teacher need coordination by the group in order to ensure effective implementation? (Wynn & Guditus, 1984).

Meeting time may also be viewed more positively by members if the following features characterize meetings: 1) there is a lot of discussion in which virtually everyone participates, but discussion remains relevant to the topics on the agenda; 2) the objectives of the meeting are clearly understood; 3) disagreements are not suppressed, overridden, or dismissed prematurely; 4) criticism is frequent and frank, and people are comfortable with the criticism because it is constructive and not person oriented; and 5) people are free to express feelings and ideas on both the problem and the process being used in the meeting (McGregor, 1960).

## REFERENCES

Bolton, R. (1979). *People skills*. Englewood Cliffs, NJ: Prentice-Hall.

Doyle, M., & Strauss, D. (1976). *How to make meetings work*. New York: Berkley.

Ford, A., & Black, J. (1989). The emergence of a community-referenced curriculum. In D. Biklen, D. Ferguson, & A. Ford (Eds.), *Schooling and disability* (Eighty-Eighth Yearbook of the National Society for the Study of Education) (pp. 141–167). Chicago: University of Chicago Press.

Ford, A., & Davern, L. (1989). Moving forward with school integration: Strategies for involving students with severe handicaps in the life of the school. In R. Gaylord-Ross (Ed.), *Integration strategies for persons with handicaps* (pp. 11–31). Baltimore: Paul H. Brookes Publishing Co.

Forest, M., & Snow, J. (1986). *McGill action planning system (MAPS)*. Toronto: Center for Integration, Frontier College.

Johnson, D.W., & Johnson, R.T. (1986). Mainstreaming and cooperative learning strategies. *Exceptional Children, 52*(6), 553–561.

Johnson, D.W., Johnson, R., Holubec, E., & Roy, P. (1984). *Circles of learning*. Alexandria, VA: The Association for Supervision and Curriculum Development.

McGregor, D. (1960). *The human side of enterprise*. NY: McGraw-Hill.

Provencal, G. (1987) Culturing commitment. In S.J. Taylor, D. Biklen, & J. Knoll (Eds.), *Community integration for people with severe disabilities*. New York: Teachers' College, Columbia University.

Schnorr, R., Ford, A., Davern, L., Park-Lee, S., & Meyer, L. (1989). *The Syracuse curriculum revision manual: A group process for developing a community-referenced curriculum guide*. Baltimore: Paul H. Brookes Publishing Co.

Stainback, S.B., & Stainback, W.C. (1989). Classroom organization. In D. Biklen, D. Ferguson, & A. Ford (Eds.), *Schooling and disability* (Eighty-Eighth Yearbook of the National Society for the Study of Education) (pp. 195–207). Chicago: University of Chicago Press.

Wynn, R., & Guditus, C. W. (1984). *Team management: Leadership by consensus*. Columbus, OH: Charles E. Merrill.

## ADDITIONAL READINGS AND RESOURCES

Baumgart, D., & Van Walleghem, J. (1986). Staffing strategies for implementing community-based instruction. *Journal of The Association for Persons with Severe Handicaps, 11*, 92–102.

Frank, A., Keith, T., & Steil, D. (1988). Training needs of special education paraprofessionals. *Exceptional Children*, *55*, 253–258.

Hamre-Nietupski, S., Nietupski, J., Bates, P., & Maurer, S. (1982). Implementing a community-based educational model for moderately/severely handicapped students: Common problems and suggested solutions. *Journal of The Association for the Severely Handicapped*, *7*(2), 38–43.

Nietupski, J., Hamre-Nietupski, S., Clancy, P., & Veerhusen, K. (1986). Guidelines for making simulation an effective adjunct to in vivo community instruction. *Journal of The Association for Persons with Severe Handicaps*, *11*, 12–18.

Nietupski, J., Hamre-Nietupski, S., Donder, D., Houselog, M., & Anderson, R. (1988). Proactive administrative strategies for implementing community-based programs for students with moderate/severe handicaps. *Education and Training in Mental Retardation*, *23*, 138–146.

[For additional resources on cooperative learning, write to: Interaction Book Co., 7208 Cornelia Drive, Edina, MN 55435.]

# CHAPTER 16

# Planning and Implementing Activity-Based Lessons

### Jim Black and Alison Ford

Earlier chapters in the *Guide* have presented strategies for determining priority instructional goals and activities for students. In addition, strategies have been offered to assist in translating goals and activities for each student into a manageable weekly schedule. This chapter focuses on the process of instructional planning, providing appropriate instruction, and monitoring student progress toward the achievement of priority educational goals. While careful planning and monitoring of instruction demands considerable time and energy on the part of teachers, it provides many significant benefits, including:

- *Individualized instruction.* All students, particularly students with moderate and severe handicaps, require instruction that is motivating, active, and powerful enough for them to learn. Planning and monitoring instruction helps us to select the most appropriate instructional strategies for each student, and to modify them as necessary.
- *Enhanced communication among team members.* Education for students with moderate and severe handicaps is a team effort. Planning and monitoring can help maintain ongoing communication between all team members, including: teachers, paraprofessionals, related services providers, and parents. Furthermore, community-referenced components of instructional programs often rely heavily on paraprofessionals to assist with and/or carry out instruction within community sites. An efficient classroom system of instructional planning and monitoring is essential in order for paraprofessionals to fulfill these important roles.
- *Accountability for educators.* Federal legislation requires that each student's individualized education program (IEP) contain methods for evaluating student progress on individualized instructional objectives. Appropriate monitoring strategies allow us to document the incremental progress each student makes toward the long-range goals the team envisions for him or her.

Recall Mary Z.'s schedule from Chapter 14 in this guide. Mary's weekly schedule involves instruction in a range of settings, including physical education class, art class, English class, industrial arts class, and the school cafeteria, as well as a community vocational training site, restaurant, and grocery store. The instruction provided in each of these settings can be planned and monitored using many different formats. The purpose of this chapter is *not* to discuss all possible planning formats that can be used by teachers; rather, our intent is to focus on one specific approach— an activity-based lesson-planning format. This is a format that will allow you to focus on the mastery of the steps in the activity as well as the underlying skills and concepts.

If we review the information learned about Mary Z. and her weekly schedule, we are likely to reach the conclusion that most, if not all, of her instruction will follow an activity-based lesson format. While functioning in the community (eating in a restaurant, shopping, working at a job site, etc.), the teacher will be concerned with enhancing Mary's participation in as many steps as possible in the routines. In art class, the teacher will be just as concerned about Mary's learning the routine of art class (including the steps of locating materials, setting up, performing the necessary steps, etc.), as her learning a *particular* artistic technique or expression (e.g., shading with charcoal). In English class, the teacher will be concerned more with Mary's ability to perform the steps in the routine of constructing a "photo journal" (with the goal of contributing to Mary's recreation/leisure repertoire), than with her learning a particular grammatical structure. How, then, do we proceed with planning for these activity-based lessons?

## ACTIVITY-BASED LESSONS: A THREE-STEP PROCESS

Figure 16.1 presents an overview of the three-step instructional planning and monitoring process. Step 1 involves *conducting an initial activity-based assessment* to determine current levels of student performance, and to target the short-term objectives leading to greater competence. Step 2 uses the assessment information to *determine general instructional procedures* that communicate how a lesson will be structured. Step 3 involves gathering and using information about each student's progress *using a planning and data card system*. (This three-step process is illustrated with sample forms completed for two different students: Ken, who represents students with moderate to severe levels of disability; and Mary Z., who represents students with severe multiple disabilities.)

### Step 1: Conduct an initial activity-based assessment.

IEP goals and objectives give us the general direction of instruction for the year. For example, both Ken and Mary have goals and objectives pertaining to the activity of

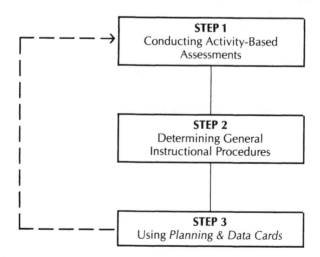

Figure 16.1.   Three-step planning and monitoring process.

grocery shopping (see Figure 16.2). These *priority* goals and objectives will be instructionally addressed and monitored during the weekly trips to the grocery store. A thorough, initial assessment will help you determine which skills the student currently has in his or her repertoire before receiving systematic instruction. This, in turn, will enable you to: 1) establish a clear "baseline" performance from which to evaluate progress at later points in the school year, 2) determine which skills to target for instruction, 3) identify necessary adaptations, and 4) begin to make decisions about what types of instructional cues match the student's learning and performance style.

What might an initial assessment of "grocery shopping" look like for Mary Z. and Ken? First, we would begin by identifying the actual store(s) in which they will

---

KEN: a student whose instructional needs represent those of many students who experience moderate to severe disabilities

*Goal*

Ken will purchase four items from four different sections of the grocery store using a written shopping list and the calculator subtraction method.

*Objectives*

• After entering the store, Ken will independently take out his shopping list and calculator and prepare to grocery shop (successfully, on three consecutive shopping trips).

• When searching for items on his shopping list, Ken will stop in each section, look at his list for items that might be found in that section, and locate the items that he needs by independently scanning the grocery aisle (successfully, for each of the four items in the section, on two consecutive opportunities).

• Once he has located an item on his list, Ken will independently use the calculator subtraction method to determine if he has "enough" or "not enough" money for the purchase (successfully, for entire list, on five consecutive shopping trips).

• Once he has obtained all of the items on his list that he has "enough" money for, Ken will independently pay for his purchases at the checkout line using appropriate social skills and a next-dollar strategy (e.g., if the cashier says, "That will be $5.76," Ken will hand over six $1 bills) (successfully, on five consecutive shopping trips).

MARY Z: a student whose instructional needs represent those of many students who experience severe multiple disabilities

*Goal*

Mary will increase her level of active participation in grocery shopping for two to three familiar items using picture-symbol shopping cards (an adapted shopping list) and money envelopes (an adaptation consisting of envelopes containing the amount of money necessary to purchase an item represented by a picture symbol on the outside).

*Objectives*

• When positioned in front of the grocery section containing the item for which she has a picture-symbol card, Mary will visually scan (horizontally) the shelf for an area of about 3 feet (successfully, on five consecutive shopping trips).

• Once the desired item is located, Mary will remove it from the shelf and place it in her shopping basket (successfully, with a given item, on four of five consecutive store trips).

• When positioned in front of the cashier, Mary will hand over her money envelope to the cashier (within 5 seconds of clerk requesting payment, for five consecutive opportunities).

---

Figure 16.2. Grocery-shopping goals and objectives for Ken and Mary Z.

learn to shop. Since instruction for both students will take place in the "Big M Super-market," we will conduct our assessment there. Using an approach that has been referred to as an "ecological inventory strategy" or "nonhandicapped person inventory" (Brown et al., 1979), we would actually visit the store and record the particular behaviors and skills performed by nonhandicapped persons engaged in the activity of shopping. To be as accurate as possible, it is usually advisable to directly observe or perform the activity under consideration. If we attempt to rely on our memory of how an activity is actually performed, we often inadvertently omit important steps.

We must then decide how much to break down the activity into its component steps. For example, the way that a nonhandicapped person purchases a soda from a vending machine can be broken down into anywhere from 5 to 100 discrete steps! A five-step breakdown will probably not provide us with enough detailed information to conduct an assessment of a student's performance, while a 100 step breakdown will likely prove unmanageable. The degree to which we break down an activity into its component steps will depend on the learning style of the student we are assessing. For some students with severe multiple handicaps, a highly detailed nonhandicapped person inventory may be required in order to obtain meaningful baseline performance data. Figure 16.3 compares skill inventories of grocery shopping based on the different learning styles of Ken and Mary Z. and their individualized goals and objectives.

The grocery-shopping inventory that will be used to assess Ken's baseline performance level is typical of the level of detail often required by persons who experience "moderate" handicaps. The component steps remain fairly large in scope (e.g., "enters price on calculator"), and include virtually all the steps required to complete the activity. The assumption is that Ken will eventually be able to master most or all of the steps in the sequence. In contrast, the inventory designed for Mary Z. *targets* just a few steps in the sequence. These are the specific steps that Mary Z. will be expected to master—she will partially participate in the others (Baumgart et al., 1982). The inventory provides a manageable number of steps in important areas and will yield a useful amount of information. If we find that our breakdown of the activity is not detailed enough, we can always reinventory the activity for a particular student to further break down specific steps for which we need more detailed information.

Once the inventory has been written, an initial assessment of student performance can be made. Continuing with our example, Ken and Mary Z. would actually go shopping at the Big M Supermarket. The teacher would structure the situation so that Ken and Mary Z. can demonstrate the extent to which they can perform the targeted skills *without* any assistance. During assessment, an independent opportunity to perform *each* step of the nonhandicapped person inventory is provided. In the event of an obvious error or no response, the teacher should be prepared to provide the least amount of assistance required by the student to help him or her move on to the next step of the inventory. Once the performance is recorded for all steps, it can be compared to the steps listed on the inventory. Discrepancies in the performance of students as compared to the original inventories can be noted, and decisions made about what to teach or adapt.

It is important that a student be somewhat familiar with the environment and activity *prior* to the actual assessment session. The goal of assessment is to get the most accurate picture of the student's current level of proficiency and target specific steps that will require instruction and/or adaptations. A student who is reacting to the novelty of the situation is not likely to give you a true indication of his or her abilities.

Student: Ken

*Steps include all requirements for participating in grocery shopping.*

1. Enters store
2. Locates/obtains cart
3. Moves out of the way and takes out all grocery-shopping materials (e.g., shopping list, calculator)
4. Enters dollar amount on calculator
5. Reviews shopping list
6. Searches for and obtains items on shopping list
   a. Stops at each section
   b. Scans list to determine if anything is needed from section
   c. If not, moves to next section
   d. If yes, locates/obtains item from shelf
7. Subtracts items on calculator
   a. Locates price tag on item
   b. Presses minus (−) sign on calculator
   c. Enters price on calculator
   d. Presses equal (=) sign
   e. Looks at calculator display
8. Determines "enough" or "not enough" money to purchase the item
   a. If "enough," places item in shopping cart
   b. If "not enough," returns item to shelf and proceeds to the checkout line
9. Checks out
   a. Gets in line at an open checkout counter
   b. Puts items from cart on counter
   c. Gets money ready
   d. Greets cashier
   e. Gives money to cashier using "next-dollar amount"
   f. Waits for and receives change
   g. Exits with bag of purchased items and personal belongings

Student: Mary Z.

*Steps are carefully selected and broken down in greater detail to allow for skill mastery. * = instructional targets.*

1. Enters store
2. *Locates/obtains basket
   a. Looks toward basket
   b. Reaches toward basket
   c. Grasps basket
   d. Pulls onto lap
   e. Releases grasp
3. Takes out necessary shopping materials (e.g., picture symbols)
4. *Searches for and obtains grocery items
   a. Holds picture symbol in hands and looks at it once positioned in front of correct section
   b. Slowly tracks with eyes from right to left looking for item that matches her picture-symbol card
   c. Reaches toward correct item
   d. Grasps item
   e. Lifts item
   f. Places item in basket
5. Repeats steps 4–5 for all remaining picture symbols
6. Prepares to check out when positioned in line
   a. Places items in cart on counter
   b. Greets cashier
7. *Pays cashier with predetermined money envelopes
   a. Reaches into knapsack
   b. Grasps envelope with picture symbol of selected item (envelope contains the amount of money required for the item and a note to the cashier asking him or her to "please place my change back in this envelope")
   c. Removes envelope from knapsack
   d. Maintains grasp on envelope
   e. Extends envelope toward cashier
   f. Releases envelope when cashier grasps it
   g. Reaches toward cashier when he or she extends envelope with change
   h. Places envelope in knapsack
8. Exits store with bag of purchased items and personal belongings.

Figure 16.3.   Comparison of two skill inventories for grocery shopping.

If you wait a session or two, you might get a more accurate picture of his or her performance. A summary of the procedures for conducting an activity-based assessment and filling out the *Activity-Based Assessment Form* is presented below. (Sample forms for Mary Z. and Ken are found in Forms 16.1 and 16.2.)

*First,* fill in the top of the form indicating the student's name, the environment and activity in which the assessment will occur, the priority instructional goal, and the staff member completing the assessment.

*Second,* conduct a nonhandicapped person inventory of the activity following these procedures:

- Perform the activity/task or watch someone else perform the task a few times.
- Write down all of the observable steps in performing the activity. Break down the steps to the degree that seems appropriate for the student for whom you are conducting the inventory. If unsure, perform a less detailed breakdown of steps. You can always reinventory selected steps if necessary.
- Review the steps in your written inventory: Are they described in observable terms? Are they sequenced in the order required to perform the activity? Are they inclusive of all steps required for initiating, preparing for, participating in, and terminating the activity?

*Third,* observe the student of concern as he or she engages in the activity. Record a ( + ) for acceptable performance. Put a ( − ) next to the skills that the student performed incorrectly and note what the student did instead. Notice from Form 16.1 that Mary Z.'s errors stemmed from: 1) making no response, 2) performing the right action but at an unacceptable rate, and 3) performing a different action.

*Fourth,* fill out the final column entitled "Decisions." Use the assessment information to decide:

- *Which steps will be targeted for instruction:* When reviewing the steps where errors are noted on the assessment form, consider the student's learning style and the number of errors. Based on this information, determine whether *all* of these steps will be targeted in upcoming instructional sessions, or only *some.*
- *Whether to teach or adapt:* For each error you need to decide whether you will *teach* the skills required by that step or *adapt* the actual performance requirements by changing the sequence, developing an aid, and so forth. (For information on adaptations, see York & Rainforth, 1987.)

### Step 2: Determine the general instructional procedures.

Planning for instruction can be a time-consuming task. However, it is extremely important to plan in order to provide systematic learning experiences for students. Written planning is particularly important when paraprofessionals will have the responsibility of delivering the actual on-site instruction. Many activity-based lessons (e.g., grocery shopping) are characterized by fast-paced action and a multitude of potential distractions for students and staff. Effective planning will help ensure that instructors are prepared to help students focus on the relevant features of the activity.

The amount of detail included in a lesson plan depends on at least the following factors: 1) your experience and skills as well as those of your instructional assistants, 2) the number of students for whom you are responsible for planning, and 3) the specific learning styles of your students. Let's return to the examples of Ken and Mary Z. The weekly schedule (see Form 16.3) indicates that Mary will receive instruction at the grocery store on Fridays. Ken is also scheduled to receive this type of instruc-

Student: __Mary Z.__

Date: __October 2__

Environment/Activity: __Big M. Grocery Shopping__

Staff: __Harriet (T.A.)__

| Skill inventory | (+, −) | What did student do? | Decisions |
|---|---|---|---|
| 1. Enters store | → | Was wheeled in by peer | |
| *2. Locates/obtains cart | | | |
|   a. Looks toward basket | − | Did not look purposefully | Teach to orient towards baskets |
|   b. Reaches toward basket | + | Fully | |
|   c. Grasps basket | + | | |
|   d. Pulls onto lap | + | Needed assistance removing from stack | Continue to assist |
|   e. Releases grasp | | | |
| 3. Takes out necessary shopping materials (e.g., picture symbols) | → | With help from peer | |
| **4. Searches for and obtains grocery items ✻ | | | |
|   a. Holds picture symbol in hands and looks at it once positioned in front of correct section | + | | Teach scanning procedures and reaching for item |
|   b. Slowly tracks with eyes from right to left looking for item that matches her picture-symbol card | − | Breadsticks were at eye level, but had trouble focusing | |
|   c. Reaches toward the correct item | + | | |
|   d. Grasps item | + | | |
|   e. Lifts item | + | | |
| 5. Repeats steps 4–5 for all remaining picture symbols | → | With help from peer | |
| 6. Prepares to check out when positioned in line | | | |
|   a. Places items in cart on counter | − | Didn't seem to know what was expected | Teach her to reach in backpack as soon as she is in cashier line |
|   b. Greets cashier | | | |
| *7. Pays cashier with predetermined money envelopes | | | |
|   a. Reaches into knapsack | + | | |
|   b. Grasps envelope with picture symbol of selected item (envelope contains the amount of money required for the item and a note to the cashier asking him or her to "please place my change back in this envelope") | + | Dropped envelope twice | Adapt envelope for better grip. |
|   c. Removes item from knapsack | − | | |
|   d. Maintains grasp on envelope | + | Needed full prompt | Continue prompts with ongoing reductions |
|   e. Extends envelope toward cashier | − | | |
|   f. Releases envelope when cashier grasps it | + | Very delayed response | Provide instruction to increase rate |
|   g. Reaches toward cashier when he or she extends envelope with change | | | |
|   h. Places envelope in knapsack | + | | |
| 8. Exits store | → | Wheeled by peer | |

* = instructional targets

✻ = One item – breadsticks (a favorite food item)

Student: __Ken__

Date: __October 16__

Environment/Activity: __Big M. Grocery Shopping__

Staff: __Harriet (T.A.)__

| Skill inventory | (+, −) | What did student do? | Decisions |
|---|---|---|---|
| 1. Enters store | + | | |
| 2. Locates/obtains cart | + | Stood by row of carts and blocked others' access to carts | Teach Ken to get cart and move to first aisle *before* he takes out materials. |
| 3. Moves out of the way and takes out all grocery shopping materials (e.g., shopping list, calculator) | − | | |
| 4. Enters dollar amount on calculator | − | Had $6.00 - entered "600" | Teach and provide *repeated* practice. Teach him to read entire list. |
| 5. Reviews shopping list (3 items; bread, pretzels, milk - written by Ken) | − | Only looked at first item on list | |
| 6. Searches for and obtains items on shopping list | | Was not systematic | Teach him to move up and down each aisle, pausing at sections to review entire list. |
|   a. Stops at each section | − | Needed reminders | |
|   b. Scans list to determine if anything is needed from section | − | | |
|   c. If not, moves to next section | + | + bread | |
|   d. If yes, locates/obtains item needed from shelf | 2/3 | + milk | |
| 7. Subtracts items on calculator | 2/3 | − pretzels | |
|   a. Locates price tag on item | + | M. did not have a price tag - placed in cart without subtracting | Teach problem-solving strategies for unmarked items |
|   b. Presses minus (−) sign on calculator | + | | |
|   c. Enters price on calculator | + | | |
|   d. Presses equal (=) sign | | | |
|   e. Looks at calculator display | | | |
| 8. Determines "enough" or "not enough" money to purchase the item | + | Got upset because last item (pretzels) produced a (−) sign. He really wanted these. | Teach problem-solving strategies (first get most important items, then others if you still have money — may need to reorganize order of list). |
|   a. If "enough," places item in shopping cart | − | | |
|   b. If "not enough," returns item to shelf and proceeds to the checkout line | | | |
| 9. Checks out | + | Took too long | Teach Ken to get money out while waiting in line. |
|   a. Gets in line at an open checkout counter | + | | |
|   b. Puts items from cart on counter | − | Responded to clerk's greeting | Teach Ken to initiate. |
|   c. Gets money ready | + | Handed over all of his money | Teach "next-dollar" strategy. |
|   d. Greets cashier | | | |
|   e. Gives money to cashier using "next-dollar" amount | − | | |
|   f. Waits for and receives change | + | | |
|   g. Exits with bag of purchased items and personal belongings. | + | | |

General Instructional Procedures

STRUCTURAL INFORMATION

Environment:   Big M Supermarket on Westcott St.
Activity:   Grocery shopping
Students:   Ken and Mary Z.
Teacher:   Harriet
Day of Week/Time:   Fridays—9:14 A.M. to 10:54 A.M.
Transportation:   Walking
Materials:   Picture symbols (Mary); Written list (Ken); Money envelope (Mary); Calculator (Ken); Money

PROCEDURES

*Preparation (9:14–9:25)*
Encourage Ken to seek Mary out and meet you near their lockers. Prompt Mary to look at the picture on her schedule to remind her that she is going to the store. Assist her in the locker routine. Meet them back at the classroom.

Before sitting at the table, the students should have secured their shopping materials. Have Ken refer to the "Shopping Preparation Checklist" on the clipboard to make sure he is ready to go. Mary should select the picture of the item that she will purchase today and put it in her shopping booklet that contains her money envelope.

*Review/Introduction (9:25–9:35)*
Have Ken review his list and count his money. Encourage Mary to watch him. Mary should then check her money envelope to make sure she has money (you should also check to make sure it is the right amount). Both students should be responsible for handling their own money.

Check data card from last trip and inform students of what they did well (e.g., "Mary, you found the baskets; Ken, you did a nice job using your calculator."). Then point out two or three things that they need to focus on today.

*Walking to the Store (9:35–9:50)*
(Teacher refers to street-crossing plan for Ken.)

*Grocery Shopping (9:50–10:20)*
The students will use the little shopping baskets that are stacked up near the entrance. They should move over to the first aisle before arranging their materials. Be sure they do not block the aisle. Ken should stay with Mary for most of the lesson, but you should also arrange for a time when he goes off on his own to find an item.

The "search strategy" that they should use involves:
1.   Go to the first aisle.
2.   Review *entire* list.
3.   Scan the aisle and identify sections. (You may need to help Ken identify sections. For example, you might say, "This is bread section; anything on your list from here?" Mary should not be expected to identify the sections.)
4.   Stop, if that section contains something from the list; move on if it doesn't.
5.   Continue procedure, moving up one side of the aisle and down the other, moving from aisle 1, to 2, to 3, and so forth.

Encourage both students to socialize with clerks and cashier. Ken should be learning to ask for help from a clerk when he can't find an item. Prompt Mary to look at people and smile in return to their greetings (be subtle).

See the data card for the instructional targets and specific cues to use for a given day.

*Walking back to School and Using Lockers (10:20–10:40)*
(Follow established routine)

*Ending the Lesson (10:40–10:54)*
Have students put materials away, including grocery items. Have them sit together to review the lesson. Highlight at least one "success" for each student. Encourage Ken to use the picture schedule with Mary to determine the next activity.

tion. The actual time allotted to this activity is from 9:14 to 10:54 (second and third periods). When developing a plan for this session, it's important to establish some basic instructional procedures that will followed *each time* this session is carried out. We have presented an example planning form entitled *General Instructional Procedures* (Form 16.3) that is designed to communicate "structural information" (e.g., location, instructor's name, students, time of lesson, transportation, materials) and "procedures" (e.g., preparation, review, introduction of the lesson, participation in the activity, termination). Many questions need to be considered when completing the "procedures" section of the form, including:

- How will you generate interest in the activity?
- How will students be positioned during different portions of the lesson?
- How will mutual attending and responding by the student be encouraged throughout the lesson?
- How will individualized objectives be addressed?
- Will each student perform all the steps in the sequence, or will only a part of the sequence be performed by a student?
- How will you maintain a high level of active participation throughout the activity?
- How will peer-to-peer interaction be encouraged?
- Should special attention be given to particular communication, motor, or social behaviors?
- Are there special, positive techniques that are being used with a student who presents challenging behavior?
- Have you written down the amount of time planned for this part of the lesson to ensure proper pacing?
- How will the lesson be brought to a close?
- How will the students be given feedback on their performance?
- What will the students need to do to get ready for the next activity?
- How much time will you devote to this part of the lesson?

Considerations such as these should be reflected on the *General Instructional Procedures* form. This information does not need to be rewritten for each instructional session, but will remain functional for a longer time period. Adopting any particular format for lesson planning will most likely require an investment of training time with classroom staff so that they understand, follow, and contribute to the planning system. Teachers are often frustrated by the lack of time available to demonstrate general teaching procedures in community settings. One option to consider is using a videotape of a community-based lesson to be shown to paraprofessionals as a supplement to your written lesson plans and discussions.

## Step 3: Use a planning and data card system.

A delineation of general lesson procedures will be helpful in determining your *general* approach to the lesson. It will not, however, provide the detailed instructional strategies needed to ensure that progress is made from lesson to lesson. Consider the following scenario:

Gene is learning to order a beverage at a fast-food restaurant. He receives instruction at a restaurant near school every Wednesday afternoon with two other students. Last Wednesday when he entered the restaurant he went directly to the closed cash register that was nearest to the door. His teacher noticed him standing there and asked him to move to a cash register that was open. Gene's teacher thought to herself, "Gene seems to make that error every time."

Ideally, a planning system should assist Gene's teacher in organizing her instruction so that in the next instructional session she has a planned strategy for intervening with Gene to prevent error and *ensure success*. Without a more precise planning tool, we often find ourselves reacting to what happens during instruction, rather than being proactive in our approach. Thus, a final step in the three-step instructional planning and monitoring process involves: 1) identifying specific performance targets, 2) determining the appropriate instructional cues, and 3) collecting and analyzing data so that appropriate instruction takes place.

Students like Gene, in our example above, often require precise "cuing procedures" in order to perform a skill successfully. There are a variety of cues that could be used to teach Gene to locate the correct cash register. Of course, the most desirable cue is a natural one. For example, he might locate the cash register that is open by noticing that the "light is on" (a natural visual cue) or that "people are lined up in front of it" (another natural visual cue). If Gene is not responding to the natural cue(s), the teacher may need to add an instructional cue (e.g., gesturing, providing verbal instructions, modeling) to draw his attention to the natural cue. An outline of the these and other available instructional cues is presented in Table 16.1. The selection of instructional cues depends heavily on the learning style of a student and the specific skill being taught. Furthermore, the teacher will need to decide *when* to provide the cue—before, during, or after Gene has made a response. If you have reason to believe that an error will occur (the data card reveals that errors have been made during the previous two sessions), then provide instruction *before* a response is required. In other words, set the student up for success. And, finally, the teacher will need to determine the intensity of the cue. Will she or he make a *subtle* or *exaggerated* gesture? Will she or he give *direct* instructions (e.g., "Look here for the light.") or *indirect* (e.g., "What should you look for?").

To make planning, implementing, and monitoring lessons manageable, we suggest an approach that combines the planning of instructional cues on the same card (or form) that will be used to collect instructional data—the *Planning & Data Card* (see sample cards in Forms 16.4 and 16.5). A card is suggested because of the ease with

---

Table 16.1.   Instructional cues

**Partial physical (PP)** prompt or **full physical (FP)** prompt: The teacher places his or her hands and/or body in direct contact with the student's, and puts the student through the correct performance of a response. It is *critical* that the student's hands and/or body are in direct contact with the activity materials and that the movements of the student's hands and/or body, not the teacher's, create a change in the materials.

**Gestural (G)** response: The teacher moves his or her hands or body to suggest a response.

**Verbal (V)**: The teacher addresses statements or words (in the student's primary language/communication system) directly to the student to assist in a response.

**Modeling (M)**: The teacher demonstrates an appropriate response for the student.

Adapted from Wuerch and Voeltz (1982).

*Note*: Rather than viewing these as hierarchical, an individualized choice would be made based upon student learning characteristics and a comparison to the natural cues of the situation. Also, a time-delay procedure may be used in combination with one of these instructional cues whenever errorless learning is a goal (see Snell & Gast, 1981).

Planning & Data Card

Student: _Mary Z._

Activity: _Grocery Shopping_

Staff: _Harriet_

What Cue Did You Actually Use?

| Instructional Target | Planned Instructional Cue | 10/9 | 10/16 | 10/23 | 10/30 | 11/6 | 11/13 | 12/2 | 12/9 |
|---|---|---|---|---|---|---|---|---|---|
| Looks toward stack of baskets upon entering store. | Let Mary orient to store, then gesture to baskets | – M V PP (G) FP | – M V PP (G) FP | – M V PP (G) FP | (–) M V PP G FP | (I) M V PP G FP | (I) M V PP G FP | (I) M V PP G FP | MASTERED  (I) M V PP G FP |
| Scans array for items (once positioned in front of array) | Draw Mary's attention to items as you reach them | – M V PP (G) FP | – M V PP (G) FP  BREADSTICKS | – M V PP (G) FP | M V PP (G) FP | M V PP (G) FP | (I) M V PP G FP | (I) M V PP (G) FP | (I) M V PP G FP |
| Locates and reaches for item | Point out the item and physically prompt her to reach | – M V (PP) G FP | – M V PP G (FP) | – M V (PP) G FP | – M V (PP) G FP | – M V (PP) G FP | – M V (PP) G FP | (I) M V PP G FP | (I) M V PP G FP |
| Reaches in backpack for money envelope (once positioned in cashier line) | Open pack and position for easy reach | – M V PP (G) FP | – M V PP (G) FP | (I) M V PP G FP | (I) M V PP G FP | – M V PP (G) FP | (I) M V PP G FP | (I) M V PP G FP | (I) M V PP G FP |
| Maintains grasp on envelope | Touch her hand occasionally - say "Good—you still have your money" | M V (PP) G FP | M V (PP) G FP | – M V (PP) G FP | – M V (PP) G FP | – M V PP G FP | (I) M V PP G FP | (I) M V PP G FP | MASTERED  (I) M V PP G FP |
| Reaches toward envelope with change (handed over by cashier) | Physically prompt this | M V PP G (FP) | M V PP G (FP) | M V PP G (FP) | (FP) M V PP G | M V (PP) G FP | M V (PP) G FP | M V (PP) G FP | (I) M V PP G FP |
| Looks up and smiles at cashier to return greeting | Encourage her to look at cashier (subtitle) | M (V) PP G FP | M (V) PP G FP | M (V) PP G FP | (I) M V PP G FP | M (V) PP G FP | M (V) PP G FP | M (V) PP G FP | M (V) PP G FP |

Planning & Data Card

Student: _Ken_

Activity: _Grocery Shopping_    Staff: _Harriet_

What Cue Did You Actually Use?

| Instructional Target | Planned Instructional Cue | 10/23 | 10/30 | 11/6 | 11/13 | 11/20 | 12/2 | 12/5 |
|---|---|---|---|---|---|---|---|---|
| Moves out of way to assemble materials | Model this | I Ⓜ V PP G / FP | I Ⓜ V PP G / FP | Ⓘ M V PP G / FP | Ⓘ M V PP G / FP | Ⓘ M V PP G / FP | MASTERED I / M V PP G / FP | I / M V PP G / FP |
| Enters correct dollar amount | Model first, clear calculator, have Ken do it | I M V PP Ⓖ / FP $7 | I M V PP Ⓖ / FP $5 | I M V PP Ⓖ / FP $4 | I M V PP G / FP $5 | I M V PP G / FP $4 | I M Ⓥ PP G / FP $7 | I M V PP G / FP $7 |
| Reviews shopping list | Tell him to read all of it | I Ⓥ PP G / FP | I Ⓥ PP G / FP | I Ⓥ PP G / FP | I Ⓥ PP G / FP | Ⓘ M V PP G / FP | MASTERED | MASTERED I / M V PP G / FP |
| Moves up and down the aisle systematically | Show him first aisle - gesture through | I M V PP Ⓖ / FP | I M Ⓥ PP G / FP | I M Ⓥ PP G / FP | Ⓘ M V PP G / FP | Ⓘ M V PP G / FP | Ⓘ M V PP G / FP | MASTERED I / M V PP G / FP |
| Scans section | Gesture to items - using "scanning motion" | I M V PP Ⓖ / FP | I M V PP Ⓖ / FP | I M V PP Ⓖ / FP | I M V PP Ⓖ / FP | I Ⓥ M PP G / FP | I Ⓥ M PP G / FP | I Ⓥ M PP G / FP |
| Returns item to shelf if not enough money | Remind him that he may not have "enough" and it's ok | I Ⓥ PP G / FP | I M Ⓥ PP G / FP | Ⓘ M V PP G / FP | I M V Ⓟ G / FP | I M V Ⓟ G / FP | I M V Ⓟ G / FP | I Ⓥ M PP G / FP |
| Gives cashier the "next dollar" amount | Demonstrate this just before entering cashiers line | I Ⓜ V PP G / FP | Ⓘ M V PP G / FP | Ⓘ M V PP G / FP | Ⓘ M V PP G / FP | Ⓘ M V PP G / FP | Ⓘ M V PP G / FP | MASTERED I / M V PP G / FP |

307

which data can be collected during community-based sessions. Not only can data be more conveniently recorded, but instructional assistants will be able to refer to it at times during the session in order to more accurately provide the planned instructional cues. Below are some procedures for filling out the card.

*First,* write your instructional targets in the appropriate column.

*Second,* adopt a coding system with which you are comfortable. Consider using the following "cue codes" (you may also want to record the minimum level of assistance that the student required): FP (full physical assistance), PP (partial physical assistance), M (model), G (gesture), V (verbal), and I (independent).

*Third,* make a notation of your "planned instructional cue" based on the student's previous performance.

*Fourth,* write anecdotal comments on the back of the card.

*Fifth,* graph data to show overall progress. In our examples, a graphing system was built into the design of the card. It is possible to graph each skill listed to see if students are requiring less assistance (e.g., from FP to PP). It is also possible to keep track of overall progress by marking the skills in which mastery has been reached (e.g., by December 9th, Mary had reached mastery on two of the seven skills listed and Ken had mastered four out of seven skills).

Remember, performance data must be analyzed and used in order to have any value! In most instructional contexts it is not necessary to collect data on every trial, or even during every instructional session. We suggest that instructional data be collected on a regular basis, but on a schedule that will be sensitive to changes in performance.

## FADING PROCEDURES

Fading procedures are used to systematically decrease the amount of assistance provided to students. These strategies are appropriately used once the student has achieved some degree of mastery of the steps in the activity sequence. The fading of instructional cues in community environments can be accomplished in a variety of ways.

One way to fade instructional cues is by gradually decreasing the amount and timing of information provided to students. The goal is to gradually decrease the instructional input provided to the student so that he or she relies less and less on the information provided by the teacher. Teachers may use indirect verbal cues ("What do you have to do next?"), instead of direct verbal cues ("Next you have to get out your membership card."); or increase the amount of time inserted between the presentation of the natural cue and the instructional cue. (For a discussion of time-delay procedures, see Snell & Gast, 1981. This procedure can also be thought of as an errorless prompting procedure—not just a fading technique.)

Another fading strategy involves increasing the physical distance between the teacher and the student. Though relatively simple, a strategy designed to fade one's physical presence is often overlooked even after students have mastered select skills. Proximity fading is a useful strategy that can be used unobtrusively in many community environments.

## GENERALIZATION AND MAINTENANCE

What if a student masters all of the skills targeted for a particular setting? Does instruction end at this point? It may—if that is the only setting in which the student will need to perform the newly learned skills. But, rarely is this the case. For example, Ken and Mary Z. have gained a marked degree of proficiency at the Big M Supermarket. However, although the Big M Supermarket is where Mary's family usually shops, it is not where Ken is likely to shop after school or on the weekends. It is highly probable that both students will find themselves in a different grocery store some day, and the question is, "Will they be able to generalize their performance to these settings?" Rather than merely "hoping" that this will occur (Stokes & Baer, 1977, call this the "Train and Hope Strategy") you might want to teach in several different grocery stores. With this multiple-site approach, you would have an opportunity to highlight the cues that occur in a reasonable range of settings (The Big M, Peter's Grocery, and Hank's Supermarket), thereby increasing the likelihood that the student can respond in yet another new situation (Leroy's Market). Horner and his colleagues refer to this as "general case" instruction (for more information see Horner, McDonnell, & Bellamy, 1986; and Horner, Sprague, & Wilcox, 1982).

Not only do we need to be concerned about the generalization of skills, but we also need to ensure their *maintenance* over time. Mary Z., for example, will soon master the skill of "locating breadsticks," one of her favorite snacks. Presumably, this item will then be replaced with a different one. It would be unfortunate, however, if, after the passage of time, she was no longer able to find the breadsticks. To prevent this from happening, the teacher might build in sessions where previously acquired skills are reintroduced to ensure maintenance.

## CONCLUSION

The proposed model for planning and implementing activity-based lessons completes a full circle. When instructional data indicate that the instructional targets have been mastered (or significant progress is *not* being made), a new cycle of determining targets, planning, instructing, and monitoring begins. At this point, time lines may have to be re-established, baseline data evaluated, and new plans developed. Our experience tells us that teachers must adopt a system of planning and monitoring instruction in the community living areas that provides them with the data needed by members of the classroom team to make instructional decisions — yet the system must be as simple and practical as possible. The system must require a minimum of paperwork, collect only necessary information, use all of the information collected, and be structured so that paraprofessionals and other team members can assist with data collection and analysis. We hope that this chapter has provided you with some practical strategies that you can build into your existing planning system.

## QUESTIONS AND ANSWERS

Q:  I find it difficult to collect data while I am teaching. Any suggestions?

A:  Many teachers feel the same way. Whatever you do, don't give up on data collection. The trick is to make it manageable for you. One question to ask is, "Am I trying to collect too much data?" The data cards presented in this chapter are purposely designed to limit the amount of data that could be collected. A second question to consider is, "Can I set aside a minute or so at the end of the lesson for the purpose of recording data?" Try to convince yourself that it is worth it to use an extra minute or so at the end of the lesson to finish your record keeping. This will alleviate your concerns about interfering with the lesson, yet allow you to record information at a time when it is fresh in your mind.

Q: This chapter addressed "cuing procedures," but what about feedback systems? I use a lot of positive reinforcement in my teaching.

A: Great! Providing positive feedback is a critical teaching technique. However, our involvement in more integrated settings has prompted us to take another look at some of our practices such as token systems, hugs, lavish praise, and food rewards. If the use of such "artificial" procedures is justifiable for a particular student, nonstigmatizing methods for dispensing the reinforcements should be devised. Whenever possible, the use of such procedures should be paired with the naturally occurring reinforcers available in a particular setting.

# REFERENCES

Baumgart, D., Brown, L., Pumpian, I., Nisbet, J., Ford, A. Sweet, M., Messina, R. & Schroeder, J. (1982). Principle of partial participation and individualized adaptations in educational programs for severely handicapped students. *Journal of The Association for Persons with Severe Handicaps, 7*(2), 17–27.

Brown, L., Branston, M.B., Hamre-Nietupski, S., Pumpian, I., Certo, N., & Gruenewald, L. (1979). A strategy for developing chronological age appropriate and functional curricular content to severely handicapped adolescents and young adults. *Journal of Special Education, 13,* 81–90.

Horner, R., McDonnell, J., & Bellamy, T. (1986). Teaching generalized skills: General case instruction in simulation and community settings. In R.H. Horner, L.H. Meyer, & H.D.B. Fredericks (Eds.), *Education of learners with severe handicaps: Exemplary service strategies* (pp. 289–314). Baltimore: Paul H. Brookes Publishing Co.

Horner, R., Sprague, J., & Wilcox, B. (1982). Constructing general case programs for community activities. In B. Wilcox & G. T. Bellamy, *Design of high school programs for severely handicapped students* (pp. 61–98). Baltimore: Paul H. Brookes Publishing Co.

Snell, M.E., & Gast, D.L. (1981). Applying time delay procedure to the instruction of the severely handicapped. *Journal of The Association for the Severely Handicapped, 6*(3), 3–14.

Stokes, T.R., & Baer, D.M. (1977). An implicit technology of generalization. *Journal of Applied Behavior Analysis, 10,* 341–367.

Wuerch, B.B., & Voeltz, L.M. (1982). *Longitudinal leisure skills for severely handicapped learners. The Ho'onanea curriculum component.* Baltimore: Paul H. Brookes Publishing Co.

York, J., & Rainforth, B. (1987). Developing instructional adaptations. In F.P. Orelove & D. Sobsey, *Educating children with multiple disabilities: A transdisciplinary approach* (pp. 183–217). Baltimore: Paul H. Brookes Publishing Co.

# ADDITIONAL READINGS AND RESOURCES

Ault, M., Wolery, M., Doyle, P., & Gast, D. (1989). Review of comparative studies in the instruction of students with moderate and severe handicaps. *Exceptional Children, 55,* 346–356.

Falvey, M., Brown, L., Lyon, S., Baumgart, D., & Schroeder, J. (1980). Strategies for using cues and correction procedures. In W. Sailor, B. Wilcox, & L. Brown (Eds.), *Methods of instruction for severely handicapped students* (pp. 109–134). Baltimore: Paul H. Brookes Publishing Co.

Ford, A., & Mirenda, P. (1984). Community instruction: A natural cues and corrections decision model. *Journal of The Association for Persons with Severe Handicaps, 9,* 79–88.

Gold, M. (1980). *"Did I say that . . . ?" : Articles and commentary on the "try another way" system.* Champaign, IL: Research Press.

Gold, M.W. (1980). *Try another way. Training manual.* Champaign, IL: Research Press.

Guess, D., & Siegel-Causey, E. (1983). Behavioral control and education of severely handicapped students: Who's doing what to whom? and why? In D. Bricker & J. Filler (Eds.),

*Serving the severely retarded: From research to practice* (pp. 230–244). Reston, VA: Council for Exceptional Children.

Haring, N., Liberty, K., & White, D.R. (1980). Rules for data-based strategy decisions in instructional programs: Current research and instructional applications. In W. Sailor, B. Wilcox, & L. Brown (Eds.), *Methods of instruction for severely handicapped students* (pp. 159–192). Baltimore: Paul H. Brookes Publishing Co.

Holvoet, J., Mulligan, M., Schussler, N., Lacy, L., & Guess, D. (1982). *The KICS model: Sequencing learning experiences for severely handicapped children and youth.* Lawrence: University of Kansas, Department of Special Education.

Jones, V., & Jones, L. (1986). *Comprehensive classroom management: Creating positive learning enviroments* (2nd ed.). Newton, MA: Allyn and Bacon.

Liberty, K., Haring, N., & Martin, M. (1981). Teaching new skills to the severely handicapped. *Journal of The Association for the Severely Handicapped, 6*(1), 5–13.

McDonnell, J. (1987). The effects of time delay and increasing prompt hierarchy strategies on the acquisition of purchasing skills by students with severe handicaps. *Journal of The Association for Persons with Severe Handicaps, 12,* 227–236.

Shevin, M., & Klein, N.K. (1984). The importance of choice-making skills for students with severe disabilities. *Journal of The Association for Persons with Severe Handicaps, 9,* 159–166.

Snell, M. (1987). *Systematic instruction of persons with severe handicaps.* (3rd ed.). Columbus, OH: Charles E. Merrill.

# Parent Input Forms

The following forms are examples of ways to gather information for individualized education program (IEP) development. As mentioned throughout the *Guide*, it is important that teachers maintain a flexible attitude toward gathering and sharing information with families. Some parents/guardians prefer to share information over the phone or in person as opposed to filling out forms. Teachers should be sensitive to parent preferences and refrain from assuming that families who do not respond to information requests in written formats are any less concerned about their children's educational program than those who do respond. Included in this appendix are the following forms:

1. *Parent Preferences for Home-School Communication*
2. *The IEP Conference: Participants and Meeting Arrangements*
3. *Student Preference and Choice Questionnaire*
4. *Parent Input: Determining Priorities in the Community-Living Areas*
   a. *Self-Management/Home Living*
   b. *Vocational*
   c. *Recreation/Leisure*
   d. *General Community Functioning*

The *Parent Preferences for Home-School Communication* form can be used to determine *what types of information* parents are interested in sharing with school personnel on a day-to-day basis and *how* they prefer to share it (e.g., telephone calls, notebooks).

The *IEP Conference: Participants and Meeting Arrangements* form is one example of how information can be obtained regarding who should attend the conference, as well as which days, times and locations are convenient.

The *Student Preference and Choice Questionnaire* can provide valuable information about how the student expresses preferences and makes choices at home and in other settings. Such information can have a significant impact on the education program to be developed. It is important to note that siblings and friends as well as parents will be able to contribute to such information-gathering efforts. Of course the primary source of input will come from the student himself/herself.

The *Parent Input: Determining Priorities in the Community Living Areas* forms can be useful in helping parents to consider activities that might be included in the IEP. This is actually a "packet" of four forms, one for each community living domain: self-management/home living, vocational, recreation/leisure, and general community functioning. We also recommend that you attach the appropriate scope and sequence

---

The set of forms contained in this appendix were adapted in part from: Turnbull, A.P., Turnbull, H.R., Summers, J.A., Brotherson, M.J., & Benson, H.A. (1986). *Families, professionals and exceptionality: Creating a special partnership.* Columbus, OH: Charles E. Merrill; reprinted by permission.

charts (from Appendix B) to these forms so that parents have a list of activities to review before completing the form.

It is unlikely that you would send an entire packet of forms home at one time. Indeed, this would be overwhelming. It is more likely that you would select an appropriate form or two to send at a particular point in time. For example, one of the first forms you might send home is the *Parent Preferences for Home-School Communication* since it will help you establish your procedure for day-to-day communication with parents.

FORM A.1

Parent Preferences for Home-School Communication

To ensure that your child is receiving the best possible education program, it is important that there be ongoing communication between your family and school personnel. It is our experience that families have different preferences for what kinds of information should be shared. In addition, families have different preferences regarding how and how often such information will be shared.

Listed below are a number of different types of information that can be shared. There are also a number of different methods that can be used to communicate this information. Please check your priorities.

_____                    _____
Person completing form                         Student's name

_____
Date

A.  Information that you would like to have shared be-   How often you would like to have this
    tween home and school: (check priorities)              information shared:

| | Daily | Weekly | Monthly |
|---|---|---|---|
| ____ Eating habits | ____ | ____ | ____ |
| ____ Bathroom habits | ____ | ____ | ____ |
| ____ Sleeping/napping habits | ____ | ____ | ____ |
| ____ Social interactions | ____ | ____ | ____ |
| ____ Difficult behaviors | ____ | ____ | ____ |
| ____ Other _____ | ____ | ____ | ____ |

As they may occur:

____ Special accomplishments
____ Special activities (restaurants, assemblies, etc.)
____ Other (please specify): _____
     _____
     _____

B.  How would you like to have this information shared on a day-to-day basis?
    ____ Notes or a notebook
    or
    ____ Brief phone calls to school staff
    or    (____ day ____ evening)
    ____ Brief phone calls from school staff
    or    (____ day ____ evening)
    ____ Other _____

C.  What other ways of sharing information would you be interested in?

|                          | How Often? | | |
|---|---|---|---|
|                          | Monthly | 4x/year | Twice/year |
| ____ Informal school visits | ____ | ____ | ____ |
| ____ Home visits | ____ | ____ | ____ |
| ____ Individual conferences | ____ | ____ | ____ |
| ____ Parent group meetings | ____ | ____ | ____ |
| ____ Newsletters | ____ | ____ | ____ |
| ____ Telephone calls | ____ | ____ | ____ |
| ____ Other(s): | ____ | ____ | ____ |
| _____ | ____ | ____ | ____ |
| _____ | ____ | ____ | ____ |

### The IEP Conference: Participants and Meeting Arrangements

A. Who would you like to have attend the conference?

Consider those people whom you feel can be helpful in planning an education program for your son or daughter. You may bring anyone you feel may be helpful (e.g., student, family members, family or student's friend, advocate).

The following school personnel will be scheduled to attend the conference:

Name                                                          Role

_____                    _____
_____                    _____
_____                    _____
_____                    _____

Please indicate any additional school personnel you would like to attend the meeting:

_____
_____
_____

B. Where would you like the conference to be held?

____ School      ____ Your home      ____ Other _____

C. When is it most convenient for you to attend?

Mon. ____      Tues. ____      Wed. ____      Thurs. ____      Fri. ____

8 A.M. ____      9 A.M. ____      10 A.M. ____      11 A.M. ____      12 P.M. ____

1 P.M. ____      2 P.M. ____      3 P.M. ____      4 P.M. ____      5 P.M. ____

Other time ____

D. Please note here if you need help making arrangements to attend a conference.

____ I need help arranging for transportation.

____ I need assistance with child care in order to attend.

____ Other _____

_____

Please return this form to school as soon as possible. We will use this information to choose arrangements that will be most convenient for you. Thank you for your assistance.

Student Preference and Choice Questionnaire                FORM A.3

Student: _____    Date: _____
Completed by: _____

1.  How does your son or daughter communicate with friends and family members?
    ____ Sign language    ____ Speech    ____ Gesture (pointing, eye gaze)
    ____ Communication device        ____ Gestures and sounds
2.  When your son or daughter likes something, which of the following will he or she do?
    ____ Say something              ____ Look at something
    ____ Laugh or smile             ____ Move body
    ____ Imitate you                ____ Point or reach out
    ____ Change facial expression   ____ Make sounds
    ____ Look at someone            ____ Other (please fill in) _____
3.  When your son or daughter dislikes something, which of the following will he or she do?
    ____ Say something              ____ Look away
    ____ Cry                        ____ Pull away
    ____ Change facial expression   ____ Push object or person away
    ____ Scream                     ____ Make sounds
    ____ Throw tantrum              ____ Gesture
    ____ Look away                  ____ Other (please fill in) _____
4.  What are your child's favorite:          Foods                    Activities

    _____     _____
    _____     _____
    _____     _____

5.  How often does your son or daughter choose:

|  | Frequently | Occasionally | Seldom |
|---|---|---|---|
| When to eat | ____ | ____ | ____ |
| What to eat | ____ | ____ | ____ |
| What to wear | ____ | ____ | ____ |
| When to get up (weekends, etc.) | ____ | ____ | ____ |
| When to go to bed | ____ | ____ | ____ |
| What chores to do | ____ | ____ | ____ |
| What to buy with his or her money | ____ | ____ | ____ |
| How to spend free time | ____ | ____ | ____ |
| Whom to do things with | ____ | ____ | ____ |
| Other (please fill in) _____ | ____ | ____ | ____ |

6.  Please list some examples of how your son or daughter spends free time at home or in the community:

| Activities | With whom? | Times per week |
|---|---|---|
| _____ | _____ | _____ |
| _____ | _____ | _____ |
| _____ | _____ | _____ |
| _____ | _____ | _____ |

7.  Your child's friends: Who are they?

| Name | Explain relationship (e.g., neighbor) |
|---|---|
| _____ | _____ |
| _____ | _____ |
| _____ | _____ |
| _____ | _____ |

8.  Anything else we should know about your child's interests, likes, and dislikes?
    _____
    _____

Parent Input: Determining Priorities in the
Community Living Areas—Self-Management/Home Living

The attached chart lists many activities that children of different ages engage in related to self-management and home living. Find your child's age group on the following chart and review the activities. Are you concerned about any of these activities? Which ones do you think we should include in your child's IEP?

1. _____

_____

_____

_____

_____

_____

2. _____

_____

_____

_____

_____

_____

3. _____

_____

_____

_____

_____

_____

*Note:* Attach the scope and sequence chart for self-management/home living from Appendix B.

Parent Input: Determining Priorities in
the Community Living Areas—Vocational

The attached chart lists many activities that children of different ages engage in related to work. Find your child's age group on the following chart and review the activities. Are you concerned about any of these activities? Which ones do you think we should include in your child's IEP?

1. _____
   _____

2. _____
   _____

3. _____
   _____

Has your son or daughter ever indicated what kind of job he or she would like to have? If so, what is it?

   _____
   _____

If your son or daughter is in middle or high school, job training in the community might be appropriate. What kinds of jobs would you like to see him or her experience before graduation (e.g., office work, restaurants)?

   _____
   _____

List, in order of importance, two to three vocational activities that you believe your son or daughter would be interested in (e.g., preparing food in a restaurant, packaging items, stocking in a store, cleaning).

1. _____
   _____

2. _____
   _____

3. _____
   _____

Note: Attach the scope and sequence chart for vocational from Appendix B.

Parent Input: Determining Priorities in the
Community Living Areas—Recreation/Leisure

The attached chart lists many activities that children of different ages engage in related to recreation/
leisure. Find your child's age group on the following chart and review the activities. Which ones do you
think we should include in your child's IEP?

1. _____

_____

2. _____

_____

3. _____

_____

If your son or daughter is in middle or high school, what are your thoughts about his or her involvement
in extracurricular activities (e.g., clubs, dances, sports)? _____

_____

_____

_____

_____

List, in order of importance, several leisure activities that you believe your son or daughter would like to
be involved in during his or her school day.

1. _____

_____

2. _____

_____

3. _____

_____

*Note:* Attach the scope and sequence chart for recreation/leisure from Appendix B.

FORM A.7

Parent Input: Determining Priorities in the
Community Living Areas—General Community Functioning

The attached chart lists many activities that children of different ages engage in related to functioning in the general community. Find your child's age group on the following chart and review the activities. Are you concerned about any of these activities? Which ones do you think we should include in your child's IEP?

1. _____

   _____

2. _____

   _____

3. _____

   _____

List, in order of importance, several activities from the general community functioning area that you would like your daughter or son to be involved in during her or his school day. Under each activity, describe what you feel she or he needs to learn that would enable her or him to perform in the activity more independently.

1. _____

   _____

2. _____

   _____

3. _____

   _____

*Note:* Attach the scope and sequence chart for general community functioning from Appendix B.

# Scope and Sequence Charts: Extended Versions

The scope and sequence charts in this appendix are extensions of those included in the body of the *Guide*. These charts contain activities for which instructional opportunities typically occur apart from school—before school, in the evenings, and on the weekends. These "extended activities" are listed in the shaded portions of each chart.

Although these "extended activities" may be better suited to instruction during nonschool hours, they may be incorporated into the school day—particularly if a parent makes a specific request. In Appendix A, it was suggested that you attach these charts to the appropriate *Parent Input Forms* so that parents can have a chance to consider the full range of community living activities.

Chart B.1. Scope and sequence for self-management/home living (see key for shading on p. 330)

| | | Age and grade levels | | | | |
|---|---|---|---|---|---|---|
| | | Elementary school | | | | |
| Goal areas | Kindergarten (age 5) | Primary grades (ages 6–8) | Intermediate grades (ages 9–11) | Middle school (ages 12–14) | High school (ages 15–18) | Transition (ages 19–21) |
| Eating and food preparation | Eat meals and snacks | Eat balanced meals | Eat balanced meals with appropriate manners | Eat balanced meals with appropriate manners | Eat balanced meals with appropriate manners | Eat balanced meals with appropriate manners |
| | Prepare simple snack for self; pour own drink | Prepare simple snack for self; pour own drink | Plan and prepare simple snacks for self | Plan and prepare snacks for self | Plan and prepare snacks for self and others | Plan menu for self/ family/roommates |
| | Serve snack to peers | Serve snack to peers | Serve food items to others | Serve food items to others | Serve food items to others | Serve food items to others |
| | Clean own place after snack/meal | Clean up table after snack | Clean up preparation area and table after snack | Clear table and do dishes after food preparation | Clear table and do dishes after food preparation | Clean up after meals |
| | | | | Prepare simple meals: breakfast, lunch (some cooking) | Prepare various types of meals | Prepare meal for self/ others |
| | | Choose nutritious foods: snack | Choose nutritious foods: snack | Choose nutritious foods: breakfast, lunch, snacks | Choose nutritious foods: breakfast, lunch, snacks | Choose nutritious foods (including when eating out) |
| | | | | Store food and leftovers | Store food and leftovers | Store food and leftovers |
| | | | | | | Make weekly grocery list |
| | | Set table for family meal | Set and clean table for family meal | Set and clear table for family meal | Set and clear table for family meal | Set and clear table for family meal |
| | | Do dishes after family meal | Do dishes after family meal | Do dishes after family meal | Do dishes after family meal | Do dishes after family meal |
| | | Help pack bag lunch | Pack bag lunch | Pack bag lunch | Pack bag lunch | Pack bag lunch |
| | | | | Put groceries away | Put groceries away | Put groceries away |

| Domain | | | | | | |
|---|---|---|---|---|---|---|
| Grooming and dressing | Brush/comb hair with reminders<br><br>Get dressed/undressed (school: shoes, outer clothes) | Brush/comb hair with reminders<br><br>Get dressed/undressed (school: shoes, swimming, outer clothes)<br><br>Maintain neat appearance throughout school day with reminders | Brush/comb hair when needed<br><br>Get dressed/undressed (school: shoes, swimming, outer clothes)<br><br>Maintain neat appearance throughout school day | Brush/comb and style hair (also choose hairstyle)<br><br>Get dressed/undressed (physical education, outer clothes)<br><br>Maintain neat appearance throughout school day<br><br>Use skin care products (cosmetics if desired)<br><br>Care for eyeglasses/contact lenses | Brush/comb and style hair (also choose hairstyle)<br><br>Get dressed/undressed (physical education, outer clothes)<br><br>Maintain appearance throughout school day<br><br>Use skin care products (cosmetics if desired)<br><br>Care for eyeglasses/contact lenses | Manage hair care<br><br>Get dressed/undressed<br><br>Maintain appearance<br><br>Manage skin care<br><br>Manage eye care needs |
| | Get dressed and undressed for the day and bedtime | Get dressed and undressed<br><br>Choose clothing for routine activities and special events | Get dressed and undressed<br><br>Choose casual/formal clothes based upon style/activity | Get dressed and undressed<br><br>Plan wardrobe, choosing most clothes | Get dressed and undressed<br><br>Plan wardrobe and purchase own clothes | Manage wardrobe<br><br>Plan and purchase own wardrobe |
| Hygiene and toileting | Use private and public toilets<br><br>Wash hands and face with reminders<br><br>Blow nose and dispose of tissue with reminders | Use private and public toilets<br><br>Wash hands and face: routine times (e.g., after toilet, before eating)<br><br>Blow nose and dispose of tissue as needed | Use private and public toilets<br><br>Wash hands and face: routine times and for specific activities (food preparation)<br><br>Follow acceptable hygiene practices | Use private and public toilets<br><br>Wash hands and face: routine times and for specific activities (food preparation)<br><br>Follow acceptable hygiene practices<br><br>Manage menstrual care | Use private and public toilets<br><br>Wash hands and face: routine times and for specific activities (food preparation)<br><br>Follow acceptable hygiene practices<br><br>Manage menstrual care | Use private and public toilets<br><br>Wash hands and face<br><br>Follow acceptable hygiene practices<br><br>Manage menstrual care |

*(continued)*

325

Chart B.1. (continued)

| | Age and grade levels | | | | | |
| | Elementary school | | | | | |
| Goal areas | Kindergarten (age 5) | Primary grades (ages 6–8) | Intermediate grades (ages 9–11) | Middle school (ages 12–14) | High school (ages 15–18) | Transition (ages 19–21) |
|---|---|---|---|---|---|---|
| Hygiene and toileting (continued) | Brush teeth<br>Take bath<br>Shampoo hair | Brush teeth<br>Take bath/shower<br>Shampoo hair | Brush and floss teeth<br>Take bath/shower<br>Shampoo hair<br>Clean and clip nails | Brush and floss teeth<br>Shower/bathe<br>Shampoo hair<br>Clean and clip nails<br>Wear deodorant<br>Shave | Brush and floss teeth<br>Shower/bathe<br>Shampoo hair<br>Clean and clip nails<br>Wear deodorant<br>Shave | Care for teeth<br>Shower/bathe<br>Shampoo hair<br>Care for nails<br>Wear deodorant<br>Shave |
| Safety and health | Follow safety rules on playground equipment and near traffic<br>Exit building for emergency/alarm<br>Show care with sharp or breakable objects<br>Inform adult when sick/injured<br>Take medicine with assistance<br>Avoid/report sexual abuse<br>Report emergency to adult<br>Use caution with strangers<br>Make emergency phone calls | Follow safety rules (playground, traffic, poison, etc.)<br>Exit building for emergency/alarm<br>Show care with sharp or breakable objects<br>Inform adult when sick/injured<br>Take medicine with assistance<br>Avoid/report sexual abuse<br>Report emergency to adult<br>Use caution with strangers<br>Make emergency phone calls | Follow safety rules<br>Exit building for emergency/alarm<br>Take care with utensils, appliances, and tools<br>Inform adult when sick/injured<br>Take medicine with adult supervision<br>Avoid/report sexual abuse<br>Report emergencies<br>Use caution with strangers<br>Make emergency phone calls<br>Avoid alcohol and other drugs | Follow safety rules<br>Exit building for emergency/alarm<br>Take care with utensils, appliances, and tools<br>Inform adult when sick/injured<br>Take medicine with supervision<br>Avoid/report sexual abuse<br>Report emergencies<br>Use caution with strangers<br>Use phone to obtain emergency help<br>Avoid alcohol and other drugs | Follow safety rules<br>Exit building for emergency/alarm<br>Take care with utensils, appliances, and tools<br>Inform adult when sick/injured<br>Take medicine as needed<br>Avoid/report sexual abuse<br>Report emergencies<br>Use caution with strangers<br>Use phone to obtain emergency help<br>Avoid alcohol and other drugs | Follow safety rules<br>Exit building for emergency/alarm<br>Take care with utensils, appliances, and tools<br>Inform other(s) when sick/injured<br>Take medicine as needed<br>Avoid/report sexual abuse<br>Report emergencies<br>Use caution with strangers<br>Use phone to obtain emergency help<br>Avoid alcohol and other drugs |

| | | | | | |
|---|---|---|---|---|---|
| Avoid electricity, poisons, matches, and other common household dangers<br>Follow water/swimming safety rules | Avoid electricity, poisons, matches, and other common household dangers<br>Follow water/swimming safety rules<br>Use caution answering phone | Use caution around electricity, poisons, and other common household dangers<br>Follow water/swimming safety rules<br>Use caution answering phone<br>Use caution when at home alone<br>Use care with small appliances<br>Follow safety rules: biking | Use appropriate first-aid procedures: minor injuries (cuts, burns)<br><br>Maintain good personal health habits (diet, exercise) with supervision<br><br>Use caution around electricity, poisons, and other common household dangers<br>Follow water/swimming safety rules<br>Use caution answering phone<br>Use caution when at home alone<br>Use care with small appliances<br>Follow safety rules: biking | Use appropriate first-aid procedures: minor, major incidents (choking, bleeding, artificial respiration)<br>Maintain good personal health habits<br><br>Manage birth control as needed<br><br>Use caution around electricity, poisons, and other household dangers<br>Follow water/swimming safety rules<br>Use caution answering phone<br>Use caution when at home alone<br>Use care with appliances<br>Follow safety rules: biking | Know appropriate first-aid procedures: minor, major incidents (choking, bleeding, artificial respiration)<br>Maintain good personal health habits<br><br>Manage birth control as needed<br><br>Use caution around electricity, poisons, and other household dangers<br>Follow water/swimming safety rules<br>Use caution answering phone<br>Use caution when at home alone<br>Use care with appliances<br>Follow safety rules: biking |
| **Assisting and taking care of others (examples)**<br>Help classmate clean up<br>Help teacher get materials<br>Help classmate learn game | Help classmate clean up<br>Help teacher with materials<br>Help classmate learn game | Help classmate clean up<br>Help teacher with materials<br>Help peer learn game | Help someone clean up<br>Help instructor with materials<br>Help peer learn game | Help someone clean up<br>Help instructor with materials<br>Help peer learn game | Help someone clean up<br>Help co-worker with materials<br>Help peer learn game |

*(continued)*

Chart B.1. *(continued)*

| Goal areas | Age and grade levels | | | | | |
|---|---|---|---|---|---|---|
| | Kindergarten (age 5) | Elementary school | | Middle school (ages 12–14) | High school (ages 15–18) | Transition (ages 19–21) |
| | | Primary grades (ages 6–8) | Intermediate grades (ages 9–11) | | | |
| Assisting and taking care of others (examples) (continued) | Help new student learn routine; Share materials | Help new student learn routine; Share personal belongings | Help new student learn routine; Share personal belongings | Help new student learn routine and meet people; Share personal belongings; Do favor for classmate/peer | Help new student learn routine and meet people; Share personal belongings; Do favor for classmate/peer | Help newcomer learn routine and meet people; Share personal belongings; Do favor for someone |
| | Get something parent needs from another room | Run errand for parent; Help with care of younger sister/brother | Run errand for parent; Help with care of infant/toddler sister or brother (e.g., watching in backyard) | Run errand for parent; Help with care of siblings (including infants); Help neighbor with chore; Help when family member is ill | Run errand for parent; Babysit at home or for others; Help neighbor with chore; Help when family member is ill; Be community volunteer | Run errand for another person; Babysit for family or friends; Help neighbors (e.g., give a ride, with a task); Care for ill family member or parent; Be community volunteer |
| Budgeting and planning/scheduling | Gather belongings for outings/activities; Carry lunch/milk money | Gather belongings for outings/activities; Carry lunch/milk money | Gather belongings for outings/activities; Carry money for small purchases: not only routine | Plan and gather items for outings/activities; Manage allowance and other money for personal purchases and gifts | Plan and gather items for outings/activities; Manage own money for routine personal expenses and gifts | Plan and gather items for outings/activities; Manage budget to cover personal expenses |

| | | | | | |
|---|---|---|---|---|---|
| | Follow daily/weekly schedule | Manage weekly/monthly schedule<br>Make plans with friends on daily basis<br>Participate in fundraising activities<br>Take care of personal belongings | Manage weekly/monthly schedule<br>Arrange activities with friends and family<br>Participate in fundraising activities<br>Take care of personal belongings | Manage weekly/monthly schedule<br>Arrange activities with friends and family<br>Participate in fundraising activities<br>Take care of personal belongings<br>Pay bills (credit card, magazine subscription) | Manage weekly/monthly schedule<br>Arrange activities with friends and family<br>Participate in fundraising activities<br>Take care of personal belongings<br>Pay bills (credit card, phone) |
| Save money in piggy bank | Save money in piggy bank<br>Participate in family plans for special events (e.g., holidays, vacation) | Save money in piggy bank<br>Participate in family plans for special events (e.g., holidays, vacation) | Save money for major purchases<br>Participate in family plans for special events (e.g., holidays, vacation) | Manage bank savings account<br>Help plan family events and vacations | Manage checking/savings account<br>Help plan events and vacations with family or friends<br>Contribute to meeting household expenses<br>Manage household expenses<br>Manage credit cards<br>Use tax return preparation service |
| **Household maintenance** | | | | | |
| Pick up toys<br>Put dirty clothes in hamper | Pick up toys and belongings around house and yard<br>Put dirty clothes in hamper | Pick up around house and yard<br>Put dirty clothes in hamper | Pick up around house and yard<br>Put dirty clothes in hamper | Pick up around house and yard<br>Put dirty clothes in hamper | Pick up around house and yard<br>Put dirty clothes in hamper |

(continued)

Chart B.1. (continued)

| | | Age and grade levels | | | | |
|---|---|---|---|---|---|---|
| | | Elementary school | | | | |
| Goal areas | Kindergarten (age 5) | Primary grades (ages 6–8) | Intermediate grades (ages 9–11) | Middle school (ages 12–14) | High school (ages 15–18) | Transition (ages 19–21) |
| Household maintenance (continued) | | Keep bedroom neat (hang up clothes, make bed) <br> Feed pets | Keep bedroom neat: straighten weekly <br> Care for pets <br> Put clean clothes away <br> Take out garbage <br> Dust furniture | Keep bedroom neat <br> Care for pets <br> Help with laundry <br> Take out garbage <br> Dust furniture <br> Vacuum and dust as assigned | Keep bedroom neat <br> Care for pets <br> Do laundry <br> Take out garbage <br> Dust <br> Floor care: vacuum and mop | Keep bedroom neat <br> Care for pets <br> Do laundry <br> Take out garbage <br> Dust <br> Clean floors <br> Clean bathroom |
| Outdoor maintenance | | | Sweep: outdoors <br> Shovel snow <br> Water lawn | Sweep: outdoors <br> Shovel snow <br> Water lawn <br> Mow lawn | Sweep: outdoors <br> Clear snow (including snowblower) <br> Water lawn <br> Mow lawn (including rider mower) <br> Paint <br> Handle basic toilet/sink repairs <br> Reset circuit breaker/change fuse | Sweep: outdoors <br> Clear snow <br> Water lawn <br> Mow lawn and trim <br> Paint <br> Handle basic repairs <br> Reset circuit breaker/change fuse |

*Note:* Unshaded activities are those that can be incorporated in the school day; shaded activities are those that are better suited to instruction during *nonschool* hours.

Chart B.2. Scope and sequence for vocational (see key for shading on p. 332)

| Goal areas | Kindergarten (age 5) | Primary grades (ages 6–8) | Intermediate grades (ages 9–11) | Middle school (ages 12–14) | High school (ages 15–18) | Transition (ages 19–21) |
|---|---|---|---|---|---|---|
| | | Elementary school | | | | |
| Classroom/school job and community-based work experiences (examples) | Carry out assigned classroom chores, such as: Take attendance slip to office Get milk from cafeteria for snack Serve snack | Carry out assigned classroom chores, such as: Erase boards Collect papers Water plants Deliver messages to other locations | Carry out assigned classroom or school jobs, such as: Erase and wash boards Clean erasers Pass back papers Take/record/deliver lunch count | Carry out assigned school jobs, such as: Work in school store Deliver/pick-up A-V equipment Do clerical tasks in main office Sell lunch tickets Work at circulation desk in library  Have at least one community-based work experience: Prepare mailings in office building Bag groceries at supermarket Stamp forms at city hall Price records at music store | Carry out assigned school jobs, such as: Work in school store Work in guidance office (prepare passes) Work as teacher's assistant Work in athletic department (equipment manager) Have at least four different community-based work experiences: Enter data into computer at insurance company Stock shelves in store Prepare food in restaurant Sterilize equipment in hospital Wash cars at police/fire station Work as assistant in day-care center | Enroll in specific job-training program Assume apprenticeship in particular trade Enroll in community college or university Work at community job (see examples under goal area "Community Jobs") |

(continued)

Chart B.2. (continued)

| | Age and grade levels | | | | | |
| | Elementary school | | | | | |
| Goal areas | Kindergarten (age 5) | Primary grades (ages 6–8) | Intermediate grades (ages 9–11) | Middle school (ages 12–14) | High school (ages 15–18) | Transition (ages 19–21) |
|---|---|---|---|---|---|---|
| Neighborhood jobs (examples) | | | Fundraising in neighborhood for school activities<br><br>Deliver newspapers<br><br>Shovel or rake for neighbors | Fundraising in neighborhood for school activities<br><br>Have a paper route<br><br>Shovel or rake for neighbors<br>Mow lawns<br>Babysit<br>Care for neighbors' pets during vacations | Fundraising in neighborhood for school activities<br><br>Distribute campaign leaflets<br>Shovel or rake for neighbors<br>Mow lawns<br>Babysit<br>Care for neighbors' pets during vacations | Fundraising: community group, club<br><br>Distribute campaign leaflets<br>Do house maintenance (painting)<br>Do yard work<br>Babysit/yard work<br>Care for neighbors' pets during vacations |
| Community jobs (examples) | | | | Work as a:<br>Day camp or junior counselor; playground leader; volunteer: hospital, church, library | Work at:<br>Summer camp; supermarket; restaurant; mall: department store or other; park; hospital; political campaign office (volunteer); gas station | Work at:<br>Supermarket or other store; restaurant; hospital; office; factory; day-care center; school |

Note: Unshaded activities are those that can be incorporated in the school day; shaded activities are those that are better suited to instruction during *nonschool* hours.

332

Chart B.3. Scope and sequence for recreation/leisure (see key for shading on p. 337)

| | | Age and grade levels | | | | | |
|---|---|---|---|---|---|---|---|
| | | Elementary school | | | | | |
| Goal areas | Kindergarten (age 5) | Primary grades (ages 6–8) | Intermediate grades (ages 9–11) | Middle school (ages 12–14) | High school (ages 15–18) | Transition (ages 19–21) |
| School and extracurricular (examples) | Look at books<br><br>Play computer games<br>Use crayons<br><br><br>Play catch<br><br>Engage in imaginary play | Read and look at books<br>Play computer games<br>Make simple crafts<br><br><br>Play catch<br><br>Play games at recess | Read books and magazines<br>Play computer games<br>Take art class<br><br><br>Shoot baskets/play catch<br>Play games at recess<br><br>Take instrumental lessons<br>Participate in school musical programs | Read books, magazines, newspapers<br>Play computer/electronic games<br>Take elective class in interest area (music, art)<br>Shoot baskets/play catch<br>"Hang out" with friends<br>Take instrumental lessons<br>Participate in school musical programs<br>Attend special events as spectator (games)<br>Attend school dances<br>Participate in clubs/activities (yearbook, newspaper) | Read books, magazines, newspapers<br>Play computer/electronic games<br>Take elective class in interest area (photography, electronics)<br>Shoot baskets/play catch<br>"Hang out" with friends<br>Take instrumental lessons<br>Participate in sports/chorus/band<br>Attend special events as spectator (sports, shows)<br>Attend school dances<br>Participate in clubs/activities (yearbook, pep rally, assemblies, science fair, student council) | Read books, magazines, newspapers<br>Play computer/electronic games<br>Take elective class in interest area (ceramics, drama)<br>Shoot baskets/play catch<br>"Hang out" with friends<br>Take instrumental lessons<br>Participate in sports/chorus/band<br>Attend special events as spectator (sports, concerts)<br>Attend school dances<br>Participate in clubs/activities (pep rally, assemblies, mock U.N.) |

(continued)

Chart B.3. *(continued)*

|  | Age and grade levels | | | | | |
|---|---|---|---|---|---|---|
|  | | Elementary school | | | | |
| Goal areas | Kindergarten (age 5) | Primary grades (ages 6–8) | Intermediate grades (ages 9–11) | Middle school (ages 12–14) | High school (ages 15–18) | Transition (ages 19–21) |
| Activities to do alone: at home and in the neighborhood (examples) | Look at books<br>Listen to music<br>Play computer games<br>Play musical instrument<br>Draw or color pictures | Read and look at books<br>Listen to music<br>Play computer games<br>Play musical instrument<br>Draw or color pictures | Read books and magazines<br>Listen to music<br>Play computer games<br>Play musical instrument<br>Write cards, letters | Read books, magazines, newspapers<br>Listen to music<br>Play computer/electronic games<br>Play musical instrument<br>Write cards, letters | Read books, magazines, newspapers<br>Listen to music<br>Play computer/electronic games<br>Play musical instrument<br>Write cards, letters<br>Cook/bake | Read books, magazines, newspapers<br>Listen to music<br>Play computer/electronic games<br>Play musical instrument<br>Write cards, letters<br>Cook/bake |
|  | Watch television/videos | Watch television/videos<br>Ride bike | Watch television/videos<br>Ride bike/skateboard | Watch television/videos<br>Walk/hike/bike/skateboard<br>Take photos<br>Pursue hobby (collecting baseball cards, crafts) | Watch television/videos<br>Walk/hike/bike<br>Take photos/videos<br>Pursue hobby (sewing, painting) | Watch television/videos<br>Walk/hike/bike<br>Take photos/videos<br>Pursue hobby (painting, drawing) |
| Activities to do with family and friends: at home and in the neighborhood (examples) | Play card games (fish, old maid)<br>Play simple board games (Chutes and Ladders)<br>Use swings/other playground equipment | Play card games (Uno, war)<br>Play board games (Sorry, Parchesi)<br>Use swings/other playground equipment | Play card games (rummy, crazy 8's)<br>Play board games (Jr. Trivia, Monopoly, checkers)<br>Shoot baskets/play catch | Play card games (rummy, hearts)<br>Play board games (Pictionary, checkers/chess)<br>Shoot baskets/play catch | Play card games (pinochle, hearts)<br>Play board games (Trivial Pursuit, Pictionary)<br>Shoot baskets/play catch | Play card games (bridge, poker, gin rummy)<br>Play board games (Trivial Pursuit, Pictionary, chess)<br>Shoot baskets/play catch |

| Physical fitness (examples) | | | | | |
|---|---|---|---|---|---|
| | Play kickball | Play dodgeball, kickball | Play ball games (softball, basketball) | Play ball games (softball, soccer) | Play ball games and yard games (croquet, volleyball, Bocce, basketball) |
| | Play computer games | Play computer games | Play computer/video games | Play computer/video games | Play computer/video games |
| Swim/play in backyard pool<br>Watch television/videos | Swim in backyard pool<br>Watch television/videos<br>Ride bike<br>Play bean bag toss<br>Invite friends over<br>Participate in playground program (summer) | Swim in backyard pool<br>Watch television/videos<br>Ride bike/skateboard<br>Play ring toss<br>Invite friends over<br>Participate in playground program (summer) | Swim in backyard pool<br>Watch television/videos<br>Ride bike/skateboard<br>Play ping pong, darts<br>Invite friends over<br>Use local parks<br>Talk on telephone | Swim in backyard pool<br>Watch television/videos<br>Ride bike<br>Play ping pong, shoot pool<br>Invite friends over/have party<br>Use local parks<br>Talk on telephone | Swim in backyard pool<br>Watch television/videos<br>Ride bike<br>Play ping pong, shoot pool<br>Invite friends over/have party<br>Use local parks<br>Talk on telephone |
| Participate in exercise routine | Participate in exercise routine | Participate in exercise routine | Participate in exercise routine in physical education class<br>Participate in conditioning for team sport (soccer, track, football)<br>Play sport regularly for exercise (volleyball, basketball, cross-country skiing) | Participate in exercise routine in physical education class<br>Participate in conditioning for team sport (soccer, track, football)<br>Play sport regularly for exercise (tennis, basketball)<br>Lift weights<br>Participate in aerobic dance/exercise class | Participate in exercise routine in physical education class<br>Bike/swim/jog/walk for exercise<br>Play sport regularly for exercise (tennis, basketball)<br>Lift weights<br>Participate in aerobic dance/exercise class |

(continued)

Chart B.3. *(continued)*

| Goal areas | Age and grade levels | | | | | |
| | Elementary school | | | Middle school (ages 12–14) | High school (ages 15–18) | Transition (ages 19–21) |
| | Kindergarten (age 5) | Primary grades (ages 6–8) | Intermediate grades (ages 9–11) | | | |
|---|---|---|---|---|---|---|
| Physical fitness (examples) (continued) | | | | | Bike/swim/jog/walk regularly for exercise<br>Do workout routine to videotape/music | Bike/swim/jog/walk regularly for exercise<br>Do workout routine to videotape/music |
| Activities to do alone: in the community (examples) | | | Use public library | Use public library<br>Ride bike<br><br>Walk/hike<br>Shop | Use public library<br>Ride bike, all-terrain vehicle (ATV, snowmobile)<br>Go for drive<br>Shop | Use public library<br>Ride bike, ATV, moped, snowmobile<br>Go for drive<br>Shop |
| Activities to do with family and friends: in the community (examples) | | | | Go to restaurant with friends | Go to restaurant with friends<br>Go to shopping mall with friends | Go to restaurant with friends<br>Go to shopping mall with friends |

| | | | | | |
|---|---|---|---|---|---|
| Use parks and playgrounds | Use parks and playgrounds | Use parks | Use parks | Use parks | Use parks |
| Use public library | Use public library | Use public library | Use public library | Use public library | Use public library |
| Go to shopping malls with family | Go to shopping malls with family | Go to shopping malls with family | Go to shopping malls with family and/or friends | Hang out at shopping mall with friends | Hang out at shopping mall with friends |
| | Use public pool | Use public pool | Use public pool | Use public pool | Use public pool |
| | Take lessons (dance, gymnastics, swimming) | Take lessons (dance, gymnastics, swimming) | Take lessons (karate, horseback riding, music) | Take lessons (music, dancing) | Take lessons (music, ceramics) |
| | Go to day camp | Go to summer camp (overnight) | Go to sports camp | Go to camps (sports, band) | Go to retreats, conferences |
| | Participate in Cub Scouts/Brownies | Participate in Boy Scouts/Girl Scouts | Join youth group | Join youth group | Join community group |
| | | Play on recreation team (soccer, football) | Play on recreation team (soccer, baseball) | Play on recreation team (soccer, bowling, swimming) | Play on recreation team (soccer, bowling, swimming) |
| | | Attend spectator events (sports, ice skating shows) | Attend spectator events, sports, concerts | Attend spectator events (sports, concerts) | Attend spectator events (sports, concerts) |
| | | | Go camping (family/youth groups) | Go camping with friends (supervised) | Go camping with friends |
| | | | Go to teen center | Go to teen center | Go to church group/meeting |
| | | | Go boating/fishing | Go fishing/boating | Go fishing/hunting |
| | | | Go to movies | Go to movies | Go to movies |
| | | | | Go dancing: clubs Ski, skate, snowmobile | Go dancing: clubs Ski, skate, snowmobile |
| | | | | | Attend work-related social events |

*Note:* Unshaded activities are those that can be incorporated in the school day; shaded activities are those that are better suited to instruction during *nonschool* hours.

Chart B.4. Scope and sequence for general community functioning (see key for shading on p. 340)

| Goal areas | Kindergarten (age 5) | Elementary school Primary grades (ages 6–8) | Elementary school Intermediate grades (ages 9–11) | Middle school (ages 12–14) | High school (ages 15–18) | Transition (ages 19–21) |
|---|---|---|---|---|---|---|
| Travel | Walk or ride bus to and from school | Walk or ride bus to and from school | Walk, ride bus, or ride bike to and from school | Walk, ride bus, or ride bike to and from school | Walk, ride bus, or ride bike to and from school | Walk, ride bus, or ride bike to and from home and community sites |
| | Walk to and from school bus and to points in school (classroom, office) | Walk to and from school bus and to points in school (classroom, cafeteria, office, music room) | Walk to various destinations in school and in community (neighborhood grocery store, mailbox) | Walk to various destinations in school and in community (store, restaurant, job site) | Walk to various destinations in school and in community (store, restaurant, job site) | Walk to various destinations |
| | Cross street: stop at curb | Cross street: familiar, low-traffic intersections | Cross streets safely | Cross streets safely | Cross streets safely | Cross streets safely |
| | | | | Use public bus/subway for general transportation | Use public bus/subway for general transportation | Use public bus/subway for general transportation |
| | | | Ride public bus or subway: highly familiar routes | Use taxi with supervision | Use taxi | Use taxi |
| | | | | Use planes, trains with supervision | Use planes, trains with supervision | Use planes, trains |
| | | | Problem solve if lost in new places Use caution with strangers | Problem solve if lost in new places Use caution with strangers | Problem solve if lost in new places Use caution with strangers | Problem solve if lost in new places Use caution with strangers |
| Community safety | Do not talk to strangers | Ask official person in charge for help (e.g., bus driver, clerk)—but do not talk to other strangers or ac- | Ask official person in charge for help | Ask official person in charge for help | Ask official person in charge for help | Ask official person in charge for help |

338

| | | | | | | |
|---|---|---|---|---|---|---|
| | Do not accept food or rides from anyone other than family or close family friend | cept rides or food from others unless prearranged by parents; Do not accept food or rides from anyone other than family or close family friend | Do not accept rides/food from others unless well known and prearranged by parent; Tell parent/adult where he or she is going (e.g., friend's home, park) | Do not accept rides/food from others unless well known and/or prearranged; Tell parent/adult where he or she is going (e.g., friend's home, park) | Do not accept rides/food from others unless well known and/or prearranged; Tell parent/adult where he or she is going (e.g., friend's home, park) | Do not accept rides/food from others unless well known and prearranged; Tell parent/roommates where he or she is going (e.g., friend's home, park) |
| Grocery shopping | Accompany parent to grocery store | Grocery shop with adult: locate familiar item | Buy two–three items at neighborhood store for self (snack) or classroom snack activity; Buy groceries with family | Buy items needed for specific planned menu; Buy groceries with family | Buy items needed for specific meal or special event; Buy groceries with family | Buy items needed for specific meal or special event; Buy weekly groceries for household; Replenish household with items needed on daily basis |
| General shopping | Accompanies parent to stores | Buy item at school store; Buy small item for self (stickers); Accompanies parent to stores | Buy item at school store | Buy item for self (baseball cards, markers); Buy card or gift for family member (birthday, Mother's Day); Buy gifts for others (e.g., holiday shopping); Buy specific clothing items (shoes, clothes) | Buy few items in store with limited money amount; Purchase personal care items; Buy gifts for others, including holiday shopping; Buy all needed clothes, shoes | Shop for desired items in shopping center; Purchase personal care items; Buy gifts for others, including holidays; Buy all needed clothes, shoes |

(continued)

Chart B.4.  (continued)

| | | Age and grade levels | | | | |
|---|---|---|---|---|---|---|
| | | Elementary school | | | | |
| Goal areas | Kindergarten (age 5) | Primary grades (ages 6–8) | Intermediate grades (ages 9–11) | Middle school (ages 12–14) | High school (ages 15–18) | Transition (ages 19–21) |
| Eating out | Carry milk/lunch money<br>Follow school cafeteria routine | Carry milk/lunch money<br>Follow school cafeteria routine | Carry milk/lunch money<br>Follow school cafeteria routine<br>Order and pay—familiar fast food restaurants, snack stand<br>Buy snack/drinks from vending machine | Budget/carry money for lunch/snacks<br>Eat in school cafeteria<br>Order and eat in fast food restaurant<br>Buy snack/drinks from vending machine | Budget/carry money for lunch/snacks<br>Eat in school/public cafeteria<br>Order and eat in fast food restaurant<br>Buy snack/drinks from vending machines | Budget/carry money for meals and snacks<br>Eat in public cafeteria<br>Order and eat in fast food restaurant<br>Buy snack/drinks from vending machines |
| | Eat in restaurant with family | Order and eat in restaurant with family and friends | Order and eat in restaurant with family and friends | Purchase food from take-out restaurant | Purchase meal for self/family from take-out restaurant | Purchase meal for family/roommates from take-out restaurant<br>Arrange for a special event meal out for a group of family and/or friends |
| Using services | Mail letter at corner mailbox | Mail letter at corner mailbox<br>Use pay phone with help | Mail letters<br>Use pay phone | Use post office<br>Use pay phone<br>Ask for assistance in stores | Use post office<br>Use pay phone<br>Ask for assistance in stores, information booth | Use post office<br>Use pay phone<br>Ask for assistance appropriately in store, information booth |
| | Choose a video to rent<br>Go to dentist/doctor | Choose a video to rent<br>Go to dentist/doctor | Choose a video to rent<br>Go to dentist/doctor | Use hair styling salon<br>Go to dentist and doctor<br>Use a bank<br>Make operator-assisted phone calls | Use hair styling salon<br>Go to dentist/doctor<br>Use a bank<br>Make operator-assisted phone calls | Use hair styling salon<br>Go to dentist/doctor<br>Use a bank<br>Make operator-assisted phone calls<br>Use laundromat and dry cleaner as needed<br>Order newspaper, utilities, cable TV services, as appropriate |

Note: Unshaded activities are those that can be incorporated in the school day; shaded activities are those that are better suited to instruction during nonschool hours.

# Blank Repertoire Charts

Blank repertoire charts are included in this appendix for self-management/home living, vocational, recreation/leisure, and general community functioning domains for each of the following age levels:

- Kindergarten (age 5)
- Primary grades (ages 6–8)
- Intermediate grades (ages 9–11)
- Middle school (ages 12–14)
- High school (ages 15–18)
- Transition (ages 19–21)

Form C.1

Repertoire chart for: ___**Kindergarten (age 5)**___     Student: _____

Domain: ___Self-Management/Home Living___     Age: _____     Date: _____

| Goal area | Present activities | Assistance on most steps | Assistance on some steps | Independent | Has related social skills? | Initiates as needed? | Makes choices? | Uses safety measures? | Note priority goal areas |
|---|---|---|---|---|---|---|---|---|---|
| | | Performance level — Check one | | | | Critical features — Check all that apply | | | |
| Eating and food preparation | Eat meals and snacks | | | | | | | | |
| | | | | | | | | | |
| | Prepare simple snack for | | | | | | | | |
| | self; pour own drink | | | | | | | | |
| | | | | | | | | | |
| | | | | | | | | | |
| | Serve snack to peers | | | | | | | | |
| | | | | | | | | | |
| | Clean own place after | | | | | | | | |
| | snack/meal | | | | | | | | |
| | | | | | | | | | |
| | | | | | | | | | |
| | | | | | | | | | |
| Grooming and dressing | Brush/comb hair with | | | | | | | | |
| | reminders | | | | | | | | |
| | | | | | | | | | |
| | Get dressed/undressed | | | | | | | | |
| | (school: shoes, outer | | | | | | | | |
| | clothes) | | | | | | | | |
| | | | | | | | | | |
| | | | | | | | | | |
| Hygiene and toileting | Use private and public | | | | | | | | |
| | toilets | | | | | | | | |
| | | | | | | | | | |
| | Wash hands and face with | | | | | | | | |
| | reminders | | | | | | | | |
| | | | | | | | | | |
| | | | | | | | | | |
| | Blow nose and dispose of | | | | | | | | |
| | tissue with reminders | | | | | | | | |
| | | | | | | | | | |
| | | | | | | | | | |

(continued)

FORM C.1
(*continued*)

| Goal area | Present activities | Performance level — Check one | | | | Critical features — Check all that apply | | | | Note priority goal areas |
|---|---|---|---|---|---|---|---|---|---|---|
| | | Assistance on most steps | Assistance on some steps | Independent | Has related social skills? | Initiates as needed? | Makes choices? | Uses safety measures? | | |
| Safety and health | Follow safety rules on playground equipment and near traffic | | | | | | | | | |
| | Exit building for emergency/alarm | | | | | | | | | |
| | Show care with sharp or breakable objects | | | | | | | | | |
| | Inform adult when sick/ injured | | | | | | | | | |
| | Take medicine with assistance | | | | | | | | | |
| | Avoid/report sexual abuse | | | | | | | | | |
| | Report emergency to adult | | | | | | | | | |
| Assisting and taking care of others (examples) | | | | | | | | | | |
| | | | | | | | | | | |
| | | | | | | | | | | |
| | | | | | | | | | | |
| | | | | | | | | | | |
| Budgeting and plan-ning/sched-uling | Gather belongings for outings/activities | | | | | | | | | |
| | Carry lunch/milk money | | | | | | | | | |
| | | | | | | | | | | |
| | | | | | | | | | | |

Repertoire chart for: _____**Kindergarten (age 5)**_____     Student: _____

Domain: _____Vocational_____     Age: _____     Date: _____

| Goal areas and experiences | Performance level | | | | Critical features | | | | Note priority goal areas |
|---|---|---|---|---|---|---|---|---|---|
| | Check one | | | | Check all that apply | | | | |
| List the vocational experiences in the student's repertoire to the present date. Specify the environment, task, and sessions per week. | Assistance on most steps | Assistance on some steps | Independent | Has related social skills? | Broadens repertoire | Challenging | Student preference | Provides interactions with nonhandicapped co-workers | |
| Kindergarten and elementary school classroom/school jobs | | | | | | | | | |
| | | | | | | | | | |
| | | | | | | | | | |
| | | | | | | | | | |
| | | | | | | | | | |
| | | | | | | | | | |
| Middle school vocational training experiences | | | | | | | | | |
| | | | | | | | | | |
| | | | | | | | | | |
| | | | | | | | | | |
| High school vocational training sites | | | | | | | | | |
| | | | | | | | | | |
| | | | | | | | | | |
| | | | | | | | | | |
| Transition to community employment | | | | | | | | | |
| | | | | | | | | | |
| | | | | | | | | | |

Repertoire chart for: **Kindergarten (age 5)** Student: _____

Domain: _____ Recreation/Leisure _____ Age: _____ Date: _____

| Goal area | Present activities | Assistance on most steps | Assistance on some steps | Independent | Has related social skills? | Obviously enjoys | Age appropriate | Interacts w/non-handicap peers | Note priority goal areas |
|---|---|---|---|---|---|---|---|---|---|
| | | Performance level — Check one | | | | Critical features — Check all that apply | | | |
| School and extra-curricular (examples) | | | | | | | | | |
| | | | | | | | | | |
| | | | | | | | | | |
| | | | | | | | | | |
| | | | | | | | | | |
| | | | | | | | | | |
| Activities to do alone: at home and in the neighbor-hood (examples) | | | | | | | | | |
| | | | | | | | | | |
| | | | | | | | | | |
| | | | | | | | | | |
| | | | | | | | | | |
| | | | | | | | | | |
| Activities with family and friends: at home and in the neighborhood (examples) | | | | | | | | | |
| | | | | | | | | | |
| | | | | | | | | | |
| | | | | | | | | | |
| | | | | | | | | | |
| Physical fitness (examples) | | | | | | | | | |
| | | | | | | | | | |
| | | | | | | | | | |
| | | | | | | | | | |
| | | | | | | | | | |
| Activities to do alone: in the community (examples) | | | | | | | | | |
| | | | | | | | | | |
| | | | | | | | | | |
| | | | | | | | | | |
| | | | | | | | | | |
| | | | | | | | | | |
| Activities with family and friends: in the community (examples) | | | | | | | | | |
| | | | | | | | | | |
| | | | | | | | | | |
| | | | | | | | | | |
| | | | | | | | | | |

Repertoire chart for: _____**Kindergarten (age 5)**_____   Student: _____

Domain: _____General Community Functioning_____   Age: _____   Date: _____

| Goal area | Present activities | Assistance on most steps | Assistance on some steps | Independent | | Has related social skills? | Initiates as needed? | Makes choices? | Uses safety measures? | Note priority goal areas |
|---|---|---|---|---|---|---|---|---|---|---|
| | | Performance level — Check one | | | | | Critical features — Check all that apply | | | |
| Travel | Walk or ride bus to and from school | | | | | | | | | |
| | | | | | | | | | | |
| | Walk to and from school bus and to points in school (classroom, office) | | | | | | | | | |
| | | | | | | | | | | |
| | Cross street—stop at curb | | | | | | | | | |
| | | | | | | | | | | |
| Community Safety | | | | | | | | | | |
| | | | | | | | | | | |
| | | | | | | | | | | |
| Grocery shopping | | | | | | | | | | |
| | | | | | | | | | | |
| | | | | | | | | | | |
| General shopping | | | | | | | | | | |
| | | | | | | | | | | |
| | | | | | | | | | | |
| Eating out | Follow school cafeteria routine | | | | | | | | | |
| | | | | | | | | | | |
| | Carry milk/lunch money | | | | | | | | | |
| | | | | | | | | | | |
| Using services | Mail letter at corner mailbox | | | | | | | | | |
| | | | | | | | | | | |

FORM C.5

Repertoire chart for: __**Primary Grades (ages 6–8)**__  Student: _____

Domain: ____Self-Management/Home Living____  Age: _____  Date: _____

| Goal area | Present activities | Performance level — Check one | | | | Critical features — Check all that apply | | | | Note priority goal areas |
|---|---|---|---|---|---|---|---|---|---|---|
| | | Assistance on most steps | Assistance on some steps | Independent | Has related social skills? | Initiates as needed? | Makes choices? | Uses safety measures? | | |
| Eating and food preparation | Eat balanced meals | | | | | | | | | |
| | | | | | | | | | | |
| | Choose nutritious foods: | | | | | | | | | |
| | snack | | | | | | | | | |
| | | | | | | | | | | |
| | | | | | | | | | | |
| | Prepare simple snacks for | | | | | | | | | |
| | self; pour own drink | | | | | | | | | |
| | | | | | | | | | | |
| | | | | | | | | | | |
| | | | | | | | | | | |
| | Serve snack to peers | | | | | | | | | |
| | | | | | | | | | | |
| | | | | | | | | | | |
| | Clean up table after snack | | | | | | | | | |
| | | | | | | | | | | |
| | | | | | | | | | | |
| Grooming and dressing | Brush/comb hair with | | | | | | | | | |
| | reminders | | | | | | | | | |
| | | | | | | | | | | |
| | Get dressed/undressed | | | | | | | | | |
| | (school: shoes, swim- | | | | | | | | | |
| | ming, outer clothes) | | | | | | | | | |
| | | | | | | | | | | |
| | | | | | | | | | | |
| | | | | | | | | | | |
| | Maintain neat appearance | | | | | | | | | |
| | throughout school day | | | | | | | | | |
| | with reminders | | | | | | | | | |
| | | | | | | | | | | |
| | | | | | | | | | | |
| | | | | | | | | | | |
| | | | | | | | | | | |

*(continued)*

FORM C.5
(*continued*)

| Goal area | Present activities | Performance level — Check one | | | | Critical features — Check all that apply | | | | Note priority goal areas |
|---|---|---|---|---|---|---|---|---|---|---|
| | | Assistance on most steps | Assistance on some steps | Independent | Has related social skills? | Initiates as needed? | Makes choices? | Uses safety measures? | |
| Hygiene and toileting | Use private and public toilets | | | | | | | | | |
| | | | | | | | | | | |
| | Wash hands and face: routine times (e.g., after toilet, before eating) | | | | | | | | | |
| | | | | | | | | | | |
| | | | | | | | | | | |
| | Blow nose and dispose of tissue as needed | | | | | | | | | |
| | | | | | | | | | | |
| | | | | | | | | | | |
| Safety and health | Follow safety rules (playground, traffic, poison, etc.) | | | | | | | | | |
| | | | | | | | | | | |
| | Exit building for emergency/alarm | | | | | | | | | |
| | | | | | | | | | | |
| | Show care with sharp or breakable objects | | | | | | | | | |
| | | | | | | | | | | |
| | Inform adult when sick/ injured | | | | | | | | | |
| | | | | | | | | | | |
| | Take medicine with assistance | | | | | | | | | |
| | | | | | | | | | | |
| | Avoid/report sexual abuse | | | | | | | | | |
| | | | | | | | | | | |

(*continued*)

| Goal area | Present activities | Performance level — Check one | | | Has related social skills? | Critical features — Check all that apply | | | Note priority goal areas |
|---|---|---|---|---|---|---|---|---|---|
| | | Assistance on most steps | Assistance on some steps | Independent | | Initiates as needed? | Makes choices? | Uses safety measures? | |
| Safety and health (continued) | Report emergency to adult | | | | | | | | |
| | | | | | | | | | |
| | | | | | | | | | |
| | Use caution with strangers | | | | | | | | |
| | | | | | | | | | |
| | | | | | | | | | |
| | | | | | | | | | |
| | Make emergency phone calls | | | | | | | | |
| | | | | | | | | | |
| | | | | | | | | | |
| Assisting and taking care of others (examples) | | | | | | | | | |
| | | | | | | | | | |
| | | | | | | | | | |
| | | | | | | | | | |
| | | | | | | | | | |
| | | | | | | | | | |
| | | | | | | | | | |
| | | | | | | | | | |
| | | | | | | | | | |
| Budgeting and planning/scheduling | Gather belongings for outings/activities | | | | | | | | |
| | | | | | | | | | |
| | | | | | | | | | |
| | Carry lunch/milk money | | | | | | | | |
| | | | | | | | | | |
| | | | | | | | | | |
| | Follow daily/weekly schedule | | | | | | | | |
| | | | | | | | | | |
| | | | | | | | | | |
| | | | | | | | | | |
| | | | | | | | | | |

Repertoire chart for: __**Primary grades (ages 6–8)**__   Student: _____

Domain: _____Vocational_____   Age: _____   Date: _____

| Goal areas and experiences | Performance level | | | | Critical features | | | | | Note priority goal areas |
|---|---|---|---|---|---|---|---|---|---|---|
| | Check one | | | | Check all that apply | | | | | |
| List the vocational experiences in the student's repertoire to the present date. Specify the environment, task, and sessions per week. | Assistance on most steps | Assistance on some steps | Independent | Has related social skills? | Broadens repertoire | Challenging | Student preference | Provides interactions with nonhandicapped co-workers | | |
| Kindergarten and elementary school classroom/school jobs | | | | | | | | | | |
| _____ | | | | | | | | | | |
| _____ | | | | | | | | | | |
| _____ | | | | | | | | | | |
| _____ | | | | | | | | | | |
| _____ | | | | | | | | | | |
| Middle school vocational training experiences | | | | | | | | | | |
| _____ | | | | | | | | | | |
| _____ | | | | | | | | | | |
| _____ | | | | | | | | | | |
| High school vocational training sites | | | | | | | | | | |
| _____ | | | | | | | | | | |
| _____ | | | | | | | | | | |
| _____ | | | | | | | | | | |
| Transition to community employment | | | | | | | | | | |
| _____ | | | | | | | | | | |
| _____ | | | | | | | | | | |

FORM C.7

Repertoire chart for: __**Primary Grades (ages 6–8)**__   Student: _____

Domain: _____**Recreation/Leisure**_____   Age: _____   Date: _____

| Goal area | Present activities | Performance level — Check one | | | | Critical features — Check all that apply | | | | Note priority goal areas |
| | | Assistance on most steps | Assistance on some steps | Independent | Has related social skills? | Obviously enjoys | Age appropriate | Interacts w/non-handicap peers | |
|---|---|---|---|---|---|---|---|---|---|
| School and extra-curricular (examples) | | | | | | | | | |
| Activities to do alone: at home and in the neighborhood (examples) | | | | | | | | | |
| Activities with family and friends: at home and in the neighborhood (examples) | | | | | | | | | |
| Physical fitness (examples) | | | | | | | | | |
| Activities to do alone: in the community (examples | | | | | | | | | |
| Activities with family and friends: in the community (examples) | | | | | | | | | |

Repertoire chart for: __**Primary Grades (ages 6–8)**__  Student: _____

Domain: ____General Community Functioning____  Age: _____  Date: _____

| Goal area | Present activities | Performance level — Check one | | | | Critical features — Check all that apply | | | | Note priority goal areas |
|---|---|---|---|---|---|---|---|---|---|---|
| | | Assistance on most steps | Assistance on some steps | Independent | Has related social skills? | Initiates as needed? | Makes choices? | Uses safety measures? | | |
| Travel | Walk or ride bus to and from school | | | | | | | | | |
| | | | | | | | | | | |
| | | | | | | | | | | |
| | Walk to and from school bus and to points in school (classroom, cafeteria, office music room) | | | | | | | | | |
| | | | | | | | | | | |
| | | | | | | | | | | |
| | Cross street: familiar, low-traffic intersections | | | | | | | | | |
| | | | | | | | | | | |
| | | | | | | | | | | |
| Community safety | | | | | | | | | | |
| | | | | | | | | | | |
| | | | | | | | | | | |
| Grocery shopping | | | | | | | | | | |
| | | | | | | | | | | |
| General shopping | Buy item at school store | | | | | | | | | |
| | | | | | | | | | | |
| | Carry milk/lunch money | | | | | | | | | |
| | | | | | | | | | | |
| Eating out | Follow school cafeteria routine | | | | | | | | | |
| | | | | | | | | | | |
| Using services | Mail letter at corner mailbox | | | | | | | | | |
| | | | | | | | | | | |
| | Use pay phone with help | | | | | | | | | |
| | | | | | | | | | | |
| | | | | | | | | | | |

FORM C.9

Repertoire chart for: **Intermediate Grades (ages 9–11)**  Student: _____

Domain: _____ Self-Management/Home Living _____  Age: _____  Date: _____

| Goal area | Present activities | Performance level — Check one | | | | Critical features — Check all that apply | | | | Note priority goal areas |
|---|---|---|---|---|---|---|---|---|---|---|
| | | Assistance on most steps | Assistance on some steps | Independent | Has related social skills? | Initiates as needed? | Makes choices? | Uses safety measures? | | |
| Eating and food preparation | Eat balanced meals with appropriate manners | | | | | | | | | |
| | Choose nutritious foods: snack | | | | | | | | | |
| | Plan and Prepare simple snacks for self | | | | | | | | | |
| | Serve food items to others | | | | | | | | | |
| | Clean up preparation area and table after snack | | | | | | | | | |
| | | | | | | | | | | |
| Grooming and dressing | Brush/comb hair when needed | | | | | | | | | |
| | Get dressed/undressed (school: shoes, swimming, outer clothes) | | | | | | | | | |
| | Maintain neat appearance throughout school day | | | | | | | | | |

(continued)

| Goal area | Present activities | Performance level Check one | | | | Critical features Check all that apply | | | | Note priority goal areas |
|---|---|---|---|---|---|---|---|---|---|---|
| | | Assistance on most steps | Assistance on some steps | Independent | Has related social skills? | Initiates as needed? | Makes choices? | Uses safety measures? | | |
| Hygiene and toileting | Use private and public toilets | | | | | | | | | |
| | | | | | | | | | | |
| | | | | | | | | | | |
| | Wash hands and face: routine times and for specific activities (food preparation) | | | | | | | | | |
| | | | | | | | | | | |
| | Follow acceptable hygiene practices | | | | | | | | | |
| | | | | | | | | | | |
| | | | | | | | | | | |
| Safety and health | Follow safety rules | | | | | | | | | |
| | | | | | | | | | | |
| | Exit building for emergency/alarm | | | | | | | | | |
| | | | | | | | | | | |
| | | | | | | | | | | |
| | Take care with utensils, appliances, and tools | | | | | | | | | |
| | | | | | | | | | | |
| | | | | | | | | | | |
| | Inform adult when sick/ injured | | | | | | | | | |
| | | | | | | | | | | |
| | | | | | | | | | | |
| | Take medicine with adult supervision | | | | | | | | | |
| | | | | | | | | | | |
| | | | | | | | | | | |
| | Avoid/report sexual abuse | | | | | | | | | |
| | | | | | | | | | | |
| | | | | | | | | | | |
| | Report emergencies | | | | | | | | | |
| | | | | | | | | | | |
| | | | | | | | | | | |

Form C.9
(*continued*)

| Goal area | Present activities | Performance level — Check one | | | | Critical features — Check all that apply | | | | Note priority goal areas |
|---|---|---|---|---|---|---|---|---|---|---|
| | | Assistance on most steps | Assistance on some steps | Independent | Has related social skills? | Initiates as needed? | Makes choices? | Uses safety measures? | | |
| Safety and health (*continued*) | Use caution with strangers | | | | | | | | | |
| | | | | | | | | | | |
| | Make emergency phone calls | | | | | | | | | |
| | | | | | | | | | | |
| | | | | | | | | | | |
| | Avoid alcohol and other drugs | | | | | | | | | |
| | | | | | | | | | | |
| Assisting and taking care of others (examples) | | | | | | | | | | |
| | | | | | | | | | | |
| | | | | | | | | | | |
| | | | | | | | | | | |
| | | | | | | | | | | |
| Budgeting and planning/scheduling | Gather belongings for outings/activities | | | | | | | | | |
| | | | | | | | | | | |
| | Take care of personal belongings | | | | | | | | | |
| | | | | | | | | | | |
| | | | | | | | | | | |
| | Carry money for small purchases: not only routine | | | | | | | | | |
| | | | | | | | | | | |
| | | | | | | | | | | |
| | Manage weekly/monthly schedule | | | | | | | | | |
| | | | | | | | | | | |
| | | | | | | | | | | |
| | Make plans with friends on daily basis | | | | | | | | | |
| | | | | | | | | | | |
| | | | | | | | | | | |
| | Participate in fundraising activities | | | | | | | | | |
| | | | | | | | | | | |

Repertoire chart for: **Intermediate Grades (ages 9–11)**   Student: _____

Domain: _____ Vocational _____   Age: _____   Date: _____

| Goal areas and experiences | Performance level | | | | Critical features | | | | | Note priority goal areas |
|---|---|---|---|---|---|---|---|---|---|---|
| | Check one | | | | Check all that apply | | | | | |
| List the vocational experiences in the student's repertoire to the present date. Specify the environment, task, and sessions per week. | Assistance on most steps | Assistance on some steps | Independent | Has related social skills? | Broadens repertoire | Challenging | Student preference | Provides interactions with nonhandicapped co-workers | | |
| Kindergarten and elementary school classroom/school jobs | | | | | | | | | | |
| | | | | | | | | | | |
| | | | | | | | | | | |
| | | | | | | | | | | |
| | | | | | | | | | | |
| | | | | | | | | | | |
| Middle school vocational training experiences | | | | | | | | | | |
| | | | | | | | | | | |
| | | | | | | | | | | |
| | | | | | | | | | | |
| High school vocational training sites | | | | | | | | | | |
| | | | | | | | | | | |
| | | | | | | | | | | |
| | | | | | | | | | | |
| Transition to community employment | | | | | | | | | | |
| | | | | | | | | | | |
| | | | | | | | | | | |

FORM C.11

Repertoire chart for: **Intermediate Grades (ages 9–11)**    Student: _____

Domain: _____ Recreation/Leisure _____    Age: _____    Date: _____

| Goal area | Present activities | Performance level — Check one | | | | Critical features — Check all that apply | | | | Note priority goal areas |
|---|---|---|---|---|---|---|---|---|---|---|
| | | Assistance on most steps | Assistance on some steps | Independent | Has related social skills? | Obviously enjoys | Age appropriate | Interacts w/non-handicap peers | | |
| School and extra-curricular (examples) | | | | | | | | | | |
| | | | | | | | | | | |
| | | | | | | | | | | |
| | | | | | | | | | | |
| | | | | | | | | | | |
| | | | | | | | | | | |
| Activities to do alone: at home and in the neigh-borhood (examples) | | | | | | | | | | |
| | | | | | | | | | | |
| | | | | | | | | | | |
| | | | | | | | | | | |
| | | | | | | | | | | |
| Activities with family and friends: at home and in the neighborhood (examples) | | | | | | | | | | |
| | | | | | | | | | | |
| | | | | | | | | | | |
| | | | | | | | | | | |
| | | | | | | | | | | |
| Physical fitness (examples) | | | | | | | | | | |
| | | | | | | | | | | |
| | | | | | | | | | | |
| | | | | | | | | | | |
| | | | | | | | | | | |
| Activities to do alone: in the community (examples) | | | | | | | | | | |
| | | | | | | | | | | |
| | | | | | | | | | | |
| | | | | | | | | | | |
| | | | | | | | | | | |
| Activities with family and friends: in the community (examples) | | | | | | | | | | |
| | | | | | | | | | | |
| | | | | | | | | | | |
| | | | | | | | | | | |

FORM C.12

Repertoire chart for: **Intermediate Grades (ages 9–11)**   Student: _____

Domain: _____ General Community Functioning _____   Age: _____ Date: _____

| Goal area | Present activities | Performance level — Check one | | | | Critical features — Check all that apply | | | | Note priority goal areas |
|---|---|---|---|---|---|---|---|---|---|---|
| | | Assistance on most steps | Assistance on some steps | Independent | Has related social skills? | Initiates as needed? | Makes choices? | Uses safety measures? | | |
| Travel | Walk, ride bus, ride bike | | | | | | | | | |
| | to and from school | | | | | | | | | |
| | | | | | | | | | | |
| | | | | | | | | | | |
| | Walk to various destina- | | | | | | | | | |
| | tions in school and in | | | | | | | | | |
| | the community (neigh- | | | | | | | | | |
| | borhood grocery store, | | | | | | | | | |
| | mailbox) | | | | | | | | | |
| | | | | | | | | | | |
| | Cross streets safely | | | | | | | | | |
| | | | | | | | | | | |
| | | | | | | | | | | |
| Community safety | | | | | | | | | | |
| | | | | | | | | | | |
| | | | | | | | | | | |
| | | | | | | | | | | |
| | | | | | | | | | | |
| | | | | | | | | | | |
| | | | | | | | | | | |
| Grocery shopping | Buy two to three items at | | | | | | | | | |
| | neighborhood store for | | | | | | | | | |
| | self (snack) or classroom | | | | | | | | | |
| | snack activity | | | | | | | | | |
| | | | | | | | | | | |
| | | | | | | | | | | |
| | | | | | | | | | | |
| | | | | | | | | | | |
| General shopping | Buy item at school store | | | | | | | | | |
| | | | | | | | | | | |
| | | | | | | | | | | |
| | | | | | | | | | | |
| | | | | | | | | | | |
| | | | | | | | | | | |
| | | | | | | | | | | |

(continued)

FORM C.12
(continued)

| Goal area | Present activities | Performance level — Check one | | | | Critical features — Check all that apply | | | | Note priority goal areas |
|---|---|---|---|---|---|---|---|---|---|---|
| | | Assistance on most steps | Assistance on some steps | Independent | Has related social skills? | Initiates as needed? | Makes choices? | Uses safety measures? | | |
| Eating out | Follow school cafeteria routine | | | | | | | | | |
| | | | | | | | | | | |
| | | | | | | | | | | |
| | | | | | | | | | | |
| | | | | | | | | | | |
| | Order and pay: familiar fast-food restaurants, snack stand | | | | | | | | | |
| | | | | | | | | | | |
| | | | | | | | | | | |
| | | | | | | | | | | |
| | Use vending machine | | | | | | | | | |
| | | | | | | | | | | |
| | | | | | | | | | | |
| | | | | | | | | | | |
| | Carry milk/lunch money | | | | | | | | | |
| | | | | | | | | | | |
| | | | | | | | | | | |
| | | | | | | | | | | |
| | | | | | | | | | | |
| Using services | Mail letter at corner mailbox | | | | | | | | | |
| | | | | | | | | | | |
| | | | | | | | | | | |
| | | | | | | | | | | |
| | | | | | | | | | | |
| | Use pay phone | | | | | | | | | |
| | | | | | | | | | | |
| | | | | | | | | | | |
| | | | | | | | | | | |
| | | | | | | | | | | |
| | | | | | | | | | | |
| | | | | | | | | | | |
| | | | | | | | | | | |
| | | | | | | | | | | |

FORM C.13

Repertoire chart for: __Middle School (ages 12–14)__   Student: _____

Domain: ___Self-Management/Home Living___   Age: _____   Date: _____

| Goal area | Present activities | Performance level — Check one | | | | Critical features — Check all that apply | | | | Note priority goal areas |
|---|---|---|---|---|---|---|---|---|---|---|
| | | Assistance on most steps | Assistance on some steps | Independent | Has related social skills? | Initiates as needed? | Makes choices? | Uses safety measures? | | |
| Eating and food preparation | Eat balanced meals with | | | | | | | | | |
| | appropriate manners | | | | | | | | | |
| | | | | | | | | | | |
| | | | | | | | | | | |
| | | | | | | | | | | |
| | Choose nutritious foods: | | | | | | | | | |
| | breakfast, lunch, snacks | | | | | | | | | |
| | | | | | | | | | | |
| | | | | | | | | | | |
| | | | | | | | | | | |
| | Plan and prepare snacks | | | | | | | | | |
| | for self | | | | | | | | | |
| | | | | | | | | | | |
| | | | | | | | | | | |
| | | | | | | | | | | |
| | Prepare simple meals: | | | | | | | | | |
| | breakfast, lunch (some | | | | | | | | | |
| | cooking) | | | | | | | | | |
| | | | | | | | | | | |
| | | | | | | | | | | |
| | | | | | | | | | | |
| | Serve food items to others | | | | | | | | | |
| | | | | | | | | | | |
| | | | | | | | | | | |
| | | | | | | | | | | |
| | Clear table and do dishes | | | | | | | | | |
| | after food preparation | | | | | | | | | |
| | | | | | | | | | | |
| | | | | | | | | | | |
| | | | | | | | | | | |
| | Store food and leftovers | | | | | | | | | |
| | | | | | | | | | | |
| | | | | | | | | | | |
| | | | | | | | | | | |
| | | | | | | | | | | |

(continued)

| Goal area | Present activities | Performance level — Check one | | | | Critical features — Check all that apply | | | | Note priority goal areas |
|---|---|---|---|---|---|---|---|---|---|---|
| | | Assistance on most steps | Assistance on some steps | Independent | Has related social skills? | Initiates as needed? | Makes choices? | Uses safety measures? | | |
| Grooming and dressing | Brush/comb and style hair | | | | | | | | | |
| | (also choose hairstyle) | | | | | | | | | |
| | | | | | | | | | | |
| | | | | | | | | | | |
| | Use skin care products | | | | | | | | | |
| | (cosmetics if desired) | | | | | | | | | |
| | | | | | | | | | | |
| | | | | | | | | | | |
| | Care for eyeglasses/contact | | | | | | | | | |
| | lenses | | | | | | | | | |
| | | | | | | | | | | |
| | | | | | | | | | | |
| | Get dressed/undressed | | | | | | | | | |
| | (physical education, | | | | | | | | | |
| | outer clothes) | | | | | | | | | |
| | | | | | | | | | | |
| | | | | | | | | | | |
| | Maintain neat appearance | | | | | | | | | |
| | throughout school day | | | | | | | | | |
| | | | | | | | | | | |
| | | | | | | | | | | |
| | | | | | | | | | | |
| Hygiene and toileting | Use private and public | | | | | | | | | |
| | toilets | | | | | | | | | |
| | | | | | | | | | | |
| | | | | | | | | | | |
| | Wash hands and face: | | | | | | | | | |
| | routine times and for | | | | | | | | | |
| | specific activities (food | | | | | | | | | |
| | preparation) | | | | | | | | | |
| | | | | | | | | | | |
| | Follow acceptable hygiene | | | | | | | | | |
| | practices | | | | | | | | | |
| | | | | | | | | | | |
| | | | | | | | | | | |
| | Manage menstrual care | | | | | | | | | |
| | | | | | | | | | | |
| | | | | | | | | | | |

(continued)

| Goal area | Present activities | Performance level | | | | Critical features | | | | Note priority goal areas |
|---|---|---|---|---|---|---|---|---|---|---|
| | | Check one | | | | Check all that apply | | | | |
| | | Assistance on most steps | Assistance on some steps | Independent | Has related social skills? | Initiates as needed? | Makes choices? | Uses safety measures? | | |
| Safety and health | Follow safety rules | | | | | | | | | |
| | Exit building for emergency/alarm | | | | | | | | | |
| | | | | | | | | | | |
| | Take care with utensils | | | | | | | | | |
| | Inform adult when sick/ injured | | | | | | | | | |
| | Take medicine with supervision | | | | | | | | | |
| | Avoid/report sexual abuse | | | | | | | | | |
| | Report emergencies | | | | | | | | | |
| | Use caution with strangers | | | | | | | | | |
| | Use phone to obtain emergency help | | | | | | | | | |
| | Avoid alcohol and other drugs | | | | | | | | | |
| | Use appropriate first-aid procedures: minor injuries (cuts, burns) | | | | | | | | | |
| | Maintain good personal health habits (diet, ex- ercise) with supervision | | | | | | | | | |

(*continued*)

FORM C.13
(continued)

| Goal area | Present activities | Performance level — Check one | | | | Critical features — Check all that apply | | | | Note priority goal areas |
|---|---|---|---|---|---|---|---|---|---|---|
| | | Assistance on most steps | Assistance on some steps | Independent | Has related social skills? | Initiates as needed? | Makes choices? | Uses safety measures? | | |
| Assisting and taking care of others (examples) | | | | | | | | | | |
| | | | | | | | | | | |
| | | | | | | | | | | |
| | | | | | | | | | | |
| | | | | | | | | | | |
| | | | | | | | | | | |
| | | | | | | | | | | |
| | | | | | | | | | | |
| | | | | | | | | | | |
| | | | | | | | | | | |
| | | | | | | | | | | |
| Budgeting and planning/scheduling | Plan and gather belongings for outings/activities | | | | | | | | | |
| | | | | | | | | | | |
| | Take care of personal belongings | | | | | | | | | |
| | | | | | | | | | | |
| | Manage allowance and other personal purchases and money for personal gifts | | | | | | | | | |
| | | | | | | | | | | |
| | Manage weekly/monthly schedule | | | | | | | | | |
| | | | | | | | | | | |
| | Arrange activities with friends and family | | | | | | | | | |
| | | | | | | | | | | |
| | Participate in fundraising activities | | | | | | | | | |
| | | | | | | | | | | |

Repertoire chart for: __Middle School (ages 12–14)__    Student: _____

Domain: _____Vocational_____    Age: _____    Date: _____

| Goal areas and experiences | Performance level | | | | Critical features | | | | |
|---|---|---|---|---|---|---|---|---|---|
| | Check one | | | | Check all that apply | | | | |
| List the vocational experiences in the student's repertoire to the present date. Specify the environment, task, and sessions per week. | Assistance on most steps | Assistance on some steps | Independent | Has related social skills? | Broadens repertoire | Challenging | Student preference | Provides interactions with nonhandicapped co-workers | Note priority goal areas |
| Kindergarten and elementary school classroom/school jobs | | | | | | | | | |
| | | | | | | | | | |
| | | | | | | | | | |
| | | | | | | | | | |
| | | | | | | | | | |
| | | | | | | | | | |
| Middle school vocational training experiences | | | | | | | | | |
| | | | | | | | | | |
| | | | | | | | | | |
| | | | | | | | | | |
| High school vocational training sites | | | | | | | | | |
| | | | | | | | | | |
| | | | | | | | | | |
| | | | | | | | | | |
| Transition to community employment | | | | | | | | | |
| | | | | | | | | | |
| | | | | | | | | | |

FORM C.15

Repertoire chart for: __**Middle School (ages 12–14)**__ Student: _____

Domain: _____ Recreation/Leisure _____ Age: _____ Date: _____

| Goal area | Present activities | Performance level — Check one | | | Has related social skills? | Critical features — Check all that apply | | | Note priority goal areas |
|---|---|---|---|---|---|---|---|---|---|
| | | Assistance on most steps | Assistance on some steps | Independent | | Obviously enjoys | Age appropriate | Interacts w/non-handicap peers | |
| School and extra-curricular (examples) | | | | | | | | | |
| Activities to do alone: at home and in the neighborhood (examples) | | | | | | | | | |
| Activities to do with family and friends: at home and in the neighborhood (examples) | | | | | | | | | |
| Physical fitness (examples) | | | | | | | | | |
| Activities to do alone: in the community (examples | | | | | | | | | |
| Activities with family and friends: in the community (examples) | | | | | | | | | |

FORM C.16

Repertoire chart for: __Middle School (ages 12–14)__    Student: _____

Domain: ___General Community Functioning___    Age: _____    Date: _____

| Goal area | Present activities | Performance level — Check one | | | | Critical features — Check all that apply | | | | Note priority goal areas |
|---|---|---|---|---|---|---|---|---|---|---|
| | | Assistance on most steps | Assistance on some steps | Independent | Has related social skills? | Initiates as needed? | Makes choices? | Uses safety measures? | | |
| Travel | Walk, ride bus, ride bike to and from school | | | | | | | | | |
| | | | | | | | | | | |
| | | | | | | | | | | |
| | Walk to various destinations | | | | | | | | | |
| | | | | | | | | | | |
| | | | | | | | | | | |
| | Cross streets safely | | | | | | | | | |
| | | | | | | | | | | |
| | | | | | | | | | | |
| | Use public bus/subway for general transportation | | | | | | | | | |
| | | | | | | | | | | |
| | | | | | | | | | | |
| | | | | | | | | | | |
| Community safety | Problem solve if lost in new places | | | | | | | | | |
| | | | | | | | | | | |
| | | | | | | | | | | |
| | | | | | | | | | | |
| | Use caution with strangers | | | | | | | | | |
| | | | | | | | | | | |
| | | | | | | | | | | |
| | | | | | | | | | | |
| | | | | | | | | | | |
| Grocery shopping | Buy items needed for specific planned menu, with help | | | | | | | | | |
| | | | | | | | | | | |
| | | | | | | | | | | |
| | | | | | | | | | | |
| | | | | | | | | | | |

(continued)

FORM C.16
(*continued*)

| Goal area | Present activities | Performance level — Check one | | | | Critical features — Check all that apply | | | Note priority goal areas |
|---|---|---|---|---|---|---|---|---|---|
| | | Assistance on most steps | Assistance on some steps | Independent | Has related social skills? | Initiates as needed? | Makes choices? | Uses safety measures? | |
| General shopping | Buy few items in store | | | | | | | | |
| | with limited money | | | | | | | | |
| | amount | | | | | | | | |
| | | | | | | | | | |
| | | | | | | | | | |
| | Purchase personal care | | | | | | | | |
| | items | | | | | | | | |
| | | | | | | | | | |
| | | | | | | | | | |
| Eating out | Eat in school cafeteria | | | | | | | | |
| | | | | | | | | | |
| | | | | | | | | | |
| | | | | | | | | | |
| | Order and eat in fast-food | | | | | | | | |
| | restaurant | | | | | | | | |
| | | | | | | | | | |
| | | | | | | | | | |
| | Buy food/drinks from | | | | | | | | |
| | vending machines | | | | | | | | |
| | | | | | | | | | |
| | | | | | | | | | |
| | Budget/carry money for | | | | | | | | |
| | lunch/snacks | | | | | | | | |
| | | | | | | | | | |
| | | | | | | | | | |
| | | | | | | | | | |
| Using services | Use post office | | | | | | | | |
| | | | | | | | | | |
| | | | | | | | | | |
| | | | | | | | | | |
| | Use pay phone | | | | | | | | |
| | | | | | | | | | |
| | | | | | | | | | |
| | | | | | | | | | |
| | Ask for assistance in stores | | | | | | | | |
| | | | | | | | | | |
| | | | | | | | | | |
| | | | | | | | | | |

Repertoire chart for: __**High School (ages 15–18)**__   Student: _____

Domain: ___Self-Management/Home Living___   Age: _____   Date: _____

| Goal area | Present activities | Performance level — Check one | | | Has related social skills? | Critical features — Check all that apply | | | Note priority goal areas |
|---|---|---|---|---|---|---|---|---|---|
| | | Assistance on most steps | Assistance on some steps | Independent | | Initiates as needed? | Makes choices? | Uses safety measures? | |
| Eating and food preparation | Eat balanced meals with appropriate manners | | | | | | | | |
| | | | | | | | | | |
| | | | | | | | | | |
| | | | | | | | | | |
| | Choose nutritious foods: breakfast, lunch, snacks | | | | | | | | |
| | | | | | | | | | |
| | | | | | | | | | |
| | | | | | | | | | |
| | Plan and prepare snacks for self | | | | | | | | |
| | | | | | | | | | |
| | | | | | | | | | |
| | | | | | | | | | |
| | Prepare various types of meals | | | | | | | | |
| | | | | | | | | | |
| | | | | | | | | | |
| | | | | | | | | | |
| | Serve food items to others | | | | | | | | |
| | | | | | | | | | |
| | | | | | | | | | |
| | | | | | | | | | |
| | Clear table and do dishes after food preparation | | | | | | | | |
| | | | | | | | | | |
| | | | | | | | | | |
| | | | | | | | | | |
| | Store food and leftovers | | | | | | | | |
| | | | | | | | | | |
| | | | | | | | | | |
| | | | | | | | | | |
| | | | | | | | | | |

(continued)

FORM C.17
(continued)

| Goal area | Present activities | Performance level — Check one — Assistance on most steps | Assistance on some steps | Independent | Has related social skills? | Critical features — Check all that apply — Initiates as needed? | Makes choices? | Uses safety measures? | Note priority goal areas |
|---|---|---|---|---|---|---|---|---|---|
| Grooming and dressing | Brush/comb and style hair | | | | | | | | |
| | (also choose hairstyle) | | | | | | | | |
| | | | | | | | | | |
| | Use skin care products | | | | | | | | |
| | (cosmetics if desired) | | | | | | | | |
| | | | | | | | | | |
| | Care for eyeglasses/contact | | | | | | | | |
| | lenses | | | | | | | | |
| | | | | | | | | | |
| | Get dressed/undressed | | | | | | | | |
| | (physical education, | | | | | | | | |
| | outer clothes) | | | | | | | | |
| | | | | | | | | | |
| | Maintain appearance | | | | | | | | |
| | throughout school day | | | | | | | | |
| Hygiene and toileting | Use public and private | | | | | | | | |
| | toilets | | | | | | | | |
| | | | | | | | | | |
| | Wash hands and face: | | | | | | | | |
| | routine times and for | | | | | | | | |
| | specific activities (food | | | | | | | | |
| | preparation) | | | | | | | | |
| | | | | | | | | | |
| | Follow acceptable hygiene | | | | | | | | |
| | | | | | | | | | |
| | Manage menstrual care | | | | | | | | |
| Safety and health | Follow safety rules | | | | | | | | |
| | | | | | | | | | |
| | Exit building for | | | | | | | | |
| | emergency/alarm | | | | | | | | |
| | | | | | | | | | |
| | Take care with utensils, | | | | | | | | |
| | appliances, and tools | | | | | | | | |
| | | | | | | | | | |
| | Inform adult when sick/in- | | | | | | | | |
| | jured | | | | | | | | |

(continued)

| Goal area | Present activities | Performance level — Check one — Assistance on most steps | Assistance on some steps | Independent | Has related social skills? | Critical features — Check all that apply — Initiates as needed? | Makes choices? | Uses safety measures? | Note priority goal areas |
|---|---|---|---|---|---|---|---|---|---|
| Safety and health (*continued*) | Take medicine as needed | | | | | | | | |
| | Avoid/report sexual abuse | | | | | | | | |
| | | | | | | | | | |
| | Report emergencies | | | | | | | | |
| | Use caution with strangers | | | | | | | | |
| | Use phone to obtain emergency help | | | | | | | | |
| | Avoid alcohol and other drugs | | | | | | | | |
| | Use appropriate first-aid procedures: minor, major incidents (choking, bleeding, artificial respiration) | | | | | | | | |
| | Maintain good personal health habits | | | | | | | | |
| | Manage birth control as needed | | | | | | | | |
| Assisting and taking care of others (examples) | | | | | | | | | |
| | | | | | | | | | |
| | | | | | | | | | |
| | | | | | | | | | |
| | | | | | | | | | |
| | | | | | | | | | |
| | | | | | | | | | |
| | | | | | | | | | |

(*continued*)

FORM C.17
(continued)

| Goal area | Present activities | Performance level | | | | Critical features | | | Note priority goal areas |
|---|---|---|---|---|---|---|---|---|---|
| | | Check one | | | | Check all that apply | | | |
| | | Assistance on most steps | Assistance on some steps | Independent | Has related social skills? | Initiates as needed? | Makes choices? | Uses safety measures? | |
| Budgeting and plan-ning/sched-uling | Plan and gather items for outings/activities | | | | | | | | |
| | | | | | | | | | |
| | | | | | | | | | |
| | Take care of personal belongings | | | | | | | | |
| | | | | | | | | | |
| | | | | | | | | | |
| | Manage own money for routine personal expenses and gifts | | | | | | | | |
| | | | | | | | | | |
| | | | | | | | | | |
| | | | | | | | | | |
| | Manage weekly/monthly schedule | | | | | | | | |
| | | | | | | | | | |
| | | | | | | | | | |
| | Arrange activities with friends and family | | | | | | | | |
| | | | | | | | | | |
| | | | | | | | | | |
| | Participate in fundraising activities | | | | | | | | |
| | | | | | | | | | |
| | | | | | | | | | |
| | Pay bills (credit card, magazine subscription) | | | | | | | | |
| | | | | | | | | | |
| | | | | | | | | | |
| | | | | | | | | | |

Repertoire chart for: __High School (ages 15–18)__     Student: _____

Domain: _____Vocational_____     Age: _____     Date: _____

| Goal areas and experiences | Performance level | | | | Critical features | | | | Note priority goal areas |
|---|---|---|---|---|---|---|---|---|---|
| | Check one | | | | Check all that apply | | | | |
| List the vocational experiences in the student's repertoire to the present date. Specify the environment, task, and sessions per week. | Assistance on most steps | Assistance on some steps | Independent | Has related social skills? | Broadens repertoire | Challenging | Student preference | Provides interactions with nonhandicapped co-workers | |
| Kindergarten and elementary school classroom/school jobs | | | | | | | | | |
| | | | | | | | | | |
| | | | | | | | | | |
| | | | | | | | | | |
| | | | | | | | | | |
| | | | | | | | | | |
| Middle school vocational training experiences | | | | | | | | | |
| | | | | | | | | | |
| | | | | | | | | | |
| | | | | | | | | | |
| High school vocational training sites | | | | | | | | | |
| | | | | | | | | | |
| | | | | | | | | | |
| | | | | | | | | | |
| Transition to community employment | | | | | | | | | |
| | | | | | | | | | |
| | | | | | | | | | |

FORM C.19

Repertoire chart for: **High School (ages 15–18)**   Student: _____

Domain: _____ Recreation/Leisure _____   Age: _____   Date: _____

| Goal area | Present activities | Performance level (Check one) | | | | Critical features (Check all that apply) | | | | Note priority goal areas |
|---|---|---|---|---|---|---|---|---|---|---|
| | | Assistance on most steps | Assistance on some steps | Independent | Has related social skills? | Obviously enjoys | Age appropriate | Interacts w/non-handicap peers | |
| School and extra-curricular (examples) | | | | | | | | | |
| | | | | | | | | | |
| | | | | | | | | | |
| | | | | | | | | | |
| | | | | | | | | | |
| Activities to do alone: at home and in the neighborhood (examples) | | | | | | | | | |
| | | | | | | | | | |
| | | | | | | | | | |
| | | | | | | | | | |
| Activities to do with family and friends: at home and in the neigh-borhood (examples) | | | | | | | | | |
| | | | | | | | | | |
| | | | | | | | | | |
| | | | | | | | | | |
| | | | | | | | | | |
| Physical fitness (examples) | | | | | | | | | |
| | | | | | | | | | |
| | | | | | | | | | |
| | | | | | | | | | |
| Activities to do alone: in the community (examples) | | | | | | | | | |
| | | | | | | | | | |
| | | | | | | | | | |
| | | | | | | | | | |
| Activities to do with family and friends: in the community (examples) | | | | | | | | | |
| | | | | | | | | | |
| | | | | | | | | | |
| | | | | | | | | | |

Repertoire chart for: ___**High School (ages 15–18)**___   Student: _____

Domain: ___General Community Functioning___   Age: _____   Date: _____

| Goal area | Present activities | Performance level — Check one | | | | Critical features — Check all that apply | | | | Note priority goal areas |
|---|---|---|---|---|---|---|---|---|---|---|
| | | Assistance on most steps | Assistance on some steps | Independent | Has related social skills? | Initiates as needed? | Makes choices? | Uses safety measures? | |
| Travel | Walk, ride bus, ride bike to and from school | | | | | | | | | |
| | | | | | | | | | | |
| | | | | | | | | | | |
| | Walk to various destinations in school and in the community (store, restaurant, job site) | | | | | | | | | |
| | | | | | | | | | | |
| | | | | | | | | | | |
| | | | | | | | | | | |
| | Cross streets safely | | | | | | | | | |
| | | | | | | | | | | |
| | | | | | | | | | | |
| | Use public bus/subway for general transportation | | | | | | | | | |
| | | | | | | | | | | |
| | | | | | | | | | | |
| | | | | | | | | | | |
| Community safety | Problem solve if lost in new places | | | | | | | | | |
| | | | | | | | | | | |
| | | | | | | | | | | |
| | Use caution with strangers | | | | | | | | | |
| | | | | | | | | | | |
| | | | | | | | | | | |
| | | | | | | | | | | |
| Grocery shopping | Buy items needed for specific meal or special event | | | | | | | | | |
| | | | | | | | | | | |
| | | | | | | | | | | |
| | | | | | | | | | | |
| | | | | | | | | | | |
| | | | | | | | | | | |
| | | | | | | | | | | |

(continued)

FORM C.20
(*continued*)

| Goal area | Present activities | Performance level — Check one | | | | Critical features — Check all that apply | | | Note priority goal areas |
|---|---|---|---|---|---|---|---|---|---|
| | | Assistance on most steps | Assistance on some steps | Independent | Has related social skills? | Initiates as needed? | Makes choices? | Uses safety measures? | |
| General shopping | Shop for desired items in shopping center | | | | | | | | |
| | | | | | | | | | |
| | | | | | | | | | |
| | Purchase personal care items | | | | | | | | |
| | | | | | | | | | |
| | | | | | | | | | |
| Eating out | Eat in school/public cafeteria | | | | | | | | |
| | | | | | | | | | |
| | | | | | | | | | |
| | Order and eat in fast-food restaurant | | | | | | | | |
| | | | | | | | | | |
| | | | | | | | | | |
| | Buy food/drinks from vending machines | | | | | | | | |
| | | | | | | | | | |
| | | | | | | | | | |
| | Budget/carry money for lunch/snacks | | | | | | | | |
| | | | | | | | | | |
| | | | | | | | | | |
| Using services | Use post office | | | | | | | | |
| | | | | | | | | | |
| | Use pay phone | | | | | | | | |
| | | | | | | | | | |
| | Ask for assistance in stores, information booth | | | | | | | | |
| | | | | | | | | | |
| | | | | | | | | | |
| | | | | | | | | | |
| | | | | | | | | | |

Repertoire chart for: __**Transition (ages 19–21)**__   Student: _____

Domain: __Self-Management and Home Living__   Age: _____   Date: _____

| Goal area | Present activities | Performance level — Check one | | | | Critical features — Check all that apply | | | | Note priority goal areas |
|---|---|---|---|---|---|---|---|---|---|---|
| | | Assistance on most steps | Assistance on some steps | Independent | Has related social skills? | Initiates as needed? | Makes choices? | Uses safety measures? | | |
| Eating and food preparation | Eat balanced meals with appropriate manners | | | | | | | | |
| | Choose nutritious foods (including when eating out) | | | | | | | | |
| | Plan menu for self/family/ roommates | | | | | | | | |
| | Prepare meal for self/ others | | | | | | | | |
| | Clean up after meals | | | | | | | | |
| | Store food and leftovers | | | | | | | | |
| | Make weekly grocery list | | | | | | | | |
| Grooming and dressing | Manage hair care | | | | | | | | |
| | Manage skin care | | | | | | | | |
| | Manage eye care needs | | | | | | | | |
| | Get dressed/undressed | | | | | | | | |
| | Maintain appearance | | | | | | | | |

(continued)

| Goal area | Present activities | Performance level — Check one | | | | Critical features — Check all that apply | | | | Note priority goal areas |
|---|---|---|---|---|---|---|---|---|---|---|
| | | Assistance on most steps | Assistance on some steps | Independent | Has related social skills? | Initiates as needed? | Makes choices? | Uses safety measures? | | |
| Hygiene and toileting | Use public and private toilets | | | | | | | | | |
| | | | | | | | | | | |
| | | | | | | | | | | |
| | Wash hands and face: routine times and for specific activities (food preparation) | | | | | | | | | |
| | | | | | | | | | | |
| | | | | | | | | | | |
| | | | | | | | | | | |
| | | | | | | | | | | |
| | Follow acceptable hygiene practices | | | | | | | | | |
| | | | | | | | | | | |
| | | | | | | | | | | |
| | Manage menstrual care | | | | | | | | | |
| | | | | | | | | | | |
| | | | | | | | | | | |
| | | | | | | | | | | |
| | | | | | | | | | | |
| Safety and health | Follow safety rules | | | | | | | | | |
| | | | | | | | | | | |
| | Exit building for emergency/alarm | | | | | | | | | |
| | | | | | | | | | | |
| | | | | | | | | | | |
| | Take care with utensils, appliances, and tools | | | | | | | | | |
| | | | | | | | | | | |
| | | | | | | | | | | |
| | Inform other(s) when sick/ injured | | | | | | | | | |
| | | | | | | | | | | |
| | | | | | | | | | | |
| | Take medicine as needed | | | | | | | | | |
| | | | | | | | | | | |

| Goal area | Present activities | Performance level — Check one | | | | Critical features — Check all that apply | | | | Note priority goal areas |
|---|---|---|---|---|---|---|---|---|---|---|
| | | Assistance on most steps | Assistance on some steps | Independent | Has related social skills? | Initiates as needed? | Makes choices? | Uses safety measures? | | |
| Safety and health (*continued*) | Avoid/report sexual abuse | | | | | | | | | |
| | | | | | | | | | | |
| | Report emergencies | | | | | | | | | |
| | | | | | | | | | | |
| | | | | | | | | | | |
| | Use caution with strangers | | | | | | | | | |
| | | | | | | | | | | |
| | | | | | | | | | | |
| | Use phone to obtain emergency help | | | | | | | | | |
| | | | | | | | | | | |
| | | | | | | | | | | |
| | Avoid alcohol and other drugs | | | | | | | | | |
| | | | | | | | | | | |
| | | | | | | | | | | |
| | | | | | | | | | | |
| | Know appropriate first-aid procedures: minor, major incidents (choking, bleeding, artificial respiration) | | | | | | | | | |
| | | | | | | | | | | |
| | | | | | | | | | | |
| | Maintain good personal health habits | | | | | | | | | |
| | | | | | | | | | | |
| | | | | | | | | | | |
| | Manage birth control as needed | | | | | | | | | |
| | | | | | | | | | | |
| Assisting and taking care of others (examples) | | | | | | | | | | |
| | | | | | | | | | | |
| | | | | | | | | | | |
| | | | | | | | | | | |
| | | | | | | | | | | |
| | | | | | | | | | | |
| | | | | | | | | | | |

(*continued*)

FORM C.21
(*continued*)

| | | Performance level | | | | Critical features | | | |
| | | Check one | | | | Check all that apply | | | |
| Goal area | Present activities | Assistance on most steps | Assistance on some steps | Independent | Has related social skills? | Initiates as needed? | Makes choices? | Uses safety measures? | Note priority goal areas |
|---|---|---|---|---|---|---|---|---|---|
| Budgeting and planning/sched-uling | Plan and gather belongings for outings/activities | | | | | | | | |
| | | | | | | | | | |
| | | | | | | | | | |
| | Take care of personal belongings | | | | | | | | |
| | | | | | | | | | |
| | | | | | | | | | |
| | | | | | | | | | |
| | Manage weekly/monthly schedule | | | | | | | | |
| | | | | | | | | | |
| | | | | | | | | | |
| | | | | | | | | | |
| | Arrange activities with friends and family | | | | | | | | |
| | | | | | | | | | |
| | | | | | | | | | |
| | | | | | | | | | |
| | Participate in fundraising activities | | | | | | | | |
| | | | | | | | | | |
| | | | | | | | | | |
| | | | | | | | | | |
| | Pay bills (credit card, magazine subscription, phone) | | | | | | | | |
| | | | | | | | | | |
| | | | | | | | | | |
| | | | | | | | | | |
| | | | | | | | | | |
| | | | | | | | | | |
| | | | | | | | | | |
| | | | | | | | | | |
| | | | | | | | | | |

Repertoire chart for: __**Transition (ages 19–21)**__    Student: _____

Domain: _____Vocational_____    Age: _____    Date: _____

| Goal areas and experiences | Performance level | | | | Critical features | | | | | |
|---|---|---|---|---|---|---|---|---|---|---|
| | Check one | | | | Check all that apply | | | | | |
| List the vocational experiences in the student's repertoire to the present date. Specify the environment, task, and sessions per week. | Assistance on most steps | Assistance on some steps | Independent | Has related social skills? | Broadens repertoire | Challenging | Student preference | Provides interactions with nonhandicapped co-workers | | Note priority goal areas |
| Kindergarten and elementary school classroom/school jobs | | | | | | | | | | |
| | | | | | | | | | | |
| | | | | | | | | | | |
| | | | | | | | | | | |
| | | | | | | | | | | |
| | | | | | | | | | | |
| Middle school vocational training experiences | | | | | | | | | | |
| | | | | | | | | | | |
| | | | | | | | | | | |
| | | | | | | | | | | |
| High school vocational training sites | | | | | | | | | | |
| | | | | | | | | | | |
| | | | | | | | | | | |
| | | | | | | | | | | |
| Transition to community employment | | | | | | | | | | |
| | | | | | | | | | | |
| | | | | | | | | | | |

Repertoire chart for: **Transition (ages 19–21)** Student: _____

Domain: _____ Recreation/Leisure _____ Age: _____ Date: _____

| Goal area | Present activities | Performance level — Check one | | | | Critical features — Check all that apply | | | | Note priority goal areas |
|---|---|---|---|---|---|---|---|---|---|---|
| | | Assistance on most steps | Assistance on some steps | Independent | Has related social skills? | Obviously enjoys | Age appropriate | Interacts w/non-handicap peers | | |
| School and extra-curricular (examples) | | | | | | | | | | |
| | | | | | | | | | | |
| | | | | | | | | | | |
| | | | | | | | | | | |
| | | | | | | | | | | |
| | | | | | | | | | | |
| Activities to do alone: at home and in the neigh-borhood (examples) | | | | | | | | | | |
| | | | | | | | | | | |
| | | | | | | | | | | |
| | | | | | | | | | | |
| | | | | | | | | | | |
| | | | | | | | | | | |
| Activities to do with family and friends: at home and in the neighbor-hood (examples) | | | | | | | | | | |
| | | | | | | | | | | |
| | | | | | | | | | | |
| | | | | | | | | | | |
| | | | | | | | | | | |
| Physical fitness (examples) | | | | | | | | | | |
| | | | | | | | | | | |
| | | | | | | | | | | |
| | | | | | | | | | | |
| | | | | | | | | | | |
| | | | | | | | | | | |
| Activities to do alone: in the community (examples) | | | | | | | | | | |
| | | | | | | | | | | |
| | | | | | | | | | | |
| | | | | | | | | | | |
| | | | | | | | | | | |
| | | | | | | | | | | |
| Activities to do with family and friends: in the community (examples) | | | | | | | | | | |
| | | | | | | | | | | |
| | | | | | | | | | | |
| | | | | | | | | | | |
| | | | | | | | | | | |

Repertoire chart for: **Transition (ages 19–21)** Student: _____

Domain: _____General Community Functioning_____ Age: _____ Date: _____

| Goal area | Present activities | Performance level Check one | | | | Critical features Check all that apply | | | | Note priority goal areas |
|---|---|---|---|---|---|---|---|---|---|---|
| | | Assistance on most steps | Assistance on some steps | Independent | Has related social skills? | Initiates as needed? | Makes choices? | Uses safety measures? | | |
| Travel | Walk, ride bus, ride bike | | | | | | | | | |
| | to and from home and | | | | | | | | | |
| | community sites | | | | | | | | | |
| | | | | | | | | | | |
| | | | | | | | | | | |
| | Walk to various destina- | | | | | | | | | |
| | tions in job site, neigh- | | | | | | | | | |
| | borhood, and | | | | | | | | | |
| | community | | | | | | | | | |
| | | | | | | | | | | |
| | | | | | | | | | | |
| | Cross streets safely | | | | | | | | | |
| | | | | | | | | | | |
| | | | | | | | | | | |
| | Use public bus/subway | | | | | | | | | |
| | | | | | | | | | | |
| | | | | | | | | | | |
| | | | | | | | | | | |
| Community safety | Problem solve if lost in | | | | | | | | | |
| | new places | | | | | | | | | |
| | | | | | | | | | | |
| | | | | | | | | | | |
| | Use caution with strangers | | | | | | | | | |
| | | | | | | | | | | |
| | | | | | | | | | | |
| | | | | | | | | | | |
| | | | | | | | | | | |
| | | | | | | | | | | |
| Grocery shopping | Buy items needed for | | | | | | | | | |
| | specific meal or special | | | | | | | | | |
| | event | | | | | | | | | |
| | | | | | | | | | | |
| | | | | | | | | | | |
| | | | | | | | | | | |
| | | | | | | | | | | |

(continued)

Form C.24
(continued)

| Goal area | Present activities | Performance level — Check one | | | | Critical features — Check all that apply | | | | Note priority goal areas |
|---|---|---|---|---|---|---|---|---|---|---|
| | | Assistance on most steps | Assistance on some steps | Independent | Has related social skills? | Initiates as needed? | Makes choices? | Uses safety measures? | | |
| General shopping | Shop for desired items in shopping center | | | | | | | | | |
| | | | | | | | | | | |
| | | | | | | | | | | |
| | Purchase personal care items | | | | | | | | | |
| | | | | | | | | | | |
| | | | | | | | | | | |
| Eating out | Eat in public cafeteria | | | | | | | | | |
| | | | | | | | | | | |
| | Order and eat in fast-food restaurant | | | | | | | | | |
| | | | | | | | | | | |
| | | | | | | | | | | |
| | Buy food/drinks from vending machines | | | | | | | | | |
| | | | | | | | | | | |
| | | | | | | | | | | |
| | Budget/carry money for meals and snacks | | | | | | | | | |
| | | | | | | | | | | |
| | | | | | | | | | | |
| | | | | | | | | | | |
| Using services | Use post office | | | | | | | | | |
| | | | | | | | | | | |
| | Use pay phone | | | | | | | | | |
| | | | | | | | | | | |
| | Ask for assistance appropriately in store, information booth | | | | | | | | | |
| | | | | | | | | | | |
| | | | | | | | | | | |
| | | | | | | | | | | |
| | | | | | | | | | | |

# Example Vocational Training Site Agreement and Brochure

## EXAMPLE COMMUNITY-BASED VOCATIONAL TRAINING SITE AGREEMENT

The _____ has the authority to conduct community-based
(School District)
training programs for its students, and the _____ is will-
(Cooperating Business)
ing to allow community-based training of students according to the provisions outlined below:

1.  The Cooperating Business shall allow community-based vocational training of
    students in accordance with the following:
    Days and Hours of Training: _____
    Primary Work Activities: _____
    Names of Students: _____
    _____
    Name of School Staff Member: _____
2.  The School District is responsible for:
    a.  Providing on-site supervision and instruction, with an emphasis on safety,
        production, and appropriate work behavior
    b.  Maintaining quality control of all work performed by students
    c.  Maintaining signed parent consent forms for all students receiving training
        on site
3.  The student shall not be made or considered an employee of the Cooperating
    Business by reason of training, but shall be considered a student deriving voca-
    tional training from a course of study with the _____
    School District without compensation from the Cooperating Business.
4.  The Cooperating Business is responsible for:
    a.  Providing on-site space and materials for vocational training
    b.  Notifying the on-site staff in event of any problems or dissatisfactions
5.  Upon completion of the agreement, the Cooperating Business is not obligated to
    provide employment for the student.

*(continued)*

385

6.  a.  The _____ School District agrees that it will hold
        the Cooperating Business harmless from any claim of liability arising out of
        the program resulting from the negligence of the School District, its agents,
        servants, employees, or students.
    b.  The Cooperating Business agrees to hold the _____
        School District harmless from any claim or liability arising out of negli-
        gence of the Cooperating Business, its agents, servants, or employees in
        regard to students while students are receiving vocational training on site.
7.  This agreement shall be in effect from _____ to _____.
                                           date      date

FOR  _____        FOR  _____
              (School District)                          (Cooperating Business)


     _____             _____
                 Title                                       Title


     _____             _____
                 Date                                        Date

## EXAMPLE VOCATIONAL BROCHURE

The text of the brochure reproduced below illustrates the various points to be discussed in a brochure for a community-based vocational training program.

---

### Purpose of the Program

The community-based vocational training program for students, offered through the Syracuse City School District's Special Education Department, utilizes both school and community instruction. The purpose of the community-based component of the program is to provide students with realistic vocational training within Syracuse-area businesses and organizations. The students receive training in these community-based job training sites as part of their overall educational program. Many area businesses, industries, and organizations are currently participating in the program.

### Students

All of the students have disabilities and attend middle and high schools throughout Syracuse. The interests, abilities, and past performance of each student help determine the type of vocational training site he or she may experience.

### School Staff

The supervision and training of students on the job site is performed by school district staff. A supervisory person is present at all times while the students are working. School personnel are responsible for the quality control of all the work done by the students.

### Community Job Sites

The job site provides students with the opportunity to learn actual vocational skills in a realistic work environment. This experience cannot be duplicated by any other means available to the Syracuse City School District. Job-site personnel are encouraged to become involved with the students to the degree that they feel comfortable.

### Days/Times/Number of Students

The days and times that a job site is utilized, as well as the number of students at the site, is negotiated between each individual job site and school staff.

### Examples of Participating Job Sites and Jobs Performed

*Burnet Market, Inc.*
Two students receive training on tasks, including pricing and shelving items and bagging groceries.

*Steele Hall—Syracuse University*
Three students receive training in the distribution center. The primary task performed by the students is preparing graduate applications.

*J & T Automotive*
Students receive training on the task of labeling and packaging automotive pieces.

*St. Joseph's Hospital, Central Sterile Processing Center*
One student receives training in packaging surgical supplies.

*Pizza Hut*
One student works on the dishwashing machine.

# Example Individualized Education Program Goals and Objectives

The goals and objectives for Mary Z. that have been presented in different chapters throughout this guide are consolidated here. (It should be noted that this is not a sample IEP, but rather a listing of sample goals and objectives only. A complete IEP would contain additional information, including: a description of present level of performance, materials and methods, and time lines for implementation.) Mary's listing of goals and objectives are drawn from a range of content areas including language arts, art, industrial arts, home economics, and physical education as well as the community living areas: vocational, self-management/home living, general community functioning, and recreation/leisure. A separate section is not provided for social, communication, and motor skills. Although in some situations it may be appropriate to list goals in these areas separately, we have decided to embed them within the major content areas.

Each goal states the behavior to be learned as well as the frequency and instructional location of the activity. Many objectives state with whom the activity will occur. Criteria for mastery are stated for those objectives that are conducive to measuring a discrete behavior or set of skills. We tried to avoid using pat criterion statements that have little or no meaning (e.g., the student will order food at a restaurant successfully "70% of the time").

Finally, it should be noted that an IEP specifies *priority* goals for a student in a given school year. It is not a comprehensive listing of everything that a student will be learning. As with all students, when an environment is rich and stimulating, learning is ongoing—and certainly not limited to what is projected on an IEP.

## IEP GOALS AND OBJECTIVES FOR MARY Z.

### Language Arts

#### Goal

While participating daily in English 8, Mary will select and look at books and magazines.

#### Objectives

- When presented with three books or magazines by a classmate (from the classroom bookshelf), Mary will indicate her preference by pointing/reaching.

- Mary will turn pages one at a time and look at pictures as a classmate points and comments (for 10 minutes, on three consecutive tries).

### Goal

While participating in English 8, Mary will construct a photo journal of a familiar school scene or event with a classmate during each journal-writing session.

### Objectives

- When a classmate presents pairs of photos from a familiar school scene or event (e.g., an assembly, a recent school dance), Mary will select photos to be included by touching or pointing to one of each pair.
- Mary will look at individual photos as her partner points to each and reads each caption.
- Mary will grasp and turn each page independently or when her partner indicates.

### Goal

While participating in English 8, Mary will listen to a small group of classmates as a story or passage is read orally (e.g., small group rehearsals of *Romeo and Juliet*).

### Objectives

- When positioned approximately 5 feet from the group's table, Mary will wheel to join the group (within 1 minute, for five consecutive classes).
- Mary will orient to the speaker.

### Goal

During English 8 class, Mary will use the school library two times per week.

### Objectives

- Mary will make a choice between listening to an audio tape, using the computer, or looking at a book by pointing to a line-drawn symbol on her communication board (within 15 seconds of prompt, for four consecutive opportunities).
- When presented with three choices of library books or magazines related to her personal interests, Mary will indicate a preference by pointing to one item.
- As needed by members of her English 8 class, Mary will accompany a partner to check out research materials. After her partner has located the item, Mary will assist in checking it out by holding the item while being wheeled to the counter, placing it on the counter, and retrieving it from the librarian at the appropriate time.

### Goal

Mary will produce a written signature as needed by using a stamp carried in her pack (at library, marking projects, putting name on forms).

### Objectives

- As a teacher or peer helps to set the stamp up, Mary will look at the surface to be stamped.
- Mary will place the stamp on the spot indicated by a teacher or peer (successfully, within 10 seconds of gesture, on five consecutive opportunities).

# Art

## Goal

While participating daily in Art 8, Mary will be encouraged to express herself creatively by contributing to the completion of individual and group art projects.

## Objectives

- When positioned approximately 5 feet from her table, Mary will wheel to the table and greet classmates who share her table by smiling at them (within 1 minute, for five consecutive classes).
- Mary will use a variety of art materials and tools to create artwork with her classmates (e.g., pottery, printmaking, papier-mâché).
- When a supply or assistance is needed, Mary will gesture to a nearby classmate to request help and, if necessary, point to the appropriate line drawing on her communication board.

## Industrial Arts

## Goal

While participating in industrial arts class, Mary will contribute to the completion of woodworking projects with a classmate or group of classmates.

## Objectives

- Mary will use an adapted sender to smooth over the surfaces of pieces of a woodworking project.
- Mary will grasp an opened bottle of glue and respond to a request to squeeze the bottle as a classmate/instructor guides her hand over the surface to be joined.
- Mary will grasp the built-up handle of a foam paint brush to apply paint or stain to completed wood projects with her group.
- Mary will greet familiar classmates in her group by smiling at them as they join the table.
- After wearing a palmar splint for 10 minutes while handling individual fasteners, Mary will maintain a pincer grasp as she hands fasteners to a classmate during assembly of projects (for next five opportunities, on four consecutive classes).
- While sanding or finishing projects, Mary will be positioned in a parapodium stander for 10 minutes of each class. During this time she will stand with her knees straight.

## Home Economics

## Goal

During home economics class (3 days/week), Mary will increase her participation in the preparation of snacks and meals with one to four classmates.

## Objectives

- When presented with premeasured amounts of liquid or dry ingredients in a 1- or 2-cup measuring cup (no more than half full) Mary will grasp the handle of the cup and pour ingredients into a mixing bowl or food processor positioned next to the cup (successfully, with minimal spillage, for five consecutive opportunities).

- When stirring ingredients, Mary will accept assistance from a peer/instructor to use a hand-over-hand method to assist her.
- Mary will request help to open a container by holding the container out to a classmate in the kitchen.
- In response to a question about what she wants, Mary will indicate whether she wants something to eat or drink using line drawings from her communication board (within 15 seconds, on four consecutive opportunities).
- Mary will assist in washing dishes with a partner after meal/snack preparation by placing rinsed items in the drainer. (Mary will be positioned in a parapodium stander with her knees straight during this activity.)

## Physical Education—Swimming

### Goal

While preparing for swim class (four times/week), Mary will increase her level of participation, as well as her interactions with her classmates.

### Objectives

- When positioned approximately 5 feet from her locker (which will be situated at the end of a bench) Mary will wheel to her locker (within 1 minute, on five consecutive opportunities).
- Mary will greet familiar classmates by smiling at them.
- Mary will request help opening her locker by gesturing to a familiar classmate (within 30 seconds, during four consecutive opportunities).
- (See the "Self-Management/Home Living" section for objectives related to dressing/undressing.)

### Goal

While participating in Swimming 8 (four times/week), Mary will increase her individual and group participation skills.

### Objectives

- After being assisted to travel part of the width of the pool (while wearing a life jacket), Mary will use her arms to propel herself the last 6 feet to the side of the pool (within 2 minutes, on four consecutive opportunities).
- While supported by an adapted innertube, Mary will participate in water polo games by watching the ball and pushing it toward another student when it is nearby (for four of five opportunities, during four consecutive games).

## Vocational

### Goal

When packaging and labeling items in the central supply department of Mercy Hospital (two sessions/week), Mary will increase her rate and accuracy.

### Objectives

- When presented with plastic envelopes and corresponding supplies, Mary will place one item in each envelope.

- Mary will use a pincer grasp to place each package under the labeling machine, and remove it after labeling.
- When positioned standing with a belt supporting her hips, Mary will stand with her knees straight for 12 minutes out of each hour of her work session.
- After wearing a palmar splint for 20 minutes of packaging, Mary will maintain use of a pincer grasp (for the next three opportunities, for five consecutive sessions).

## Goal

Mary will look at symbols on a picture schedule to follow a prescribed routine at the hospital work site, including break.

## Objectives

- When presented with a horizontal display of three work activities, Mary will look at the symbol for the next scheduled activity as pointed to by a co-worker or teacher.
- After being shown the symbol for "break," and being presented with her purse, Mary will remove her money envelope (within 10 seconds, on five consecutive opportunities).
- During her break, Mary will choose a snack or drink by pointing to a symbol on her communication board (from three choices, for five consecutive opportunities).
- Mary will order the desired items by pointing to a picture symbol (in plastic folder) for the cafeteria worker (within 5 seconds of clerk's attention, for five consecutive opportunities).
- Mary will pick up the money envelope (predetermined amount) from her tray and hand it to the cashier (within 5 seconds of clerk requesting payment, on five consecutive opportunities).

## Goal

While working at Mercy Hospital, Mary will increase her interactions with co-workers.

## Objectives

- Mary will greet familiar co-workers with a smile when she arrives at work and will wave goodbye to them at the end of her shift.
- Mary will seek help from a nearby co-worker (Ann or Julie) by vocalizing and then pointing to a symbol on her board when she needs more work (as needed, for five consecutive work sessions).

## Self-Management/Home Living

## Goal

When positioned at her school locker (approximately four to five times daily), Mary will remove or replace her outer clothing and gather belongings to prepare for the next scheduled activity.

*Objectives*

- Mary will request help opening her locker by gesturing to a familiar classmate.
- When positioned at her locker before homeroom, Mary will grasp and remove her school bag for morning classes and replace it before lunch.
- When using her school locker, Mary will greet familiar students nearby by smiling at them.

*Goal*

Mary will follow a picture schedule throughout each day to prepare belongings for transitions to activities in school and community settings.

*Objectives*

- At the end of each period or activity, Mary will point (in response to a request) to the symbol on her picture schedule for the current activity and look at the symbol to the right for the next scheduled activity (successfully, throughout the day, for 5 consecutive days).
- After orienting to the next activity on her picture schedule, Mary will participate in gathering the appropriate belongings or items as needed.

*Goal*

During daily situations that involve eating and drinking (home economics class, school cafeteria, and Burger King), Mary will increase her mealtime skills.

*Objectives*

- Mary will pick up an appropriate amount of food (e.g., french fries), and complete chewing and swallowing before reaching for more (successfully, on four consecutive occasions).
- Mary will use an adapted spoon to eat soft food, independently (e.g., pudding, applesauce) ($\frac{1}{2}$-cup portion, on four consecutive occasions, with minimal spillage).
- When drinking from a glass (half full), Mary will take an appropriate amount of liquid into her mouth and pause between drinks (successfully, on four consecutive opportunities).
- When given her napkin by a peer or instructor, Mary will bring it to her mouth and wipe (successfully, on four consecutive opportunities).
- Mary will seek eye contact with peers at her table.

*Goal*

Mary will use public restrooms daily in familiar locations at school and in the community (hospital work site, Burger King).

*Objectives*

- Mary will look at the communication board symbol for "restroom" as pointed to by her instructor before wheeling to the restroom.
- When positioned inside of a familiar restroom (school or hospital), Mary will identify the accessible stall by wheeling to it (within 30 seconds, for five consecutive opportunities).

- When positioned next to the toilet, Mary will transfer from her wheelchair to the toilet by bearing weight while pivoting with assistance.
- When positioned in front of the air hand-dryer at the hospital or Burger King, Mary will push the button and hold her wet hands under the warm air (for at least 10 seconds, for three consecutive opportunities).

### Goal

Mary will increase her participation and speed in daily situations that require dressing and undressing (outerwear during arrivals and departures; swimwear for physical education class).

### Objectives

- While preparing for swim class, Mary will remove a pullover shirt by grasping and pulling it after her arms are removed from the sleeves (within 10 seconds of prompt, on five consecutive opportunities).
- Mary will participate in removing outerwear by pulling her hat off, pulling her mittens off, and pulling her coat off after it has been partially removed by a peer or instructor.
- Mary will participate in putting outerwear on by reaching for her coat in her locker, lifting her hat to her head, and pulling her mittens up after a peer or instructor has placed them partway on her hands.

### Goal

Mary will increase her participation when shampooing (twice weekly) after swimming class.

### Objectives

- When shampoo is applied to her hair, Mary will use both hands to rub and lather her hair (for 20 seconds, for four consecutive occasions).
- Mary will hold a blow dryer to assist in drying her hair (for 60 seconds, on four consecutive opportunities).

### Goal

Mary will increase her participation in the preparation of snacks and meals with several classmates in home economics class (daily).

### Objectives *(See the "Home Economics" section.)*

## General Community Functioning

### Goal

When preparing to buy a school lunch or a snack (at work or a fast-food restaurant), Mary will review available menu items to plan her purchase and use a picture-symbol strategy and gestures to communicate her request.

### Objectives

- When presented with picture-symbol cards of food items, Mary will point to the items she would like to buy before entering the serving or ordering line (from three choices, on five consecutive opportunities).

- Mary will point for the food service worker to picture-symbol cards (displayed in a clear plastic folder) for items that she has selected (within 5 seconds of worker's attention, for five consecutive opportunities).
- After receiving the items she ordered, Mary will smile to thank the clerk.
- At the approriate time in a given routine, Mary will hand her money envelope to the cashier (within 5 seconds of clerk requesting payment, on five consecutive opportunities).

### Goal

When making routine purchases (school cafeteria, school store, snacks in community settings, store purchases), Mary will select the correct money envelope for the situation (predetermined-amount strategy).

### Objectives

- When presented with two money envelopes with picture symbols for routine purchase situations, Mary will take the envelope she needs for the current situation (successfully, four of five times, for five consecutive opportunities).
- When making multiple purchases (when practical), Mary will choose the correct money envelopes and pool the money to cover the cost of all items (successfully, four of five times, for five consecutive opportunities).
- At the appropriate time in a given routine, Mary will hand her money envelope to the cashier (within 5 seconds of clerk requesting payment, on five consecutive opportunities).

### Goal

Mary will increase her level of active participation in grocery shopping for two to three familiar items using pictures-symbol shopping cards (an adapted shopping list) and money evelopes (an adaptation consisting of envelopes containing the amount of money necessary to purchase an item represented by a picture symbol on the outside).

### Objectives

- When positioned in front of grocery section containing the item for which she has a picture-symbol card, Mary will visually scan (horizontally) the shelf for an area of about 3 feet (successfully, on five consecutive shopping trips).
- Once the desired item is located, Mary will remove it from the shelf and place it in her shopping basket (successfully, with a given item, on four of five consecutive store trips).
- When positioned in front of the cashier, Mary will hand over her money envelope to the cashier (within 5 seconds of clerk requesting payment, for five consecutive opportunities).

## Recreation/Leisure

### Goal

Mary will increase her individual and group participation skills through activities in eighth-grade swim class (four times/week).

**Objectives** *(See the "Physical Education—Swimming" section.)*

### Goal

While participating in art class (daily), Mary will express herself creatively by contributing to individual and group art projects.

**Objectives** *(See the "Art" section.)*

### Goal

Mary will increase her participation in using a cassette tape player in the school library when selected as a free-time activity (opportunities throughout week).

### Objectives

- Mary will greet the librarian, request headphones by pointing to symbols on her communication board, and thank the librarian by smiling (successfully, on four of five consecutive opportunities).
- Mary will demonstrate her music preference by pointing to one of three tapes offered (from three choices, on four consecutive opportunities).
- Mary will gesture when a change in tape or activity is desired.
- After the tape is placed in the tape player, Mary will press the lid down as indicated by her partner (within 10 seconds, on four consecutive opportunities).

### Goal

Mary will participate in table games with eighth-grade friends during free time at school (several opportunities per week).

### Objectives

- When playing Pictionary with two pairs of familiar classmates, Mary will roll the dice for her team when requested.
- Mary will explore new leisure activities that are introduced to her by her peers. She will communicate her level of interest through facial responses, body language, and the amount of physical effort she puts forth to participate.

### Goal

In the computer room during after-school computer club (twice/week) and daily school-day opportunities, Mary will participate in computer games with another student.

### Objectives

- Upon entering the computer room with a peer, Mary will point to a symbol on her board to show interest in playing a computer game (from two familiar choices, within 10 seconds of questions, on four consecutive opportunities).
- While playing a computer game with a friend, Mary will respond to a friend's reminder of her turn by pressing the keyboard (single-switch games will be used) (within 10 seconds, on five consecutive opportunities).

### Goal

During the second semester, Mary will use the public library weekly.

## *Objectives*

- When presented with choices of books, Mary will indicate a preference by pointing or taking the desired book.
- Mary will return the librarian's greeting by looking at her and extending her library card.
- While an instructor or friend holds her pack open, Mary will place her library book in her pack (within 15 seconds, on four consecutive opportunities).

# Index

Academic skills, 89–92
    alternative functional sequences and, 90–91
    curriculum adaptation and, 89–90
    mathematics, 117–129, 149–158
        see also Money handling; Time management
    program determination and, 91–92
    reading and writing, 93–106
        see also Reading and writing skills
Access to knowledge of resources, for parents, 19–20
Accountability, activity-based lessons and, 295
Action
    reciprocal, 195
    request for, 194
Activity
    adequate time scheduling for, 250
    flow of, 249–250
    interrupted, indication of, 195
    see also specific types
Activity-based lessons, 292, 295–310
    data collection and, 304–308, 309
    fading procedures and, 308
    feedback systems and, 310
    generalization and maintenance and, 308–309
    individualized objectives and, 285–286
    three-step process for, 296–308
        general instructional procedure determination in, 300,
            303–304
        initial assessment in, 296–300, 301–302
        planning and data card system in, 304–308
Adaptive devices, see Assistive devices
Addition system, subtraction system versus, money handling
    and, 128
Adults, unnecessary interference by, 251
Age
    general community functioning and, 86–87
    money handling and, 127
    recreation/leisure inappropriate for, 74
    peer interactions and, 185–186
    vocational training and, 55
Arithmetic, see Money handling; Time management
Art, instructional goals in, 9, 391
Assessment
    activity-based, 296–300, 301–302
    in development of augmentative communication system,
        198–201
    of motor skills, 214, 219
    of reading and writing skills, 99–100, 101–102
        inventory for, 107–115
Assistance, request/acceptance of, 176
    communication and, 193
Assisting and taking care of others
    instruction in, 43
    repertoire chart for, 37
    scope and sequence chart for, 32, 327–328
    social skills and, 176
Assistive devices
    communication and, 191
        see also Communication skills, communication system
            and
    for feeding and self-care activities, 43
    motor skills and, 222–223
    group activities and, 227

Attention
    to object/referent, 195
    request for, 193
Augmentative Communication News, 206
Augmentative communication systems, 191
    development of, 196–202
        see also Communication skills, communication system and

Barriers, to communication, 197
Behavior, inappropriate, communication skills and, 204–205
Budgeting
    repertoire chart for, 37
    scope and sequence chart for, 32, 328–329
        see also Money handling; Planning/scheduling

Calculator strategy for money handling, 121, 145–147
    addition versus subtraction system and, 128
    calculator selection and, 128–129
Caring for others, see Assisting and taking care of others
Carry-over sessions, for recreation/leisure skills, 74
Choices
    communication of, 194–195
        see also Preferences
Classroom operation management, 281–293
    group decision making and, 292–293
    instructional session structure and, alternative methods of,
        283–286, 292
    integration and, 289–292
    logistical concerns and, 287–289
    physical layout and, 287
    teamwork and, 281–283
Classroom/school jobs, 45, 331
        see also Vocational domain
Clocks, telling time by, 150, 162–168
    digital time pieces and, 157–158
Cognitive/language skills, communication system and, 200–
        201
Collaboration
    home-school, 17–27
        see also Home-school collaboration
    in problem solving, 282–283, 284–285, 292–293
Comments, communication skills and, 193
Communication
    home-school, 22, 23
        see also Home-school collaboration
    parent-to-parent, 19, 20–22
    teamwork and, 282
        activity-based lessons and, 295
Communication skills, 169–170, 189–206
    assessment of, 199–200
    barriers to, 197
    communication books and, 205
    communication system and, 191–196
        changes in, 205–206
        development of, skill selection for instruction and, 196–
            202
        funding sources for, 206
        major components of, 192
        resources for, 206
        functions and examples of, 193–195

Communication skills—*continued*
    gestures and, 205
    goals and objectives for, 202–203
    inappropriate behaviors and, 204–205
    meaningful contexts for teaching of, 203–204
    opportunities for use of, 189–190
    sensory stimulation versus, 204
Community, recreation/leisure activities in, 67,
    336–337
Community-based instruction, with heterogeneous group, 286
*Community-Based Vocational Training Site Agreement*, 60,
    385–386
Community-based work experiences, 45, 331
Community functioning, general, *see* General community
    functioning
Community jobs, 46, 332
    *see also* Vocational domain
Community living domains, 25–27
    activity selection for, 25–26
    definition of instructional conditions for, 27
    general community functioning, 77–88
    recreation/leisure, 63–74
    self-management/home living, 29–43
    vocational, 45–61
    *see also specific domains*
Community safety, 78, 338–339
Community service use, 78, 340
Compliance, lack of, social skills and, 185
*Conference Planning Form*, 26, 236–238, 242–243
Contexts, meaningful
    communication systems and, 203–204
    motor skills and, 224–225
Cooperative learning strategies, 283, 285, 292
Coping, negative situations and, 177
Counting skills, *see* Money handling
Co-workers, 55–56, 57
Cross-age tutoring, 105, 286
Cues
    instructional, 305
        fading of, 308
    obtainment of, 176
Curriculum(a)
    expanded, recommendations for, 9
    implicit, 11
    overall, community-referenced instruction as part of, 7–11
    regular, *see* Regular curriculum
    scope of, 5
    sequence of, 5
Curriculum decision making, 10, 11
Curriculum materials, up-to-date, IEP and, 234

Daily social routines, 250–251
Data collection, for activity-based lessons, 304–308, 309
Decision making
    curriculum, 10, 11
    instructional conditions and, 27
        *see also* Instructional conditions
    student involvement in, communication and, 190
Disabilities
    communication opportunities and, 190
    motor skills and, *see* Motor skills
Dressing, *see* Grooming and dressing

Eating and food preparation
    assistive devices for, 43
    eating out and, 78, 82–83, 84, 340
    goals and objectives for, 41, 42
    instructional sites for, 39
    motor skills and, 221
    repertoire chart for, 34
    scope and sequence chart for, 30, 324

Elementary school
    general community functioning and, 86–87
    money handling opportunities in, 122
    reading and writing opportunities in, 98
    repertoire charts for, 347–359
    time-management opportunities in, 154
    vocational training in, 46, 47, 55
Employment, *see* Vocational domain
Environment
    instructional, selection of, *see* Site selection
    integrated, motor skills and, 221–222
Environmental-cue strategy, for time management, 153, 160
Excess behaviors, communication skills and, 204–205
Expanded curriculum, recommendations for, 9
Extracurricular recreation/leisure activities, 66, 333
Eye contact, 185
Eyes, motor skills and, 218

Fading procedures, 308
Family
    recreation/leisure activities with, 67, 334–335,
        336–337
    *see also* Home-school collaboration; Parent *entries*
Feedback
    negative, 176
    positive, 175
        activity-based lessons and, 310
Feeding, *see* Eating and food preparation
Fine arts, instructional goals in, 9, 391
Fine motor skills, 217
    communication system and, 198–199
    *see also* Motor skills
Food preparation, *see* Eating and food preparation
Friends, recreation/leisure activities with, 67, 72,
    334–335, 336–337
Friendships
    encouragement of, 186–187
    facilitation of, 184
    *see also* Social skills
Functional academic skills, *see* Academic skills
Functional–embedded money-handling skills, 118, 120
Functional–embedded symbol usage, reading and writing skills
    and, 95, 97, 101
Functional–embedded time-management skills, 150, 152
Functional–language experience, reading and writing skills
    and, 95, 97, 101
Functional–money-handling sequence, 118, 120
Functional scheduling, 253
Functional–time-management sequence, 150, 152
Funding
    for communication devices, 206
    for general community functioning activities, 87
    logistical concerns involving, 288

Games, *see* Recreation/leisure
General community functioning, 77–88
    activity selection for, 79–82
        *see also* Repertoire chart, for general community
            functioning
    age and, 86–87
    conditions of instruction for, 82–85
    funding and, 87
    goals and objectives for, 85–86
        example of, 395–396
    nonhandicapped peers and, 87–88
    scope and sequence of, 77–79, 338–340
*General Instructional Procedures*, 303, 304
Generalization, maintenance and, 308–309
Gestures, 205
    *see also* Communication skills
Goals, instructional, *see* Instructional goals
Greeting/closing, communication and, 193

Grocery shopping, 77, 78, 79, 83, 86, 339
Grooming and dressing
  facilitation of, 43
  goals and objectives for, 41–42
  independence level in, 42–43
  instructional sites for, 39
  repertoire chart for, 35
  scope and sequence chart for, 30, 325
Grouping
  activities involving, assistive devices and, 227
  heterogenous, community-based instruction with, 286
  homogeneous, 289
  large, with individualized objectives, 286
  for math curriculum, 129
  range of skills in, 248–249
  for reading curriculum, 105
  scheduling and, 266–267, 278–279
  for vocational training, 58

Head control, motor skills and, 226–227
Health, see Safety, health and
Heterogeneous grouping
  community-based instruction with, 286
  for reading curriculum, 105
  scheduling and, 266–267, 278–279
  for vocational training, 58
High school
  general community functioning and, 87
  money handling opportunities in, 122
  reading and writing opportunities in, 98
  repertoire charts for, 368–375
  time-management opportunities in, 154
  vocational training in, 47, 48, 55
Home, recreation/leisure activities for, 66, 67,
    334–335
Home economics, IEP goals in, 391–392
Home living, 29–43
  see also Self-management/home living
Home-school collaboration, 17–27
  communication in
    initial strategies for, 22
    ongoing strategies for, 23
    parent preferences for, 22, 313, 315
    parent-to-parent, 20–22
  IEP planning and, 22, 234–236
  practices of, 20–23
  principles of, 18–20
  timelines for, 21
Homogeneous groups, 289
Household maintenance, 329–330
Hygiene
  assistive devices for, 43
  goals and objectives for, 41
  instructional sites for, 39
  repertoire chart for, 35
  scope and sequence chart for, 31, 325–326

IEP, see Individualized education program
IEP Conference: Participants and Meeting Arrangements,
    238–239, 313, 316
Implementation strategies, 231
  activity-based lessons, 295–310
  classroom operation management, 281–293
  IEP development, 233–245
  scheduling, 247–254
  see also specific strategies
Implicit curriculum, 11
Inclusion, strategies for, 8–9
Individualized education program (IEP), 9
  community living domains in, 25–26
    see also Community living domains; specific domain,
      e.g., Recreation/leisure

development of, 233–245
  conducting IEP conference in, 240–241
  evaluating most recent IEP in, 236–238
  preparing for IEP conference in, 238–240
  reviewing current information in, 233–234
  securing parent involvement in, 234–236, 244
  securing parent signatures in, 241
  updating IEP in, 241, 243
  writing formal IEP in, 241
goals and objectives in
  criteria for, 244–245
  example of, 389–398
  see also Instructional goals
for money handling, 125–126
planning of, parent involvement in, 18–19, 22
for reading and writing, 95, 99–102
Individualized instruction, activity-based lessons and, 295
Individualized transition plan (ITP), development of, 50
Industrial arts, IEP goals in, 391
Information
  access to, for parents, 19–20
  provision of
    social skills and, 176
    to student's communication partner, 190
  see also Data collection, for activity-based lessons
Initiation skills, 175
Instructional conditions
  decisions about, 27
  for general community functioning, 82–85
  for recreation/leisure, 65, 69–71
  for self-management/home living, 38–40
  for vocational domain, 54–56
  see also Classroom operation management; Scheduling;
    Teaching
Instructional cues, 305
  fading of, 308
Instructional goals
  for communication skills, 202–203
  different, for different students, 8–9
    scheduling and, 252–253
  example of, 389–398
  for general community functioning, 85–86
  individualized
    activity-based sessions with, 285–286
    large group lessons with, 286
  for money handling, 125–126
  for motor skills, 223–224
  for reading and writing, 102–104
  for recreation/leisure, 71–73
  scheduling and, 258–261, 270–273
  for self-management/home living activities, 40–42
  for social skills, 183
  for time management, 156
  for vocational domain, 56–57
Instructional procedures, planning for, activity-based lessons
  and, 300, 303–304
Integrated environments, participation in, motor skills and,
    221–222
Integrated therapy model, 225
  scheduling and, 254
Integration, moving forward with, 289–292
Interactions, see Relationships; Social skills; specific type,
    e.g., Friendships
Interdependent support network, 17–18
Isolated therapy model, 225
ITP (individualized transition plan), development of, 50

Jobs
  classroom/school, 45, 331
  community, 46, 332
  neighborhood, 46, 332
  see also Vocational domain

Kindergarten
    repertoire charts for, 342–346
    vocational training in, 55

Language skills, *see* Communication skills; Reading and writing skills
Large group lessons, with individualized objectives, 286
Least dependent alternative strategy, 26
Leisure, *see* Recreation/leisure
Logistics, 287–289
    general community functioning and, 85
    recreation/leisure and, 71
    vocational training and, 56

Maintenance, generalization and, 308–309
Manipulation skills, 217
    communication system and, 198–199
*Many Faces of Funding, The*, 206
Mathematics, *see* Money handling; Time management
*McGill Action Planning System (MAPS)*, 238–239
Mealtimes, *see* Eating and food preparation
Middle school
    general community functioning and, 87
    money handling opportunities in, 122
    reading and writing opportunities in, 98
    repertoire charts for, 360–367
    time-management opportunities in, 154
    vocational training in, 46, 47, 51, 55
Mobility, 216
    communication system and, 198
    *see also* Motor skills
Money-card strategy, for money handling, 121, 134
Money handling, 117–129
    addition versus subtraction system for, 128
    calculator strategy for, 121, 145–147
    calculator types and, 128–129
    existing repertoire in, evaluation of, 122–123
    general community functioning and, 86
    goals and objectives for, 125–126
    individual programs for, determination of, 122–125
    money-card strategy for, 121, 134
    monitoring progress in, 126–127
    numberline strategy for, 118, 121, 135–145
    opportunities for use of, 122
    predetermined-amount strategy for, 121, 132–133
    "prerequisites" and, 128
    scope and sequence of, 118–122
    skill sequences for, 130–147
        calculator use for multiple-item purchase in, 145–147
        money-card strategy in, 134
        numberline strategy for single-item purchase in, 135–145
        predetermined-amount strategy in, 132–133
    student grouping and, 129
Motor skills, 169–170, 211–228
    equipment and, group activities and, 227
    fine, 217
        communication system and, 198–199
    functions of, 213–214, 215–218
    goals and objectives for, 223–224
    head control and, 226–227
    meaningful contexts for teaching of, 224–225
    opportunities for use of, 212–213
    oral, 218
    physical prompting and, 226
    physical therapy and, 227–228
    selection of, for instruction, 214, 219–223
    sensory stimulation and, progress measurement and, 226
    task analyses of, 227
    visual, 218
Multilevel adaptations, 8

Negative feedback, provision of, social skills and, 176
Negative situations, coping with, 177
Neighborhood, recreation/leisure activities for, 66, 67, 334–335
Neighborhood jobs, 46, 332
    *see also* Vocational domain
Noncompliance, social skills and, 185
Nonhandicapped peers, *see* Peers, involvement of
Numberline strategy, for money handling, 118, 121
Nurturance, family and, 18

Object
    acceptance of, 194
    attention to, 195
    request for, 194
Objectives, *see* Instructional goals
Oral motor functions, 218
Outdoor maintenance, 330

Paraprofessionals, logistical concerns involving, 288
Parent(s)
    and funding of general community functioning activities, 87
    priorities of, 22, 313–314, 318–321
    signatures of, on IEP, 241
    *see also* Family
*Parent Input: Determining Priorities in the Community Living Areas*, 22, 313–314, 318–321
Parent input forms, 313–321
    *see also specific forms*, 313–321
Parent involvement
    in IEP process, 234–236, 244
    in vocational training, 46, 48
    *Parent Preferences for Home-School Communication*, 22, 313, 315
Parent-professional interactions
    IEP planning and, community living domains in, 26
    *see also* Home-school collaboration
Parent-to-parent communication, 19, 20–22
Pedestrian traveling, *see* Travel
Peers, involvement of, 27
    age-appropriate activities and, 185–186
    facilitation of, 184
    general community functioning and, 84, 87–88
    recreation/leisure and, 60, 71
Perceptual abilities, communication system and, 199
Personal relationships, *see* Relationships
Personnel, *see* Staff *entries*; Teacher(s)
Philosophical principles, 3–4
    shared, teamwork and, 281–282
Physical disabilities
    communication opportunities and, 190
    motor skills and, *see* Motor skills
Physical education, instructional goals in, 9, 392
Physical fitness activities, 67, 335–336
Physical layout of classroom, 287
Physical prompting, motor skills and, 226
Physical therapy, 227–228
Picture-symbol schedule strategy, for time management, 153, 161
Planning and data card system, activity-based lessons and, 304–308
Planning/scheduling, 32
    goals and objectives for, 40–41
    instructional sites for, 39
    *see also* Budgeting; Scheduling; Time management
Positioning
    communication system and, 198
    motor skills and, 215
Positive feedback
    activity-based lessons and, 310
    provision of, social skills and, 175

Predetermined-amount strategy, for money handling, 121,
    132–133
Preferences
    indication of, 177
    recreation/leisure and, 65, 73
    student, 313, 317
    see also Choices
Priorities
    IEP, 236–238
    parent, 22, 313–314, 318–321
    student, 26
Problem solving, collaborative process of, 282–283, 284–285,
    292–293
Professional-parent interactions
    IEP planning and, community living domains in, 26
    see also Home-school collaboration
Protest, communication and, 194
Public transportation, vocational training and, 58
"Pull-out" activities, minimization of, 249

Reading and writing skills, 93–106
    combined approaches to, 105–106
    existing repertoire in, evaluation of, 99–100
    goals and objectives for, 102–104
        example of, 389–390
    grouping of students and, 105
    individual programs for, determination of, 95,
        99–102
    inventory of, 107–115
        basic sight-word vocabulary in, 110–111
        expansive sight-word vocabulary in, 112–115
        line drawings/pictures in, 108–109
        monitoring progress in, 104–105
    opportunities for use of, 95, 98
    scope and sequence of, 94–95, 96–97
Reciprocal action, communication and, 195
Recreation/leisure, 63–74
    activity selection for, 64–65
        see also Repertoire chart, for recreation/leisure
    age-inappropriate, 74
    carry-over sessions and, 74
    conditions of instruction for, 65, 69–71
    goals and objectives for, 71–73
        example of, 396–398
    long-term value of, 74
    preferences and, 73
    scope and sequence of, 63–64, 66–67, 333–337
    time devoted to, 74
Regular–adapted approach
    to money handling, 118, 119
    to reading and writing, 94, 96–97, 101
    to time management, 150, 151
Regular–adapted scheduling, 253
Regular curriculum
    adaptation of, 8–9, 89–90
    money handling, 118, 119
    reading and writing, 96, 101
    time management, 150, 151
Regular–embedded scheduling, 253
Regular scheduling, 252
Rejection, communication and, 194
Relationships
    with co-workers, 57
    importance of, 17–18
    see also Social skills
Repertoire chart
    for general community functioning, 79, 80–81
        high school, 374–375
        intermediate grades, 358–359
        kindergarten, 346
        middle school, 366–367
        primary grades, 352
        transition, 382–383

    for recreation/leisure, 64–65, 68
        high school, 373
        intermediate grades, 357
        kindergarten, 345
        middle school, 365
        primary grades, 351
        transition, 381
    for self-management/home living, 34–37
        high school, 368–371
        intermediate grades, 353–355
        kindergarten, 342–343
        middle school, 360–363
        primary grades, 347–349
        transition, 376–379
    for social skills, 181–182
    for vocational domain, 50, 52–53
        high school, 372
        intermediate grades, 356
        kindergarten, 344
        middle school, 364
        primary grades, 350
        transition, 380
Resources
    augmentative communication, 206
    parent awareness of, 19–20
Responsibilities, consensus on, teamwork and, 282
Restaurants, see Eating and food preparation, eating out and
Roles, consensus on, teamwork and, 282
Rules
    following of, 175
    restrictive, communication and, 190

Safety
    community, 78, 338–339
    health and
        maintenance of, motor skills and, 220–221
        repertoire chart for, 36
        scope and sequence chart for, 31, 326–327
Scheduling, 247–254
    examples of, 256–279
        fifth grade, 256–267
        middle school, 268–279
    and functional activity incorporation in natural flow,
        264–265, 276–277
    groupings and, 266–267, 278–279
    guidelines for, 247–251
    integrated therapy model and, 254
    master list in, 258–261, 270–273
    personnel availability and, 262–263, 274–275
    problems with, communication opportunities and, 190
    weekly, design of, 251–253
    see also Planning/scheduling; Time management
School curriculum
    overall, community-referenced instruction as part of, 7–11
    see also Curriculum(a)
School-home collaboration, 17–27
    see also Home-school collaboration
School jobs, 45, 331
    see also Vocational domain
School recreation/leisure activities, 66, 333
Science, instructional goals in, 8–9
Scope and sequence charts, 5–7
    for general community functioning, 78, 338–340
    for money handling, 119–120
    purpose of, 25
    for reading and writing, 96–97
    for recreation/leisure, 66–67, 333–337
    for self-management/home living activities, 29–33,
        324–330
    for vocational domain, 47, 331–332
Secondary school, see High school
Self, request for attention to, 193

Self-management/home living, 29–43
    activity selection for, 33–38
        *see also* Repertoire chart, for self-management/home
            living
    assistive devices for, 43
    conditions of instruction for, 38–40
    goals and objectives for, 40–42
        example of, 393–395
    scope and sequence of, 29–33, 324–330
Self-regulation, social skills and, 175
Sensory/perceptual abilities, communication system and, 199
Sensory stimulation
    communication skills versus, 204
    motor skills and, progress measurement and, 226
Services, use of, 78, 83, 340
Shopping, 77, 78, 79, 83, 86, 339–340
    *see also* Money handling
Sight-word vocabulary, 95
    basic, 110–111
    expansive, 112–115
Site development, for vocational training, 59–61
Site selection, 27
    for general community functioning activities, 82–83
    for recreation/leisure, 65, 69, 70
    for self-management/home living activities, 38–39
    for vocational training, 51, 54–55, 58–59
Social networks, 172–174
Social routines, daily, 250–251
Social skills, 169–170, 171–187
    age-appropriate activities and, 185–186
    encouragement of, 186
    existing repertoire of, evaluation of, 178–180,
        181–182
    eye contact and, 185
    and facilitation of interactions and friendships, 184
    functions of, 174–178, 179
    goals and objectives for, 183
    noncompliance and, 185
    nonhandicapped peers and, 186–187
    politeness and, 186
    selection of, for instruction, 178–183
    social networks and, 172–174
Staff
    availability of, scheduling and, 262–263, 274–275
    shortages of, 288
    teamwork and, 281–283
    *see also* Teacher(s)
Staff-student assignments, consistent, 250
Stores, *see* Shopping
Street crossing, 87
Student(s)
    adult interference with, 251
    priorities of, 26
Student preference, 313, 317
    recreation/leisure and, 65, 73
*Student Preference and Choice Questionnaire*, 313, 317
Student-staff assignments, consistent, 250
Subtraction system, addition system versus, money handling
    and, 128
Support network, interdependent, 17–18
Supported employment, transition to, *see* Transition
Symbol systems, 196
    *see also* Communication skills, communication system and
Symbols, embedded, 95, 97

Task analysis, of functional motor skills, 227
Teacher(s)
    definition of, 4
    management skills of, *see* Classroom operation management
    parent interactions with, *see* Professional-parent interactions
    *see also* Staff *entries*
Teaching

conditions for, *see* Instructional conditions
in meaningful contexts
    communication systems and, 203–204
    motor skills and, 224–225
    natural times for, 248
Teaching assistants, 250
Teamwork, 281–283, 284–285, 292–293
    activity-based lessons and, 295
    *see also* Home-school collaboration
Termination skills, 177
Time management, 149–158
    clock and watch use in, 150, 157–158, 162–168
    commercially available materials and, 158
    digital watches and, 157–158
    environmental-cue strategy for, 153, 160
    existing repertoire in, evaluation of, 154–155
    goals and objectives for, 156
    individual program for, determination of, 154–156
    monitoring progress in, 157
    opportunities for use of, 153–154
    picture-symbol schedule strategy for, 153, 161
    scope and sequence of, 150–153
    skill sequence for, 159–168
        clock and watch use in, 162–168
        environmental-cue strategy in, 160
        picture-symbol schedules in, 161
Toileting, *see* Hygiene
Toys, *see* Recreation/leisure
"Train and Hope Strategy," 309
Training site, *see* Site *entries*
Transition
    repertoire charts for, 376–383
    vocational training during, 47, 48–50, 51, 55
Transportation, 288
    vocational training and, 58, 60–61
    *see also* Travel
Travel
    general community functioning and, 77, 78, 83, 338
        elementary school and, 87
    *see also* Transportation
Tutoring, cross-age, 105, 286

Visual motor functions, 218
Vocabulary
    sight-word, *see* Sight-word vocabulary
    *see also* Communication skills
Vocational brochure, example of, 387
Vocational domain, 45–61
    activity selection for, 50, 53
        *see also* Repertoire chart, for vocational domain
    conditions of instruction for, 54–56
    example sites for, 58–59
    goals and objectives for, 56–57
        example of, 392–393
    grouping for instruction in, 58
    scope and sequence of, 45–50, 331–332
        elementary school, 46, 47
        high school, 47, 48, 51
        middle school, 46, 47, 51
        transition, 47, 48–50
    securing sites for, 59–61
    student selection for, 58
    transportation and, 58

Watches, telling time by, 150, 162–168
    digital time pieces and, 157–158
Weekly schedule, design of, 251–253
Word identification, evaluation of, 99, 108, 110,
    112–114
Work, *see* Vocational domain
Writing skills, *see* Reading and writing skills